Cambridge studies in medieval life and thought

Edited by WALTER ULLMANN, LITT.D., F.B.A.
*Professor of Medieval History in the
University of Cambridge*

Third series, vol. 9

THE TWO ITALIES

CAMBRIDGE STUDIES IN
MEDIEVAL LIFE AND THOUGHT

THIRD SERIES

THE TWO ITALIES

ECONOMIC RELATIONS BETWEEN THE NORMAN KINGDOM OF SICILY AND THE NORTHERN COMMUNES

DAVID ABULAFIA

Fellow of Gonville and Caius College
Cambridge

CAMBRIDGE UNIVERSITY PRESS

CAMBRIDGE

LONDON · NEW YORK · MELBOURNE

Published by the Syndics of the Cambridge University Press
The Pitt Building, Trumpington Street, Cambridge CB2 1RP
Bentley House, 200 Euston Road, London NW1 2DB
32 East 57th Street, New York, NY 10022, USA
296 Beaconsfield Parade, Middle Park, Melbourne 3206, Australia

First published 1977

Printed in Great Britain
at the
University Printing House, Cambridge

Library of Congress Cataloguing in Publication Data

Abulafia, David, 1949–
The two Italies.

(Cambridge studies in medieval life and thought; 3d ser., v. 9)

Bibliography: p.

Includes index.

1. Italy, Northern – Commerce – Sicily – History.
2. Sicily – Commerce – Italy, Northern – History. I. Title.
II. Series.

HF411.A28   382′.0945′10458   76-11069

ISBN 0 521 21211 1

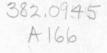

MATRI FRATRIQVE
PATRIS MEMORIAE
OPTIMIS CVSTODIBVS

ואיך ספר יכיל מהללו
לאיש אשר אלה לו

(Hebrew inscription from Toledo)

Abundanciam frumenti, vini et olei,
et omnium frugum opulenciam, ex largitate divini muneris
longa per tempora tribue ut illo regnante
sit sanitas corporum in patria,
et pax inviolata sit in regno.

From the Coronation *Ordo* of the Norman kings of Sicily
(R. Elze, 'Tre Ordines per l'Incoronazione di un Re e di una Regina del
Regno normanno di Sicilia', *Atti CISSN*, 447–8.)

CONTENTS

MAPS

PREFACE

In this book I have traced the fight of the Genoese, Pisans and Venetians for privileged commercial status in the Norman kingdom of Sicily and southern Italy; and I have traced the exercise of that status where evidence exists. I have tried to show that Sicily and southern Italy played a special and crucial rôle in the commercial expansion of the north Italian towns. Not merely was the Norman kingdom a convenient base midway between the north Italian ports and more distant destinations such as the crusader states or Andalusia; not merely were luxury items available in the markets of Sicily, Campania and Apulia; but, in addition, the need to purchase wheat and raw cotton from the Norman kingdom made that kingdom a desirable and, ultimately, a wealthy ally. Most of the detailed evidence concerns Genoa (though it also speaks eloquently for Lucca), but the activities of the Genoese can themselves only be understood in the wider context of Pisan, Venetian, Greek and, on occasion, German attitudes to the Norman kings of Sicily. No apology seems necessary for the Genoese bias of his book, given the bias of the evidence; nor does apology seem necessary for the omission of Amalfi from this book. There is simply very little to say about the activities of the south Italian merchant cities on the basis of surviving twelfth-century sources. Nor does this work pretend to provide an overall survey of the trade of Norman Sicily. Such material as the Cairo Geniza documents, or other North African sources, may one day provide enough evidence for a study of twelfth-century trade between Sicily and the Islamic lands. Apart from the fact that I do not know Arabic, there is much to be said for containing my analysis within what are effectively Italian limits; for the subject of this study has some bearing on the emergence of the lasting contrast between the economy of north and south Italy.

It will be apparent from my discussion of the sources that my tables of Genoese annual investment in overseas ports provide only a vague index of the actual proportions of investment. Commercial contracts often name a number of ports of call; and it is not always easy to discover to which sailing season, current or future, they refer. I have made some use of tables published by Erik Bach, as appendices to his study of twelfth-century Genoa. These tables are, however, divided by calendar year, rather than by sailing season; and, as they stand, they bear little relation to the rhythm of trade. Thus I have taken care to adjust his figures to the divisions of the sailing year. I have not recalculated his non-Sicilian tables, except to remove from them certain contracts that mention Sicily or southern Italy as one trading halt among a number of others. Where the Norman kingdom was clearly an early or an important port of call, it has served my purpose better to classify these documents with others that name Sicily or Campania.

I have shown rather less consistency in the spelling of names. My policy has been to convert the Latin names of the Genoese notarial documents into Italian, in accordance with the practice of Italian historians; but nobody can pretend that these versions are identical to those of twelfth-century spoken Genoese. Some names, anyhow, are impossible to contort into sensible Italian versions; and with French, Provençal and other non-Genoese merchants, I have generally abandoned Italian for a comprehensible 'native' form. Thus 'Iohannes de Leges' has become 'Jean de Liège'. In the case of Greek names I have conserved the letter 'k' and the ending '-os', even though this provides only an approximation to medieval Greek usage. I have tried to be rigid in my use of geographical terms. North Africa is properly divided into the Maghrib (far west), Ifriqiya (Tunisia, the classical 'Africa') and Barbary (Tripolitania and Cyrenaica), as well of course as Egypt. By 'Syria' I mean Israel, Lebanon and modern Syria. By 'Romania' I mean the twelfth-century Byzantine empire; north Italian merchants meant, in particular, Greece and the Bosphoros. By 'Mezzogiorno' I mean the mainland areas of southern Italy, though the name is nowadays extended to include Sicily, Sardinia and parts of Italy north of the ancient Norman frontier. The term 'the *Regno*' is a conveniently short alternative to 'Kingdom of Sicily'; it refers both to the mainland and to the island parts of the kingdom. There is, however,

deep water between Sicily and Calabria, and I have almost certainly
been sucked into it by confusing island and mainland. This book is
meant to be about both, but it will be clear that the evidence about
the island is much fuller. Generalisations about 'Sicily' are indeed
aimed at the island of Sicily; but, to add complication, the term
'Kingdom of Sicily' means both island and mainland, and where
I have slipped unconsciously from one to the other I hope the effect
has not been too disastrous.

This book provides no adequate return for the many debts I have
incurred. Dr R. C. Smail, who supervised my doctoral dissertation
on a similar theme, has inspired me with his enthusiasm and
friendship; in Genoa, Professor Geo Pistarino provided every
scholarly facility, along with a warm welcome. Professor Walter
Ullmann's constant encouragement while I prepared this book has
injected into it whatever vigour it may possess, as has the unremit-
ting support of Professor Philip Grierson and Dr Jonathan Riley-
Smith. My grateful thanks also to Mr Arthur Hibbert, Professor
Christopher Cheney (Cambridge), Dr Dione Clementi (London),
Dr Philip Jones (Oxford), Professor Eliyahu Ashtor (Jerusalem),
Professor Hans Eberhard Mayer (Kiel), Dr Anthony Luttrell (Malta),
Professor Francesco Giunta (Palermo). The late Miss Evelyn Jamison
gave my Norman Sicilian interests strong and friendly encourage-
ment.

The award of the Rome Medieval Scholarship for 1972–4, by the
Faculty of Archaeology, History and Letters of the British School
at Rome, provided me with invaluable facilities in Italy. In Cambridge, the college of my education, King's, has been very
generous. The Master and Fellows of Gonville and Caius College
have, by electing me into their company, earned my immeasurable
gratitude; they have also made it possible for me to benefit from the
services of the Fellows' research typist, Mrs P. McCullagh.

The most ancient debts are the greatest and freshest. Long ago my
father talked to me of the past; and my mother has continued to set
high standards of literary elegance that I can hardly emulate; while
my brother taught me to appreciate Italy and its contents.

Gonville and Caius College   D. S. H. A.
Cambridge
14 August 1975

A NOTE ON THE TABLES

To draw up 'statistical tables' that set out concisely the information contained in the Genoese commercial contracts demands either exceptional folly or exceptional courage. Some documents are simply ambiguous, vague either about the total sum invested in overseas trade or about the intended destination; some contain poor arithmetic, with totals that fail to tally with the itemised accounts. There is the problem whether to include stray fragments from the hand of a known notary whose cartulary is evidently an incomplete record of overseas business he recorded. These difficulties are particularly acute in the case of Giovanni Scriba (active 1154–64); each scholar who examines his evidence seems to offer a widely different total *per annum* or overall. The tables that are offered should therefore be treated as a very rough guide – rough in the sense that there are often holes in the evidence that suggest that the figures may not be a complete record even of one notary's activities; and rough in the sense that they represent only one way of adding together sums of money provided by a reasonably, but not entirely, consistent series of documents. The tables are expressed in Genoese pounds, of 240 silver *denarii*, and no attempt has been made to include sums of Sicilian *tari* nor of other coins, except where a credible current value is indicated; where, similarly, the travelling partner in a commercial expedition is to carry goods of a specified pound-value, that value in pounds has been included in the totals offered. On occasion, moreover, partners specified not the value of the money or goods they were carrying abroad, but the amount that would be produced by the travelling partner on his return, in settlement of his obligations to his partner. This was, in essence, a ruse to avoid accusations of usury, since a loan of £10 to a travelling partner might well win from £2 to £5 'commission'. Such documents are relatively rare, and the pound total offered has had to be included in the

export figures cited; for the alternative of 'adjusting' figures down-
wards seemed even less excusable than the distant ruses of Genoese
usurers. Loans that do not mention nor can be linked to known
overseas voyages have not been listed under the heading of trade for
'no stated destination'; some, to be sure, must have been used to back
commercial ventures, but others than traders needed credit in the
twelfth century.

ABBREVIATIONS

COLLECTIONS

ASLSP: *Atti della Società Ligure di Storia Patria.*

BAS, versione italiana: *Biblioteca arabo-sicula*, versione italiana, ed. and tr. M. Amari (Turin 1880–1). This was published both in a folio edition (1 vol.) and in octavo (2 vols.); references here are to the folio version.

FSI: *Fonti per la Storia d'Italia* (Istituto Storico Italiano per il Medio Evo, 101 vols.).

MGH: *Monumenta Germaniae Historica.*
 Const.: Legum Sectio IV, *Constitutiones et Acta Publica.*
 SS: *Scriptores.*

RISS: *Rerum Italicarum Scriptores.* Two series: 1st ser., ed. L. A. Muratori; 2nd ser., in course of publication.

INDIVIDUAL ITEMS: PRIMARY SOURCES

Alex. Teles.: *Alexandri Telesini Coenobii Abbatis de Rebus Gestis Rogerii Siciliae Regis Libri Quattuor*, ed. G. del Re, *Cronisti e scrittori sincroni napoletani editi e inediti*, 1: *I Normanni* (Naples, 1845), 81–156.

Ann. Ian.: *Annali Genovesi di Caffaro e de' suoi continuatori*, ed. L. T. Belgrano and C. Imperiale di Sant'Angelo. FSI; 5 vols. (Rome, 1890–1929).

Ann. Pis.: *Bernardi Maragonis Annales Pisani*, ed. M. Lupo Gentile (RISS, ser. 2, VI, part 2).

Carabellese–Zambler: *Le Relazioni commerciali fra la Puglia e la Repubblica di Venezia dal sec. X al XV*, ed. F. Carabellese, A. Zambler, 2 vols. (Trani, 1897–8).

CDG: *Codice diplomatico della Repubblica di Genova*, ed. C. Imperiale di Sant'Angelo. FSI: 3 vols. (Rome, 1936–42).

DCV: *Documenti del Commercio Veneziano nei secoli XI–XIII*, ed. R. Morozzo della Rocca and A. Lombardo, 2 vols. (Rome and Turin, 1940).

Doc. ined.: *I documenti inediti dell'epoca normanna in Sicilia*, parte prima, ed. C. A. Garufi, Documenti per servire alla storia di Sicilia, ser. 1, Diplomata, XVIII (Palermo, 1899).

F. Benev.: *Falconis Beneventani Chronicon*, repr. by Del Re, *op. cit.* 157–276.

G. *Cass.*: M. W. Hall, H. C. Krueger, R. L. Reynolds (eds.), *Guglielmo Cassinese (1190–1192)*, Notai Liguri del sec. XII, II; 2 vols. (Genoa, 1938).

GS: *Il Cartolare di Giovanni Scriba*, ed. M. Chiaudano and M. Moresco, 2 vols. (Rome and Turin, 1935).

H.Falc.: Hugo Falcandus, *La Historia o Liber de Regno Sicilie e la Epistola ad Petrum Panormitane Ecclesie Thesaurarium*, ed. G. B. Siragusa, FSI (Rome, 1897).

Hist. ducum venet.: *Historia ducum veneticorum*, ed. H. Simonsfeld, MGH. SS., XIV, 42–89.

Ibn Jubayr: *The travels of Ibn Jubayr*, tr. R. J. C. Broadhurst (London, 1952).

NDCV: *Nuovi documenti del commercio veneto dei secoli XI–XIII*, ed. R. Morozzo della Rocca and A. Lombardo (Venice, 1953).

OSM (1186): C. Jona (ed.), *Oberto Scriba de Mercato (1186)*, Notai Liguri del sec. XII, IV (Genoa, 1940). This work appeared under the name of M. Chiaudano, General Editor, in view of the Fascist race laws.

OSM (1190): M. Chiaudano and R. Morozzo della Rocca (eds.), *Oberto Scriba de Mercato (1190)*, Notai Liguri del sec. XII, I (Genoa, 1938).

Rom. Sal.: *Romualdi Salernitani Chronicon*, ed. C. A. Garufi, RISS, ser. 2, VII, part I.

Tafel-Thomas: *Urkunden zur älteren Handels- und Staatsgeschichte der Republik Venedig*, Fontes Rerum Austriacum, sectio II, vol. XII, 2 parts (Vienna, 1856).

REGISTERS OF DOCUMENTS

Caspar, Register: E. Caspar, *Roger II. (1101–1154) und die Gründung der normannisch-sicilischen Monarchie* (Innsbruck, 1904), Regesten, 475–580.

Clementi, Cal.: D. Clementi, 'Calendar of the Diplomas of the Hohenstaufen Emperor Henry VI concerning the Kingdom of Sicily', *Quellen und Forschungen aus italienischen Archiven und Bibliotheken*, XXXV (1955), 86–225.

OTHER WORKS

Atti CISSN: *Atti del Congresso internazionale di studi sulla Sicilia normanna, Palermo 1972* (Palermo, 1973).

Chalandon, *Hist.*: F. Chalandon, *Histoire de la domination normande en Italie et en Sicile*, 2 vols. (Paris, 1907).

PSIFB: *Popolo e Stato in Italia nell'Età di Federico Barbarossa – Alessandria e la Lega Lombarda, Relazioni e communicazioni al XXXIII congresso storico subalpino per la celebrazione dell'VIII Centenario della Fondazione di Alessandria, Alessandria 1968* (Turin, 1970).

Reynolds Essays: *Economy, society and government in medieval Italy: essays in memory of R. L. Reynolds*, ed. D. Herlihy, R. S. Lopez, V. Slessarev (Kent, Ohio, 1969).

Studi Luzzatto: *Studi in onore di Gino Luzzatto*, vol. 1 (Milan, 1949).

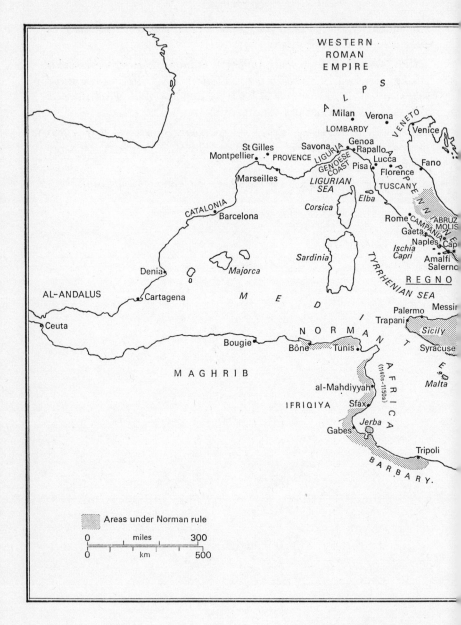

WESTERN
ROMAN
EMPIRE

A
L
P
S

Milan • Verona
VENETO
Venice
LOMBARDY

St Gilles Savona Genoa
Montpellier • PROVENCE LIGURIA • Rapallo
GENOESE Lucca
COAST Pisa Florence Fano
Marseilles LIGURIAN TUSCANY
SEA
Elba
Corsica
Rome • CAMPANIA ABRUZ
MOLIS
Gaeta • Naples Cap
Ischia APENNINE
Capri Amalfi
Salerno
Denia • MEDI REGNO
Barcelona
CATALONIA

Sardinia TYRRHENIAN SEA
Majorca

AL-ANDALUS Cartagena • MEDI
Palermo Messir
Trapani
Sicily
Ceuta • Bougie • NORMAN Syracuse
Bône • Tunis
MAGHRIB A
F
R Malta
al-Mahdiyyah • I
Sfax • C
IFRIQIYA Jerba A
Gabes • (1140s–1150s) Tripoli
B
A
R
B
A
R
Y

Areas under Norman rule

0 _____ miles _____ 300
0 _____ km _____ 500

MAP I. The Mediterranean

HUNGARY

CROATIA

SERBIA

DALMATIA

ADRIATIC SEA

Ragusa
(Dubrovnik) (1170s–1190s)

Durazzo (1185)

Via Egnatia

Thessalonika (1185)

Constantinople

Bari

APULIA

CANIA

BASIL
ICATA

Otranto

'ROMANIA'

AEGEAN SEA

Corfu
(1147)

Thebes

Ionian
Isles
(1147, 1185)

Corinth Athens

Antioch

Port St
Symeon

SYRIA

Damascus

CABRIA

RANEAN SEA

Crete

Acre

Jerusalem

KINGDOM
OF
JERUSALEM

Damietta

Alexandria

Cairo

EGYPT

twelfth century

MAP 2. The Norman Kingdom of Sicily

PART I

THE FOUNDATIONS

Chapter 1

THE SOURCES

I

The *campanile* still casts its shadow over the study of medieval Italy. For the towns and their citizens remain the focus of attention; less interest is displayed in the larger economic and political unit that comprised both the city and its surrounding countryside.[1] Predominantly rural areas such as Sicily and southern Italy have suffered especially. The influence of the *campanile* extends further: there are signs of what the Italians call *campanilismo*, an aggressive species of parochialism. The local rivalries of the Middle Ages have been succeeded by manifestations of local pride; there have, in consequence, been few attempts to examine the economic relations between individual regions of Italy. As far as a composite picture of medieval Italy is available, it is weighted towards northern Italy and is made of units that fit together rather ill. It is true that the commercial centres of the north, such as Genoa, Pisa and Venice, have been examined in the light of their overseas interests, but the more distant and 'heroic' endeavours of the mercantile cities have received most attention. Not Sicily and southern Italy but Syria and Constantinople have been favoured in studies of north Italian trade.[2] In part the explanation for this failure to consider Italy as a whole lies not in *campanilismo* but in considered attitudes to medieval Italian history. It might, for instance, be argued that Italy was

---

[1] A valuable corrective is supplied by Philip Jones, 'La storia economica: dalla caduta dell'Impero romano al secolo XIV' in R. Romano and C. Vivanti (eds.), *Storia d'Italia* (Turin, 1974), vol. II, 1469–1810; an expanded version of Dr Jones's monograph is eagerly awaited.

[2] See, e.g., R. S. Lopez, *Storia delle colonie genovesi nel Mediterraneo* (Bologna, 1938); E. H. Byrne, 'The Genoese colonies in Syria', *The Crusades and other historical essays presented to Dana C. Munro* (New York, 1928); R. Heynen, *Zur Entstehung des Kapitalismus in Venedig* (Stuttgart, 1905); meanwhile Pisa has fared better with G. Rossi-Sabatini, *L'Espansione di Pisa nel Mediterraneo* (Florence, 1935), but even though the Pisan sources are sparse, they are not fully exploited by the author.

no more an economic unity in the twelfth century than it was a political unity. Thus the study of north–south trade within Italy cannot claim any necessary priority over the study of north Italian trade with Syria or the Greek empire. To establish such priority it would be necessary to show that the wares of exchange in south Italian and Sicilian trade were of especial importance to northern merchants: as indeed they will be seen to have been. Or it would be necessary to show that Sicily and southern Italy were favoured by very heavy investment on the part of north Italian merchants: this too was the case, though intermittently. Another explanation for the failure to consider Italy as a whole undoubtedly lies in the feeling that the northern communes were an important political and cultural phenomenon that must be viewed as the context for the life of Francis of Assisi, Dante or Giotto. But the failure of communal developments in the south Italian and Sicilian towns sheds some light on the success of these developments in the north; in other words, it helps explain the mechanics of the political evolution of the northern towns. Secondly, the rôle of the north Italian merchants in the agrarian south was not simply that of trading entrepreneurs. The northern communes needed food and other raw materials from Sicily and southern Italy; the growth of the communes cannot be detached from their needs elsewhere in Italy. Finally, the lasting economic imbalance between an industrial north and an agrarian south may have had some of its roots in the early penetration of Sicily and southern Italy by the merchants of twelfth-century Genoa, Pisa and Venice. For a historian who wishes to gain a balanced view of the Italian economy in the twelfth century it does seem, therefore, that the study of north–south relations promises to be of interest; and for a historian who wishes to concentrate on events and themes of long-term importance – to dig for roots, however well hidden they may have been during the twelfth century – the same theme also promises questions and answers of value.[3]

[3] Thus Jones, 'Storia economica', p. 1,469n. announces his intention to concentrate on the 'aspetti significativi e innovatori' rather than on the 'elementi tradizionali e conservatori'. Also valuable from this point of view is the provocative essay of R. S. Lopez, *The commercial revolution of the Middle Ages* (New Jersey, 1971); while G. Luzzatto, *An economic history of Italy from the fall of the Roman empire to the beginning of the sixteenth century*, tr. P. J. Jones (London, 1961), combines both forms of treatment.

Several of the issues raised already cannot, it is true, be dealt with very adequately from the point of view of the twelfth century. Lacunae in evidence during that century, or the need for a longer perspective, provide yet further reasons for the reluctance of historians to consider these matters in a twelfth-century context. The evidence available is, in fact, balanced soundly in favour of the single city of Genoa, though Venice is also quite well served by the documents. Nevertheless the material is rich and is capable of indefinite extension into subsequent centuries too. Happily there are signs that Genoese trade with twelfth-century Sicily was particularly intensive, compared even to that of Pisa or Venice. Happily also there are signs that the Genoese broke into Sicilian and south Italian markets on a large scale only from the beginning of the twelfth century. Thus it seems defensible to take the earliest material, for all the problems of imbalance, as a starting-point for the study of the economic relationship between north and south Italy in the Middle Ages. In however partial a sense, Italy began once again to function as an economic unity in the twelfth century; a unity, certainly, based upon disparity, given the commercial rôle of the northerners and the agrarian rôle of many of the southerners, but a unity that had been shattered with the barbarian invasions and the ending of the *pax romana*.

This is not to deny that twelfth-century politicians recognised in Italy a political unit. Frederick Barbarossa claimed both southern and northern Italy for himself; and Roger II, for a brief period, styled himself 'King of Sicily and Italy'.[4] Nor is this to deny that some Italian historians have addressed themselves to aspects of these problems. Vito Vitale, for many years the presiding genius of Genoese history, was by origin an Apulian, and gave preliminary consideration to the commercial activities of the Genoese in Sicily; but he paid only limited attention to the evidence of the Genoese commercial contracts for trade in Sicily and, instead, concentrated on the grants of commercial rights by the Norman kings and by the German emperors. More recently the Genoese scholar Mario Chiaudano exhorted an audience in Bari to examine the Genoese evidence more closely; and Professor Pistarino, another Genoese scholar,

---

[4] Roger used this title for only nine years (1130–9): K. A. Kehr, *Die Urkunden der normannisch-sicilischen Könige* (Innsbruck, 1902), 416, 419, 421–2.

reminded an audience in Palermo how significant was the rôle of
the north Italians in the diplomacy of Sicily during the twelfth
century.[5] But it has not so much been these voices that others have
heard. Adolf Schaube's encyclopaedic study of the trade of the
Latins in the Mediterranean has remained the basis for comment on
south Italian and Sicilian economic history. Political relations with
the north Italians in the reign of Frederick II were analysed in an
attractive study by Heymann Chone, built entirely on the evidence
of treaties and chronicles – it was a study of commercial privileges,
not of actual commercial activity. Some attempt has been made to
link Frederick's economic policies to the economic development of
southern Italy and Sicily in studies by James Powell and Erich
Maschke, but neither has been able to pay close attention to
Frederick's Norman antecedents.[6] Meanwhile those historians who
specialised in the economic history of northern Italy have tended to
concentrate either upon the inner history of the towns or, as has been
said, on their long-distance trade; this is particularly true of the
famous Wisconsin School of medievalists, which concentrated on
the production of invaluable editions of the notarial cartularies of
twelfth-century Genoa.[7] Aspects of Venetian relations with southern

[5] V. Vitale, 'Le relazioni commerciali di Genova col Regno normanno-svevo',
Giornale storico e letterario della Liguria, n.s., III (1927), 3–29. This article is sub-
titled 'I Normanni', suggesting that a separate section on the Swabian period was
being planned, though such a sequel was never published. The first half of Vitale's
earlier study, 'Genova ed Enrico VI di Svevia', *Miscellanea di studi storici in onore
di Camillo Manfroni* (Padua, 1925), 89–102, was incorporated in 'Le relazioni
commerciali'. See also M. Chiaudano, 'Genova e i normanni', *Archivio storico
pugliese*, XIII (1959), 71–8; G. Pistarino, 'I Normanni e le repubbliche marinare
italiane', *Atti CISSN*, 241–63.
[6] A. Schaube, *Handelsgeschichte der Romanischen Völker des Mittelmeergebiets bis zum
Ende der Kreuzzüge* (Munich–Berlin, 1906); H. Chone, *Die Handelsbeziehungen
Kaiser Friedrichs II. zu den Seestädten Venedig, Pisa, Genua* (Berlin, 1902); J. M.
Powell, 'Medieval monarchy and trade: the economic policy of Emperor
Frederick II in Sicily', *Studi medievali*, ser. 3, III (1962), 420–524, with a reply by
E. Maschke, 'Die Wirtschaftspolitik Kaiser Friedrichs II. im Königreich Sizilien',
Vierteljahrschrift für Sozial- und Wirtschaftsgeschichte, LV (1966), 289–328. Work in
a rather different sphere by H. Misbach is discussed *infra*, Chapter 10, 267–73.
P. Nardone's posthumous study of Genoa, Pisa and the Mezzogiorno, based on
grants of privilege and on chronicle sources, does not range further back than
Henry VI: *Genova e Pisa nei loro rapporti commerciali col Mezzogiorno d'Italia*
(Prato, 1923). W. Heyd, *Histoire du commerce du Levant au Moyen Age*, tr. F.
Raynaud, 2 vols. (Leipzig, 1885–6) has little to say about Sicily.
[7] The interests of the Wisconsin school are well indicated in D. Herlihy, R. S.

Italy were illuminated by Francesco Carabellese early this century; while the work of Gino Luzzatto on the merchant class of medieval Venice has helped enormously in attempts to place the commercial activity of the Venetians in its Italian context.[8]

The greatness of the gap in economic history is particularly odd since work in other fields relating to Norman Sicily has been ample and excellent: Amari's translations of the Arabic sources and his monumental history of the Muslims in Sicily; Chalandon's general study of the Norman period; Caspar's painstaking account of Roger II's career; Evelyn Jamison's magisterial studies of Norman administration.[9] All these, and later, works provide a secure and substantial base for further study of Norman Sicily.[10] Much of the research has, however, been confined to the editing of important texts – a necessary preliminary, certainly; but there remain more tools than artefacts. In any case, it is inherently possible that the sources for an economic history of Norman Italy and Sicily do not survive. Economic historians are no longer content with treaties, partisan chronicles and travellers' tales as sole indices of economic developments. Trade contracts or customs accounts, sources that

Lopez and V. Slessarev, eds., *Economy, society and government in medieval Italy: essays in memory of Robert L. Reynolds* (Kent, Ohio, 1969). For the cartularies, see *infra*, 11–20.

[8] F. Carabellese and A. Zambler, *Le Relazioni commerciali fra la Puglia e la Repubblica di Venezia dal sec. X al XV*, 2 vols. (Trani, 1897–8); G. Luzzatto, *Studi di storia economica veneziana* (Padua, 1954) and his *Storia economica di Venezia dall'XI al XVI secolo* (Venice, 1961).

[9] M. Amari, *Biblioteca arabo–sicula, versione italiana*, folio ed. in one vol., 8vo ed. in 2 vols. (Turin–Rome, 1880–1); M. Amari, *Storia dei musulmani di Sicilia*, 2nd ed. prepared by C. A. Nallino, 3 vols. in 5 books (Catania, 1933–9; new edition in preparation); F. Chalandon, *Histoire de la domination normande en Italie et en Sicile*, 2 vols. (Paris, 1907); E. Caspar, *Roger II. und die Gründung der normannisch–sicilischen Monarchie* (Innsbruck, 1904); E. M. Jamison, 'The Norman administration of Apulia and Capua', *Papers of the British School at Rome*, VI (1913), 211–481, and subsequent works listed *ibid.* XXIV (1956), 1–4, and in *Atti CISSN*, 525–7.

[10] Some idea of the state of research can be gained from *Atti del Convegno internazionale di studi Ruggeriani*, 2 vols. (Palermo, 1955), and from *Atti CISSN*, recording a conference of December 1972. It is only fair to add that certain Sicilian scholars have looked at problems of Norman economic history; see I. Peri, *Città e campagna in Sicilia*, 2 vols. (Palermo, 1953–6), based largely on Idrisi's geographical description of Sicily; C. Trasselli, *Privilegi di Messina e di Trapani, 1160–1355* (Palermo, 1949) – the greater part of which, along with most of Trasselli's studies of the Sicilian economy, is concerned with the later Middle Ages.

provide a day-by-day picture of commercial movements, are called for instead.[11] From them something approaching a dynamic view of an economic system can be obtained, whereas treaties and works of geography do not tend to place commodities in accurate proportion to their production, nor can they tell much about changes of interest in the merchandise available on the commodity market. In the case of Sicily and southern Italy there are no customs records still surviving from the Norman period, and virtually no commercial contracts survive in the form in which they were registered in the ports of the *Regno*. The customs records certainly recorded the exemptions on taxes due to individual merchant groups, and probably recorded in addition the commodities or tonnage that passed through the major ports of the kingdom. Some may have been destroyed as early as 1160, others were probably discarded during the Spanish régime.[12] In consequence, the search for suitable material must obviously be directed outside the *Regno*, to the maritime republics themselves and, most of all, to Genoa, where large notarial cartularies survive from the second half of the twelfth century onwards. There are naturally great advantages and great disadvantages in having to turn for trade figures outside the *Regno* – advantages, in that comparisons can be made between trade figures for Sicily and those for other destinations; and disadvantages, in that the notaries who provide the surviving details were more concerned to settle legal obligations that might arise in Genoa than to help plan merchant voyages in any detail.

II

It was always desirable to record transactions involving money, such as transfers of land or investments in long-term projects from which financial returns were expected. Fear of default was ex-

---

[11] An extreme form of dependence on this type of material is illustrated in P. and M. Chaunu's monumental *Séville et l'Atlantique* (Paris, 1955–9).

[12] The occasion in 1160 was a riot in Palermo during which the royal palace was partly sacked and many records destroyed – Chalandon, *Hist.*, II. 277. The earliest Sicilian commercial contracts to survive in quantity date from the late thirteenth century; but acts drawn up in the *Regno* on behalf of merchants of Pisa, Genoa, Marseilles and Savona do survive from the late twelfth and early thirteenth centuries. For a contract for trade within Sicily (in Arabic) see S. Cusa, *I diplomi greci e arabi di Sicilia*, 2 vols. (Palermo, 1860–2), II, 502–4, 719. This would appear to be unique.

pressed very plainly in north Italian commercial contracts, and was a major reason for giving them documentary form at all.[13] A further reason was the considerable scale of mercantile activity, which became in the twelfth century a regular form of financial investment that stepped beyond the boundaries of family or class groups to comprehend foreign visitors to the north Italian ports, and, similarly, long-term visits by north Italians to foreign ports. The official who drew up these contracts, the notary, was, technically, an imperial civil servant, though appointed in the twelfth century by the commune; and it was for the commune and its citizens or visitors that he normally worked. His acts had legal force, so that documents enrolled in his book or charters issued by his hand were legal instruments. All these circumstances conspired to make the compilation of commercial contracts a major element in the work of Genoese and Venetian notaries, amid their traditional routine of land grants, wills and court suits.[14]

Although their internal structure is very similar, Venetian and Genoese commercial contracts have, as they survive, an important difference in presentation. What survive from Venice are individual examples of complete charters on parchment in their final form – in other words, the exact documents that partners in a deal held, one for each partner. The Venetian documents were kept among the title deeds of the great families, jumbled up with land grants and purchases. Their survival is accidental and random.[15] They have been acquired by the Archivio di Stato in Venice along with the archives of the Venetian churches into whose hands they, and the lands which many of the other deeds concern, gradually fell. Although they contain varied and often vivid accounts of trade with the Adriatic and east Mediterranean towns, they can only be used

[13] Any view of this topic will involve the incorporation of certain individual conclusions that differ in degree or as a whole from other writers' opinions. In large measure my own comments are drawn from the study of the original documents and cartularies in the Archivio di Stato at Genoa and at Venice.

[14] 'Mostra Storica del Notariato Medievale Ligure', ed. F. Borlandi, G. Costamagna, D. Pincuh, *et al.*, *ASLSP*, n.s., IV, fasc. I (1964). Commentaries, photographs and transcriptions bring out many facets of the notary's work.

[15] A comprehensive collection of commercial contracts has been made available by A. Lombardo and R. Morozzo della Rocca, *Documenti del commercio veneziano nei secoli XI–XIII*, 2 vols. (Rome–Turin, 1940); supplement by the same editors, *Nuovi documenti del commercio veneto dei secoli XI–XIII* (Venice, 1953).

with extreme caution to detect fluctuations in trade with particular regions. For the whole of the twelfth century only about five hundred of these documents have come to light; many are, in fact, quittances that cancel (and therefore repeat verbally) the original trade contract, and all claims arising therefrom. To compensate for the limitation in quantity there is the fact that the Venetian contracts are primarily concerned with the great families, the governing élite that led an active life in government and war. These were the families whose title-deeds were most likely to fall *en masse* into ecclesiastical hands by an act of charity or by dynastic extinction. A further compensation for lack of quantity is that the surviving series includes documents written in the Venetian colonies and trade-counters overseas, in Apulia, Constantinople and Syria, and even on board ship (notaries travelled in the merchant convoys as a matter of course).[16]

Although the Venetian contracts are the final, 'polished', version of the partnership agreements they represent, their physical form is frequently modest. The contracts are written in a crabbed hand on end scraps of parchment, irregular in shape and crowded with writing. The relatively poor quality of the parchment and the signs that the notary scraped and saved reflect the ephemeral nature of this material, by comparison with land grants or public acts. By now the commercial contracts are in a state of advanced decay; several of those read by Lombardo and Morozzo have been overwhelmed by fungus, though fortunately the major series from the church of San Zaccaria has been better preserved.[17] What does repay attention, however, is the series of autograph signatures by Venetian merchants who witnessed the partnership agreements. Although it is plain

[16] Genoese notarial registers compiled in the colonies on the Bosphoros and the Black Sea do survive, but all are much later in date than the period of this study.

[17] I have taken care to examine in the originals accessible material published by Lombardo and Morozzo, in the Archivio di Stato, Venice. It should be noted that the twelfth-century charters have now been reclassified. The most important single group, San Zaccaria Busta 40, is now numbered Busta 34. The only emendation to record is a possible reinterpretation of *DCV*, I, no. 251, which has been published as a contract for Peschiera (*depiscaria*); 'Pescara' would be an alternative translation, and would bring the contract into the series of trade partnerships for the *Regno* – S. Zaccaria, perg. B. 34. There is little chance that material unnoticed by Lombardo and Morozzo will come to light. I can only add one text, an apology from the Doge dated 1198, addressed to a merchant of Gaeta whose goods had been seized – Venice, Biblioteca Nazionale Marciana, MS Lat. XIV–72 (coll. 4,273), no. viii.

that some signatories had little idea of the form of letters, and could probably write only their names, it is evident too that literacy was not confined to any one group of merchants, such as the noble class.

What survives in Genoa, by contrast, is a series of paper books filled with summaries of charters, books compiled by the city notaries as a basic record for purposes of authentication in cases where documents were lost or suspect. In addition, the Commune required notaries to deposit copies of their cartularies in the city archive (no other word is possible), so that even after the notary's death reference could, if necessary, be made to his acts. Here is displayed that concern for documentation that prompted the consuls to patronise the writing of the city annals, and to bring together the public documents of the Commune in the *Liber Jurium*.[18] Obviously in this instance the main interest was land transfers and other permanent transactions, but in the process thousands of commercial contracts were preserved as well, surviving complete until 1684 when the cartularies were the victim of French bombardment of Genoa.[19] Several early volumes were destroyed and enormous disarray resulted, so that fragments of damaged cartularies are now to be found bound up haphazardly in the wrong register, and big gaps exist between groups of documents from the same hand.[20]

These cartularies represent a different stage in the production of the final contract from that represented by the Venetian material. The procedure in Genoa seems to have been this. The interested parties came to the notary in his booth or at any other place agreed upon, and declared their intention to make a business deal. The notary wrote down in rough form, either on a scrap of paper or in a manual reserved for the purpose, the details of the transaction – the amount of money involved, the names of the partners, the destination if it were a deal for overseas trade, and, of course, the names of the witnesses. A few of these paper scraps survive loose in the early cartularies, and their unusual simplicity and brevity suggests that they should not be seen simply as registrations made when the

[18] Cf. *infra*, 24–5, 28.
[19] G. P. Bognetti, *Per l'edizione dei Notai Liguri* (Genoa, 1938), 24. The name of M. Moresco, general editor, also appears on the title page.
[20] Thus MS Diversorum 102 in the Genoa State Archive binds together work by Oberto de Mercato, Oberto de Placentia and Guglielmo da Sori.

notary's books and quires were not to hand. The thirteenth century provides, in addition, several fragments of notaries' manuals, containing the first redactions of contracts subsequently entered into the cartularies. But whether in the twelfth century such manuals were also compiled is unknown. A further point is that the entries in the cartularies are not in exact chronological order. This cannot always be the result of the bombardment in 1684, because the date moves forward and back in contracts enrolled on the same page of the book. So it is reasonable to conclude that, when he had the time, the notary gathered together the notes he already had, and where possible perhaps improved the order so that ventures to Sicily or elsewhere would comprise a compact group of documents; then he entered his notes into the cartulary, still in abbreviated form. Later still the contracting parties returned to him. They notified him of any corrections (hence the frequent emendations) and informed him whether the contract was still to stand. If so the notary in due course drew up on parchment the full version of the document, expanding all the formulae and changing from the rather crabbed scrawl typical of the cartularies to a more legible hand.[21] If the partners did ask for a full version, he normally cancelled the entry in his cartulary by drawing lines across it; however, uncancelled documents need not always be aborted contracts. On occasion the notary handed over the task of making a charter to another notary, probably where complications had occurred with the other notary's customers, such as their involvement in a large-scale convoy expedition overseas. Thus Giovanni Scriba, the oldest surviving notary, sometimes cancels by writing OGER[ius] or OTOBONUS, apparently the

[21] Basing himself on thirteenth- and fourteenth-century evidence, G. Costamagna argues strongly in *La Triplice Redazione del Instrumentum Genovese* (Notai Liguri del Sec. XII e XIII, VIII, Genoa, 1961), for the use of manuals in which the first registration of the contracts occurred. Cf. Bognetti, 51–3, 58–62. Parchment versions of the commercial contracts do not survive from Genoa, only from Venice. Analogous, however, is the material presented in Chapter 8, *infra*, quittances drawn up by Ottobono Scriba in connection with loans to finance Genoese participation in Henry VI's invasion of Sicily – Genoa, Archivio di Stato, archivio segreto, Materie politiche (2721), Busta 2, no. 45 and no. 46. Bognetti, 59, argues that, in the case of Guglielmo Cassinese, there were only two redactions – first the cartulary, then the final instrument. The idea that notaries were not, or not yet, consistent in their practice makes much sense. Final redactions of non-commercial documents do survive alongside entries in the cartulary recording their second redaction: compare *GS*, I, plate II, p. xxxvi, with plate III, p. 92.

names of other notaries, in big letters over his entry.[22] In fact, Giovanni's register contains a high number of uncancelled acts. On 20 August 1156 he recorded five acts concerning maritime trade, two for Sicily and three for Alexandria. But only one of the Sicilian and one of the Alexandrian acts was cancelled.[23] Since a convoy expedition is implied by the concentration of contracts at this season and at this point in the cartulary, it may be that Giovanni was not thoroughly systematic in his cancellation, rather than that part of the convoy withdrew. The general implication derived from failure to cancel must, however, be that the voyage or payment in question very likely did not take place. The uncancelled acts are an index to the intentions of Genoese merchants and to their ideas of trade prospects, but will be differentiated from cancelled ones. Generally it is true to say, then, that the registration in the cartulary did not in itself have final legal force; it was in the relation to its charter of a parliamentary Bill to an Act.

The contracts are, of course, partnership contracts, involving two or more individuals. There is no way of knowing what proportion of trade in Genoa and Venice was financed by partnerships, and what proportion was financed by individual merchants who travelled overseas free of obligation to a second party. That merchants did carry money overseas without committing it to a partnership is, however, evident. Certain partnership contracts from Genoa end with clauses permitting the travelling partner to carry '*extra societatem*' money 'of his own', normally rather a small sum compared to his total investment in the actual partnership. Similarly, very wealthy merchants such as Solomon of Salerno travelled abroad with their colleagues' and their own funds, and it is difficult to believe that Solomon made no investments free of partnership restrictions.[24] In general, however, it does not appear that the majority of sleeping partners had recent first-hand knowledge of the destinations to which they sent funds. Although the more distinguished sleeping partners, such as the della Volta family, were probably trained in their youth as travelling merchants, they seem in later life to have exercised only remote control over their Sicilian and other investments. It may seem to be an exaggeration even to describe them as

[22] Chiaudano, Introduction to *GS*, p. xxxii.   [23] *GS* I, 61–3.
[24] For Solomon's career, see Chapter 9, 237–54, *infra*.

merchants, but that would be to ignore their rôle in the sale and exchange of goods and bullion in Genoa, and to ignore the conscious nature of the decisions they made concerning where to invest their funds overseas. Thus, even if the partnership was only one means of placing money in trade overseas, its importance far outstrips other means, such as carrying the money in one's own pocket or purchasing goods for carriage overseas under one's own supervision. For the partnerships have an added dimension, determined by the attitude of the sleeping partners to trade prospects overseas.

The legal force these contracts possessed is reflected also in their internal form. Basically it is possible to distinguish three types of commercial contract: the *societas* (sometimes, especially at Venice, termed *collegancia*), the sea-loan and the *accomendacio* or *commenda*. The difference lies in the relationship between the static partner (*socius stans*), who remained in Genoa or Venice, and the travelling partner (*socius negocians*), and in the liability of each in case of loss. In the normal *societas*, the static partner placed twice the amount his counterpart agreed to contribute in the hands of the latter. On his return from overseas the *socius negocians* divided the profits equally; in cases of loss, the risk was incurred equally too. The sea-loan involved the loan of a stated amount of capital to the *socius negocians*, who was to return it to the sleeping partner in due course along with an interest charge – this might be expressed in the same currency as the original loan, or, very often, in an 'exotic' currency such as Sicilian tari or Byzantine hyperpers (a form of sea-loan often known as the *cambium maritimum*);[25] and it should never be assumed

[25] R. de Roover, 'The Cambium Maritimum contract according to the Genoese notarial records of the XIIth and XIIIth centuries', *Reynolds Essays*, 15–33. The most sophisticated, and often the least intelligible, of these *cambia maritima* involved in addition pledges of cloth or other goods. Normally the debtor, who was also the travelling partner, would provide this material pledge. He would then take both the loan he had received and the items he had mortgaged to a foreign destination, where he would sell the merchandise and invest the money. Very frequently, too, the creditor would follow him overseas to collect his debt on a stipulated date in a named port. He would be repaid at a favourable exchange rate, made possible by his partner's deft use of the loan in the intervening period. Thus the advantage for the creditor is clear. For the debtor, the main advantage was probably the opportunity to double the amount of money he could hope to have available overseas. First, there was the debt; then there was the value of the goods. Or it could happen that the debtor would want to purchase cheaply on his arrival, prior to selling his merchandise at a later date when

that the commercial contracts express other than a highly advantageous rate of exchange for the Genoese pound. Liability rested with the sleeping partner. Finally, the *accomendacio* combined elements of the sea-loan with the opportunism of the *societas*.[26] Here the lender contributed all the capital and reserved to himself about three-quarters (the proportion varied) of the profits. Once again it was he who incurred all risks. This type of contract had distinct advantages for lender and borrower alike: it avoided the restriction on profit implied by the sea-loan, and it helped create a class of expert middle-class merchants who began their career as agents for the large-scale patrician investors. It was simpler than the *societas*, in the sense that it demanded no close adjustment of capital investment by each side, and so not surprisingly many twelfth-century *societates* included supplementary *accomendaciones* of a few pounds, raised either from the funds of the *socius stans* or from those of a third party. How much should be made of the ratio between the restrictive *societas* and sea-loan and the free *accomendacio* it is difficult to say. This ratio has been seen as an index to the fluidity of capital in medieval Genoa, or as a key to the capacity for economic expansion of patricians and bourgeoisie.[27] In fact the picture is extremely complicated. In the mid-twelfth century individual merchants without capital would still join *societates* if they had the backing of rich relatives or friends; a merchant would often be set up in business by his father, under whose wing and on whose behalf he would operate for a few years. Moreover, the *accomendacio* was not, as has been supposed, mainly a late-twelfth-century development that changed the overall character of commercial investment in Genoa, Venice and other towns. Any attempt to interpret the ratio between *societas* and *accomendacio* is further complicated by the fact that the social relationships of the notaries had a great influence on the sort of business they attracted. For the moment, therefore, a functional interpretation of their purpose, determined by the needs of north

prices were more favourable to the seller. Under these circumstances the availability of ready capital placed a merchant importing goods into foreign ports in a very strong position.

[26] M. Chiaudano, *Contratti commerciali genovesi del secolo XII* (Turin, 1925), 39–40.

[27] E. H. Byrne, 'Commercial contracts of the Genoese in the Syrian trade of the XIIth century', *Quarterly Journal of Economics*, XXXI (1916–17), 152, 168–70.

Italian businessmen at one particular moment, is all that can reasonably be applied.

After the exact type of contract had been stipulated by name, the travelling partner would promise to follow a particular route overseas and, on occasion, to travel on a particular ship. If the right to travel anywhere he might choose was to be granted him, it was normally clearly expressed; even here contracts can sometimes be ascribed primarily to trade in Sicily if something is known of the travelling partner's engagements with other investors, for it was very common for lenders and borrowers to spread their business and to send their money with several different agents in the same convoy of ships. The documents conclude with a statement of special provisions, such as their relation with other *societates* already entered into, and with certification by witnesses, unless these have been named at the start of the contract.[28]

III

For the twelfth century, work by eight Genoese notaries survives, but a number of gaps exist. The material begins in December 1154. The most serious hole is from 1165 to 1178, although other sources indicate that this was not a promising period for Genoese trade in Sicily. The years 1181, 1185, 1187, 1188, 1189, 1193 are also not accounted for; and for all the years except 1155–64 none of the notaries provides a complete survey but only groups of months or days.[29] In this respect the earliest notary, Giovanni Scriba, offers

---

28 It is perhaps worth citing at this stage a typical, and very simple, contract, an unpublished act of Oberto Scriba de Mercato, dating from 1179:
'Testes Wilielmus Rapalinus, Wilielmus de orto, Obertus de caneto, Wilielmus de sancta savina. Ego Rinaldus frater Wilielmi Rapalini confiteor me recepisse in accomandacio a te Giulia uxore Rubaldi de caneto lb. dr. ian. .xx. quos porto in Sicilia ad quartum lucri in nullo alio itinere mutato [et hac acomandacione cum lucro et capitali integre et in ea fuerit in tua vel tui nuntii potestate mitere – *inserted above the line*] Ianuam debeo venire. Dat. Ian. in caneto in domo eidem Rubaldi. Ea die [XIII die exeuntis augusti].' The idiosyncracies of grammar and spelling are noticeable. Archivio di Stato, Genoa, MS Diversorum 102, f.8r, no. 2.

29 Ministero dell'Interno, Pubblicazioni degli Archivi di Stato, XXII and XLI, *Archivio di Stato di Genova: Cartolari notarili genovesi* (Rome, 1956 and 1961). This comprises (a) a folio-by-folio analysis of the cartularies; (b) a name-by-name index to fragments of the notaries' work; (c) a year-by-year list of material available. Although the cartulary now known as MS Diversorum 102 is included in the

evidence of special completeness. The scale of business, especially mercantile, grew and grew during the twelfth century, and the notaries responded with greater numbers of contracts; the number of acts inscribed per day by Giovanni is only a small fraction of that registered at the end of the century by Guglielmo Cassinese and his colleagues. Hence the quantity of appropriate contracts increases greatly despite all the gaps there are. These gaps can, nevertheless, be filled to a minor degree. It is wrong to think in terms of years, so much as sailing seasons; by mid-October the ships bound even for nearby ports had sailed and most business after that was aimed at the next sailing season. The great concentration of business occurred well before October, in late spring and summer, when long-distance trade to the east Mediterranean – much of which took in Sicily too – was planned. While the ships were away local business naturally took priority – land sales, wills and so on; but even so there were frequently quittances, loans and exchanges to be negotiated, with a view to profiting from expected returns or simply to avoid debt; many of these concerned previous expeditions to Sicily or sums of Sicilian gold money. It is, here, proposed to divide up groups of contracts not with reference to the calendar year in which they were issued but with reference to the anticipated sailing season – apparently a novel approach. On this basis something can be said about the trade of 1185, to take one instance, even though no documents survive from that year.[30]

It is essential to identify each notary's connections and status in order to see how far his picture of urban activity is likely to have been formed by personal contacts and public duties. No single notary provides a panoramic view, nor a truly objective one so far as he is dependent on his inner coterie of constant clients. Here Giovanni Scriba (1154–64) very much comes into his own, not merely because of the exceptional antiquity of the manuscript but also because of the close links between the notary and certain members of the governing and trading élite. He appears to have been an official notary to the consuls, and during part of the year 1159 he was absent from day-to-day business on their behalf.[31] He recorded

inventory, the *Notai Ignoti*, unbound wandering fragments, are not. For these, see Bognetti, 98–103; the oldest fragments, other than some bound in error in Cart. 1, and published with the rest of that cartulary, are of 1176, sixteen acts of 'Iacobus'.
[30] Ministero dell'Interno, XLI, 157.   [31] Caffaro in *Ann. Ian.*, I, 54.

deals made by a variety of consular families – the della Volta, the Vento, the Spinola, the Embriaco. He was deeply involved with the business affairs of Solomon of Salerno, a subject of King William of Sicily who had settled in and traded from Genoa. He has something to say on commodities too. Because he was close to the leadership he drew up the wills and property inventories of the top families. The manuscript in Genoa is in a clear and consistent hand on paper of fine quality, itself one of the commodities imported from overseas, from Alexandria, by Genoese merchants.[32]

Excluding for the moment some material from Savona, the next oldest Ligurian notary whose cartularies survive is Oberto Scriba de Mercato (1179, 1180, 1182, 1183, 1184, 1186, 1190; also 1200, 1201, 1207, 1213, 1214). From 1190 he was probably official scribe of the market in Genoa.[33] His clientele included members of the larger consular families such as Embriaco and de Castello, but at the same time his registers reflect the extent to which medium-rank families were making medium-sized investments overseas, as the scale of commercial investment and, *pari passu*, the rôle of mercantile activity in the economic life of Genoa, burgeoned later in the century. He acts as guide to some critical years in Genoese–Sicilian relations, but only the years 1186 and 1190 have been published, along with a surviving fragment from 1180 which was bound with Giovanni Scriba's cartulary.[34] His handwriting, though uneven in quality, is generally legible.

December 1190 to April 1192 are covered in a continuous sequence by the busy notary Guglielmo Cassinese. This is only a tiny part of the material he must have accumulated in a career that ran from

---

[32] M. Amari, *Nuovi ricordi arabici su la storia di Genova* (Genoa, 1873; also printed in *ASLSP*, v, 1873), 85–6; *GS*, II, plates II and III. An old edition of Giovanni Scriba's cartulary (*Historiae Patriae Monumenta, edita iussu Regis Caroli Alberto, Chartarum*, II (Turin, 1853), col. 285 *et sqq.*, omits many documents and is generally less accurate than the Chiaudano–Moresco edition of 1935.

[33] Bognetti, 103–4.

[34] C. Jona (ed.), *Oberta Scriba de Mercato, 1186* (Notai Liguri del sec. XII, IV; Genoa, 1940). The title page carries only the name of M. Chiaudano, the General Editor, owing to the Fascist race laws; M. Chiaudano and R. Morozzo della Rocca, *Oberta Scriba de Mercato, 1190* (Notai Liguri del sec. XII, I; Genoa, 1938). Unpublished cartularies in the Archivio di Stato, Genoa: MS Diversorum 102, f.11–21v; Cart. 2 (only the sections from 1186 and 1190 have been printed); Cart. 4. A fragment from 1180 is printed in *GS*, II, 278–83; original bound with Giovanni Scriba as Cart. 1, f. 175r–175bis/v.

before 1180 to 1209. This career can be traced only sketchily, although it is known that he was notary to the Archbishop of Genoa and, at least on an unofficial basis, to the great Abbey of Santo Stefano; but his secular clients were also prestigious, including such prominent families as the Malocello, Mallone and de Mari. He attracted in addition business from visiting Flemish and Lucchese merchants.[35]

Guglielmo de Sauri, or da Sori, has never been published but furnishes an important dossier on the activities of the Embriaco family, with which he seems to have had particularly close relations. His work survives from 1191, 1195, 1199, 1200 and 1202. The fragment from 1191 usefully confirms the picture presented by Cassinese of heavy investment in Naples early that year.[36]

Some of the miscellaneous fragments now bound up in other notaries' books cannot be assigned to any particular hand, or be dated, or both.[37] If a contract cannot be dated to a precise sailing

[35] Chiaudano, *Contratti commerciali*, 1–26, for a full study of this notary; cf. also Bognetti, 108. Edition by M. W. Hall, H. C. Krueger, R. L. Reynolds, *Guglielmo Cassinese*, 2 vols. (Notai Liguri del sec. XII, II; Genoa, 1938). He trained a disciple, 'Iohannes filius quondam Guiberti' (Giovanni di Guiberto), whose script and range of work is very similar to his master's, and whose registers survive from 1200, 1201, 1205, 1206 and 1211 in sizeable fragments. Edited by the same team as Cassinese (2 vols., Notai Liguri, V; Genoa, 1939–40); cf. Bognetti, 109.

[36] Archivio di Stato, Genoa, MS Diversorum 102 and Cartolare 3/ii. Folios for 1191: MS 102, f.141r–143v. especially f.142r, no. 2. Later years contain important references to Markward von Anweiler, Henry VI's Seneschal and later Regent of Sicily. An edition planned by the late V. Vitale has not been published (see Bognetti, 111). Mention should also be made of Oberto de Placentia, or di Piacenza. His cartularies survive in large pieces divided between MS 102 and Cart. 56 (December 1196 to March 1198; 1200; 1201). Selected contracts have been published by R. Doehaerd, *Les Relations commerciales entre Gênes, la Belgique et l'Outremont*, 3 vols. (Brussels–Rome, 1941), II, no. 1 – no. 123 – but the texts are misdated, mistranscribed and even wrongly ascribed; her texts from Guiberto (ascribed to Cassinese) are also inaccurate. Oberto de Placentia is very valuable for the northern cloth trade, and also offers a little material on Sicilian commerce. Another contemporary notary, Bonvillano (ed. J. E. Eierman, H. C. Krueger, R. L. Reynolds, in Notai Liguri, III; Genoa, 1939), only survives from September to December 1198, and was apparently far from a master craftsman; cf. Bognetti, 109. No Sicilian trade contracts are listed by Bonvillano.

[37] It is no longer thought that any work by 'Lanfranco' belongs before 1202 (cf. Bognetti, 107; Ministero dell'Interno, XLI, 157). A pencilled note in Ministero, 157, held at Archivio di Stato, Genoa, in the main reading room, rejects the twelfth-century date of the fragments of 'Lanfranco' ascribed previously to 1188–93. For 'Iacobus' (1176), cf. note 29 *supra*, and Bognetti, 100, 110. Undated parts of Oberto Scriba: Ministero dell'Interno, XXII, 106–7.

season, or related to others drawn up the same year, it loses much of
its force and applicability. Undatable work by Oberto de Mercato
and others has, therefore been left aside. Conversely, the evidence
of the contracts gains in value as the amount of contracts gains in
size. What in fact is their importance for the study of Sicilian
economic history?

An initial analytical problem is that of quantification. It has been
seen that the cartularies do not survive in enough bulk to make it
possible to draw pictures of the overall movement of trade over a
specific number of years. Moreover, it is only occasionally that the
work of more than one notary survives for exactly the same period
of time. Here, anyway, the different interests of individual notaries
reduce the impact of direct comparisons. It may begin to appear that
no trends at all can be extrapolated from this material. There is,
however, an elementary outside test to apply. Do the commercial
movements recorded by a particular notary respond in any measure
to the granting of rights to the Genoese republic in overseas ports?
The answer is a very clear yes. There is a marked upswing in trade
with Sicily after the great Genoese–Sicilian treaty of 1156. Interest
in Constantinople developed in the 1160s as Emperor Manuel
Komnenos tried to make Byzantine markets attractive to Genoa.
All this is apparent in the notaries, though a reverse test – that
breaking of relations politically leads to complete collapse in
economic relations – interestingly enough does not always apply.[38]
Only positive tests, looking for positive effects, can be used. Even
so this type of result is very general, and often not very surprising
either. Can more specific use of the registers be made? Once again
it is important to ask the right questions. The partnerships are most
often expressed in money, more rarely in commodities. It is therefore difficult to answer in much detail problems about the movement of goods out of Sicily; though something more can be said
about trends in goods moving into Sicily, on the basis of scattered
notarial inventories and references to partnerships expressed in

---

[38] There was an eclipse of Genoese trade in Sicily after Genoa joined Henry VI's
campaign against Tancred, but no collapse when Frederick II turned on Genoa
and removed the Republic's trading privileges in the *Regno*: see Chapter 8,
193–201, *infra*; J. M. Powell, 'Genoese policy and the Kingdom of Sicily, 1220–
1240', *Mediaeval Studies*, XXVIII (1966), 346–54.

'kind'. The contracts say a certain amount about prices, but normally the products described are not, or not mainly, Sicilian in production; they tend rather to be items listed for import into Sicily and other markets, and there is, of course, no guarantee that the prices cited by the notaries do not conceal hidden interest rates, and are therefore rather higher than those a merchant could reasonably expect to pay.

Setting aside commodities, which are not the sole key to the history of medieval trade, the Genoese notaries provide a magnificent range of detailed material. First, there is the number of contracts agreed upon in one season for one region. Each contract can be seen as a single business deal based on consideration of the commercial odds at a particular moment. Therefore, to discover quite simply where the emphasis in Mediterranean trade lay during one season, a head-count of contracts can be useful. But clearly it is only a preliminary manoeuvre in their analysis, for each contract naturally concerns a different sum of money invested in one of several different ways. A second dimension is added by counting the overall investment in one enterprise or region during a particular season, with the result that the total investment in Sicily can be compared to the overall investment in overseas trade that season, or with other prominent markets such as Alexandria and Bougie. It is necessary to bear in mind the question how far difficulties of access to the more distant markets led to the concentration of investment in a small group of contracts intended for only one or two convoys; in the case of nearer ports such as Palermo it was quite common for one Genoese merchant to indulge in a series of small investments throughout the sailing season; probably this was no less profitable than one large investment in the same region. Hence a detailed analysis of personnel becomes necessary too. In this way it will be possible to see whether the number of contracts is being inflated by the partition of one man's investment in a number of ventures to the same destination. More than that, the identity of the traders will suggest a link between the commercial activity of the Genoese governing class and the initiation of friendly policies towards Sicily and other foreign powers. And, on a lower level, the identity of minor investors, their scale of investment and their choice of markets will indicate in what particular areas Genoese businessmen were expressing confidence – to what extent a particular region

constituted a gilt-edged market, and to what extent they were prepared to try their hand in opening up rather newer markets such as
those in Norman Africa. This is quite apart from the information
the documents convey about the silver to gold ratio, political relations with Sicily and its kings, the importance of individual ports in
the *Regno* – Messina as against Palermo, the Sicilian ports as against
the Campanian. To what extent, too, did Messina and the kingdom
as a whole benefit from the increased passage of trade to Alexandria,
Syria and other eastern markets? And to what extent do the notaries
provide evidence not of movement between Sicily and Genoa, but
between Sicily and Spain or North Africa or the east Mediterranean?
Given, too, the overall expansion of Genoese trade in the late
twelfth century, clearly marked in Giovanni Scriba's relative poverty
of contracts *per annum* compared to, say the richness of Guglielmo
Cassinese, it is interesting to examine how far Sicily was caught
along in this movement, how far, indeed, it provided the material
basis for a great burgeoning of capital investment. For there is one
paramount question that is not answered directly by the notaries, but
to which, through their registers, it is possible to propose the outline
of an answer: what was the value of Genoese trade to Sicily's
rulers, how far were they throwing away their revenue by allowing
the north Italians substantial privileges of tax exemption, and how far
were they acting in unison with the north Italians in order to establish a secure outlet for taxable and saleable products of the *Regno*,
such as cotton, wheat and meat? The drawbacks of the notarial
registers compared to, say, the lost customs records of Sicily are
clear; but it is equally apparent that, once the limitations have been
honestly accepted, a major source for the economic history of
Norman Sicily remains available.

IV

Certain other towns have left notarial contracts that concern Sicily.
Savona was under a Genoese protectorate in the twelfth century;
although it had its own set of consuls, Savona participated in the
trade of Genoa, and vice versa. Like Genoa, Savona preserved its
notarial cartularies, but they are rather different in form to those
from the mother-city. They include lengthy records of law suits,
especially disputes over commercial obligation, and they often

describe in detail incidents on voyages to the *Regno*. Most of the surviving material is from the first twenty years of the thirteenth century, and the extensive information contained there about the trade of the *Regno* can only, it is clear, be used with caution in a study of the commerce of Norman Sicily. On the other hand, the cartulary of Arnaldo da Cumano and Giovanni di Donato (1177 to 1188, but concentrated around the years 1178 to 1182) is closer in form to the Genoese registers. It is dominated by land sales, but does offer some interesting material on Sicilian contact with Savona.[39] Since the Genoese excluded Savona from direct trade with Sicily in 1182, the loss of late-twelfth-century Savonese cartularies may not be, from the Sicilian viewpoint, very serious.[40] Apart from Savona, Marseilles had a developed notariate by 1200, to judge from the family archive of the Manduel merchant family. But the earliest contract, although it happens to be from Messina, dates from 1200.[41] For other cities the picture is even bleaker. A handful of private charters preserved in Pisa concerns maritime activity: the appointment of an executor during absence in Sicily, for example; while two documents shed light on the Pisan colony in Messina.[42] As in Venice, such items have survived haphazardly, and the

---

[39] Archivio di Stato, Savona, Cartolare Arnaldo da Cumano. The work of later notaries is illuminating on questions such as trade routes and provisioning: Martinus (1203), who is full of good things; 'Ubertus', really two notaries, Giovanni and his assistant Guglielmo (1213–16); Saono (1216–17) – all the more so since a lacuna follows extending right across the thirteenth century. All are in the Archivio di Stato, Savona, sezione notarile; but in 1974 the staff there disclaimed knowledge of Martinus' whereabouts. Transcriptions are, however, available in the Istituto di Paleografia e di Storia medievale, University of Genoa. An edition of Arnaldo da Cumano and Giovanni di Donato is in the press, published by the Ministero dell'Interno. Although no notarial records of law-suits survive from Genoa, this is perhaps because they have since been lost.

[40] See Chapter 6, 169–71, *infra*; also F. Noberasco and I. Scovazzi, *Storia di Savona*, 2 vols. (Savona, 1926), I, *passim*.

[41] L. Blancard (ed.), *Documents inédits sur le commerce de Marseille au moyen-âge*, 2 vols. (Marseilles, 1884–5), I, 3–5, no. 1.

[42] Archivio di Stato, Pisa, Pergamene Coletti, 1170–4, for evidence of commercial activity; on non-Sicilian trade, Archivio di Stato, Diplomatico, Monastero degli Olivetani, 1170 Aug. 16 *corta*, 1180 Oct. 24 *corta*, 1186 July 24 *corta* and Archivio della Certosa di Calci, 1182 Dec. 4 (trade in Sardinia). Messina is mentioned in Archivio di Calci 1190 Oct. 9 and in Archivio di Stato, Pergamene Roncioni, 1199 March 16 *corta* (documents I have edited for publication). For Calci documents, cf. the register in Archivio di Stato, Pisa, known as Carte Lupi, Fonti I, Certosa di Calci, I.

notarial record commences very late, in 1263. Lucca and Siena furnish material from the 1220s onwards.[43] On the other hand, there is plentiful evidence about the activity of Lucchese merchants who traded with Sicily in the Genoese cartularies of Oberto Scriba and of Guglielmo Cassinese; for Genoa was Lucca's ally and its quay. Thus it will be possible and indeed proper to add Lucca to the list of north Italian towns trading with Norman Sicily.

V

This is not to deny that the chronicles and travellers' tales which constituted the diet of past historians are without a vitamin value of their own. The Sicilian chronicles have little to say about economic matters, although the presence of Archbishop Romuald of Salerno at Venice in 1177, as Sicilian ambassador, means that his account of the Peace of Venice is of especial value – particularly for the study of Venetian relations with the Norman kingdom.[44] The Genoese annals are more expansive, for they were planned as a semi-official chronicle of the consuls and of the deeds and victories of the republic. Embassies to foreign rulers, privileges received in foreign ports, and wars with Pisa or Sicily are recorded in detail; and, since the work was continued by a series of chroniclers in sequence, the

---

[43] R. S. Lopez, 'The unexplored wealth of the Notarial Archives in Pisa and Lucca', *Mélanges Louis Halphen* (Paris, 1951), 417–32; D. Herlihy, *Pisa in the early Renaissance* (New Haven, Conn., 1958), 1–20; D. Bizzari (ed.), *Imbreviature notarili* 2 vols. (Turin, 1934), an edition of the earliest Sienese material. In any case, the main interests of the Lucchese and Sienese documents are the Tuscan hinterland and the trans-Apennine plains. The lack of Pisan cartularies from the twelfth century could reflect a slower development of commercial institutions, though it is fair to add that Venice too has lost its complete cartularies from this period – if, indeed, they ever existed – and yet Venice practised very sophisticated commercial techniques. Moreover, the surviving Pisan commercial charters show that some Pisan techniques were analogous to those of Genoa or Venice.

[44] Ed. C. A. Garufi, in *RISS*, ser. 2, VII, part 1; cf. H. Hoffmann, 'Hugo Falcandus und Romuald von Salerno', *Deutsches Archiv*, XXIII (1967), 116–70, criticising Garufi's edition – the annotation of which cannot, nevertheless, be ignored. The chroniclers of Roger II's reign, Alexander of Telese and Falco of Benevento, are available in G. del Re (ed.), *Cronisti e scrittori sincroni napoletani editi e inediti*, I, *I Normanni* (Naples, 1845), 85–148, 161–252. For Hugo Falcandus, foe of Maio of Bari, and a writer of great fluency, see the edition by G. B. Siragusa, *La Historia o Liber de Regno Sicilie e la Epistola ad Petrum Panormitane Ecclesie Thesaurarium* (FSI, Rome, 1897), 3–165; also E. M. Jamison, *Admiral Eugenius of Sicily: his life and work and the authorship of the 'Epistola ad Petrum' and the 'Historia Hugonis Falcandi Siculi'* (London, 1957); against which, Hoffmann, *op. cit.*

annalists are near enough in time to the events they describe to command special respect.[45] Less detailed are the Pisan Annals of Bernardo Maragone, a patrician of the city whose work reached as far as 1174 and was continued by his son Salem; here, however, there are several lengthy passages glorying in Pisan victories in Campania or over the Genoese in the Tyrrhenian Sea.[46] There are no twelfth-century sources from Venice, however, except under the refashioned stonework of thirteenth-, fourteenth- and fifteenth-century chronicles, many of which hark back to lost twelfth-century originals.[47] For Venice the Byzantine writers Niketas Choniates and Kinnamos provide much material, however; while the scholar Eustathios, Archbishop of Thessalonika, left a graphic memoir describing the Norman attack on his city in 1185.[48] The Arabic historians knew rather less about the affairs of the north Italian republics, and their comments on Latin traders in Sicily are only of minuscule value.[49]

A second group of literary sources consists in accounts of visits to Sicily by foreigners. A group of Hebrew and Arabic eye-witness accounts stands out prominently. First, there is the record left by the Spanish Jew Benjamin of Tudela who toured the Hebrew communities of the Mediterranean in about 1160. His diary is distinguished both by clarity and brevity, and includes a colourful portrait of Norman Sicily and southern Italy.[50] Another Spaniard, ibn Jubayr, secretary to the governor of Granada, set out a few years later from

[45] L. T. Belgrano (ed.), *Annali Genovesi di Caffaro e de' suoi continuatori*, vols. I and II, (FSI; Rome, 1890–1901).

[46] M. Lupo Gentile (ed.), *Gli Annales Pisani di Bernardo Maragone*, RISS, ser. 2, VI, part 2.

[47] See, in particular, H. Simonsfeld (ed.), *Historia ducum veneticorum*, MGH. SS., XIV, 72–97; E. Pastorello (ed.), *La Cronica di Andrea Dandolo*, RISS, ser. 2, XII, part I, an early-fourteenth-century source.

[48] Io. Kinnamos, *Epitome rerum ab Ioanne et Alexio Comnenis Gestarum*, ed. A. Meineke, Corpus Scriptorum Historiae Byzantinae (Bonn, 1836); Niketas Choniates, *Historia*, ed. I. Bekker, Corpus Scriptorum Historiae Byzantinae (Bonn, 1835); Eustathios of Thessalonika, *La Espugnazione di Tessalonica*, ed. S. P. Kyriakidis and V. Rotolo (Palermo, 1961), and tr. by H. Hunger, *Die Normannen in Thessalonike* (2nd ed., Graz, 1967), with useful notes.

[49] M. Amari, *BAS, versione italiana*, supplies conscientious translations of all sources then known from the Arab world that had a bearing on Norman Sicily. I have exploited what common ground I can see in my article 'L'Attività commerciale genovese nell'Africa normanna: la città di Tripoli', *Atti CISSN*, 395–402.

[50] M. N. Adler (ed.), *The itinerary of Benjamin of Tudela* (London, 1907); also, A. Asher (ed.), *The itinerary of Rabbi Benjamin of Tudela*, 2 vols. (London–Berlin, 1840–1).

Spain on a pilgrimage to Mecca and Madinah. On his return he visited Sicily in 1184/5, and left in his diary a priceless description of the island, its ports and institutions – though, to be sure, his acquaintance with the island was short and his comments need not be representative of the general state of affairs.[51] King Roger II's geographer al-Idrisi cannot be accused of such superficiality, on the other hand. He was set the task, he says, of describing the produce and natural resources of each region of the world. Unfortunately, his description of Sicily is fuller than that of the Norman mainland – probably because he used Arabic sources that knew Sicily, with its Muslim heritage, rather better than they knew the south of Italy. Unfortunately, again, he shows a tendency to hyperbole that seems characteristic of the Muslim sources. 'Extreme fertility' or 'severe devastation' are ascribed to many regions without reference to any possible median.[52]

Other travellers who have left descriptions of Sicily (though not, in general, of southern Italy) are the Jews of Fustat in Egypt. The documents left in their synagogue storeroom, or Geniza, include many letters from or about merchants in Sicily. However, the main concentration of letters is from the eleventh century, though some documents from the period of the Norman kingdom have been found. But the letters are hardly ever precisely dated; and some of the Sicilian letters do not concern business so much as family affairs, or religious matters. They are private communications, not diaries of wonders seen in unfamiliar parts of the world. Moreover, though they say much about the movement of commodities and of merchants, they tell much less about the activities of non-Jewish merchants, such as the north Italians. Few have been edited or even examined out of the vast mass existing in Cambridge and elsewhere.[53]

[51] R. J. C. Broadhurst (tr.), *The travels of Ibn Jubayr* (London, 1952), 335–61; M. Amari (tr.), *BAS, versione italiana*, folio ed., 35–45.

[52] *BAS, ed. cit.* 8–34 (Sicily only); M. Amari and C. Schiaparelli (ed. and tr.), *L'Italia descritta nel 'Libro del Re Ruggero' compilato da Edrisi* (Rome, 1883); also published in *Atti dell'Accademia dei Lincei, scienze morali*, ser. 2, VIII, 1883 (for Sicily and peninsular Italy); new edition in preparation in Palermo. One of his sources was probably the government surveys of Sicily known as *dafatir* – D. Clementi, 'Notes on Norman Sicilian surveys', in V. H. Galbraith, *The making of Domesday Book* (Oxford, 1961), 55–8.

[53] For an outline of the history of the Geniza material, see S. C. Reif, *A guide to the Taylor–Schechter Genizah Collection* (Cambridge University Library, 1973); also

Potentially more promising are the Geniza marriage contracts (*ketuboth*), all originally dated; they specify the contents of the bride's trousseau, and often cite prices. There are frequent references to 'Sicilian' luxury goods, such as silk mantles. But 'Sicilian' may sometimes be a generic term, as in the case of fustian, a western cloth named after the Geniza city of Fustat. In any case the *ketuboth* generally cite luxury goods, whereas Sicily attracted many merchants in search of humbler essentials, such as foodstuffs and raw cotton.[54] For this side of the picture, there is more gloom. Hope stems from the existence of North African cartularies of twelfth-century date or ancestry, that record legal verdicts of Islamic judges on matters such as commercial law. These verdicts, or *fatwas*, appear to be based on distinct and real legal cases; and those that refer to Sicilian commerce mention the import of Sicilian grain into Tunisia, against cash rather than against the export from Tunisia of textiles or other products.[55]

VI

The main worry of the economic historian of the twelfth century is to find material out of which a dynamic picture of trade developments can be created. However, there is a danger of assuming that treaties and grants of commercial privilege do no more than pro-

S. D. Goitein, *A Mediterranean society*, I, *Economic foundations* (Berkeley–Los Angeles, 1967), 1–28. A 'register'-type survey of the Geniza documents has been compiled: S. Shaked, *A tentative bibliography of Geniza documents* (Paris–The Hague, 1964). As Goitein, *Medit. society*, I, 7, points out, a Geniza 'is the very opposite of an archive', a hoard of documents that have lost all use, not a permanent record available for consultation.

54 A late-medieval marriage contract has been published by H. Bresc and S. D. Goitein, 'Un inventaire dotal de Juifs siciliens (1479)', *Mélanges d'Archéologie et d'Histoire de l'Ecole française de Rome*, LXXXII (1970), 903–7. Comparative study of the Geniza material, relating it to documents in the other Near Eastern archives and to the north Italian economic sources, has proceeded slowly. See, however, E. Ashtor, *Histoire des prix et des salaires dans l'Orient médiéval* (Paris, 1969), and *Les métaux précieux et la balance des payements du Proche-Orient à la basse époque* (Paris, 1971). The review of the latter by C. Cahen in *Revue Historique*, CCLI (1974), 173–5, argues that Ashtor's conclusions are inadequate, since they fail to take account of recent work by H. Misbach. Aspects of Misbach's work are discussed by me in Chapter 10, *infra*, 267–73; I do not believe that his work affects Ashtor's argument.

55 H. R. Idris, *La Berbérie orientale sous les Zirides*, 2 vols. (Paris–Algiers, 1962), II, 663–8.

vide weighty anchors that sink deep into the sea-bed and create a static view of medieval trade. This is not true if the privileges survive in quantity, or if they can be shown to be effectively the earliest ever granted, or if they can be related to other documents such as commercial contracts or chronicle accounts of the fluctuating fortunes of foreign merchants visiting the *Regno*. All these conditions are fulfilled by the numerous texts that survive in the form of agreements between the kings of Sicily (or the future King Roger II) and the Genoese, Savonese and Venetians; while the privileges granted by the German emperors to Genoa, Pisa and other north Italian towns say something about the merchants' commercial and territorial aspirations in the *Regno*.

The Genoese not merely kept an archive of notarial cartularies, and not merely commissioned their self-glorifying *Annales*; early in the thirteenth century, the consuls authorised the compilation of a Liber Jurium, a book of public acts, especially treaties with foreign powers. This now survives in several versions, and provides a number of important texts.[56] In addition, loose treaties survive in the State Archives at Genoa and Pisa, often providing contemporary or near-contemporary texts.[57] In 1195 the Genoese are known, for instance, to have taken their copy of Henry VI's privilege of 1191 to the emperor, to try to convince him to fulfil the promises made then. Similarly, William II's confirmation of his father's grant to Genoa did not repeat all the terms of the agreement made eighteen years earlier by William I; there was no need, since a text resided in Genoa, and, presumably, Palermo.[58] Several items concerning Venetian relations with Sicily also survive, preserved in the thirteenth-century treaty catalogues of the Venetian Commune. King William II's privilege to Venice is preserved three times in the Venetian treaty books, once in the fourteenth-century Liber Blancus,

---

[56] Edited from the texts then known in *Monumenta Historiae Patriae edita iussu Regis Caroli Alberto*, VI and VII, *Liber Iurium Reipublicae Genuensis*, but superseded for the twelfth century by C. Imperiale di Sant'Angelo, *Codice diplomatico della Repubblica di Genova*, 3 vols. (FSI, Rome, 1936–42). More recent discoveries of medieval Genoese documents are summarised by P. Lisciandrelli, 'Trattati e negoziazioni politiche della Repubblica di Genova, 958–1797', *ASLSP*, n.s., I, fasc. I (1960).

[57] For the Pisan material, see B. Casini, *Inventario dell'Archivio del Comune di Pisa (secolo XI–1509)* (Livorno, 1969), listing material in the *fondo* Atti Pubblici.

[58] *Ann. Ian.* II, 58–9; *CDG*, II, 202–4.

compiled by Doge Andrea Dandolo, and twice in the Liber Pactorum i (the second copy here is a fragment, probably inserted in error after the first copy had been made, and then apparently abandoned when the mistake was noticed). The Pactorum text seems closer to the original at several points, but no earlier text now survives.[59] Similarly, Savona preserved a register of treaties from about 1220, if not earlier; this survives, chain and all, under the descriptive title 'Registro a catena'.[60] Finally, a valuable series of trade treaties between Dubrovnik and the Adriatic ports has been preserved, and helps give an idea of smaller-scale commercial activity carried on between minor ports on either side of the Adriatic; ultimately, too, these treaties have some bearing on Sicilian relations with Venice.[61]

Strictly it is correct to distinguish between treaties between equal powers and grants or privileges by superior powers, such as the Byzantine chrysobulls for Venice and its rivals. Although the Norman grants to the Genoese and Venetians were not in any formal sense 'treaties', the Sicilian chancery took care not to give documentary offence – all of which reflects the reality of the situation in which the north Italians were something more than supplicants, and the Norman Sicilians partly supplicant themselves. In order to give weight to the economic and political reality of these privileges, they will sometimes be referred to as 'treaties'; but this is not to suggest that they were, as documents, recognisably agreements between equal parties.[62]

---

59 Archivio di Stato, Venice, Liber Blancus f.272v–273v; Liber Pactorum i, f.84v–85v; f.76v. (The numeration of Pactorum has been changed several times; the latest system adds '2' to each folio number, but is not very clearly written or of any obvious use; and the clearer style of numbering has been adopted here.)

60 Archivio di Stato, Savona, *Registro a catena piccolo*, or Registrum i. A late-thirteenth-century Registrum ii also survives; it lists only headings for the early material contained in Registrum i.

61 Historijski Arhiv, Dubrovnik, Acta Sanctae Mariae Majoris; cf. Abulafia, 'Dalmatian Ragusa and the Norman Kingdom of Sicily', *Slavonic and East European Review*, LIV (1976), 412–28.

62 H. Enzensberger, *Beiträge zum Kanzlei- und Urkundenwesen der normannischen Herrscher Unteritaliens und Siziliens* (Kallmünz, 1971), 107–8, remarks: 'daß es sich trotz der formalen Einseitigkeit um ein bilaterales Abkommen handelt, erkennen wir deutlich am Beispiel Genuas'. See also J. Riedmann, *Die Beurkundung der Verträge Friedrich Barbarossas mit italienischen Städten* (Österreichische Akademie der Wissenschaften, phil.-hist. Klasse, Sitzungsberichte, 291. Band, 3. Abhandlung; Vienna, 1973), 48–60, 161–2, *et passim*, for the diplomatic form of Barbarossa's

Eloquent in a different fashion are those artefacts that have conveniently arrived in north Italian destinations from Sicily and southern Italy, or in Sicily and southern Italy from north Europe. The Pisan doors of Monreale cathedral in Sicily present only a minor problem of dating, but objects from the *Regno* in Venetian collections are more of a difficulty, since the chronology both of their manufacture in the *Regno* and of their movement out of the *Regno* to Venice is uncertain.[63] Coin evidence goes far to show the continuing strength of the Sicilian economy, from several angles.[64]

Altogether, then, it is possible to carry the study of the Norman Sicilian economy far beyond what is conventionally on offer, both in the details revealed and in the scope of the picture presented. Indeed, the north Italian bias of the evidence will prove both convenient and revealing.

'treaties' with the Italian communes concerning the invasion of Sicily, and subsequently with the King of Sicily.

[63] The dating of the Pisan doors at Monreale is discussed by F. Bartoloni, 'La data del portale di Bonanno nel Duomo di Monreale', *Studi medievali in onore di Antonino de Stefano* (Palermo, 1956), 39–41. For a Sicilian casket in Venice and another object possibly of Sicilian manufacture, see Chapter 10 *infra*, 276–7.

[64] P. Grierson and W. A. Oddy, 'Le Titre du Tari sicilien du milieu du XIe siècle à 1278', *Revue numismatique*, ser. 6, XVI (1974), 123–34, have very convincingly shown how consistent was the gold content of the Sicilian tari or quarter-dinar throughout the Norman period. This dismisses a rumour put about by A. Sambon, in *Le Monete del reame di Napoli e di Sicilia* (printed but never published), 47, that William I brought the tari into disrepute. A further argument was that references in south Italian documents to *Papienses*, coins of Pavia, and to *Provesini*, coins of Champagne, show that there was a reluctance to cite the tari or other royal coins in financial transactions, since the tari could not be trusted: Sambon, 16, 37; A. Engel, *Recherches sur la numismatique et la sigillographie des Normands de Sicile et d'Italie* (Paris, 1882), 77. Rather does this prove that north Italian and north French silver continued to flow into the *Regno* and to be trapped there – a point made even more plausible by the increase in deposit banking in Sicily and southern Italy as the twelfth century drew to a close. See Chapter 10, *infra;* also E. Gattola, *Ad historiam abbatiae cassinenses accessiones* (Venice, 1734), I, 257, for *Papienses* in Campania in 1149. Until 1138 the Genoese carried *Papienses*; Conrad II granted Genoa a mint only that year – *CDG*, I, 106 – and so many *Papienses* could have come south in Ligurian pockets. A very large hoard of Champagne coins has recently been discovered in Basilicata, dating to the early thirteenth century: see 270–1 *infra*.

Chapter 2

THE RESOURCES

I

The Kingdom of Sicily: the very use of this title implies the existence of a political unit that possessed a specifically Sicilian identity, founded on continuity of government, culture or population, or all of these. It was, according to one historian, a 'model-state' in the twelfth and thirteenth centuries, in the sense that the Norman and Swabian kings governed the lives and affairs of their subjects with great precision and extensive controls, being blessed with a developed legislative sense that aimed to abstract and to apply a coherent series of juristic principles throughout their kingdom.[1] To this extent 'Kingdom of Sicily' means the government of the kingdom and the activities of its rulers; the definition is only incidentally concerned with the actual domains over which the Normans and their heirs ruled. But as a territorial entity, the *Regno* was something more than Sicilian. In the twelfth and for most of the thirteenth century it comprised, in addition to the island of Sicily, the southern half of peninsular Italy – the modern provinces of Calabria, Basilicata (Lucania), Apulia, Campania, Molise and the Abruzzi, a well as the trading city of Gaeta (but not the small papal enclave at Benevento). At different moments the *Regno* was stretched to include towns in what are now Algeria, Tunisia and Libya, as well as parts of Yugoslavia, Albania and Greece. Malta was incorporated into the *Regno* in 1127, but was first invaded by the Normans in 1090. Moreover, the northern land limits of the kingdom, slicing across the peninsula, were not clearly drawn and remained the subject of contention.[2]

---

[1] A. Marongiu, 'A model-state in the Middle Ages: the Norman and Swabian Kingdom of Sicily', *Comparative Studies in Society and History*, VI (1964), 307–20; also available in A. Marongiu, *Byzantine, Norman, Swabian and later institutions in southern Italy* (London, 1972), essay no. xi.

[2] D. Clementi, 'L'Atteggiamento dell'Imperatore Federico I nella Questione del

Added to the fluidity of its frontiers, inside the kingdom there existed a medley of ethnic groups – Greeks and Longobards on the mainland; Greeks, Arabs and Berbers in Sicily – whose individual political traditions and aspirations had found expression during the eleventh century in endemic civil strife. The looseness of the kingdom – in other words, the extent to which it derived its identity from the central government after its unification in the 1130s – becomes increasingly obvious. A further factor detracting from its identity is that the principal enemies of Norman Sicily, the German and Byzantine emperors, refused to recognise that it was a kingdom at all, and regarded Roger II's coronation as first King of Sicily in 1130 as an impudent usurpation of their own sovereign rights. After all, there had never been such a kingdom in the past; Bari was part of the Byzantine empire until the Normans seized it in 1071; the Hauteville dynasty was not even of royal stock nor of high feudal origin. Indeed the Norman royal title – 'King of Sicily and of the Duchy of Apulia and of the Principality of Capua' (Rex Sicilie et Ducatus Apulie et Principatus Capue) – recognised the ambiguity of contrasting claims to suzerainty in the Mezzogiorno. Technically at least mainland areas ruled by Roger belonged to the kingdom without actually being integral to it.

The distinction between mainland and island extended further than the identity of past rulers and of claimants to rule; the Normans set up in Apulia and Capua (that is, Campania) an administrative structure separate to that operating in Sicily and Calabria, the unit held and conquered by Roger II's father, Roger I the Great Count. Royal policy towards feudatories differed widely between the two regions, partly for historical reasons – the pre-existing mainland power structure was more 'feudalised' than Sicily ever had been or ever became – and partly because it was in Sicily that the Norman kings seem to have chosen to concentrate their own landed resources. This concentration of royal demesne lands in Sicily will prove to explain much about the economic affairs of the crown, quite apart from the political advantage that accrued to the Normans from not permitting any barons to establish a rival power-base on the newly-won island.[3]

Confine terrestre nel Regno normanno di Sicilia, Puglia e Capua', *PSIFB*, 479–83; E. M. Jamison (ed.), *Catalogus Baronum* (FSI; Rome, 1972), map.
[3] The exact relationship between the mainland and island administration has been

The resources

In the face of such diversity it is quite reasonable to cast doubt on the advisability of undertaking a study of the Norman kingdom. Is it, perhaps, ill-advised to generalise about the economic structure and development of areas that possessed only an artificial political link – or, in other words, to create an economic category out of a political one? There were substantial differences in economic resources between the mainland and Sicily – in the extent and rôle of agriculture, in problems of access and transport, in links with particular foreign markets. In commerce, it was particularly on the mainland that active, thriving mercantile cities existed that sent their merchants to the ends of the Mediterranean – cities such as Amalfi, Gaeta and Bari. The imbalance between the activities of each region may seem serious enough solely to permit a hinged comparative study, in which parallels are investigated and contrasts, in great quantity, recorded. At any rate it is obvious that the artificiality of the kingdom in so many respects must be a central consideration in any analysis of its history and institutions. The unifying factor was, simply, the king. Glowing contemporary reports talk of the wealth of the Norman kings; but the sources of this wealth have never been analysed in detail. The Norman kings are said to have extracted as much income from Palermo as did the Normans of England from the whole of their kingdom.[4] In part, however, the reputation for wealth of the Norman Sicilians rests on the fertility and prosperity of the island they ruled. Ibn Jubayr, a Spanish Moor, condescended to compare Sicily to his beloved Andalus – praise indeed.[5] But exactly what was the connection between the wealth of the island and that of the king? It is surprising that such a simple question, so deeply concerned with the whole mechanics of medieval royal finance, should never explicitly have been answered. It is by no means as obvious as it may appear that wealthy kingdoms bespeak wealthy kings. Anyway, the possible sources of wealth are so many – taxes, monopolies, rents, for instance – that closer definition is called for.

debated with vigour by M. Caravale, *Il Regno normanno di Sicilia* (Milan, 1966), against E. M. Jamison, 'The Norman administration', *op. cit.*; for a middle view, see E. Mazzarese Fardella, *Aspetti dell'organizzazione amministrativa nello stato normanno e svevo* (Milan, 1966).

[4] D. Mack Smith, *A history of Sicily*, II, *Medieval Sicily* (London, 1968), 30.
[5] Ibn Jubayr, ed. Broadhurst, 339, 349.

Since this study is ultimately concerned with the relations between government and economic enterprise, it seems logical to
concentrate on the period when the kingdom was united and
pacified. It would be wrong to suppose that the coronation of
Roger II symbolised the end of civil strife (in fact it created some
more), but certainly by the late 1140s baronial opposition ceased
wholly to dominate royal strategy, military and political. Increasingly, dissident elements turned to forces outside the kingdom –
especially the German and Greek emperors – as their capacity to
resist from power-bases within the *Regno* was whittled down. Meanwhile, in the south Italian countryside cultivation could be restored
and depopulated villages re-established.

At the basis of such considerations are further problems. Making
a stance in the late eleventh century, what sort of land do we find?
From the first Normans to Frederick II the *Regno* was compared to
Canaan, a land flowing with milk and honey.[6] But what did it
produce, and how was the land exploited? These are questions of
paramount importance not merely to the study of Sicilian agricultural history (obviously enough), but to the study of Sicilian trade
as well. Any analysis of the commerce of the *Regno* is deeply concerned with the export of foodstuffs; this is a basic fact of Sicilian
history from Roman or even Punic times.

The most obvious characteristic of southern Italy is the large area
covered by mountain.[7] There are no extensive internal plateaux;
the whole concentration of economic life was and remains along
the coasts, and few important towns are to be found inland. It is
therefore practical to divide mainland Italy into a number of
coastal zones, corresponding to the plains. Round Naples and Salerno,
for instance, the highlands, which jut right out into the sea, still

---

[6] Amato of Monte Cassino, *Storia dei Normanni*, ed. V. de Bartholomaeis (FSI;
Rome, 1935), 24: 'la terre qui mene lat et miel et tant belles coses'. Cf. Frederick
II's blasphemy that had God seen Sicily, He would never have sent the Children
of Israel to Canaan, attributed to the Emperor by Salimbene (MGH. SS., xxxii,
350).

[7] The following maps have been used: United Nations Food and Agriculture
Organisation, *Soil Map of Europe* (Rome, 1965–6); Consiglio Nazionale delle
Ricerche, *Carta della utilizzazione del suolo d'Italia* (1:200,000), maps 13, 15–23
(Milan, 1956–60); H.M.War Office, *Geological Map of Italy* (1:1,000,000), south
sheet (London, 1943). For changes caused by erosion, see C. Vita-Finzi, *The Medi-
terranean valleys, geological changes in historical times* (Cambridge, 1969).

bear forests while the plain is fertile and very suitable for cultivation of vegetables, vines and olives. Inland at Benevento, a papal enclave, the land is made up of a rather hard 'Brown Mediterranean' soil that is cultivable but demands careful irrigation. The area as a whole is typified by the production of grapes and olives, but cultivation of the latter was only gradually being extended during the eleventh and twelfth centuries. The same goes for a second major region, Apulia, which now consists of an almost uninterrupted sequence of olive plantations from Foggia to Brindisi. During the Middle Ages this was certainly a major grain-producing region, even though the clayey 'Red Mediterranean' soil is hard to work and tends to dry out in the summer. There were probably several practical reasons for the limitation on olive cultivation during the eleventh century, and its slow progress afterwards. Years of insecurity in Apulia had made it unsafe to invest in so easily destructible a form of cultivation.[8] It was only with the enrichment of Apulia, following Norman pacification and Venetian commercial visits, that local capital was available for investment in olive plantations. Campania and Apulia – these were the principal productive plains. To them can be added the seaside plain in the instep of Italy, but little is known about its agricultural status in the Middle Ages. It was, however, a minor target of Venetian commercial interest. The soil is alluvial and very suitable for cultivation.

Moving from the plains back to the mountains the picture changes radically. The Abruzzi and Molise were incorporated into the Norman kingdom, but very little is known about their economic life. The Abruzzi, naturally forest lands, are now much more barren than they were in the Norman period. Low-lying, alluvial soils are confined to a narrow coastal strip. High mountains make the interior difficult of access; but the activity of such coastal ports as Termoli suggests that the isolation of the Abruzzi and Molise was not as complete as the silence of the sources may lead it to be supposed.[9]

A little more is known about mountain economies further south, in the region known to the Byzantines as Lucania (basically Basilicata and northern Calabria). Here chestnut trees provided the major

8 A. Lizier, *L'Economia rurale dell'età pre-normanna nell'Italia meridionale* (Palermo, 1907), 122, 159.

9 For Termoli, see Abulafia, 'Dalmatian Ragusa', 417.

crop: chestnut flour. Stock-breeding was probably limited to pigs, and even their flesh was eaten only periodically. A certain amount of vegetable cultivation was possible too. A climate of severe contrasts, tending to extreme cold in winter and possible drought in summer, has always made life utterly miserable. Calabria, though just as hilly, seems to have been more fortunate, with limited areas suitable for agriculture. Dense forest covered much of the high ground. Here Greek monks hacked their way into the woods and forced from the soil a living. They kept goats and sheep and even, at the other end of the animal scale, silkworm, planting mulberry trees, as well as vines and fruit-trees. The produce of their mulberry trees was certainly sent south to Reggio, and in return, it must be assumed, the Calabrian monks received necessary items of food or other imports that they could not provide for themselves.[10]

The rôle of Sicily was more specialised than that of the south Italian regions. Sicily was, since the Roman empire, pre-eminently famous as a granary. In the Norman period it was the hilly hinterland that produced the main volume of grain, though certain long valleys, especially the Val di Noto and the Val di Mazara, also produced high-quality crops. The wheat seems to have been of a specially hard type, with high gluten content; its qualities included suitability to a hot, dry climate and durability in the face of damp and heat; its disadvantages were a low crop yield and the need for constant close attention. It was particularly ideal for export, since normally it could survive a long voyage in a ship's hold without fermenting. It remained an expensive, top-grade food. In fact, as will be shown, this was one of the prime attractions in growing it. Central Sicily, the main wheat-land, consists largely of 'Brown Mediterranean' soil, fertile and tractable; there are extensive uplands, though these are very frequently cultivable.[11] Here dry-farming,

[10] A. Guillou, 'La Lucanie byzantine', *Byzantion*, xxxv (1965), 138; reprinted in A. Guillou, *Studies in Byzantine Italy* (London, 1970), essay no. x. Also A. Guillou, *Corpus des actes grecs d'Italie du Sud*, fasc. ii. *S. Nicodème de Kellarana* (Vatican City, 1968), no. 3 for vines and olives; *ibid.*, fasc. iv, *Le brébion de la métropole byzantine de Région (vers 1050)* (Vatican City, 1974), for mulberries; and A. Guillou, 'Production and profits in the Byzantine Province of Italy (tenth to eleventh centuries): an expanding society', *Dumbarton Oaks Papers*, xxviii (1974), 91–109.

[11] Mack Smith, *op. cit.* 22, 30; F. Milone, *Memoria illustrativa della Carta della utilizzazione del suolo della Sicilia* (Rome, 1959), 109, 111 and 86, estimating the area of

dependent on the annual winter rains, would provide the water that farmers needed. There are signs that, in the early twelfth century at least, rainfall may have been higher in Sicily than now. The wide span of the bridge built at Palermo in 1113 by Admiral George of Antioch has been taken to show that water-courses were fuller and the climate was more congenial to cultivation of crops.[12]

The second characteristic of the island was the extent of fruit and vegetable cultivation along the coasts. Al-Idrisi provides detailed accounts of the coastal plains.[13] Broadly it was the north and east parts of the triangle that seem to have been most productive. The south has always been exposed to the drying effects of the African sirocco. Furthermore, the south could not offer so many safe harbours as north and east Sicily, because it was more exposed to Saracen attack and because the natural harbours simply did not exist. Elsewhere in Sicily, the Arabic sources convey an image of continuous orchards and gardens, extending inside the town walls and far into the countryside.[14] Irrigation canals were the norm in the towns and suburbs. Behind Messina and Catania the hills were covered in forest and protected by royal privilege. Agricultural life seems to have been diverse, active and productive. Admittedly, little is known about pasturage and livestock in Sicily, or elsewhere in the *Regno*. Goats that nibbled at the bushes and sheep moving pasture by season (transhumance) have been blamed for the destruction of Mezzogiorno and Sicilian agrarian life. In fact, the balance of agricultural production was always delicate. Irrigation demanded maintenance; no less did the orchards that were irrigated. Conditions in the Norman period were generally stable enough politically to make it possible for agricultural activity to continue unhindered, at least in Sicily. (The mainland was technologically less advanced, but produced a greater variety of items: wine and oil on a larger scale than Sicily.

grain cultivation in Sicily in the 1950s as 30% of all land, about 5% above the national average, and Milone, 93 and 169, emphasizing the general consistency of the picture since antiquity. N. Jasny, *The wheats of classical antiquity* (Baltimore, 1944), describes types of wheat grown in Italy.

[12] H. H. Lamb, *The changing climate* (London, 1966), 8.

[13] Idrisi, ed. Amari–Schiaparelli, 26–38.

[14] Ibn Jubayr, 348–51; ibn Hawqal, in *BAS, versione italiana*, folio ed., 3–6; H. Bresc, 'Les Jardins de Palerme', *Mélanges d'Histoire et d'Archéologie de l'Ecole Française de Rome*, LXXXIV (1972), for later centuries.

But there political disruption, even after Roger II's coronation, must have created innumerable local setbacks.)[15]

Other agrarian activities included the production in Sicily of silk, cotton, sugar-cane, indigo and henna. These were introduced by the Arabs. Cotton production seems to have been very high by the mid-twelfth century, since raw cotton was a favourite export of the Genoese merchants who visited Sicily. From animal hides leather and parchment were produced; but papyrus and paper were also used as writing materials – the former being manufactured out of Sicilian papyrus stems and the latter, possibly, out of Sicilian cotton.[16]

The relationship between urban and agrarian activity in the *Regno* has received little attention. Some towns in Sicily, such as Girgenti (Agrigento), seem to have acted as distribution centres for the produce of the neighbouring region. As has been seen, some agricultural activity – fruit production most notably – was carried on within the town walls; and, equally, some townsmen will have been employed in the fields outside the towns.[17]

On an institutional level, it is most common to see in the Normans the creators of south Italian feudalism, though certainly vassal relationships existed on many levels in the Mezzogiorno prior to

[15] C. Parain, 'The evolution of agricultural technique', *Cambridge economic history of Europe*, vol. 1 (2nd ed., 1966), 132; on transhumance in general, P. J. Jones, 'Medieval agrarian society in its prime: Italy', *ibid.* 380–1. M. Aymard and H. Bresc, 'Problemi di Storia dell'Insediamento nella Sicilia medievale e moderna, 1100–1800', *Archeologia e geografia del popolamento, Quaderni storici*, XXIV, fasc. 2 (1973), 945–76, adopt a pessimistic view of the Sicilian economy at the time of the Norman conquest, based on the assumption that there was serious disruption of economic activity. The Geniza texts might shed light on this; they seem not to agree that such disruption occurred. In other words, the urban and commercial situation was less grim. At any rate, it is impossible to deny the economic *potential* of Sicily to visiting merchants in search of grain or other agrarian products.
[16] Ibn Hawqal, *loc. cit.*, 6; Idrisi, 30; Peri, *Città e campagna*, 225; G. La Mantia, *Il primo documento in carta – Contessa Adelaide, 1109 – esistente in Sicilia* (Palermo, 1908). K. A. Kehr, *Die Urkunden der normannisch-sicilischen Könige* (Innsbruck, 1902), 137–47, provides conclusive evidence for the issue of papyrus as well as paper documents during the Norman period. As has been seen, Giovanni Scriba acquired his paper from Egypt – Chapter 1, note 32, *supra*. When, later on, paper was manufactured in Genoa, the cotton rag used in its manufacture could have been ultimately of Sicilian origin.
[17] I. Peri, 'Per la storia della vita cittadina e del commercio nel Medio Evo: Girgenti porto del sale e del grano', *Studi in onore di Amintore Fanfani*, 6 vols. (Milan, 1962), I, 531–616.

the Norman conquest.[18] If no more, the Normans formalised and systematised types of feudal relationship in southern Italy; the question, complex as it is, is very different from that whether feudalism was brought to island Sicily by the Normans.[19] The Arabs had never created a feudal system of land tenure in Sicily, except for the *iqta*, an approximation to the western military fief, though it involved no intermediaries between knight and sultan. Land was held directly from the ruler as a reward or retainer for services. As for labourers, their status long remained very depressed compared to that of the south Italian serfs.[20] The crucial factor in Sicilian feudalism was, however, the reservation to himself of the majority of the lands that Count Roger conquered. Sicily became predominantly crown demesne land, its hinterland covered by vast *latifundia* under the control of royal bailiffs. Knights' fees, by analogy with the *iqta*, were created, but few baronies were established between them and the sovereign.[21] The principal exceptions were family ones – a Hauteville, Tancred, was appointed Count of Syracuse; members of Roger I's wife's family, the Aleramici from Savona, were granted Paterno.[22] The holdings of the Duke of Apulia, Robert Guiscard and his heirs, were gradually absorbed into the Great Count's network:

[18] A Soviet scholar, M. L. Abramson, is, not surprisingly, insistent upon this point – see her articles in *Sredniye Vyeka (Middle Ages)*, III, 1951; V, 1954; XXVIII, 1965; XXXI, 1968; XXXII, 1969; and, most recently, 'Krestyanskiye soobshchestva v yuzhnoy Italii v X–XIII vv.', ('Information about peasants in southern Italy in the tenth to thirteenth century'), *Yevropa v sredniye vyeka: ekonomika, politika, kultura* (Moscow, 1972), 47–61.

[19] And, in addition, it is different to the question whether the *Regno* was a 'feudal state', as maintained by L. R. Ménager, 'L'Institution monarchique dans les états normands d'Italie', *Cahiers de civilisation médiévale*, II (1959), against A. Marongiu, 'Model-state'. This debate – of considerable importance, certainly – is concerned with the Norman idea of kingship, and not simply with questions of land tenure.

[20] Information I owe to the late Miss Evelyn Jamison. Cf. also Peri, *Città e campagna*, 88–9, and I. Peri, *Il Villanaggio in Sicilia* (Palermo, 1965).

[21] C. Cahen, *Le Régime féodal de l'Italie normande* (Paris, 1940), 59–60; Cahen, 32 for the *iqta*. G. Galasso, *Dal Comune medievale all'Unità* (Bari, 1969), 53, estimates the proportion of land held by the crown on the mainland at 20–30% of the total available for distribution.

[22] Cahen, 38; cf. Chapter 5, 127, 130, *infra*, for Tancred's heirs in 1162, though Cahen, 59, was apparently unaware of them. The Count Simon known from 1162 may be the son of Henry, Count of Paterno (Roger I's brother), or a natural son of Roger II. Probably he is the former. For both, see Chalandon, *Hist.*, II, 135, 297; H. Falc., 9, 11–13, 19, 20, 22, 51. Also Chapter 3, 64–5, *infra*.

Palermo, half Messina, the Val Demona nearby, all highly profitable enclaves.[23] The financial implications of this general take-over were enormous. The corn-producing hinterland became the reserve of the ruler of Sicily, a colossal source of wealth that was conscientiously exploited by the crown in alliance with buyers in north Italy, North Africa and elsewhere.

For the king did retain extensive controls over the movement of wheat. King Tancred promised Gaeta 'ut frumenta non prohibeantur vobis de Sicilia extrahere et deferre Gaietam, nisi quando generalis prohibitio facta fuerit a regia maiestate', a picture in accord with the practice of the Angevins a century later. Not just the movement but also the sale of grain could be placed under *prohibitio* in the thirteenth century, to judge from the monopolistic exploitation of the grain trade by Frederick II in 1239.[24] A story recounted by ibn al-Athir suggests that the Normans too exercised their grain interests. He writes that a crusade was planned against al-Mahdiyyah (which he confuses with the First Crusade), and that Roger I was asked to help. He was very reluctant:

Suppose they conquer the land and become masters of it, then [commerce] in foodstuffs will pass from Sicilian hands to theirs; meanwhile we shall have to send them provisions from Sicily and I shall lose the money I draw each year from the sale of my produce.[25]

There were even royal financial agents at al-Mahdiyyah by 1117, who co-ordinated the sale of grain in North Africa.[26]

[23] Chalandon, *Hist.*, I, 209.

[24] Tancred's privilege: C. Minieri Riccio, *Saggio di Codice diplomatico, formato sulle antiche scritture dell'Archivio di Stato di Napoli* (Naples, 1878–83), II, 286. Subsequent developments: Schaube, 505–9 (Frederick II); M. de Boüard 'Problèmes de subsistances dans l'état médiéval: le marché et le prix des céréales au royaume angevin de Sicile', *Annales – Histoire: Economie: Société*, X (1938), 438–510. Charles I of Anjou operated a highly sophisticated transfer system by which grain could be ordered to particular towns and provinces as soon as signs of poor harvests appeared. Some of these orders and some of his export licences were in the Naples Archive until its destruction by the Germans in 1943: E. M. Jamison, 'Documents from the Angevin Registers of Naples: Charles I', *Papers of the British School at Rome*, XVII (1949), 87–180.

[25] Ibn al-Athir, *BAS, versione italiana*, folio ed., 115.

[26] H. Wieruszowski, 'The Norman Kingdom of Sicily and the Crusades', *A history of the Crusades*, ed. K. M. Setton, II. *The later Crusades, 1189–1311* (Philadelphia, 1962; Madison, Wis., 1969), 18–20.

The king drew benefit from trade in other ways too, by way of tolls and taxes. Although the Genoese and Venetians were granted tax reductions, it is not clear that the Pisans managed to avoid payments of the κομμέρκιον, an *ad valorem* tax on merchandise normally set at 10 per cent in the *Regno*. Other taxes, *passagium*, *pedagium*, *portaticum*, *plateaticum*, *falangagium*, are little more than names at present.[27] Sometimes these names were used in documents simply to mean 'tolls and taxes', but they could also have specific applications. Payment of internal *passagium* on royal bridges, rivers and lands was abolished by William II in 1187, but the toll had, in any case, long been in the hands of tax pirates, who appropriated it for their own use. The citizens of Palermo and Messina found the payment of taxes on imports of food into their cities particularly irksome, and managed to gain relief from these taxes under William I. It is too early to be able to disentangle Byzantine, Longobard, Arab and Norman elements in the commercial tax structure of the *Regno*, though the κομμέρκιον has clear Greek affinities.[28]

Further benefit was drawn from the Sicilian economy by monopolies on the extraction of salt, iron, pitch and other mineral products, as well as tunny-fishing. The extent of royal rights is not always easy to judge, since these monopolies are known from grants of exemption that tell only fragments of the story.[29] The reservation of pitch and iron, and of the wood in the forests behind Messina, accords well with the naval needs of the Normans; into the same

[27] The κομμέρκιον is known from the privileges to Genoa: 63, 92 *infra*. A 10% κομμέρκιον was normally payable in the Byzantine empire: H. Antoniadis-Bibicou, *Recherches sur les douanes à Byzance* (Paris, 1963), 97–157. Ten per cent was also paid at Messina until 1160: 117 *infra*.

[28] Minieri-Riccio, II, 285–7, for Gaetan exemption from 'pedagium, falangagium' and the 'dirictum quod sub nomine catenaccii et pondere statere hactenus in Gaieta dabant'. Henry VI granted the Abbey of Santa Maria Latina in Jerusalem 'ut liceat singulis annis in perpetuum ducentas salmas frumenti in quoslibet portus regni nostri libere sine aliquo portatico aut plateatico mittere et abstrahere' – W. Holtzmann, 'Papst-, Kaiser- und Normannenurkunden aus Unteritalien, i', *Quellen und Forschungen aus italienischen Archiven und Bibliotheken*, XXXV (1955), 74, no. 10; cf. 70, no. 7, a more generous grant of export rights on other commodities. Abolition of internal *passagium*: text in Minieri-Riccio, Supplemento, I, 21. Palermo and Messina: 117–18 *infra*. See Powell, 'Medieval Monarchy', 432.

[29] Caspar, *Roger II.*, Register no. 7 (salt, 1109); no. 48 (pitch); no. 48 and no. 69 (tunny-fishing); A. Pratesi, *Carte latine di abbazie calabresi provenienti dall'Archivio Aldobrandini* (Vatican City, 1958), no. 89 (iron, 1208); no. 32 and no. 64 (salt).

category can be placed the expropriation of merchant ships, or embargoes on their sailing during periods of naval emergency.[30] Little is known of the royal officers who raised the taxes and super-vised royal rights. It is not even clear to which of the royal *duane* they were accountable. At the ports, the king's *portulani* seem to have collected taxes and to have kept records of tax exemptions, but these records have not survived.[31]

II

Benjamin of Tudela speaks of 'Sicilian' merchants in Barcelona and Alexandria, differentiating them from Amalfitans. The problem is whether he refers to Muslims, Greeks, Jews, Latins – or all of these. In Palermo at any rate the Muslims constituted the largest element in the mercantile population, as late as ibn Jubayr's visit in 1184/5. Messina, however, had fewer non-Christian merchants by 1160 and was active in trade with Reggio across the straits and with foreign ports. Its merchants and ship-owners are found in Genoa, Venice and Constantinople. Ibn Jubayr characterises Messina as the main mart of the 'merchant infidels', and despite the royal privileges it received, the town benefited far more from the visits of outsiders on their way to Sicily or to east Mediterranean ports, than from the activities of its natives. Its status in the eleventh century seems to have been much inferior to its position a century later. Messina was a Norman phenomenon and a phenomenon of the crusades.[32]

[30] The Gaetans were excused the duty to hand over use of their ships to royal officials should the *curia* require grain to be transferred to the mainland: Minieri-Riccio, II, 285–7. Embargoes on sailing: Ibn Jubayr, 353 (Amari, *BAS*, folio ed., 42); 163–4, 275–6 *infra*. When ibn Jubayr arrived at Trapani, he boarded a Genoese vessel bound for Spain, and then suddenly 'there arrived an order from the King of Sicily stopping all ships from sailing from the shores of his island. It seems that he is preparing a fleet, and no ships may sail until the fleet has left... The Genoese owners of the two ships hurried aboard to protect themselves from the Wali (*baiulus*?) but he relaxed as the result of a bribe the Genoese gave him, so that they remained in their ship and awaited a wind on which to sail.' A case of the commandeering of a ship is cited *infra*, 65–6; this vessel arrived in Sicily from Savona in about 1127.

[31] The *baiuli* and *portulani* are little known in this context, though the former had well-attested functions outside the ports: Jamison, 'Norman administration', 402; M. Caravale, *Il Regno normanno di Sicilia* (Milan, 1966), 370–7. Holtzmann, *art. cit.*, 70, no. 7: 'notum facimus omnibus baiulis et portulanis Messane' (privilege of William II for Santa Maria Latina).

[32] *The itinerary of Benjamin of Tudela*, ed. Adler, 2, 76; ibn Jubayr, 338, 348. For

Whatever the vitality of Sicilians overseas, during the eleventh century Sicily, especially Palermo, was the hub of the Mediterranean trade routes, visited for its own sake and as a major halt or interchange point for shipping and travellers from every end of the Mediterranean. The cosmopolitan, 'international' activity of one of the merchant groups that used Sicily both as a base and as a market, the Jews, shows how difficult it can be to divide native Sicilians from foreigners and denizens. Indeed, to avoid payment of a tithe imposed on foreign merchants by the Arab rulers of Sicily in the 1060s, many Egyptian Jews traded under the cover of their Sicilian Jewish colleagues; and throughout the eleventh and twelfth centuries Jewish immigration from Ifriqiya, in the wake of the Banu Hillal and other plagues to commerce, brought to Sicily as permanent or temporary residents many non-native Jews.[33] It might be said that evidence from cosmopolitan Jewish merchants gives little idea of the full range of local and long-distance trade, all the more so since the evidence comes from a community in Egypt, not in Sicily. Yet it is obvious from the records of the Cairo Geniza that eleventh-century Sicily was deeply involved in trade with the east, or at least with North Africa. In fact Arab Sicily and Arab–Berber Tunisia belonged in the eyes of the Cairo Jews to a single commercial circuit.

Sicily and Tunisia together were the object of a variety of commercial enterprises. Coral was shipped from Tunisia to Sicily, and it may be that none of the 'Sicilian coral' that the Cairo letters mention was collected in the island's waters, though it was sent with that label to Egypt.[34] Movement between Tunisia and Sicily was so frequent that it becomes, in consequence, difficult and even dangerous to attempt to disentangle the two regions. The journey was quick – normally much less than a week from Palermo to Tunis or al-Mahdiyyah.[35] But it was at Mazara in the eleventh century, and Trapani in the late twelfth and thirteenth, that businessmen trading to Tunisia were concentrated. Ibn Jubayr points out the value of Trapani to long-distance shipping on its way from Tunisia to

Paganus, a sailor from Messina who appears in Genoa and Venice, cf. Chapter 5, 134, *infra*.

[33] Goitein, *Medit. society*, I, 61, 344, 350, 488.

[34] Goitein, *Medit. society*, I, 47. Cf. Chapter 10, 276.

[35] Goitein, *Medit. society*, I, 325: a case of 35 days was quite exceptional.

northern Italy; Mazara was a little further out of the way, and arguably the expansion of Genoese and Pisan trade in the west Mediterranean, along with this greater accessibility, was what eventually gave Trapani its primacy. But it is wrong to suppose that most ships sailed from western Sicily via Ifriqiya to Egypt. Perhaps even more common was a Tunisia–Sicily–Alexandria route; and even if individual ships did not travel the whole way, many of the goods put on sale in Palermo eventually travelled this route.[36]

Palermo clearly retained its importance in the Ifriqiyan trade, even though it was, as it were, round the corner of Sicily. But the speciality of Palermo was long-distance trade with Egypt and the east Mediterranean. During one summer in the mid-eleventh century, ten ships carrying a grand total of five thousand persons arrived in Alexandria from Palermo; there is no reason to regard this figure as exceptional.[37] Another region much visited by the Fustat Jews was Demona – later part of Robert Guiscard's reserved demesne – which proves, interestingly enough, to have been a local centre for the manufacture of silk cloth and of carpets.[38] Its proximity to another town, Messina, makes the relative unimportance of the future arsenal of Sicily all the more surprising in the eleventh century. In the middle of that century Perahya Yiju wrote to his father, in Mazara, describing a journey round Sicily to Messina, and grumbling that 'the town is mediocre; one cannot live here… it is impossible to walk in the streets here because of the dirt'.[39] This may just be abuse against Christian standards of hygiene, but the lack of comment on the port as a commercial centre implies that at this stage it played no great rôle in trade with Egypt or elsewhere. Perahya was not the only Jew to avoid Messina when he could, for he says that the rabbi no longer held afternoon and evening prayers, which must be taken to mean he had difficulty in finding a *minyan*,

---

[36] S. D. Goitein, 'Sicily and southern Italy in the Cairo Geniza documents', *Archivio storico per la Sicilia orientale*, LXVII (1971), 10–11.

[37] Goitein, *Medit. society*, I, 215.

[38] Chalandon, *Hist.*, I, 209; Goitein, 'Sicily and southern Italy', 12, 13 – where he seems to me to underestimate the importance of Demona.

[39] Goitein, 'Sicily and southern Italy', 30 (translation of the whole document); S. D. Goitein, *Letters of medieval Jewish Traders* (Princeton, N.J., 1973), 327–30 (revised translation); Shaked, *Tentative bibliography*, 188.

a congregation of ten males. In fact the real centre of Siculo–Greek economic activity during this century proves to have been Syracuse; the Jews purchased silk there in the eleventh century and hides there in the eleventh and thirteenth centuries. Syracuse was also, by the Hohenstaufen period, a centre of cheese production, for Jewish merchants exported Sicilian cheese to Egypt, probably as a supplementary protein source for the poorer classes.[40]

The Jewish traders brought from Egypt and elsewhere a variety of luxury items. In spring 1058, a merchant bound for Sicily received in partnership from an Egyptian 186 dinars worth of oriental spices and aromatics, for sale in the island. Brazilwood was popular, as a dye for cloth; indigo, if of good quality, could be sold too, though Sicily produced its own. Lapis lazuli was brought from the east to Sicily, which suggests many questions about the supply of artistic materials in Arab and Norman Sicily. Pottery was brought from Rosetta on the Nile; in mentioning pottery, the Geniza letters only serve to confirm that the identity of style and technique between some Sicilian and Fatimid pottery has its roots in direct trade in ceramics.[41] This trade went both ways, to judge from a find of Syracusan 'developed Siculo–Norman' ware at the Geniza city of Fustat itself.[42] Goitein may be right in principle when he says that Sicily imported much the same oriental luxury goods as western Europe, even in the Arab period; but if anything the scale of imports from the east may have been higher than in Europe.

Sicily too could provide the east with highly desirable objects. In about 1100 the rabbinical court at Fustat adjudicated a suit concerning Sicilian robes sent as far as the Yemen.[43] And the Yemen was not even halfway to the destination of some Cairo Jews – India; there they obtained many of the famous oriental spices and it is perfectly reasonable to suppose they paid with western produce. Perahya Yiju, who so disliked Messina, was himself the nephew of one of the greatest India merchants in eleventh-century Cairo. But

[40] Goitein, 'Sicily and southern Italy', 19; *Medit. society*, I, 40, 124.
[41] Goitein, *Medit. society*, I, 176, 184 (spices); 210 (brazilwood, lapis lazuli); 110 (pottery).
[42] D. B. Whitehouse, 'The medieval pottery of south Italy', Ph.D. dissertation (Cambridge, 1967), 161, 163, (revised ed. in the press, Rome).
[43] Shaked, *Tentative bibliography*, 200. More instances of Sicilian links with the deeper parts of Asia can perhaps be expected in Goitein's forthcoming *India Book*.

Sicily did not produce solely for a luxury market. The emphasis in Sicilian exports was on basic materials such as leather goods and food (wheat was sent to Egypt if the Nile failed in its duty).[44]

It is impossible to say anything about Sicily's balance of payments before the mid-twelfth century, except to talk in general terms of signs of prosperity. There does, however, survive an account sheet, of about the mid-eleventh century, recording purchases made in Sicily as a result of a partnership established either in Cairo or in Ifriqiya. The *socius negocians* possessed 4,435 quarter dinars (tari). This is how he spent part of it:

63 Syracuse hides [no price given]	
20 pieces of lead, weighing 24 *qintar* [about 2,000 lb]	
Price [of lead] with customs and service charge	260
2 bales of shelled almonds [wrapped in] 21 (or 76?)	
rabbit skins, weight 10 *qintar*; price with customs	253
...3 narrow farkhas [a Sicilian textile]	23
1 wide farkha	8
1 turban [a popular export]	14
2 turbans	28
4 brocade blankets	38
238 gold leaves	68
4 Dustari gowns	110
11 Indigo-coloured wraps [shawls]	6
1 silk wrap	20
1 Dustari gown	12
19 lb silk	206[45]

However, the price evidence from the Geniza, unless applied very widely in area and time, leaves one with the uneasy feeling that nothing more than the operation of the law of supply and demand has been proved. For instance, in one year in Sicily the price of flax fluctuated from 70 tari in winter to 40 per bale in summer, not surprisingly, since it was during the summer that new supplies arrived. Or again: 'I was happy to have sold these four bales of flax', runs

[44] Goitein, 'Sicily and southern Italy', 19; based on Cambridge University Library MS T–S. 16. 13, line 11.
[45] Goitein, 'Sicily and southern Italy', 31–3; additional comments, in square brackets, are my own. Original: Cambridge University Library MS T–S., Arabic Box 54, f.88.

a report from Mazara, 'since the ship of the Binzerti [Tunisians?] arrived and the prices fell... What I had sold for 30 tari is now worth only 26–27.'[46]

Goitein has argued that the Geniza records indicate a flourishing textile industry in Sicily. Judging from the evidence so far published, this 'industry' was in fact an accumulation of small-scale enterprises of great variety. Thus there were some luxury silk cloths sent abroad; and there were exports of brocades and of other examples of Sicilian handiwork; but the emphasis in exports was not on finished textiles. Striking in the account sheet just cited is the emphasis on unprocessed goods: there are nineteen pounds of silk, fetching 206 tari; there are pieces of lead and semi-processed articles such as hides and shelled almonds wrapped in rabbit skins. But there is no evidence that the manufacture of silk cloth was of great importance in the Sicilian economy. In the twelfth century, the main effort seems to have been directed towards the creation of palace workshops that could provide silk and other luxury textiles for the royal court, without hint of commercial activity. Some silk exports there clearly were in the years before the Norman conquest of Sicily; and exports too of more modest textiles. The contrast in price between the eleven indigo-coloured shawls, at 6 tari for the lot, and the single silk shawl, at 20 tari, is one of the most striking features of the account sheet that has been cited, and yet neither represents more than a tiny proportion of the 4,435 tari the travelling partner had available for spending. Goitein points out that only a small part of the silk that was exported from Sicily, the silk called *lasin*, was of especially high quality.[47]

Elsewhere in the kingdom there was some production of textiles. There were royal dye-works at Salerno, granted out by the archbishop late in the Norman period.[48] But the emphasis, both in southern Italy and Sicily, was not, by 1150, on the export of finished

[46] Goitein, *Medit. society*, I, 302.
[47] Goitein, 'Sicily and southern Italy', 13. For the silk industry see also V. Monneret de Villard, 'La Tessitura palermitana sotto i Normanni', *Miscellanea G. Mercati*, vol. IV (Studi e Testi, cxxiii; Vatican City, 1946), 464–89. Also ibn Jubayr, 341, and Otto of Freising, MGH. SS. xx, 370, for the royal workshops. H. Fillitz, *The Crown jewels and the ecclesiastical treasure chamber, Vienna* (2nd ed., Vienna, 1963), no. 163 – no. 172, conveniently lists suriviving items from the silk coronation robes of the Norman and Hohenstaufen rulers of Sicily.
[48] Jamison, *Admiral Eugenius*, 323–32, Document iv.

textiles. Whether this means that the eleventh-century textile producers had gone into decline, or that they never existed on a large scale in the first place, is a question worthy of study; but the results would not greatly affect the twelfth-century state of affairs. It is abundantly clear from the Genoese contracts that raw cotton was a far more important export from the *Regno* than cotton cloth; in the late twelfth century large quantities of north Italian and Flemish cloth were being imported into Sicily and Campania. Few and far between are instances of raw cotton being imported into the *Regno*. Indeed, it seems that the availability of raw cotton for processing in northern looms was a prime attraction of Sicily in the eyes of the Genoese, Lucchese and rival merchants. Cotton as well as wheat received detailed treatment in the Genoese–Sicilian treaty of 1156. Wheat, after all, was needed for consumption, but cotton could be metamorphosed into cloth and sold back to those that had produced it out of the soil. The exploitation of this possibility marks a major breakthrough in the development of north Italian overseas trade; and Sicily, as seller of raw cotton and purchaser of finished cloth, had a special rôle to play. Moreover, with profits earned on textile sales, northern merchants could buy other desirables, not least wheat, without having to dig deeply into their own pockets. It is precisely the lack, or demise, of a Sicilian and south Italian textile industry that is of importance in the study of the Norman economy.[49]

III

The Amalfitans have always had a special reputation among historians of southern Italy. The eleventh century is seen as the period when Amalfi dominated Latin trade with the east, the twelfth and thirteenth that when Genoa, Pisa and Venice competed among themselves, without much concern for small fry such as Amalfi, for control of the eastern markets.[50] Such displacement did occur, but

---

[49] For further development of these points, see Chapter 10, 255–64, *infra*.

[50] See, e.g., G. Luzzatto, *Economic history of Italy*, 51. Tle classic account by M. Camera, *Memorie storico–diplomatiche dell'antica città e ducato di Amalfi*, 2 vols. (Salerno, 1876–81), has little of substance to say about commerce, especially since the dating of the documents cited is erratic. G. Galasso, 'Il Commercio amalfitano nel periodo normanno', *Studi in onore di R. Filangieri* (Naples, 1959), I, 81–103 is very valuable; also A. Citarella, 'The relations of Amalfi with the Arab world before the crusades', *Speculum*, XLII (1967), 299–312; G. Coniglio, 'Amalfi e il suo commercio nel Medioevo', *Nuova rivista storica*, XVIII/XIX (1944/5), 100–14.

whether the form it took was as direct as this summary statement
implies is a more complex problem. Pisan attack on the harbour of
Amalfi, and Venetian erosion of Amalfitan commercial rights in
Byzantium together seem to show that attempts did occur to destroy
Amalfitan commercial pre-eminence. But the city does not appear
as the destination of Genoese merchants in their contracts for trade
in the Tyrrhenian Sea. Salerno and, later on, Naples are the ports
mentioned. Amalfi hardly enters the history of north Italian relations with the Kingdom of Sicily and, in particular, it does not
seem to have been able to participate in north Italian penetration of
French and Flemish markets and thereby to gain access to continental as well as Mediterranean markets. The Amalfitans continued to
trade not necessarily on a diminished scale, but in any case on a scale
out of all proportion to the massive investment of Genoese, Pisans
and Venetians in Mediterranean trade. There was apparently an
Amalfitan quarter in Palermo during Tancred's reign, but nothing
is known of its activities. Indeed, the only city under Norman
control whose commerce is well documented in north Italian sources
is Gaeta; Gaetan merchants traded with Sicily, Sardinia, Corneto
and Liguria and engaged in a lively but bloody rivalry with the
Savonese.[51] Gaetan merchants apart, sailors and shippers from the
city seem to have been welcome in Genoa, providing useful services
in Genoese trade overseas. As for the Apulian towns, only their
trade with Dubrovnik is known in detail in this period.[52]

IV

The origins of Genoese and Pisan commercial activity are difficult
to reconstruct. In the twelfth century Genoa and Pisa were growing
cities, for whereas the former had previously constituted only part
of the area within the Roman walls of Ianua, by the 1160s it had a
new, more extensive set of walls.[53] The characteristics of Genoa are
determined by its limitations: the lack of an extensive food-producing

[51] See Chapter 6, 170–1, *infra*; for the earlier history, M. Merores, *Gaeta im frühen Mittelalter* (Gotha, 1911). Merores, 96–8 provides ample illustration of Gaetan trade in luxury items in about 1012. For Gaetans in Corneto, D. S. H. Abulafia, 'Corneto-Tarquinia and the Italian mercantile republics: the earliest evidence', *Papers of the British School at Rome*, XLII (1974), 224–34.
[52] Specifically, Molfetta, Monopoli, Bari, Bisceglie and also Termoli (Molise) – Abulafia, 'Dalmatian Ragusa', 413–18.　　[53] *Ann. Ian.*, I, 54.

hinterland, its physical confinement on the edge of the mountains where they come down to the sea. All this increased its dependence on outside sources of supply, the more so as its population grew. The first signs of its mercantile capacity are shown by the existence of a navy, which the Genoese were able to send against al-Mahdiyyah in 1087. It may be true, as Lopez suggests, that pirate activity against the Saracens and others, not solely on the Mahdiyyah scale, provided the patricians and their inferiors with a source of capital which served as a basis for their investments in trade.[54] And indeed the process of capital investment on an ever-larger scale continued throughout the twelfth century, so that the investments of the 1150s appear to be mere small change by comparison with those of 1200. And yet all this does not explain every aspect of the problem; there was a vast 'revival of trade', a 'commercial revolution', in which Genoa and Pisa were not the late starters but among the front runners. In fact Genoa was extremely well placed to indulge in large-scale commerce. First, the creation of surplus capital among the patrician landowners – quite apart from that derived from pirate plunder – made it possible for the upper rank of Genoese to transfer some of their money from land to overseas trade. Secondly, and linked to this, Genoa must always have been dependent on imports of food if its population was to survive. Rather than postulating outside, 'oriental' inspiration for the commercial growth of Genoa, we can look to the basic needs of the population and to the ability of the moneyed class to satisfy these needs to its own advantage. Thirdly, there was the emancipation of Genoa from imperial surveillance and the close co-operation between the patricians and the archbishop, resulting in the formation of an aristocratic communal government. The vicecomital families, a group of clans to which the majority of twelfth-century consuls belonged (della Volta, de Castello), concentrated political authority in their

[54] R. S. Lopez, 'The trade of medieval Europe: the south', *Cambridge Economic History of Europe*, II (Cambridge, 1952), 306, a view suggested perhaps by Karl Marx, *Capital* (Communist Party of the Soviet Union edition, Moscow, 1959), 325–6: 'merchant's capital, when it holds a position of dominance, stands everywhere for a system of robbery, so that its development among the trading nations of old and modern times is always directly connected with plundering, piracy, kidnapping slaves, and colonial conquest; as in Carthage, Rome, and later among the Venetians, Portuguese, Dutch, etc.'

own hands. As a result the decision to involve Genoa in costly but
profitable overseas expeditions lay in the hands of the one group
that stood most of all to profit. When Genoese ships went in the
wake of the crusade to Antioch and Acre, it was by mandate of
the consuls. Official policy and the desires and aims of the Genoese
nobility cannot be divorced. There were of course Genoese families
such as the Avvocato and Gavi that stood aloof from trade, but it
was not they who won control of the Commune.[55] Genoese greatness was, rather, the result of conscious endeavour.

Pisa falls into a different category. It did possess an agricultural
hinterland, though this was circumscribed by the boundaries of
other lordships. Hence its endless struggles against Lucca and
Florence to expand its local frontiers at their expense. Certainly by
the late thirteenth century the *contado* was quite insufficient for the
food needs of Pisa.[56] More characteristic of Tuscany and of the
trans-Apennine regions was the urban nature of the hinterland:
dozens of hungry cities, needing a port through which they could
draw additional supplies and where they could send for transfer
overseas their own products or those they had brought from further
north still. This lack of total dependence on foreign foodstuffs,
compared to Genoa, is reflected in the less frantic commercial
activity of Pisa. Mercantile institutions – the notariate, for example
– were less highly developed or slower to develop. Trade for Pisa
was a means to wealth, but it was not so much a means to life. In
Sicily the Pisans were content to trade without privileges for many
years. Nevertheless it was the Pisans who, during the eleventh century,
attempted a series of conquests in the central Mediterranean that
provide the first evidence for extensive north Italian interest in the
affairs of the Norman conquerors of Sicily.

During the tenth century the Tyrrhenian coast was repeatedly
assaulted by Saracen pirates, as far north as Tuscany. It was essential
for the peace of the whole littoral to prevent Islam from establishing
itself permanently anywhere on the mainland. So it is hardly surprising to find that in 970 'fuerunt Pisani in Calabria'.[57] But their
expedition there provides no evidence whatsoever for commercial

55 A. B. Hibbert, 'The origins of the medieval town patriciate', *Past and Present*,
III (1953), 24.
56 Herlihy, *Pisa in the early Renaissance*, 105–6, refers to imports of grain from Sicily
in 1283 and 1299.   57 *Ann. Pis.*, 4 (971, *stile pisano*).

activity. It could as well have been prompted by the desire to protect
the western coast of Italy as by annoyance at attacks on Pisan shipping. At any rate the preoccupation with the Saracens remained,
for in 1063 the Pisans attempted to capture Palermo single-handed.
Two years earlier Roger I had established a base at Messina, and now
he was working slowly westwards. Clearly the Pisans hoped that
Muslim power in Sicily could be cracked suddenly and permanently,
if possible in alliance with the Normans. For first of all Pisa sent
a fleet to Roger to discuss with him a combined attack on Palermo.
However, Roger did not feel he could afford to neglect his strategy
in eastern Sicily for the sake of such a grandiose scheme. In effect
this refusal put paid to any chance the Pisans may have had of taking
Palermo. Without a land base they could do little more than bom-
bard the port and ravage the gardens in its suburbs. Probably the
whole affair constituted little more than a naval skirmish in the
harbour. A handful of Saracen ships was destroyed and, as trophy of
their visit, the chain across the harbour mouth was seized. Although
this act would have secured them access to the quays, they proved
incapable of doing any more and sailed away delighted with themselves.[58] The implication is that their resources were far too slender
for them even to hope to overwhelm one of the largest cities of the
Mediterranean.

The third expedition, that to al-Mahdiyyah, followed a similar
pattern. On this occasion the Genoese joined in as partners, and
there was a small Amalfitan contingent. Once again Count Roger
was invited to participate; once again he refused owing to his Sicilian
priorities. In 1087 the Italian fleet attacked al-Mahdiyyah in the hope
of capturing it. After fierce fighting the Italians were finally beaten
off, but not before they had penetrated the town and collected a huge
haul of gold, silver and fine robes, enough to pay for the erection in
Pisa of the church of San Sisto in Cortevecchia from the proceeds
of the loot.[59] Here, as in the case of Palermo, a permanent foothold

[58] Chalandon, *Hist.*, I, 193–203; *Ann. Pis.*, 5–6 (1063 *stile comune*). Inscription in Pisa
    cathedral: *Ann. Pis.*, 5–6 and 5, n. 7.
[59] Galasso, 'Commercio amalfitano', 85, emphasises that the Amalfitans were not
    an 'official' contingent. Pisan accounts in *Ann. Pis.*, 6–7, and in the *Carmen in vic-
    toria Pisanorum Genuensium aliorumque Italianorum*, ed. L. T. Belgrano, *ASLSP*,
    IV (1867), pp. ccxvi–ccxxxvii. Cf. W. Heywood, *A history of Pisa, eleventh and
    twelfth centuries* (Cambridge, 1921), 26–44.

in Saracen territory had been envisaged, and presumably al-
Mahdiyyah was chosen because it was coming increasingly to the
fore as a terminal for the trans-Saharan gold routes, as well as participating in trade with Egypt and Sicily.[60] In addition, the Pisans
and Genoese were reacting to difficulties they had experienced in
past attempts to trade in Africa – exclusion from markets, seizure
of property, piracy on the high seas. The campaign was an attempt
not to create a commercial network but to make an existing network
more secure. The fact that the target was a Muslim city, the worthy
object of Christian hostility, merely provided a further excuse for
the attack, but did not actually bring it about.

Another important stage in the growth to maturity of Genoese
and Pisan commercial activity occurred with the First Crusade.
Once again strong parallels exist between Pisan and Genoese
behaviour then and in 1063 or 1087. Fleets from Pisa and Genoa
arrived in Syria and Palestine just when the leaders of the Crusade
were most desperate for naval aid against the Turks in Antioch and
against the Egyptians along the Palestinian seaboard. In return for
their aid the communes were promised streets and markets in the
main towns of the crusader states, as well as sections of the towns
they helped capture and some exemption from taxes. The territorial
concessions from the crusader lords proved very hard to enforce,
but the tax exemption, a 'negative' right (that is, the right not to act
in a certain way), was more easily maintained. The Genoese did
manage to set up a lordship of their own at Gibelet (Jubayl or By-
blos), which played a major part in their activities *Ultramare*. In the
Principality of Antioch, the Genoese established an important trade
counter at Port St Symeon. Altogether the list of towns where the
Italians installed themselves is particularly impressive when the overland links between St Symeon and Mosul, or Acre and Damascus,
to cite two examples, are recalled. These bases were taps at the end
of a long Middle Eastern pipeline bringing spices and drugs and dyes
and fabrics from Mesopotamia and beyond to the Frankish settlements, and thence via Messina or Palermo to continental Europe.[61]

[60] The rise of al-Mahdiyyah, relative to the decline of Qayrawan, is discussed by
M. Brett, 'Ifriqiya as a market for Saharan trade from the 10th to the 12th century
A.D.', *Journal of African History*, X (1969), 347–64.
[61] Heyd, *Histoire du commerce du Levant*, I, 133–45; J. La Monte, *Feudal monarchy in the
Latin kingdom of Jerusalem, 1100–1291* (Cambridge, Mass., 1932), 264–9.

In this account Venice has been left to one side, not because it failed to participate in these activities – it too gained substantially from the First Crusade, and even more from the siege of Tyre (1123–5) – but because the 'commercial revolution' which enveloped its west Italian rivals did not greatly affect, except in volume and in the extension of exploitable regions, Venetian interest in the east. Venice already had substantial trading commitments in Alexandria, and may have been reluctant to show more than opportunist interest in the crusader conquests. Genoa and Pisa, on the other hand, possibly came to know the Egyptian markets only as a result of their involvement in the Syrian ones. For them Alexandria was originally part of a circuit, later a trade centre in its own right. Venice may have moved in the opposite direction: its Egyptian interests encouraged it to bolster its Syrian.[62]

Venice stands out especially for its involvement in Byzantine trade. The terms on which it entered the economic structure of the Greek empire were similar to those on which its rivals entered that of the crusader states: reward for naval aid, first in 992, then on a still more exclusive basis, in 1082/4, with the chrysobull of Alexios I Komnenos.[63] This document, and the circumstances that brought it about, reflect the first clash between Venice and the Normans. When Robert Guiscard besieged Durazzo, it was the Amalfitans who opened their city gates to him, but there were Venetians in the town too, and they and the Doge's fleet resisted the Guiscard in the name of Alexios.[64] By the late eleventh century Constantinople had only a small fleet of its own; it had to rely on the support of outsiders. When its Adriatic flank was dangerously threatened, Byzantium had to call on Venice. In recompense for its naval aid, Venice received exceptional privileges in the Greek empire. The title πρωτοσέβαστος was conferred on the Doge, giving him the rank of a member of the imperial family. The claims of the (Venetian)

[62] Heyd, I, 142–5, for Venetian gains in the Levant in the first quarter of the twelfth century.

[63] Tafel-Thomas, I, 43–54. The redating of this bull from 1082 to 1084 has been the subject of much discussion; E. Frances, 'Alexis Comnène et les privilèges octroyés à Venise', *Byzantinoslavica*, XXIX (1968), 17–23; see also S. Borsari, 'Il Crisobullo di Alessio I per Venezia', *Annali dell'Istituto italiano per gli studi storici (Napoli)*, II (1970), 111–31.

[64] Anna Comnena, *Alexiadis Libri XV*, ed. L. Schopenus, Corpus Scriptorum Historiae Byzantinae, 2 vols. (Bonn, 1839, 1878), Book V, 1, i.

patriarch of Grado to authority in Dalmatia and Croatia were confirmed – a kick in the teeth for Pope Gregory VII, at that moment
Guiscard's ally; Amalfitans residing in the empire were to pay
tribute to the church of St Mark. The Venetians were given an extensive quarter in Constantinople and the right to trade unhindered
in the more important trade centres of the empire, except in those
beyond the Bosphoros. The κομμέρκιον, the sales tax of 10 per cent,
was abolished for Venetian merchants, along with several other
commercial dues.[65] Altogether Venice was established in a unique
position in the empire, a position that placed its merchants well
ahead of both foreigners and natives in terms of rights and exemptions – an impetus, in short, to expand Venetian trade in the Greek
empire on a massive scale. This Byzantine lien affected Venetian
relations with the Normans very seriously throughout the twelfth
century. On the one hand Venice wanted to keep its connections
with the Apulian ports alive, for thence it could obtain grain and
other basic supplies for its own use or consumption in Syria and
Egypt. On the other hand it hesitated to compromise itself in the
eyes of the Basileus by establishing too cordial a relationship with
the Norman 'usurpers'. It feared to antagonise the Normans because
they repeatedly sent armies across to the Balkans and might at whim
try to close the Adriatic to hostile shipping. Paradoxically, in gaining
the Aegean the Venetians risked losing their own Adriatic.

[65] Tafel-Thomas, I, 48–9.

PART II

THE DEVELOPMENT OF TRADE

Chapter 3

THE FIRST PHASE OF ALLIANCES, 1116–54

I

At the time of Roger II's coronation other Latin princes – including certain of his subjects – had no reason or desire to regard his position as permanent. The German rulers were naturally glad to see Byzantine and Arab power in southern Italy extinguished; they still hoped that the Normans would prove to have done no more than to prepare the ground for their own take-over, based on a historic and rightful claim to possession. Similarly, Byzantine and papal claims to practical or theoretical overlordship were reactivated. All this seriously compromised the interests of the north Italian republics – their commercial interests in Sicily and in Constantinople, and their defensive interests in northern Italy, where they were exposed to German attack. The alternatives were clear, and none was without its lure. The republics could defend imperial claims to southern Italy by providing the Germans with a fleet, in return for commercial concessions in conquered territory – a line held to by Pisa with fair consistency. They could offer Constantinople similar services – as did Venice, in order to protect one side of its Adriatic trade, though at the same time the city had deep commitments in Norman Apulia. Or the republics could place their interests in the *Regno* first and hope thereby to win the gratitude of the Sicilian kings, along with commercial privileges – a gamble the Genoese took as far as they could.

II

Shortly before Roger II's fleet sailed into Salerno in summer 1127, the Pisans made a treaty of friendship with Amalfi that provided both sides with shops and warehouses in each other's city, as well as the right to trade free from tolls and taxes.[1] Possibly this treaty can

---

[1] The treaty is dated October 1127, Pisan style – i.e., 1126. Printed by F. Bonaini, 'Due carte pisano–amalfitane', *Archivio storico italiano*, ser. 3, VIII (1868), 5–7; cf. Galasso, 'Commercio amalfitano', 89–90, 95.

be seen as a last-minute act of defence by both parties before Roger
had time to consolidate his power in Campania and to interfere in
the affairs of Amalfi. In trying to avoid entanglement with Roger,
Pisa only fell into the arms of his enemies who were planning to
eliminate his authority on the mainland – the Norman rebels
Robert of Capua and Rainulf of Alife; the Pope too. Pisa's fleet
became even more necessary to the rebels as the Campanian towns
were seized or besieged by Roger of Sicily.[2]

Pisa made its first promises to Robert of Capua in 1133, but was
reluctant to invade the *Regno* without Genoese participation, more
because Pisa wished to keep an eye on Genoese pretensions in Corsica than out of friendliness for its rival. Robert of Capua made
approaches to Genoa through ambassadors, but all along Roger
of Hauteville may have been bribing the Genoese, and possibly the
Pisans too, to keep out of the war. Finally Genoa, and Venice too,
gave way to the rebels' entreaties.[3] Only Pisan involvement is documented, however, beginning in 1135 when the Commune sent its
fleet south and decided, apparently contrary to rebel strategy, to
capture Amalfi. Roger riposted with a grant of licence to the
Amalfitans, permitting them to commit acts of piracy against any
hostile foreign shipping; and while Amalfitan warships scoured the
seas, the Pisans entered the harbour and sacked Amalfi and its
tributary neighbours. Pisa had established a territorial niche not
simply in southern Italy, but in one of the richest towns of southern
Italy, a prize far richer than the treaty of 1126 had offered. But a
counter-attack by Roger recovered Amalfi for the Normans within
a matter of days, and the idea of a Pisan territorial foothold in Campania, though far from forgotten, had to be deferred.[4]

---

[2] Space precludes a lengthy narrative here; cf. the accounts of Chalandon, *Hist.*, II,
32–75; Caspar, 155–208; C. Manfroni, *Storia della marina italiana dalle invasioni
barbariche al trattato di Ninfeo* (Livorno, 1899), 185–93. Sources: Falco Beneventanus, 220–32, favourable to the rebels and invaders; Alexander Telesinus, 123–40,
favourable to Roger; Romuald of Salerno, 223; *Ann. Pis.*, 9–12.

[3] F. Benev., 220, 222; Alex. Teles., 122; *Ann. Pis.*, 9–10. For the bribing of Genoa,
Caspar, 143–4, and Bernard of Clairvaux in *Patrologia Latina*, pt CLXXXII, 284,
attaching to Roger's ambassadors to Genoa the epithet of Vergil, 'Danaos et dona
ferentes'.

[4] *Ann. Pis.*, 9–11; cf. Alex. Teles., 140. Pisan possession of some of the towns in
Campania became a *sine qua non* of Pisan negotions with the Hohenstaufen
invaders of the *Regno*.

In 1137 the Pisans returned in the company of the Genoese, as the naval arm of the Emperor Lothar's assault on the *Regno*, and, remembering the rewards of 1135, they cleaned up opposition from Amalfi before moving on to yet greater gains at Salerno, which, Maragone insists, rapidly surrendered 'to Lothar and the Pisans'.[5] In its treaties with Frederick I and Henry VI, Pisa was promised Salerno whole, perhaps in memory of the events of 1137, or in memory of still earlier promises by Lothar. But victories turn sour when the question begins to be asked who the real victor is. The Pisans had hoped to plunder Salerno; its peaceful surrender was a major disappointment. Quarrels broke out between Pisans and Salernitans, and as violence increased the imperial troops refused to intervene, for the real trouble-makers were very probably the Pisan conquerors, not the conquered. The Pisan reaction was drastic indeed: far from continuing to fight, the Pisan fleet withdrew from Salerno and hurried to make peace with King Roger. Quite apart from exasperation at the situation in Salerno, the Pisans were worried about their situation in Norman-held lands. To judge from the Pisan annals, Roger was starting to take offensive measures against Pisan trade and property in the kingdom:

postea idem Rex [Rogerius] contristatus est cum Pisanis; qui Pisani miserunt unam galeam cum sapientibus, et hoc fecerunt cum consilio sapientium regis Sicilie, qui erant in Turri maiore; et sic fecerunt pacem cum eo, et postea Pisas reversi sunt XIII Kal. Octubris.[6]

Why it took Roger so long to take action against Pisan business is unclear. He may have resorted to bribes or commercial promises, but no documentary evidence for this survives. At any rate, Lothar had been undermined at a critical moment. His failure to satisfy his naval arm was followed by major military and diplomatic triumphs for the Norman Sicilians. After the capture of Pope Innocent by

---

[5] *Ann. Pis.*, 12. Caffaro, *Ann. Ian.*, I, 27, shows Genoa as a loyal supporter of Lothar and Innocent. D. Clementi, 'Some unnoticed aspects of the Emperor Henry VI's conquest of the Norman Kingdom of Sicily', *Bulletin of the John Rylands Library*, XXXVI (1954), 337, n.1, suggests that Lothar promised the Genoese rights in Sicily and the Mezzogiorno similar to those promised in writing by Barbarossa and Henry VI. The idea of an unwritten pact is not contrary to possibility, but the terms of the 1162 agreement will be seen (*infra*, 127–31), to refer quite specifically to that year, and any earlier promises are unlikely to have been quite so elaborate in scope. [6] *Ann. Pis.*, 12; cf. Rom. Sal., 223.

Roger II in 1139 the legitimacy of the Sicilian crown was at last recognized by the papacy. The imperial invaders would henceforth have to turn to new allies – even, indeed, to Constantinople.

The legacy of Pisan hostility was a multiple and serious one. First, Amalfi may have suffered seriously from the attack on its installations and shipping. As Idrisi said, the harbour was good, but easily taken by storm, and, to judge from the Genoese notarial acts, Salerno and later Naples were from the 1150s the principal commercial centres of Campania.[7] Secondly, the attacks on Amalfi and Salerno strengthened Pisan desires for a territorial base in southern Italy – desires manifested as long ago as the Pisan attack on Palermo (1063). Pisa became harder for the emperors to buy, too: it would only help conquerors on the understanding that it too was a conqueror – which was just what Maragone had affirmed from the start. On the Pisan side, patience was required, and at a real price: Pisa continued to trade in the *Regno* without any known commercial rights or concessions; but the Sicilian kings can hardly have begrudged Pisa the taxes its merchants poured into the royal coffers at Palermo, Messina or Naples.

III

Genoa, like Pisa, had reason to fear royal expropriation of its property in the *Regno*. Its commercial relations with the island of Sicily are documented from 1116 when, as a reward for their loyalty to Count Roger, the Genoese consul Ogerio and his brother Amico received a piece of waste-ground beyond the castle of Messina, ten cubits broad, and stretching down to the beach. Here they were allowed to rebuild a pre-existing ὁσπίτιον, or sailors' rest and merchant hostel. Count Roger's grant to the brothers was a private one, in the sense that its terms cannot necessarily be extended to include all Genoese residents. Thus Ogerio and Amico, or their

7 Idrisi, ed. Amari–Schiaparelli, 96. Evidence for Pisan devastation is provided by an Amalfitan document of 1142 that refers to the loss of a charter recording the sale of a house at Atrani '[quando] fuit capta Rabelli ab ipsi Pisani' – R. Filangieri di Candida (ed.), *Codice diplomatico amalfitano*, 2 vols. (Naples, 1917; Trani, 1951), I, 253. Cf. G. Rossi Sabatini, 'Relazioni tra Pisa e Amalfi nel Medioevo' and R. di Tucci, 'Relazioni commerciali fra Amalfi e Genova', both in *Studi sulla Repubblica marinara di Amalfi*, a cura del comitato per la 'Celebrazione di Amalfi imperiale' (Salerno, 1935), 55–67, 68–78.

nominees, were to receive a pound of gold each *per annum* and freedom from the κομέρκιον up to a value of 60 tari on their imports and exports through Messina. By mid-century standards, it is true, 60 tari was only a small amount of money. Genoese merchants normally reckoned that there were 28 or 30 tari to the ounce of gold. Thus a commercial contract from Genoa dated 4 September 1159 cites a 'racio de tarenis 28 per unciam' for gold of Palermo; a total of 22 oz was to be carried, or 616 tari – that is, ten times the tax-free allowance of 1116. Possibly, then, the charter originally cited 60 ounces of tari, not 60 tari as such; and, since only a Greek text survives, an error in transmission may have occurred in translation from its presumed Latin original.[8]

The extent to which the grant was a private favour to Ogerio and his brother bears on a second issue, the meaning of the title κούνσολος γένουας attached to Ogerio. Understandably there has been great keenness to show that the Genoese commune possessed overseas consulates as early as 1116.[9] According to this interpretation, Ogerio was a resident official appointed from Genoa to adjudicate the affairs of the city's merchants in Messina. That in itself would speak for a sizeable trade between Genoa and Messina; and it might also imply that the Genoese had already been granted some degree of exemption from the authority of Sicilian courts. All this is possible, for from 1127 and, more particularly, 1156, the Genoese possessed certain judicial rights in Sicily; and it is known that later in the century, in 1189, the Pisans had a consulate at Messina. But to date forward the existence of these rights and institutions to a time when Genoese trade was still relatively undeveloped is very hazardous. Schaube insisted that Ogerio was in fact Oglerius Capra, 'der 1114–1117 dem Kollegium der städtischen Konsuln angehörte'; Ogerius was a very common Genoese name but the attribution makes sense. An 'Ougerius cap.' appears in the Sicilian–Savonese treaty of 1127, named among a group of Genoese patricians; and this too may be

---

[8] S. Cusa, *I diplomi greci e arabi di Sicilia*, 2 vols. (Palermo, 1860–82), I, 359. For the 616 tari, see *GS*, II, 314. Tari were not constant in weight, and were measured in ounces and pounds of weighed gold, not by counting individual tari. The tari was both a notional and a real coin. Quite apart from the low number of tari cited, the ten cubits of wasteland is not exceptionally impressive: Goliath was six cubits tall.

[9] Heyd, I, 182, n.2 and 123; Caspar, 54.

the consul of 1114 to 1117.[10] In any case, this Ogerio must have been a frequent visitor to Sicily during the eleven years from Roger's accession to the grant of 1116. By the middle of the century the most distinguished patrician merchants tended to stay at home, commissioning agents to perform their tasks overseas; but urgent diplomatic needs, or a less highly developed factorial system, could have sent Ogerio to Sicily several times. During the years of Countess Adelaide's regency some insurgent elements were active, and Ogerio may have given the regent his support against them; after all, the Countess was herself a Ligurian Aleramico, and she had brought other Ligurians south to Sicily with her at the time of her marriage to Roger I.[11]

The privilege of 1116 does not make it clear whether the ὁσπίτιον building was to be enlarged or rebuilt on its former scale. As ships passed through Messina bound for Syria and Alexandria, the Genoese in Sicily may have required more extensive facilities; alternatively, a catastrophe could have destroyed the old hospice. Particularly valuable was the direct access to the sea that the Genoese now gained. Ibn Jubayr's account of the port of Messina, written in 1185, explains why:

Messina leans against the mountains, the lower slopes of which adjoin the entrenchments of the town. To its south is the sea, and its harbour is the most remarkable of maritime ports, since large ships can come into it from the seas until they almost touch it. Between them and the shore is thrown a plank over which men come and go and porters take up the baggage; thus no boats are needed for loading and unloading save for ships anchored far out. You will observe ships ranged along the quay like horses lined at their pickets or in their stables. This is all because of the great depth here of the sea which forms the strait, some three miles wide, that separates the island from the continent.[12]

Since the site of the hospice, if not its size, was to be extended as a result of the count's grant, it does seem that the Genoese were thereby able to acquire their own quays or landing-stations.

The Genoese breakthrough in Sicilian trade may be said to have occurred not with the extension of the merchants' rights in the ports,

[10] Schaube, *Handelsgeschichte der Romanischen Völker*, 464–5, n. 7. Cf. *Ann. Ian.*, I, 15; Olivieri, 'Serie dei Consoli del Comune di Genova', *ASLSP*, I (1858), 240. For the treaty with Savona, see 65–9 *infra*.

[11] Chalandon, *Hist.*, I, 356.   [12] Ibn Jubayr, 339.

but with the establishment of inland settlements. Tradition reports that there were Genoese, Savonese and other 'Lombards' from Liguria at Caltagirone in Sicily; they had come as mercenaries, merchants or marriage-relations.[13] Roger I, as has been seen, married into the Savonese nobility and his wife's family acquired Sicilian fiefs. Meanwhile other members of the same Aleramico clan were marrying other members of the Hauteville family: thus Roger II's half-brothers and his natural sister all had Ligurian consorts.[14] It is in this context, partly fabulous and partly historical, that the pacts of 1127 or 1128 between Roger II and the Savonese must be examined.[15] Three charters survive; the first is longest, and begins by saying that some Savonese came to Roger, 'ducem Sicilie et Calabrie', to ask him to release a compatriot galley and crew, held by him in Messina. The Savonese made their call in the name of the Bishop of Genoa and of the consuls and citizens of the same town, to which Savona was tributary. Roger agreed to their request out of courtesy to Genoa, and in gratitude the Savonese swore that they would never in future do any harm to any of the Duke's subjects who came by land or by sea, whatever their business and whether they encountered them in Savona or elsewhere – in 'totum mare quod est a Numidia usque ad Tripolim et totum mare et totam terram que inter nos et eos sunt'.[16] A time-table was established for the adjudication of legal cases arising from breach

13 Amari, *Storia dei Musulmani*, III, 235–7, rightly wonders whether there is much substance to the story of a Genoese colony at Caltagirone; no documentary evidence survives any longer, and certain elements in the tale are clearly fictitious. Savonese Ligurians rather than Genoese settlers do, as Amari says, make the best sense. But T. Fazello, *De rebus Siculis decas prima*, ed. V. M. Amico (Catania, 1749), 445–6, claims: 'hoc oppidum ut Caltagironei predicant et diplomate attestantur, Sarracenis Sicilia potientibus a Genuensibus cum classe Camerinam appulsis, atque inde in mediterranea progressis magna vi receptum est…'; and F. Aprile, *Della cronologia universale della Sicilia* (Palermo, 1725), 65, reports a lost inscription. These writers date the Genoese occupation to a ridiculous year 1000.

14 Cf. 39 *supra*; Amari, *Storia dei Musulmani*, III, 231–2; Noberasco–Scovazzi, *Storia di Savona*, I, 253.

15 Printed by G. Filippi, 'Patto di pace tra Ruggiero II Normanno e la Città di Savona', *Archivio storico per le provincie napoletane*, XIV (1889), 750–7. Care has, however, been taken to consult the surviving text in the Archivio di Stato, Savona, Registro a catena piccolo, f.5v–6v.

16 Registro a catena piccolo, f.5v, followed by Filippi, reads 'a Nubia usque ad Tripolim'. Wieruszowski, 'Sicily and the Crusades', 22, n. 31, wisely emends 'Nubia' into 'Numidia', to create a little more geographical sense.

of their oath, and it was arranged that the entire citizenry of Savona should guarantee the pact by swearing to observe its terms. As for the captured galley and crew, they must offer forty days' service to Roger just for that year: this suggests that Roger's officials had originally seized them in a press-gang operation, to help in a forthcoming naval expedition, aimed undoubtedly at North Africa.[17] A second document in this series of pacts expresses Roger's side of the agreement. He promised protection to any Savonese travelling in his lands, 'ut ipsi sint securi in terra sue potestatis de personis et rebus preter illos qui causa predandi mari vel terra ierint'.[18] A third document states that the requisitioning of naval equipment (*gaforium* and *sartores*, anchor, rigging and sails) would not be classed by the Savonese as piracy if Duke Roger appropriated them 'moderate et cum ratione' – further proof that in the 1120s the Normans had not yet created the vast and victorious fleet that brought them their African and Greek victories in the decades after Roger was crowned king.[19] The document now reverts to Savona, stating that the Savonese swore their oath to Duke Roger 'salva amicitia januensium atque fidelitate suorum marchionum', that is, their Genoese overlords and the Aleramici. Should Genoa and Roger go to war with one another, Savona will remain bound by its oath. This means that the Savonese could fight on the side of Genoa or another master, but that at the close of conflict the terms of the treaty of protection between Roger and Savona would come once again into force; such stipulations are common in commercial treaties of the twelfth century, and they served an important purpose. The rights of a vassal (such as the Commune of Savona) could be protected, both vis-à-vis that vassal's lord and vis-à-vis the second party in the treaty relationship. If anything, such clauses confirm the permanence rather than the temporariness of these treaties. What they say is that both parties wish to remain on good terms even though

---

[17] Malta was reoccupied by Roger II in 1127: A. T. Luttrell, 'Malta nel periodo normanno', *Atti CISSN*, 471–2. But Wieruszowski, 21–2, overstates the case of Roger preparing 'for his future rôle as lord of the African sea by concluding a treaty with Savona…containing…the promise of one Savonese galley to police the sea', since the galley was required for only a single year of campaigning.

[18] *Registro a catena*, f.5v.

[19] *Registro a catena*, f.6r–v. Part of f.5v and f.6r is occupied by an extraneous 'Carta inter Saonenses et Rozolinum et Ugonem Ferrum de Massilia'.

some day circumstances may force them into opposing camps; and if that happens it will be the result of conflicting or overriding obligations and pressures which may eventually emerge. But such clauses cannot be taken to mean that these difficulties will necessarily emerge.

Next, this third charter hurtles away from Savona to outline a machinery of judicial inquiry that would prevent conflicts between Genoese (*sic*) and Sicilian interests from becoming serious before the opportunity for arbitration had arisen; this seems to refer to legal and commercial disputes in the markets and ports, rather than to military and diplomatic strife between the Norman rulers of Sicily and the German overlords of Genoa. Then, in its typically wayward manner, the document reverts to specifically Savonese questions:

Et si aliquid huic carte additum vel demptum fuerit secundum voluntatem predicti ducis ac comitis et duorum saunensium, quibus a suis consulibus quibus injunctum fuerit, huic deprecationi et addicioni totum consilium saunensium acquiescit, exceptis his tribus: amicitia januensium, et fidelitate suorum marchionum, et gafori galearum.

This seems to say that the rights of Duke Roger regarding *gaforium* and *sartores* were an agreed concession, made to balance the Savonese reservation regarding their Genoese and Aleramico neighbours.

After this the names of the witnesses to the documents are cited; and striking is the presence of the Genoese consuls of 1127, as well as some other Genoese names:

Testes hanc cartam: Iterius [?] consul et Octo de mari et Marchio de Cafara et Raynaldus Sardena et Wilielmus de Volta, Petrus de Castello. Et Cunradus de Sancta Michanta [?] et Ougerius cap[ra?] et Lanfrancus Guertius. Et Obertus Guercius.

Filippi's edition adds confusion by printing Casara, Sartena; but the *Registrum a catena* of Savona, the sole manuscript source, is very badly rubbed on this folio, and the letters are often hard to read.[20]

---

[20] Registro a catena, f.6r. Filippi, 757: '...[*sic*] consul et Octo de Mari et Marcho de casara et Raynaldus Sartena et Vilelmus de Volta...[*sic*] de Castello et Curadus de sancta nichanda et Ongerius...[*sic*] et Lafrancus Gaervius et Obertus Guercius'. Cf. Olivieri, 242; *Ann. Ian.*, I, 23.

Nevertheless, here the letters do stand out clearly, for the firm impressions of the scribe's pen remain even where the ink has been worn away. By failing to pay attention to these names, Filippi was, in fact, led into slight but significant error. The presence of the Genoese consuls of 1127 sets in doubt his redating of the Savonese documents to 1128. The documents do claim to be of 1127, but the indiction is wrong, reading VI where V would be correct. Moreover, Roger is described as Duke of Apulia before his cousin William had died and left the duchy vacant for possession by the Count of Sicily. To remove both difficulties, Filippi wisely argued that 1128 would make best sense as date.[21] Of course, the whole question of inconsistencies in dating has great bearing on the problem of authenticity of these texts. Their manuscript tradition is not, in fact, as solid as may appear from their inclusion in the treaty-book of the Savonese Commune. The *Registrum a catena* was compiled in the early thirteenth century, although additions were made throughout the Middle Ages. That confusion occurred at some time in the century after 1127 is perfectly clear, but whether this confusion was the result of incompetent forgery or of incompetent transcription is far less certain. A forger could easily have obtained the names of the consuls of 1127 and of other eminent Genoese – 'Ougerius cap.' may well be Ogerio Capra and thus a veteran of the 1116 agreement, a point that would, if less subject to alternative readings, speak loudly for the authenticity of the texts, since he is just the man who might have been expected to appear in the Genoese party negotiating with Roger of Sicily. Similarly Lanfrancus Guercius was a colleague of Ogerio as consul from 1114 to 1117, and his appearance in the 1127 document need hardly cause surprise.[22]

However, even to refer to a Genoese 'party' may be begging several questions. The Savonese texts do not state that the '*testes*' from Genoa actually travelled to Messina; indeed, it is highly unlikely that a large group of consuls would have abandoned their home duties to witness a relatively trivial accord that concerned the Savonese far more directly than it did the Genoese. The most that could be claimed is that the Genoese consuls rubber-stamped, as it were, the Savonese pact with Roger of Sicily, on the basis of reports from their own representatives or from the Savonese themselves.

---

[21] Filippi, 752–3. [22] Olivieri, 240; *Ann. Ian.*, I, 15.

The Genoese Annals say nothing about the affair, as they might be expected to have done if the consuls had been deeply involved. Thus the texts combine many faults and invite condemnation as forgeries.

There is, however, another answer to the question of their authenticity that makes full allowance for the interval between 1127 and their registration in the treaty-book that now survives. The texts are certainly copies, but it would be wrong to suppose that they are copies of original diplomata of 1127. They could be a wayward, often rather incoherent, attempt at the reconstruction of lost documents, or at the construction of documents where none earlier ever existed. In the first place, they are oddly enough phrased for it to be clear that their source was not the Sicilian chancery. Apart from their haphazard style and construction, the reference to Roger as 'duke' of Apulia, Calabria and Sicily is unlikely to have emanated from Roger's own draftsmen. In the second place, there is the innocuous nature of the treaty. It is not a set of commercial privileges involving particular tax exemptions, but a promise of protection against the seizure of ships and persons, based on one instance recounted in the first of the three texts. Indeed, some of the clauses do not especially favour Savona: the right of the Duke to claim *gaforium* and *sartores* seems unlikely to have been conceded in a totally false Savonese privilege. Rather is this a friendly agreement that makes good sense in the light of Roger's links with the Aleramici and with Consul Ogerio and his fellow Genoese. Nor is it likely that Genoa could be the source of forgery; the clauses that concerned the Genoese added nothing new to their status in Sicily, as far as can be seen.

There is a final point in favour of the idea that the Savona texts are reconstructions of lost or non-existent documents, reflecting real circumstances. For it was not necessary for a grant or treaty to be in writing, especially where it concerned mercantile affairs. There are no signs that Emperor Lothar made a written pact with Pisa or with Genoa. Similarly, in 1211 Bisceglie and Dubrovnik drew up a treaty reaffirming the age-old commercial rights of their citizens in each other's town, which had previously operated by custom and had only recently been questioned anew.[23] There may be hints of

---

[23] Clementi, 'Unnoticed aspects', 337, n.1; Abulafia, 'Dalmatian Ragusa', 417–18.

the same pattern in William I's reference to the customs enjoyed by the Genoese in the *Regno* during his father's reign:

> deprecati sunt nos ut usus et consuetudines quas per civitates regni nostri, habere sunt soliti, et nunc nos eis concessimus, in scriptis redigeremus.[24]

A change of ruler would encourage privilege holders to demand confirmation of their rights, which would pass into writing; and meanwhile the royal *duana* kept accurate records of who owed what for what. Later in William I's grant we read of the 'customary rights' of the Genoese without any further description being supplied; and so it is clear that a variety of exemptions and rights applied specifically to the Genoese, quite apart from the sundry clauses that are known from 1116 and 1127.

What were these rights during Roger's reign? The text of the 1156 treaty undoubtedly refers primarily to the state of affairs in William I's reign – the promise to exclude Provençal shipping, for example, fits best into the political context of the 1150s. There are no signs that the charter is a re-issue, suitably updated, of a Rogerian text, neither in the charter nor in what the *Annales Ianuenses* said about it. Moreover, the appendix to the 1156 charter, promising protection of Genoese shipping 'exceptis galeatorum predonibus', bears no verbal resemblance to the Savona privilege, and makes no reference to King Roger or to Savona.[25] Before William I's day the Genoese may have had special privileges in a number of towns, such as Salerno and Messina, but they were still, as it were, streets ahead of Pisa which had no known hospices or tax rights at this period. In any case the Genoese do not seem to have been very popular in Messina. In 1129 a Genoese fleet of sixteen galleys began to harry some Pisan ships at sea. The Pisans fled south and took cover in Messina. There they assembled their forces (including, presumably, Pisan ships and merchants already in port), and won the support of the native Messinese. Thus strengthened, they turned on their pursuers. The Genoese, however, put up a spirited defence. They disembarked and seized part of the town – according to Caffaro, 'they had in their power the town (*burgum*) and its wealth

---

[24] *CDG*, I, 339.
[25] For an analysis of these texts, see Chapter 4 *infra*, 92–8. Caffaro's comments: *Ann. Ian.*, I, 47.

(*peccuniam*), but for love of the king and at the request of the king's representatives, they returned the money and property of the townspeople'.[26] Why the Messinese supported the Pisans is far from clear. But, to judge from events thirty years later, when Messina received its own royal commercial privileges, there was a long-standing or long-brewing hostility to the favoured foreigners from Liguria, with their hospice and beach. And, however great this resentment, it is clear that the Pisans and Genoese were already at each other's throats over their own Sicilian interests. The King's intervention in 1129 is worth stressing. The Genoese clearly feared to lose their current reputation for loyalty to King Roger, and King Roger was evidently horrified at the prospect of chaos in one of his principal ports and arsenals. Meanwhile, further north in the *Regno* it was the Pisans who found themselves unpopular with the King's subjects. Merchants of the trading city of Gaeta seized a Pisan ship during this same year.[27]

A valuable document, the *Registrum curiae Archiepiscopalis Januae* of November 1143, tells much about Genoese overseas trade, in the form of a table of tithes and taxes due to the archbishop's *curia* on imports from Sicily and elsewhere. For each ship from Syria, Alexandria, Byzantium and North Africa or Spain, a 'tithe' of $22\frac{1}{2}$s was to be paid; but if a ship carried grain, one *mina* (*c* 105 lb) of grain per person on board was payable. By contrast, ships from Sicily had to pay 'pro decimis' 11s 3d, half the more general 'tithe', but this reduction was not carried over to the grain ships, from which once again a *mina* was hungrily demanded – an indication of the value of basic foodstuffs to the *curia*, as against the industrial and luxury products of the island. Shipping from Sardinia and Corsica was to pay a mere 8s and 7s respectively, but one *mina* in the case of grain. In the instance of grain-carrying vessels that arrived from Calabria or Provence 'ultra portum pisanum vel ultra portum monachum', that is, arrived anywhere between the limits of Genoese territory bounded by the Pisan *contado* and by Monaco, each man had to hand over one *quartinum* of grain, with the exception of two of the sailors and anyone who was bound for St Raphael or Fréjus. If

[26] *Ann. Ian.*, I, 24.
[27] *Tabularium Cassinense*, Codex diplomaticus Cajetanus, I, part 2 (Montecassino, 1891), 144–5.

there were fewer than nine people in each boat, one *mina* must be given, instead; and if there were nine or ten or eleven or twelve, two *minae*; otherwise, one *quartinum*.[28] In the summary of this statement of dues appended by the scribe at the end of his list, he adds the name of Sicily to Calabria, Maremma and Provence; and since Messina was one of the main outlets for Calabrian produce, and indeed since Calabria was ruled from Palermo and not from the mainland government departments, the mention of Sicily and Calabria together makes good sense.[29] Whereas taxes were imposed on imports of salt from Sardinia and Provence, in other instances such as Sicily this commodity received no special mention. So, although Sicily and southern Italy were major salt producers, and although the crown had a monopolistic interest in the salt-pans of the *Regno*, there are no signs here or elsewhere that large quantities were sent to Genoa. (North Africa, which bought salt for gold, is a more likely market.) In 1175 and 1228 the same 'tithes' were applied, 11s 3d for Sicily and 22s 6d for beyond. The only modification that concerns Sicily was that the parish priest at Rapallo was granted in the 1190s the right to tithe the tithe, as it were – to take a tenth part for himself, and to send nine parts to the archbishop's *curia* – in the case of shipping manned by men of Rapallo which travelled 'in provinciam, in sardiniam, in corsicam, messini, napoli, et ubicumque extra predictum terminum, et redeuntes similiter portum fecerint in Rapallo'.[30] From this it appears that Messina and Naples became the main loading centres for south Italian, or 'Calabrian', grain, though of course there were plenty of minor centres between, and important ones in the Salerno region. Whether Naples played so eminent a rôle in the early twelfth century is another matter: in the 1190s, but not the 1150s, it was a favourite Genoese port of call.

The Archbishop's Registers indicate that it was the central Mediterranean islands, along with Provence (with which the Genoese had stormy relations) that provisioned the city of Genoa, and they serve to emphasise the importance of the struggle for Corsica, Sardinia and Sicily during the twelfth century. Sicily produced the best grain,

---

[28] Printed by L. T. Belgrano, *ASLSP*, II, fasc. 2 (1870), 9, 10.
[29] Belgrano, *Reg. Curiae*, 366 (summary compiled in 1149).
[30] Belgrano, *Reg. Curiae*, 456 (1175); 270–2 (1194); 450, 452, 455 (1228); 384 (Rapallo).

and offered in addition a market for selling and buying a great variety of other things, so its value was composite in a sense that the other islands' value was not; moreover, Corsica and Sardinia were virtually without rulers and became the object of direct competition between Genoa and Pisa.[31]

Another striking element in the Register is that many of the boats carrying grain along the Tyrrhenian coast were very small – manned by twelve men or less. These are not the sea-going, fairly rapid ships in which the big Genoese financiers placed their money, though they too had ample space for grain; rather are they the twelfth-century equivalent of tramp-steamers – a crucial and easily forgotten element in both Tyrrhenian and Adriatic trade. Much of Rapallo's trade reached no further than the Tiber. Contracts are quite common in the Genoese notarial books for trade in the Maremma, especially at Corneto (Tarquinia), and much of this must have been carried in small coast-hugging boats.[32] It is generally accepted that many of the smaller or lonelier investments made by middle-class Genoese were not registered in the notaries' books; in particular, the cartularies only tell of trade financed by partnerships. Free agents, such as the skippers of coastal boats, were unhampered by the need to preserve legal obligations and to guard one's risks, for they performed principally on their own behalf. But in the context of south Italian trade these movements, individually minute but massive *in toto*, need not be disconcerting. If anything, they show that the quantity of ships bound for the *Regno* from Genoa and its rivals was greater than the contracts reveal, and that sales in the *Regno* to north Italians were consequently higher too. Clearly, then, there is an inherent imbalance in the commercial contracts towards long-distance, high-value trade; but this imbalance can be counted to the advantage of the *Regno* and to the disadvantage of Syria or Egypt, which could not be reached by light coastal shipping.

[31] E.g. in 1127: Caffaro, *Ann. Ian.*, I, 23–4. A full study of Genoese commercial and political relations with Sardinia is much required; Pisa has fared better with F. Artizzu, *Pisani e Catalani nella Sardegna medioevale* (Padua, 1973); and F. Artizzu (ed.), *Documenti inediti relativi ai rapporti economici tra la Sardegna e Pisa nel Medioevo*, 2 vols. (Padua, 1961–2).

[32] Belgrano, *Reg. Curiae*, 10, and 384, referring to those who 'cum rapallinis navigant a Rapallo usque in Tiberi'. Also Abulafia, 'Corneto–Tarquinia', 224–32.

IV

Much of the shipping referred to by the curial registers was not even Genoese, in the sense that boats, crews or merchants might be non-Ligurian. Throughout the twelfth century southern Italy remained a great repository of nautical skills – the home of professional captains and ship-owners both Campanian and Apulian. Maritime law, in the form of the Νόμος Ῥωδικός, the Rhodian Sea-Law, was widely known and studied in juristic circles in southern Italy.[33] And, although the mercantile towns of the south failed to make a great impact on commercial developments after about 1130, the professional sailors of Norman Italy were known and respected in northern ports. From a Commune tariff list of 1128 it is clear that Gaetans, Neapolitans, Amalfitans and Salernitans used the harbour at Genoa. 'Per unumquemque' – apparently per person on board – they paid the Commune 12d, 12½d, 10½d, and 10½d respectively. The lower rate for Salerno and Amalfi is significant, and it may imply sufficient volume of trade, or the hope for such volume, that reciprocal reductions in tariff were in force.[34]

Evidence from the 1130s shows how unexceptional it was for Genoese businessmen to travel overseas in south Italian boats. An *ars dictandi*, in a late twelfth-century hand, preserved in Vienna includes two letters by Genoese merchants amid a series of other examples of good letter writing.[35] The purpose of the collection was clearly didactic; probably it was a handbook for the teaching of rhetoric, and not a guide to daily practice, for many of the letters are between kings or emperors and popes or bishops. The imperial letters purport to be from Emperor Lothar, and their place of issue dates them between 1132 and 1136, along, apparently, with the rest of the collection; moreover, the imperial letters seem to contain a genuine core.[36] Frequent references to Cremona suggest Lombardy

[33] E. H. Freshfield, *A manual of later Roman law: the Ecloga ad Procheiron mutata* (Cambridge, 1927), prints a south Italian law-book of the twelfth century that includes the Rhodian sea law. See also W. Ashburner, *The Rhodian sea-law* (Oxford, 1909).   [34] *CDG*, I, 61.

[35] Vienna, Österreichische Nationalbibliothek, MS Bibl. Pal. Vind. 2507; the *ars dictandi*, but not the whole MS, was printed by W. Wattenbach, 'Iter austriacum, 1853', *Archiv für Kunde österreichischer Geschichtsquellen*, xxiv (1855). Cf. C. H. Haskins, *Studies in medieval culture* (Oxford, 1929), 181, 184.

[36] Wattenbach, 46–50.

as a likely source of the manuscript as it stands; it is clearly a cheap student's edition, copied from earlier collections of rhetoric – it is written in a small hand on scraped leaves, through which traces of an earlier, Caroline, hand can be detected. On these conditions, it is possible to take seriously the merchants' letters:

a) G. son of Guglielmo Ebriaco [Embriaco] to his colleague and fellow-citizen F., who is now in Constantinople. G. asks for news of him, having heard he may have fallen ill. He asks F. to continue business until he has come out to Constantinople in the ship of the men of Bari (*in navi Barensium*); meanwhile, F. is asked to reply through an itinerant Venetian merchant, Vitale. F.'s wife and children request through G. that F. send various spices and robes back to them in Genoa.[37]

b) F. writes to G., explaining that while in Egypt he fell ill, but has since returned to his business, and places an order for cloth of Piacenza, which he asks G. to bring out with him to Constantinople.[38]

The language of these letters is high-flown; any interpretation of them as literal copies of real originals must be held suspect. Arguably they are stylised versions of real letters – themselves possibly transmitted through the intermediary of Genoese notaries at Constantinople and Genoa. But it would be wrong to suppose that Genoese merchants had no training in letters or in Latin. Many of them must have wished to read the documents they carried; and the notary's rôle was more than that of a scribe. His most important asset was the legal force his registration gave the documents he composed. For tasks outside the legal domain, merchants may have relied on their own talents as early as the 1130s – as they certainly did by the early thirteenth century.[39] In any case, the image that the *ars dictandi* presents, altogether gratuitously, of a member of the distinguished Embriaco family bringing Placentine cloth to Byzantium on board a south Italian vessel, is perfectly credible. Venetian contracts of the twelfth century refer to 'Longobard' ships, probably

[37] MS 2507, f.52v, headed 'negociatoris ad alium'; Wattenbach, 79, no. xix.
[38] MS 2507, f.52v–53r, headed 'responsio'; Wattenbach, 80, no. xx.
[39] Autograph signatures of witnesses occur on many Venetian commercial contracts – thus Archivio di Stato, Venice, S. Zaccaria pergamene, Busta 34, quittance from Obertino son of Guglielmo de la Caçaira of Verona, September 1176; *ibid*. contract for Pescara or Peschiera, November 1173. A series of accounts of 1211 survives from Florence, written in the Tuscan vernacular: A. Castellani, 'Frammenti d'un libro di banchieri fiorentini del 1211', *Studi di filologia italiana*, XVI (1958), 19–95.

south Italian; and Genoese and Savonese notarial acts from the late twelfth and early thirteenth centuries show that Gaetan boats were also regular visitors to northern Italy.[40]

V

The Venetian colonies in Apulia were at least as firmly established there as were those of the Genoese in Sicily. For Venetian support of Alexios Komnenos had no lasting effect on the right to trade in the *Regno*, though periodically Constantinople would reinvoke the chrysobull and on each occasion, as will be seen, the Venetians had to decide their priorities. Venice remained anxious not to compromise its relations with Constantinople by means of its commercial interests in Apulia and Sicily, and equally anxious not to provoke the Normans into attempting to close the Adriatic. It was a flimsy tightrope, and in the 1140s it snapped. Basically, then, it is necessary to distinguish Venetian interests in Apulia and other parts of the *Regno* from Venetian dependence on an open Adriatic; the latter need resulted in lengthy struggles with the Normans and other forces beyond the confines of the kingdom. Nevertheless these struggles were of crucial importance in the formulation of Venetian policy towards the kings of Sicily and yet greater rulers.

Until Venice and Sicily made peace in the mid-twelfth century, the Republic continually hoped to detach some of the Apulian towns from their Sicilian allegiance and to make them independent junior partners in Venetian overseas trade – as Venice managed to do with striking success in Istria and Dalmatia, or, less domineering here, in its relations with Fano in central Italy.[41] Bari was the main target of Venetian interest, but all down the coast, as far as Otranto, Venetians negotiated their affairs in the Adriatic and in the eastern Mediterranean, with fellow countrymen, native Apulians, Amalfitans and Dalmatians. The earliest commercial contract relating to the Norman territories is a quittance of February 1104, in which

---

40 *DCV*, I, no. 217, 'cum nave de Longobardis'; *OSM* (*1190*), no. 640 for Gaeta; also Archivio di Stato, Savona, Registro a catena piccolo, f.10v; *ibid.* Cart. Martino, f.146v–149r (Gaetan attack on Savonese citizens in Savona, 1203).

41 Archivio di Stato, Venice, Codex diplomaticus Lanfranchi, 1000–1199, anno 1141, p. 11 (Fano, 1 March) – transcript from Liber Pactorum i, f.187v–188r; Cod. dipl. Lanfranchi, anno 1145, p. 160 (Pola, December); Pactorum i, f.139r–v (other Istrian towns).

Domenico Michiel settled all claims arising out of a *societas* ('collegancia') between himself and Giovanni Baro.[42] This was composed of £100 belonging to the wealthy patrician Domenico Michiel and £50 belonging to his factor, to be carried by Baro in the ship of Stefano Marango 'in taxegio de Odrento [Otranto] ad caricandum de victualis et inde ad Antiocham'. It had been arranged that if Domenico were already at Antioch by the time his partner arrived, the proceeds of the sale of foodstuffs would be divided there; but it does not seem that Domenico travelled east, for the quittance was drawn up at the Rialto. This document shows clearly that food supplies were being brought from the heel of Italy to the young Latin states in the east by Venetian merchants. But whether the Latins in Syria drew a regular or intermittent supply of foodstuffs from the *Regno* at this period is uncertain. Only in the thirteenth century did Latin Syria become so short of agricultural land that Sicilian grain became the prime requirement of the settlers in the east.[43]

The value of the Michiel contract is magnified by a second charter of Domenico Michiel, issued when he had been elected Doge of Venice. In this document, of May 1122, he forbade that any harm be done to the life, limb or property of any citizen of Bari, and promised to make amends for any abuses of his decree that occurred in Venice.[44] And indeed there was every reason for Doge Michiel to interest himself in Bari. Bari had risen against Duke William of Apulia, with great success: the archbishop was assassinated and a certain Grimoald was appointed first and last 'Prince of Bari', holding out until 1129.[45] The charter was a gesture of support for the rebels; and if, as seems the case, Venice did nothing further to help Bari, it must have been because Venice felt that there was

---

[42] *DCV*, I, no. 31.

[43] There is no guarantee that Sicilian royal privileges permitting Palestine-based monasteries to export certain quantities of grain and other items from the *Regno* were intended to cover the export of grain from the *Regno* to Sicily. The Palestinian monasteries may simply have expected their Sicilian daughter houses to raise a cash crop. San Salvatore, a Greek monastery at Messina, was permitted in 1134 to carry up to 200 *salmae* of wheat to Africa free of duty (Caspar, *Register*, no. 95), and the Palestinian houses, except in years of dearth, may have sold their produce in Africa or to visiting merchants. See, e.g., Holtzmann, 'Urkunden aus Unteritalien', I, 74, no. 10 (Santa Maria Latina), and C. A. Garufi (ed.), *I documenti inediti dell'epoca normanna in Sicilia* (Palermo, 1899), 201 (Santa Maria della Valle Josaphat). [44] Carabellese–Zambler, II, no. 1.

[45] *Rom. Sal.*, 210 and n.8; 217, 219; cf. *Alex. Teles.*, 108.

nothing further that its help could achieve. The Doge clearly thought that his Apulian and Adriatic difficulties were settled by the Bari insurrection, for the next year (1123) he appeared off Tyre with a fleet, offering the crusader kingdom his help in exchange for commercial privileges.[46]

Early in the days of the insurrection other Venetian patricians had been doing business at Bari. During February 1119, Giovanni Morosini, Viviano da Molin and Matteo Scoli drew up an agreement in Bari with Pietro Caracia Canape of Torcello. They received on loan from Pietro an anchor weighing 270 lb, three-fifths divided unequally among Giovanni, Viviano and Matteo, and the remaining two-fifths held by another well-born Venetian, Vitale Navigaioso. This anchor may not have been intended for sale, but was possibly transferred as a security for a sea-loan. Vitale was to captain their ship, bound for Damietta and Constantinople. Once again the vitality of the Venetian commercial settlements in Apulia in east Mediterranean trade is amply demonstrated.[47]

Although Venice offered opportunist support to the Apulians in 1122 and to the Campanian rebels in 1134, the Republic was equally quick to make its peace with the victor, Roger. Roger II certainly granted Venice a charter of privilege, for mention of it occurs in his grandson's charter, dated 1175, but no date for the first charter is given.[48] The most likely period is after the King and the Pope made peace in 1138, since before that Venice was aligned with the Germans and after 1147 it was at war with Sicily on Manuel Komnenos' behalf. Moreover, it was in 1144 that Roger granted the Venetians in Palermo permission to establish a church of St Mark. A date before 1134 is unlikely, for William II's charter calls Roger 'dominus gloriosissimus rex', which leaves only a few years of mounting tension between 1130 and 1134 for his grant.[49] The contents of

---

[46] Tafel-Thomas, I, 84–9.

[47] *DCV*, I, no. 41. For the use of anchors as security, see R. Heynen, *Zur Entstehung des Kapitalismus in Venedig* (Stuttgart, 1905), 79, and his Appendix I, 128.

[48] Archivio di Stato, Venice, Liber Blancus, f.272v–273v; Liber Pactorum I, f.84v–85v, f.76v; Tafel-Thomas, I, 174.

[49] For the 1144 grant, see 79 *infra*. Another possible date for Roger II's agreement is 1154, in the last months of his life; negotiations between William I and the Doge are recorded which must date from 1154, and which could, in consequence, be a continuation of Roger's negotiations rather than a new diplomatic enterprise– H.Falc., 66–7; 86–9 *infra*.

Roger's privilege are, however, plain from King William's document. Only half the taxes normally due from Venetian shipping would in future be paid at Messina, but full taxes elsewhere. The reduction at Messina covered all taxes, not simply the *commercium*, for William's charter refers to *iustitiis*, a wide term suggesting that rights were not limited to one special tax. At this stage, however, there is no evidence for special tax status in Bari and the rest of Apulia.

Venetian merchants visited Sicily proper with large sums in their pockets, even while Apulia was in arms. In August 1119 Viviano da Molin, who has been encountered at Bari, received from Domenico Grilioni a formal quittance of a *collegancia* of £300. This had been divided two to one between Domenico and Viviano, and was for trade in Sicily and then in Constantinople. Though Viviano remained a junior partner, his own share in such large investments is impressive. He belonged to a wealthy family that did not neglect the opportunities for enrichment offered by Sicily.[50] In 1127 two of the da Molin clan agreed to a sea-loan for a mere £20, to be carried 'in taxegio de Sichilia cum navi in qua Uberto Faledro nauclerus ivit'. The terms of the deal were that the second, junior, da Molin was to repay £6 for every £5 borrowed, an interest rate of 20 per cent. From the evidence of the 1119 and 1127 contracts it is, then, clear that ships bound for the east would often 'divert' to Sicily before moving to Romania or Egypt.[51]

That Palermo as well as Messina was frequented by the Venetians is clear from a royal grant of 1144 which permitted certain Venetian citizens to rebuild an old Greek church in Palermo that had been destroyed long ago by the Saracens. This church became an important centre for the Venetians in Palermo, as will be seen; it may even have acted as a focus for commercial activity, if Slessarev's assumptions about *ecclesiae mercatorum* carry any weight.[52] Apart from their Palermitan church of St Mark, in the Seralkadi quarter, the Venetians may have possessed churches dedicated to their patron saint elsewhere in the *Regno*. It seems very likely that Venetian

[50] *DCV*, I, no. 40.   [51] *DCV*, I, no. 50.

[52] *Doc. ined.*, 44, no. 18; Caspar, Register, no. 163; cf. Schaube, 457. Its further fortunes are traced *infra*, 135, 204. *Ecclesiae mercatorum*: V. Slessarev, '*Ecclesiae mercatorum* and the rise of merchant colonies', *Business History Review*, XLI (1967), 177–97.

settlements were most heavily concentrated in Apulia rather than Sicily, and the Apulian historian Carabellese ascribed the surviving church of San Marco in Bari to Venetian patrons. The building was constructed in the early twelfth century in the heart of old Bari, north of the Norman cathedral. But its antecedents are unknown, and it must be remembered that St Mark was revered in Bari as well as Venice before his relics were stolen from Egypt. The most generous conclusion must be that the Venetians probably had a church in Bari and that, of all the surviving medieval churches in the city, this was most probably theirs.[53]

VI

In the 1140s Norman attacks on the coasts of Greece once again aroused fear among the Venetians. The background to these events belongs properly to the history of the Second Crusade, which Roger of Sicily tried to divert if not necessarily against Constantinople, at least away from all possibility of crusader co-operation with Constantinople.[54] As the French sat encamped outside Constantinople, the westernmost shores of the empire were savagely assaulted by a massive Sicilian fleet – an attempt at the disruption of the western provinces in the hope that simultaneously the French crusaders would be crossing swords with Manuel Komnenos in Constantinople, or so preoccupying the Basileus that the Sicilians would have a totally free hand in their attack on Greece.[55] During these months the overt hostility of the Sicilians and the doubtful attitude of the French encouraged Manuel to revitalise Alexios' alliance with Venice, and to formulate with King Conrad of Germany a programme of joint action against the 'tyrant dragon' in Sicily. But the situation in the Adriatic was too critical to be dealt with solely by alliances and future plans. During 1147 Roger's fleet captured Corfu, and then seized Cephalonia; his navy sailed past Modon to raid Monemvasia and attacked Nafplion, Euboea, Negropont and probably Athens too. Inland it raided Thebes and carried off its silk-workers. Corinth too was attacked: it was well known

[53] F. Carabellese, *Bari* (Bergamo, 1909), 85, 86, with illustrations.
[54] Odo of Deuil, *De profectione Ludovici VII in orientem*, ed. V. Berry (New York, 1948), 10, for Roger's attitude to the crusade.
[55] All this was much to the delight of Odo of Deuil, 82. Cf. Niketas Choniates, 97; Kinnamos, 92.

as a commercial centre that traded 'with Asia and with Italy', especially with Venice. The city was sacked and piles of luxury goods were stolen: 'if anyone had seen the Sicilian triremes laden with so many beautiful objects, and submerged down to the oars, he would truly have said they were not pirate ships but merchant ships carrying goods of every sort.'[56]

Lacking more than the smallest fleet of their own, the Byzantines called in their old naval mainstay, Venice. Manuel offered as reward for Venetian aid the confirmation and extension of the privileges permitting the Venetians free trade in the empire. The range of towns where there were to be Venetian settlements was enlarged, and the Amalfitan quarters were to be abolished everywhere to make more room for the Venetians. After all, the Amalfitans were now King Roger's subjects, no longer those of the Basileus. The Venetians were, in return, to provide naval aid until September of the same year (1148) – a mere six months. Not merely were they to resist Roger's forces in the Ionian Islands, but they were expected to participate in a planned invasion of Apulia itself.[57] After some successful engagements against Sicilian shipping, the Venetians joined their Byzantine allies in an assault on Corfu, but they grew increasingly impatient at the failure to arrive of a major Greek land army. In exasperation the Venetians sailed south, seizing some imperial warships on their way. The Greeks recognised how much slimmer were their chances of dislodging the Normans from Corfu, and hastened to make their peace with the Venetians. Together they stormed the island.[58]

---

[56] As Niketas Choniates, 100, remarks. For the Siculo–Greek war see: Kinnamos, 87–98; Niketas Choniates, 97–102; Rom. Sal., 227; *Hist. ducum venet.*, 73. Cf. F. Chalandon, *Les Comnène: Jean II Comnène et Manuel Ier Comnène* (Paris, 1912), 319–20, 327, 361; H. Ahrweiler, *Byzance et la mer* (Paris, 1966), 242–3; Manfroni, 201–7. Athens: K. Setton, 'The archaeology of medieval Athens', *Essays in medieval life and thought presented in honour of A. P. Evans* (New York, 1955), 251 – a layer of mid-century ash excavated in a medieval industrial zone given over to textile dyeing may record the Normans' destructive presence. Textile workers were carried off, too: Otto of Freising, *Gesta Frederici*, MGH. SS., xx, 370. For Corinthian trade with Venice, *DCV*, I, nos. 67–9 *et passim*.

[57] Tafel–Thomas, I, 109–13, 114–124; Kinnamos, 98; *Hist. ducum venet.*, 75; A. Dandolo, 242.

[58] Kinnamos, 101; Niketas Choniates, 114–17 (describing a Venetian masquerade based on Byzantine court ceremonial); *Hist. ducum venet.*, 75. Did Corfu remain Greek? Byzantine sources are very insistent on this, but they are propaganda poems

Roger's Adriatic activities did not stop with this defeat, but the Venetians were anxious to make a settlement with him now that their stipulated service to Manuel was over. There were several reasons for this. First, Venice had seen at Corfu how the Greeks made bigger demands on its resources than the Republic could satisfy; meanwhile Constantinople had held back its own military contribution. Secondly, the prospect of a successful Byzantine invasion of Apulia aroused the same fears as that of Norman penetration of Greece and the Balkans – that is, the possibility that Manuel or Roger would gain a stranglehold over Venice by controlling its Adriatic exit. So during the summer of 1150 a Venetian fleet took part in the campaign to land troops in Apulia, but its artful procrastination and intrigue delayed the Byzantines until autumn storms destroyed part of the allied fleet and a mass invasion became impossible.[59] Third, and most urgent, of the reasons for a settlement was the effect of Venetian policy on the commercial interests of its citizens in the *Regno*. It is hardly surprising that no contracts either for Apulian or for Sicilian trade survive from Venetian collections in the years 1144 to 1159. And the *Historia ducum veneticorum* explains why:

Cum ergo propter hec rex predictus Venetos valde odiret, cepit eos per se et per quos poterat in personis et rebus offendere. Sed cum diu inter regem et Venetos hujusmodi werra durasset et plurimi hinc inde ducerentur captivi, duxque predictus pacis quietisque fuisset amator, faciente Deo, qui malis finem imponit ad pacem venerunt uterque.[60]

By this should be understood not merely the official confiscation of Venetian goods in the *Regno*, but deliberate acts of piracy by the

produced at the imperial court: M. Mathieu, 'La Sicile normande dans la poésie byzantine', *Bollettino del Centro di studi filologici e linguistici siciliani*, II (1954), 1–28; P. Rassow, 'Zum byzantinisch-normannischen Krieg', *Mitteilungen des Institut für österreichisches Geschichtsforschung*, LXXII (1954), 213–18. Compare, however, Benjamin of Tudela's declaration (Adler, 10; Asher, I, 46): 'From Otranto it is a voyage of two days to Corfu, where only one Jew, of the name of R. Joseph, lives, and here ends the Kingdom of Sicily. Thence it is two days voyage to the land of Larta (Arta), which is the beginning of the dominions [of Manuel] sovereign of the Greeks.' Asher, II, 34, provides an unsatisfactory alternative explanation. For the later history of Sicilian control of Corfu and the Ionian Sea, see now J. Hoffmann, *Rudimente von Territorialstaaten im byzantinischen Reich (1071–1210)*, Miscellanea Byzantina Monacensia, XVII (Munich, 1974), 54–6.

[59] Kinnamos, 102; Niketas Choniates, 125–31.
[60] *Hist. ducum venet.*, 75.

royal fleet against Venetian trade, and war damage committed in Corinth and elsewhere in Greece. A contract of October 1151, drawn up in Venice, testifies to this. Vitale Urso and Vitale Senatori are found declaring that they knew of the existence of a series of lost Greek charters sent by Leonardo Fradello to Marino Bembo, authorising him to take from Sparta to Constantinople a quantity of oil provided by the archon of Sparta. But the oil, and presumably the charters, travelled 'cum illis navibus quae fuerunt captae a galeis regis Rugeri'.[61] And indeed it is with an almost self-congratulatory air that the *Historia ducum* sets the violence of relations with Roger against the friendliness of relations with William I.[62]

The Serenissima had survived a difficult, dangerous experience. Yet the basic dilemma remained: two hostile powers faced each other across the Adriatic; their activities compromised or affected a variety of other political units, imperial, royal and communal, whose own movements could upset the delicate balance that the Venetian rulers sought to obtain in the interests of the Republic's trade. There was, of course, an answer, and Roger II had suggested it at the time of the Second Crusade. The conquest of Constantinople became an increasingly attractive proposition to Latin Christians, not least to Venetians, as Greek military feebleness grew more glaringly obvious.

Genoa and Pisa too could not entirely avoid the Siculo–Byzantine war which was waged in their trading waters. Both republics had recently made satisfactory trading arrangements in the *Regno* itself,

[61] *NDCV*, no. 11. This must indicate that the Venetian boats were attacked by Sicilian warships in the Aegean, between the Peloponnese and Constantinople.

[62] *Hist. ducum venet.*, *loc. cit.* This passage argues for the cessation and then resumption of existing Venetian rights in the *Regno* – i.e., it does not suggest that Roger II's original privilege should be dated to the 1150s, but merely that it was renewed then. It is worth adding a fourth reason why Venice could welcome better relations with Sicily – the failure of Sicilian diplomatic initiatives in Germany, Serbia and Hungary, the last of which was competing with Venice for domination over the Dalmatian ports and over Istria. Cf. 76, n. 41, *supra*; Chalandon, *Hist.*, II, 146–7; S. Guldescu, *History of medieval Croatia* (The Hague, 1964), 190–1; 246. Earlier in the century Hungary had joined an alliance with Venice against the Normans: Tafel-Thomas, II, 65 (1101); but, from the 1140s, Sicilian friendship with Hungary remained firm and was highly valued – C. A. Garufi (ed.), 'Liber successionum episcopi Agrigenti', *Archivio storico siciliano*, ser. 2, XXVIII (1903), 148–9; *Monumenta Hungariae Historica*, Diplomata, VI, 63; *Historia Welforum Weingartensis*, MGH. SS., XXI, 468.

as has been seen; the fighting in the Adriatic and Aegean should not have greatly disturbed access to Syria and Egypt. Nevertheless the desire to keep out of the conflict led the two communes to establish a pact of what could be called positive neutrality (17 April 1149). Pisa and Genoa agreed to join forces against 'any power or city or inhabited place' that might take offensive action against either signatory. They defined the region where the treaty was to take force in fairly universal terms: all western Italy as far as Reggio Calabria, all Sicily, the heel of Italy and the whole eastern coast, as well as Greek, Syrian, Egyptian, North African and Spanish waters – in fact, the whole Mediterranean except for the disputed territories of Sardinia and Corsica. The pact makes no attempt to single out any particular or likely foe amid the myriad struggling groups; it represents general fear of entanglement or commitment.[63]

[63] *CDG*, I, 243–7. In this chapter I have not attempted to make use of Venetian accusations against Roger II made at the Diet of Merseburg in 1135. Venetian claims that goods worth 40,000 talents had been seized by Sicilian pirates were clearly exaggerated, and their verbal assaults on Roger were what the Germans and Greeks present wished to hear, rather than a statement of policy. See H. Wieruszowski, 'Roger II, *Rex-Tyrannus*', *Speculum*, XXXVIII (1963), 60–1; *Annales Erphesfurtenses*, MGH.SS., VI, 540; Caspar, 168–9.

Chapter 4

THE MARITIME ALLIANCE OF 1156 AND
ITS AFTERMATH

I

During Roger II's reign foreign policy remained substantially in the King's hands. For his struggle with the papacy, with the German rulers and with the Campanian rebels was in large measure a personal one, in the sense that Roger had to fight for recognition of his kingly title and of his lordship in southern Italy. Such ministers as George of Antioch and Robert of Selby were executive officers, agents of the royal will rather than directors of the affairs of state. After Roger's death in 1154 the picture becomes more complex. King William I entrusted control of the government to a group of omnicompetent royal ministers, headed by Maio of Bari. Maio's appointment and actions provoked bitter opposition in many sections of the Sicilian community – among his social superiors, the Norman barons, as well as among curial officials both Greek and Latin. Thomas Brown from England found the new atmosphere in government too stifling; he left the service of the Norman Sicilian King to join that of the new Angevin lord of England.[1] Hugo Falcandus too did not like what he saw, pouring eloquent scorn on Maio's parentage – Maio, he says, was the son of a Bari oil merchant (and very probably, for all the insults, a member of the Apulian urban aristocracy); but Falcandus makes it clear that Maio's unpopularity stemmed at least as much from avarice, from lack of achievement and from his domination over the King.[2] There may have been an attempt to enforce payment to the crown of taxes that, in King Roger's time, had been allowed to lapse, under pressure of war or out of royal tact. Roger at least knew how tenuous was support on the mainland, and may not always have insisted on his

---

[1] C. Johnson (ed.), *Dialogus de Scaccario: the course of the Exchequer by Richard, son of Nigel* (London, 1950), 35–6; cf. 18 and xxxiv.   [2] H.Falc., 17 *et passim*.

rights of income. If indeed Maio was as avaricious as Falcandus affirmed, this was probably with good reason: the erosion of the Sicilian empire in Africa may have diminished treasury income substantially. During the period of direct Norman rule in Africa a number of sources of payment from al-Mahdiyyah and elsewhere existed: port dues, market taxes and the poll-tax on non-Christians, as well as payment of tribute by local emirs. It does seem that the Normans encouraged Italian merchants to travel to their African possessions and to help build up commercial life after years of devastation and famine.[3] More to the point, Africa was a source of supply for gold, providing metal for the tari of Sicily and Salerno. Arguably, then, the tax measures were linked to the Almohad conquest of Norman Africa. The fall of Tripoli and al-Mahdiyyah threatened to break the supply-line bringing gold from inner Africa to Sicily, and the crown may have reacted by trying to enforce payment of dues inside Sicily and southern Italy. After all, rule in Africa had meant that Norman ships were able to police the straits between Sicily and Ifriqiya, and to demand payment of dues by all shipping that stopped in subject ports on either side of the straits, on the way from one end of the Mediterranean to another. Nevertheless, the signs are that the crown survived these financial pressures without substantial loss of income: the gold coinage remained as stable in precious metal content as ever, as the financial burden shifted from the African towns to Sicily and mainland Italy.[4]

Amid these pressures some supporters were gained, even though others were permanently alienated. In 1154 a new privilege was conferred upon the Venetians; in 1156 the Genoese received even fuller favours. These grants of commercial rights may seem at variance with the financial policy or needs of Maio of Bari, particularly in the light of Hugo Falcandus' hostile narrative. Indeed, some historians have argued that the privileges granted to the Genoese and the Venetians reveal an attempt by the crown to build up support among the bourgeoisie, in the context of a programme of opposition

---

[3] D. S. H. Abulafia, 'L'Attività commerciale genovese nell'Africa normanna: la città di Tripoli', *Atti CISSN*, 395–402. For the history of Norman Africa in general, see Amari, *Storia dei Musulmani*, III, 368–494; F. Cerone, *L'Opera politica e militare di Ruggero II in Africa ed in Oriente* (Catania, 1913); Wieruszowski, 'Sicily and the Crusades', 16–32.

[4] Grierson–Oddy, 'Le Titre du Tari sicilien', 123–34.

to the feudal aristocracy. It would, however, be difficult to argue that the floating population of north Italians in the *Regno* constituted a powerful middle class: it would also be difficult to show that the crown neglected sources of support among the baronage.[5] Moreover, such an interpretation of Maio's privileges leaves out of account the other perfectly adequate explanations of their issue, based on the diplomatic and commercial situation in the 1150s.

The grant to Venice is difficult to disentangle from events reported to have occurred late in Roger II's reign. Roger had, as has been seen, come to terms with the Venetians in the last years of his life, after threatening the exclusion of Venetian merchants from his lands. Hugo Falcandus does, however, mention an embassy sent by William I to Venice shortly after his accession. He writes that, shortly after Maio of Bari was appointed Emir of Emirs, the King decided to appoint Roberto di San Giovanni, Canon of Palermo Cathedral, as his new chancellor, to fill a gap created by Maio's promotion. Roberto was well known for his efficiency and loyalty, but the King decided to test his competence formally before appointing him to high office. So he sent him to Venice as his ambassador; he was to take ship from Apulia. Maio, however, regarded Roberto with much less favour; and, Hugo relates, he sent a letter to the King's *capitaneus* in Apulia in which he asked this officer to provide Roberto with a leaky ship and an unreliable crew, in the hope that the embassy would, literally, founder in mid-Adriatic. But Roberto came to hear of the plot and hired an alternative ship and crew, at his own expense, so that, 'exhausted by many dangers, he nevertheless avoided Maio's trap'. Hugo is at his most eloquent in this passage, and it is easy to see that its purpose was as much to condemn Maio as to praise Roberto.[6] So it is not the best evidence that treaty negotiations took place in Venice at the start of William's reign; and, in particular, it is not very good evidence that Maio was a party to these negotiations. Although there are references to a treaty with Sicily in Venetian eulogies of Doge Domenico Morosini, who died in February 1156, it is more likely

---

[5] In this I am in agreement with A. Ancora, 'Alcuni aspetti della politica di Maione da Bari', *Studi storici in onore di Gabriele Pepe* (Bari, 1969) 303–4; cf. J. Powell, 'Medieval monarchy and trade', 434–8; M. Caravale, 'La Feudalità nella Sicilia normanna', *Atti CISSN*, 48–50.

[6] H.Falc., 66–7. For Roberto's later career, *ibid*. 120, 145.

that they concern his decision to come to terms with King Roger than his pact with King William. His epitaph was copied by Marino Sanudo, whose transcription states: 'this most noble Doge made peace with the king of Sicily, because Venice was in deep discord with the king of Sicily over the matter of the Emperor Manuel' – an account closer to Venetian descriptions of the treaty with King Roger than to Falcandus' description of the negotiations with King William.[7]

Andrea Dandolo possibly holds the key to understanding the sequence of events. He relates that the Doge made peace with King William I in 1154/5, 'terrasque Venetorum a Ragusio infra, et eos similiter, exceptis illis quos in favorem imperatoris Constantinopolitani inveniret, securos redit, et inmunitates plurimas in suo regno negociatoribus venetis indulsit'.[8] This account stands close to the wording of the privilege granted by William II to the Venetians in 1175, and that privilege was said to be a renewal of grants made by Roger II and William I. Andrea Dandolo knew the 1175 grant in Venice, and included it in his *Liber Blancus*, where it can still be read; and he may have used the wording of the 1175 privilege to reconstruct that of 1154/5. Indeed, the reference to Ragusa makes good sense only in the context of the 1175 treaty; twenty years earlier the town seems to have been under Byzantine control.[9] What carries most weight, therefore, is not his summary of the grant but his insistence that it was arranged between Domenico Morosini and King William I. The treaty was an attempt to show that, despite the continuing aggression of the German and Greek emperors, the Sicilian *Regno* remained in high esteem at Venice; it was an attempt to indicate that the death of King Roger did not affect the Venetian acceptance of the legitimacy of the kingdom he had created, and of William's succession by hereditary right. Whether, in addition, Roger II's privilege was granted very late in his life, and possibly only formalised after William's accession, is another, less fruitful, question. Roger had already, it seems, granted Venice commercial rights as long ago as the 1130s or early 1140s, and there may not have been time in the 1150s for him to issue a new grant of rights prior to his death. That, however, is to introduce a thoroughly

---

[7] M. Sanudo, *Vita dei Dogi di Venezia*, ed. G. Monticolo (RISS, ser. 2, XXII, part 4), 237–8.   [8] A. Dandolo, 245.   [9] Abulafia, 'Dalmatian Ragusa', 419–20.

speculative element into a chronology which can, in essentials, be reconstructed as follows:

(1) In the 1150s, while Roger was still alive, the Venetians agreed to make peace with the King of Sicily, and recovered in consequence their trading rights, probably in the form granted to them ten or twenty years before;

(2) After Roger II's death King William reissued King Roger's privilege, be it that of the 1140s or that of *circa* 1154.

Maio's rôle in all this was probably not discreditable. Alvaro Ancora has, indeed, seen fit to list the Sicilian–Venetian pact of 1154/5 as one of Maio's positive achievements.[10] Given that Apulia rebelled in 1155 at the instigation of the Germans and Greeks, and given that Venetian support for King William seems to have remained firm, it is clear that this pact was indeed a solid one, that could weather serious storms. The Genoese were a little more patient, but, once the King had shown his hand in Apulia and rooted out the rebels, Genoa too became convinced that Roger's son deserved to stay as king, and came to terms.

II

The end of the Sicilian war with Germany, Byzantium and Venice enabled the Genoese to make diplomatic approaches to a variety of desirable trading partners, without running too great a risk of compromising themselves in one court through their activities at another. The emissary of Manuel Komnenos, Demetrios Makrembolites, came to Genoa; meanwhile Sicilian emissaries had travelled to Constantinople in the hope that the change of ruler in Palermo might induce a change of heart in Manuel. Hostilities were resumed during the south Italian revolt against William of Sicily, and it was not until 1158 that a Byzantine–Sicilian treaty was signed. Genoese relations with Constantinople appeared to fare better: on 12 October 1155 Makrembolites agreed with the Genoese consuls that a quarter in Constantinople should henceforth be made available to the Genoese, 'sicuti Pisani habent, et hec in partibus quibus ipsi Pisani et Veneti habent'.[11] Visits, partly commercial, partly diplomatic, took place on several occasions in the next decade from Genoa to the imperial court; nevertheless, trade in Romania re-

[10] Ancora, 315.　　　　　　　[11] *CDG*, I, 328.

mained restricted in scale and in operators, and the implementation
of Manuel's promise to provide a Genoese quarter took time.
Venice and even Pisa had better privileges and an older establishment of denizen families in Byzantium, whose rôle in Byzantine
trade completely outstripped that of the Genoese. Unable to com-
pete in Greece, the Genoese found ample compensation nearer
home, in the Kingdom of Sicily.[12]

During November 1156 Ansaldo Auria and Guglielmo Vento
negotiated on behalf of the Genoese Commune the renewal and
extension of Genoese privileges in Sicily. Both were high-born
Genoese of consular rank, though not, at the time of the treaty,
consuls. They came to Palermo, where the king, 'amore predictorum
consulum et comunis Ianue karissimorum amicorum nostrorum',
readily provided them with a grant of commercial rights. The hand
of Maio of Bari is quite literally visible, for the original privilege
from which the surviving authentic copy was made was certified
'per manus Maionis magni ammirati ammiratorum'.[13] Now, the
Genoese can hardly have been unaware that Maio had recently
survived a major rebellion directed specifically at himself (or so the
rebels assured the King); nor can they have been unaware that
King William had ruthlessly and vigorously crushed the revolt –
they must have known how the Sicilian King razed the mercantile
centre of Bari to the ground in 1155, so that it was still desolate when
Benjamin of Tudela travelled from Spain via Genoa through Apulia
in about 1160.[14] In June 1156 the Sicilian King had brought the
papacy to terms, in the advantageous Treaty of Benevento.

[12] I have not been able to discover the source of the statement of J. W. Franklin,
The cathedrals of Italy (London, 1958), 146, where it is stated that William I made
a donation towards the cost of constructing the Baptistery at Pisa, in about 1155.
The *Nuova guida per la città di Pisa*, introd. by P. Serri (Pisa, 1833), 50–1, makes a
similar claim for Roger II, again without citing a reference. There is no visible
inscription mentioning the Sicilian king or kings in the Baptistery, though some
twelfth-century inscriptions do survive there. Were this true, it might provide
evidence of a continuing *rapprochement* between Pisa and the Normans; the *fedus*
of 1137 did, of course, remain in force, and was not even disturbed by the Sicilian
assault on the Pisan colony at Almyra in Greece (*Ann. Pis.*, 17), in summer 1157.
[13] *CDG*, I, 338–41 (citing 339 and 340); original in Genoa, Archivio di Stato, Materie
politiche, mazzo I; facsimile in A. de Stefano and F. Bartoloni, 'Diplomata Regum
Siciliae de gente normannorum', *Archivio paleografico italiano*, XIV (1954–5), fasc. 60,
plate vii. Cf. *Ann. Ian.*, II, 45–7.
[14] Benjamin of Tudela, ed. Adler, 9; cf. H.Falc., 21.

William's victory over internal opposition, as over papal and Byzantine, had reaffirmed the legitimacy of Roger's creation, the Kingdom of Sicily, and had brought the *Regno* security on many of its frontiers. In Africa, the Sicilians had begun to lose ground, but the Genoese soon began to hope that they could obtain extensive concessions in the great Almohad empire which rapidly absorbed the Norman African towns. Under these conditions, the Genoese clearly felt that the recognition of King William's authority in the *Regno* in exchange for commercial rights was a highly practicable purpose.[15]

Implicitly, then, the Genoese recognised the real successes that Hugo Falcandus insisted on denying to Maio. And for Sicily too the Genoese treaty had clear political advantages. Sicily did not need to buy a Genoese fleet, rather as the Byzantines and the crusaders had 'bought' Italian fleets with which to fight their naval wars or besiege enemy strongholds; King William's need was quite the opposite, given the size of the Sicilian royal fleet – an assurance that Genoa would no longer lend its fleet to his potential enemies, should battle once again be joined with either emperor. Such an assurance could not, of course, be obtained for nothing; and yet it is arguable that the commercial needs of Genoa and the financial needs of Sicily were not out of step, so that the surface cost of William's concessions was soon balanced by economic advantages that accrued from more intensive commercial activity both in the towns and in the fields of the *Regno*. The rôle of the crown as demesne lord of the greater part of Sicily bore fruit – or rather, indeed, grain and pastoral products, made available to north Italian visitors for sale, so that the King could convert a healthy surplus into Genoese silver or, if first the merchants had gone east, into oriental gold. And it was not simply any grain that the King made available: primacy was given to wheat, *frumentum*, with specially low tariffs to encourage its purchase and export by the Genoese. Barley, no doubt, formed the staple food of the tillers of the soil; but wheat was more durable, especially the island variety, and was possibly more commonly consumed in courts and by townspeople than inferior grains.

[15] For the Treaty of Benevento, see J. Deér, *Papsttum und Normannen*, Studien und Quellen zur Welt Kaiser Friedrichs II., I (Cologne, 1972), 246–52; Ancora, 312–13. Genoese privileges in Africa: *Ann. Ian.*, I, 62.

The privilege of 1156 is a major source of information about commodities as well as tariffs, so the terms must be carefully analysed.[16] In the first place, it was stipulated that ships coming into Messina were to pay nothing in tax, unless they had come directly from Genoa, in which case 1 *solidus* was to be paid for each man, and for each *apotheca* (presumably, each merchant's load) 2 *solidi* of Genoese silver. On the way out of Messina, 1 tari of Sicilian gold was to be paid on every two bales of goods. For every 4 *saumae* (the standard grain measure) 1 gold tari was payable, so long as the grain was carried directly to Genoa.[17] Here the King was obviously trying to ensure that the Genoese came in search of provisions they themselves needed, rather than as speculators in the grain market. In the latter instance there was a danger that they might interfere with royal rights over the shipment of grain inside the *Regno* in times of famine, or even, if Frederick II's actions carry weight, interfere with the possibility that the crown could operate its own overseas commerce in grain.[18] For every four pigs, in other words salted carcasses, 1 tari was to be paid; not surprisingly, the Genoese were assigned these 'bacon rights' only in Messina, since the Arab population of western Sicily would not have raised pigs.[19] As further concessions, the Genoese were granted the enviable right to use their own weights and measures for business between their citizens, and to use the royal weights and measures for business with Sicilians without payment of commission for their use. Finally, ships arriving in Messina from Alexandria, Syria, 'vel a terra Christianorum vel Saracenorum' were bound to pay a *commercium* of only 3 per cent and to pay nothing at all should they make no sales on the island.

To the evidence of the charter of 1156 can be added evidence from 1116, to show that the Genoese had long possessed a hospice in Messina. Thus the privilege of King William did not provide the Genoese with a corporate identity in Messina, for they had established a continuously occupied base there in 1116; rather did the

---

[16] For what follows, *CDG*, I, 338–341.
[17] One *salma* or *sauma* equalled 315½ lb at Messina, 239 lb in Apulia, but 263 lb elsewhere in the *Regno* – Schaube, 815.
[18] *Supra*, 40.
[19] Compare too the privileges to the Messina monasteries, e.g. *Doc. ined.*, no. 82, which also confer 'bacon rights'.

new privilege exempt the Genoese community in Messina from incidental financial exactions that resulted directly from the fact of residence in a foreign kingdom – the obligation to use the royal weights and measures, for example. King William's charter thus differs markedly from privileges conferred on the north Italians by the German rulers or by the leaders of the First Crusade, which involved a promise of rights and quarters in lands to be conquered, rather than the conferment of favour on a well-established mercantile group.[20] That the Genoese were trading substantially in Sicily before 1156 will be shown shortly.

Palermo too was dealt with in detail. On their entry into the port travelling in from the country villages (*a casalibus*) the Genoese were to pay 1½ tari per *cantarium* (80 kg) of cotton – by implication, raw cotton. Nothing was to be paid on cotton brought into the countryside, no doubt as an encouragement to internal trade. For a hundred lambs, presumably lamb fleeces, the merchants must pay 1½ tari; parchment was much valued in Sicily, as elsewhere, and Sicily was a rich source of supply. And for each *cantarium* of wool, ½ a tari was to be paid, if the wool were 'brought from their own land', a phrase which could mean Liguria or Genoese estates inside Sicily. As for products brought into the city of Palermo for sale, but never actually sold, the Genoese were to be free of customs duty on them. However, the tax on wheat was to be higher than at Messina: 1 tari per 2 *modii*, not 1 tari per 4 *saumae*.

At Girgenti (Agrigento) the royal officials were to differentiate between cotton bought by the Genoese outside and inside the town. When they bought within the city, with the intention of exporting the produce, they would pay ½ a tari per *cantarium*, but 1 full tari when they bought outside Here, perhaps, is visible an attempt to strengthen the commercial rôle of Girgenti by attracting merchants to the town, and by encouraging them to buy raw cotton for export overseas. Lambskins and other hides could also be had, at 1 tari per *sauma* that the Genoese exported; and for every 2 *modii* of wheat that 'they wished to carry to Genoa' the visitors would pay 1 tari, as at Palermo. Lack of reference to Girgenti in the Genoese notarial acts means that the effect of these measures is unknown; the

---

[20] La Monte, 261–75, for a useful hand-list of crusader privileges; *infra*, Chapter 5, 127–31, and Chapter 7, 191, for imperial privileges to Genoa.

charter of 1156 is the only strong evidence that Girgenti was a desirable target for north Italian merchants.

At Mazara the Genoese were to give 10 tari on the quayside (*ad mare*) for each merchant on board ship – in contemporary terms, about £1 Genoese per head. Half a tari tax was to be imposed on each sack (*saccum*) of cotton; and the same rate of taxation would be paid on wheat and skins as at Girgenti. The King clearly hoped to exploit the passage of ships bound for North Africa by imposing higher port taxes at Mazara than he applied on Genoese visitors to Palermo, Messina or Girgenti; this was some compensation, no doubt, for the increased pressure on the Norman towns in Africa, which fell to the Almohads soon after the treaty between Sicily and Genoa. But – since the rate of taxation at other Sicilian towns visited by the Genoese, such as Trapani, is quite unknown – it would be foolhardy to assert that 10 tari per merchant constituted an especially high or low rate.

In Messina, and presumably throughout the *Regno*, the purchase or hire of royal ships and ships belonging to the King's subjects was only to be permitted by crown licence. Not merely were the Sicilian kings shipping entrepreneurs in their own right (if Frederick II's example carries weight); in addition the crown relied on merchant vessels to provide a peacetime naval reserve for the war fleet, and very possibly the products of the royal arsenals at Messina and Palermo were rented out to native traders. However, it seems clear that the King merely restricted the Genoese to the practice and rights of other merchants, none of whom had automatic exemption from licences. Later in the treaty King William promised that Genoese vessels would not be detained unless the royal fleet were ready to sail; in any case the Genoese were constrained to say nothing about naval movements that might embarrass the King or his heirs. The practical application of this regulation can be witnessed in 1185, when ibn Jubayr's Genoese captains paid their way out of such a detention clause at Trapani. Such embargoes can hardly have been a Sicilian speciality; in any well-policed land they must have functioned to the frustration and confusion of visiting merchants (the word 'embargo' is, in fact, of naval or mercantile origin). And merchants made good informers, if not spies: it was Genoese traders who bore witness to the identity of the child emperor Alexios when William II invaded the Byzantine empire. By all accounts their identification was wrong, but at least they had provided the answer the King most wished to hear.[21]

A clause of the 1156 treaty that has been much discussed is the promise of King William, at the plea of the Genoese, to forbid Provençal and French shipping access to the kingdom, nor to send Sicilian merchant ships to Provence.[22] The notarial acts do seem to show that merchants of Toulouse were trading through Genoa with Sicily; in that case, the clause may have been directed against merchants of Provence, Champagne and further north, rather than visitors from lands west of the Rhône. Equally, the Genoese may simply have hoped to channel Provençal and French trade with Sicily through their city, rather than to exclude all Provençal merchants from Sicilian trade – the reference is to shipping between Provence and Sicily and need not have included personnel as well. The Genoese had reason to fear that an alternative trade route that bypassed Liguria would be established, linking Sicily to Champagne and other attractive markets where Genoese ambitions were directed. An analogy is provided within Liguria: in 1181 the Genoese forbade Savona to send its shipping to Sicily unless the Savonese first sent their vessels to Genoa. That way carrying capacity was increased without home interests being undermined.[23] Certain other considerations behind the Genoese ban on the Provençaux are clearer: rivalry with Marseilles and other Provençal ports concerned not simply long-distance trade, but domination in the Ligurian Sea. One of the cardinal points of Genoese negotiations with the German emperors was always recognition of the Republic's right to control the sea-coast between Monaco and Portovenere. Thereby Genoa could hope to establish a virtual monopoly in Ligurian trade, and to extend further its markets in Liguria – the more so since the only sizeable competitor, Savona, traded under what was effectively a Genoese flag. More than this, the Genoese may have been aiming an indirect blow at Pisa. During the twelfth century the Pisans carried

---

[21] Ibn Jubayr, 352–4, both for the embargo and the Genoese spies; *supra*, 40, for controls of grain movements.

[22] *CDG*, I, 340; H. E. Mayer, *Marseilles Levantehandel und ein akkonensisches Fälscheratelier des XIII. Jahrhunderts* (Tübingen, 1972), 61; Pistarino, 251–2. Cf. the remarkable essay of A. B. Hibbert, 'The economic policies of towns', *Cambridge economic history of Europe*, III, 166.   [23] *CDG*, II, 263–5.

much of Marseilles' trade with the Holy Land; for although Marseilles later claimed that the kings of Jerusalem had granted the city extensive commercial privileges, the documents in question are now known to be forgeries.[24] If Genoa had had its way, Marseilles' rôle in west Mediterranean trade would have been confined to Languedoc, Catalonia and other areas of secondary competitive importance. Nor need Provençal exclusion have reduced Sicilian access to continental European markets; Genoese enthusiasm would have provided ample compensation.

Less is known from the treaty of 1156 about Genoese trade with the mainland parts of the *Regno*. The privileges granted in the past to the Genoese for trade in 'Salerno and other cities' were confirmed, but it is not specified in the new treaty what these privileges were. Some appear to have been customary rights, not conferred by royal charter – reciprocal agreements between towns, for instance. The tariff list of 1128 from Genoa shows that Salernitans and Amalfitans paid the commune 2d less per person than the Neapolitans and Gaetans on the arrival of their ships in port; and discrimination in favour of individual trading partners does speak for the existence of commercial agreements.[25] Moreover, Salerno attracted the attention of a good number of Genoese merchant ships in the 1150s and 1160s; Naples was apparently less favoured. And Salerno provided Genoa with one of its richest merchants, Solomon, who flourished in the time of Giovanni Scriba. Thus it is not surprising to find Salerno singled out from the 'other cities' of the Mezzogiorno.

Separate from the commercial agreement, but appended to it, there exists another treaty of the same place and date, in which William promises Genoa protection at sea and on land, excepting only Genoese pirates or those who act against the interests of the crown. Judicial arrangements in the event of breach of this pact were also made. For, even should any individual Genoese break it, the treaty was to remain firm, as would remain the promise of the kings of Sicily to observe forever its terms.[26]

These charters were each drawn up twice, once for the Genoese to carry back home, and once for the King's records. The legates were back in Genoa by January 1157, for during that month the consuls demanded that three hundred *de melioribus* of Genoa should

[24] Mayer, 61–2 and *passim*.   [25] *CDG*, I, 61; cf. 74 *supra*.   [26] *CDG*, I, 341–2.

swear with them to observe firmly and faithfully the treaty of friendship with King William. In addition the consuls decreed that no
Genoese citizen was to go and join the service of the Byzantine
emperor in order to fight the King of Sicily. Then they reiterated
the treaty of safe protection at sea and on land. King William's ambassadors – two Sicilians, Richard, bishop-elect of Syracuse, and
Rainaldo de Tusa, and one Genoese, Ansaldo de Nigrone – were
present at the oath-taking. To the opening statement of the oath-
record are then attached the names of the consuls, the two legates
sent to Palermo, the judges (*consules de placiti*) and the three hundred
'good men', all drawn up in the hand of 'Iohannis notarii publici
scriba', or Giovanni Scriba.[27] Of him more in a moment.

The Genoese were confident they had done very well out of the
treaty: 'unde quidem multa maiora et pulchriora Ianuenses accepisse
quam fecisse, longe lateque a sapientibus per orbem dicitur et
tenent'.[28] Here Caffaro is expressing not just his own view but, as
he insists, that of Genoese and foreigners alike. Nevertheless this
outwardly categorical statement deserves analysis. The argument
propounded by Caffaro is that the Genoese received much for little
labour – by comparison with, say, their efforts in the Holy Land,
where naval aid had to be supplied to gain commercial concessions.
That is not quite the same as saying that the Sicilian King had been
almost irresponsibly generous. King William, unlike the Genoese,
did not see the treaty as a way to balance financial and military needs.
His appears to have been a longer-term view. In the first place, a
rival naval power had been won away from the German king, or
the Basileus – irrespective of whether William would be able to
call upon that navy for aid. In the second place, the King had secured
a market for the produce of the island of Sicily: regular purchases
by the Genoese would swell the King's coffers, particularly if the
produce being sold were grown on the crown estates. To reduce
taxes on such produce would be simply to make it more attractive
to Genoese buyers, while the crown lost little by reducing imposts
on goods that it had ultimately put up for sale itself. Increased demand for Sicilian goods should easily counteract the tax reduction.
Of course, there are so few clues about the normal level of taxation
of visiting merchants that the effects of the new taxes cannot be

[27] *CDG*, I, 344–9. Giovanni Scriba: *CDG*, I, 349. [28] *Ann. Ian.*, I, 47.

measured in any real way; however, there are signs of renewed interest in Sicilian trade in the wake of the 1156 treaty; so, arguably, beneficial effects were rapidly visible. Finally, there was a combined economic and military advantage in the treaty for the Sicilian King: so long as the Genoese stood against Sicily, they threatened not merely the security of the kingdom, but the ability to keep Sicilian markets open under stress of war. To judge from Pisan pirate activity against Sicilian-bound shipping in the 1160s and 1170s, interference in trade by outsiders could be a serious irritant.[29] Thus peace with mercantile cities had distinct advantages for the Sicilian treasury as well as for the money-bags of northern merchants.

Nevertheless, the treaty of 1156 did not settle all current and outstanding matters. Diplomatic activity continued, with exchanges of embassies. Probably William and Maio required assurances that the moves to placate Constantinople in no way committed Genoa against Sicily, and that the Republic would do its best to resist Barbarossa's demands in northern Italy. Thus in 1157 Gionata Crispino was sent 'to eastern parts and to William king of Sicily', while Amico Mirto went to Constantinople to ensure the realisation of the privileges granted there. Crispino must have recounted to William the oath-taking by three hundred Genoese, with its clause forbidding citizens to serve the Greek emperor against the King of Sicily. Caffaro's phrasing when he says that Amico Mirto went to guarantee Genoese rights in Byzantium could be extended to cover Crispino's visit to Sicily too – his syntax is not clear here.[30] In that case it may be that William was slow to put his promises into effect, prior, at least, to receiving news of the oath ceremony. Further evidence of embassies can be gleaned from the commercial contracts: in October 1158 Elia, 'nuncio Ammirati' – the legate perhaps of Maio of Bari, Emir of Emirs – is found in Genoa making a sea-loan of £155 18s 6d, to be paid back in Palermo as 81 oz of tari gold (at $16\frac{1}{3}$ carats), plus 66 oz of purer *paiole* gold from the Sahara (at $20\frac{1}{2}$ carats). In 1160, also, there are indications that Genoese ambassadors to Constantinople might have visited the King of Sicily on their way east.[31] But merchants could hope for more gains at court than continuing

---

[29] *Ann. Pis.*, 27 (1162), 36 (1165), 50 (1170), 53 (1171). [30] *Ann. Ian.* I, 48.
[31] *GS*, II, 310, no. xviii, for Elia; *GS*, I, no. 615, no. 666 for embassies to Sicily and Constantinople – cf. 115–16 *infra*.

Table 1. *Genoese contracts by apparent first place of destination, 1155–64 (after E. Bach)*

Destination	Number of contracts
The *Regno*	
Sicily	84
South Italy	9
Maremma, Rome or Lombardy	9
Sardinia	14
Western Mediterranean	
North Africa	73
Provence and Languedoc	17
Spain	17
Eastern Mediterranean	
Syria (‘*Ultramare*’)	34
Alexandria	58
Byzantine empire	20
Total	335

Table 2. *Genoese investments by region, 1155–64 (£)*

Syria	10,075	N. Africa	6,103
Egypt	9,031	Byzantium	2,007[32]
SICILY	6,689		

exchange of pleasantries or adjudication of difficulties: the royal court was plainly the prime centre of demand for top-grade luxury goods. For a merchant laden with fine merchandise, access to a king's eyes was at least as important as access to a king's ears.

III

How well Genoa responded to the Sicilian incentive is plain from Giovanni Scriba's cartulary. A head-count of contracts by first place of destination for the years 1155–64 is shown in Table 1. On this basis Erik Bach was prompted to write 'que la Sicile est la relation commerciale la plus importante de Gênes quand aucune guerre n'y fait obstacle'. Nevertheless, as he himself was aware, the total sums invested in each region provided a different order of priorities, as is shown in Table 2.

[32] These figures are drawn from the excellent book of E. Bach, *La Cité de Gênes au XIIe siècle* (Copenhagen, 1955), 50–1.

The average amount invested in Sicily is therefore £79.63, less than a third of the average per contract for Syria, £296.32. This contrast can, in part, be explained by the longer journeys and greater risks that investments in Syria and Egypt involved. Money sent to Syria was best invested in the convoys of ships that went out in spring and autumn, to return after about six months, rather than in the random departures that occurred throughout spring, summer and autumn for places nearer home. The patricians and professionals, those who had the capital available or who could raise loans on good securities, were thus more able to place their substantial funds in long-distance, high-risk and slowly maturing commercial enter-prises, whereas Sicily and nearer destinations attracted both large and tiny investments. And the risks of the Syrian trade were prob-ably nicely balanced by handsome financial rewards: rare goods with high overheads demanded stiff prices and brought sturdy profits. In this respect the raw materials market of Sicily may have been less attractive financially, however necessary its products were to Genoese bellies and bodies. A second consideration in the comparison of Syrian and Sicilian trade is that the security of the Sicilian market saw a marked decline during the period of Giovanni Scriba's surviving records. Between 1154 and 1164 Genoa switched from friendship with King William to an alliance with Frederick Barbarossa. A constant, stable market in Sicily must therefore be counted, in retrospect, an unreality.

A season-by-season analysis of Genoese trade with Sicily can only seriously begin in 1156, since the evidence for the 1155 season is fragmentary and the evidence from 1154 dates to the last months of the year, looking forward to the 1155 sailing season. For March 1155 only two commercial contracts for anywhere survive. The first is an uncancelled act, recording a *societas* between Peire de Tolosa and Otone Bono, under the terms of which Peire was to carry £127 to Salerno or directly to Sicily; in the second act, cancelled, Otone Bono sent Aucello with a *societas* of £93 on the same route. The de Tolosa family, or persons 'de Tolosa', from Toulouse, appear several times in Scriba's cartulary, and have marked commercial interests in Provence – a fact which makes the attribution to Toulouse a little safer.[33]

[33] *GS*, I, no. 11, no. 12.

The summer ended with a contract for trade to Mazara ('ante Masarium'), drawn up on 19 September 1155 between Ribaldo de Sarafia, an eminent merchant, and Ferro de Campo. Although many of the other Sicilian contracts of the twelfth century may have been aimed at business in Mazara, this item is unique in its specification of the port by name – a reference that makes sense in the light of the 1156 treaty. Further interest is provided by the fact that the travelling partner, Ferro de Campo, was to carry £75 plus, 'extra societatem', 90 tari that belonged to Ribaldo, to be exchanged 'for the fortune and profit of the same Ribaldo'. Ninety tari was 3 oz of gold, or about £10 at most; so that this document indicates that Sicilian gold coinage was at this point being held by Genoese merchants for reinvestment, along with the city's own money, in Sicilian trade. Similarly, Genoese merchants had goods on deposit in Sicily, stored against future ventures and prospects: on 6 November 1155 Stabile *bancherius* and Rainaldo Margon made a contract of £100 for a voyage to Sicily and back, the profit from which was to be placed in the hands of Ansaldo Auria, the future ambassador to William's court. In addition Rainaldo was to receive in Sicily £50 worth of Stabile's goods, which he was to sell, and from the proceeds of which he was permitted to take one quarter of the profit.[34]

The next sailing season, that of 1156, culminated in the legates' departure for Palermo. It saw a marked growth of interest in Sicilian trade. Knowledge that a group of ships was on its way to the kingdom to negotiate a treaty encouraged commercial investment, even though the outcome of the expedition was not yet entirely certain. Naturally, many of the investments known were made by those personally involved in the embassy, as legates or as consuls during the year when the treaty negotiations were planned. An uncancelled contract of 2 May 1156 shows Ingo della Volta and Opizo coming together to form a *societas* of £484 10s 0d for trade in Sicily and beyond – a truly massive investment, even though the sum spent in Sicily cannot be named. Ingo della Volta, as a member of the leading political faction in the Commune of Genoa, had access both to vast funds of money and to vast funds of information about diplomatic prospects. And indeed his *societas* with Opizo was only part of the

[34] *GS*, I, no. 34, no. 35.

story; a certain Eustachio, whom Bonogiovanni Malfigliastro engaged to carry £52 4s 0d to Sicily in *accomendacio*, had already established a *societas* with Ingo for trade in Sicily. This *societas* was apparently registered by another notary than Giovanni Scriba, or listed in a lost section of his cartulary, since the only reference to its existence is a statement that Ingo had given his assent to Eustachio's deal with Malfigliastro, inserted in Eustachio's *accomendacio* (2 May 1156). On 3 May Guglielmo Vento, legate to Palermo, entrusted a quantity of textiles valued at £24 10s 0d to two factors who were to carry the cloth to Salerno and thence to Alexandria should they so desire – a sign, perhaps, of uncertainty about the market for northern textiles ('sagie et volgia') in southern Italy.[35]

Bonogiovanni Malfigliastro's partnership with Eustachio was followed by further business directed at the *Regno*. On 9 August 1156 Malfigliastro lent Bonus Senior and his colleagues £33, for carriage to Salerno and from there to Sicily and then back to Genoa. Should Malfigliastro's agents remain in the kingdom over the winter, they were, nevertheless, to send repayment back to him at the end of the summer. Sea-loans had their interest rate fixed at the time of contracting the partnership, and Bonogiovanni Malfigliastro was to receive £41 for the £33 he had lent. It would be up to the travelling partners to find still further profit for themselves within the stipulated period of time.[36]

But travelling partners were not always so co-operative, to judge from an uncancelled contract of 19 August 1156.[37] That day Solomon – as will be seen, a Salernitan by origin – arranged to travel to Alexandria for business there. He entrusted Ogerio de Ripa with some outstanding tasks in Sicily – Ogerio was to recover 1,254 tari, nearly 42 oz of gold, owed to Solomon by Giordano de Molino. Should the money be recovered 'in that place where the court of the king and of the legates will be held', Ogerio may have 100 tari in commission; should he manage to recover less than $35\frac{1}{3}$ oz of gold, his profit on the debt collection will be reduced proportionately; but if he should recover less than half the 42 oz,

---

[35] *GS*, I, no. 71 (uncancelled), no. 72 (cancelled), no. 73 (cancelled). Cf. also no. 68, a £50 *accomendacio* for Sicily, invested by Guglielmo Filardo.

[36] *GS*, I, no. 106.

[37] *GS*, I, no. 112. I emend '.cc. uncias' to '.cc. tarenos' – an obvious error that leads the figures actually cited into arithmetical chaos.

he is to have 2 oz (60 tari) of gold for himself in any case. Should he
need to go to Syracuse ('apud Saragosam': patently not Saragossa)
or beyond the royal court in order to collect the money, he shall
have his provisions paid for by Solomon and his fee shall rise to
150 tari. Should he in the process miss the ship back home ('if you
cannot come back in the ship of the legates') his food and lodging
will have to be paid for out of the proceeds of the other goods he is
carrying – whether his own or Solomon's or other people's is not
stated. And in the meantime he is free to use whatever money he
has recovered for investment in Sicilian business, so long as he
brings it back in the end. An added inducement is that he can keep
for himself one-fifth of the profit earned by investing Solomon's
money in commercial enterprises. Now, none of the three individuals named in Solomon's deed appears in the list of *meliores homines*
who swore in February 1157 to observe the treaty with King
William – Solomon was a denizen merchant, not a citizen; Giordano,
having already disappeared abroad, seems to have stayed there;
and Ogerio de Ripa either remained in Sicily after the legates' ship
had returned, or was not of sufficient standing to be included among
the named three hundred. But, irrespective of his origin or social
status, he was clearly of some commercial distinction: earlier in
1156 he placed as security for the purchase of a house in Genoa a
quantity of pepper and brazilwood.[38] No doubt he was entrusted
with his task in Sicily because he had already arranged to travel
there for business, and because Solomon had confidence in his
ability and reliability. Nor is it surprising that Syracuse was one
place where Giordano might be located; for although no contracts
survive that name Syracuse as destination, merchants travelling
through Messina must have had cause to call there – if only because
during the minority of Frederick II the Genoese had sufficient interest in the town to seize it. Its cheese and leather industries are
known from the Geniza letters.[39]

Business aimed at Sicily was particularly active in late August and
early September of 1156. On 20 August 1156 two *societates* were

[38] *GS*, I, no. 88.
[39] D. S. H. Abulafia, 'Henry, Count of Malta, and his Mediterranean activities,
1203–1230', in A. T. Luttrell (ed.), *Medieval Malta: Studies on Malta before the
Knights* (Supplementary Monograph of the British School at Rome; London,
1975), 111–12; Goitein, *Medit. society*, I, 40, 124, and 'Sicily and southern Italy', 19.

formed, each of £60, and each specifying a journey to Sicily and then back to Genoa; and the next day a longer-term partnership was established when Gandolfo lent Lanfranco Malagronda £32, to be used in Sicily, against the obligation to return £40 the next summer.[40] Other *cambium* contracts this season were less generous in terms of time to repay the original loan: on 13 September Bonogiovanni Tigna received from Ferro de Campo goods of an unnamed value, promising to return 5 oz of gold at the Palermo standard (16⅓ carats), following his forthcoming voyage to Sicily. In addition Bonogiovanni declared that he owed the wealthy merchant Ribaldo de Sarafia 5½ oz of gold. Both sums were to be repaid within the fortnight after Christmas. This double contract is of additional interest since it hints at the outcome of an earlier deal, the contract of 19 September 1155 for trade at Mazara. The travelling partner in that venture had returned from his voyage to Sicily within the year, having earned half the profit drawn from his earlier *societas* with Ribaldo. Now he reappears as *socius stans* in his own right, financing an *accomendacio* in merchandise – goods he may have bought beyond Sicily or in Genoa, since otherwise there would be less reason in sending them to Sicily for sale now. Unfortunately nothing else is known of Ferro de Campo – neither his origin nor his further investments. He was not, at any rate, a Genoese patrician.[41]

Sicily apart, the evidence for trade in the 1156 sailing season has to be based on a handful of contracts. Certainly, there were large investments in Alexandria, Syria and North Africa – £200 in Bougie that April, £310 plus 12 *morabitini* in Valencia and Alexandria together, £320 in Syria during August; and Sardinia, Majorca and the Maremma attracted lesser business.[42] A contract of £392 15s 0d for Constantinople, involving a visit to the court of the emperor himself, belongs to a special category, in which the delicate attempts of the Genoese to secure the rights they had been promised prompted a series of exploratory investments through which they tried to show willing.[43] Large investments in Sicily were rarer: Ingo della Volta's *societas* of £484 has been noted, but the act is uncancelled

[40] *GS*, I, no. 115, no. 116, no. 120.   [41] *GS*, I, no. 140 and no. 34.
[42] *GS*, I, no. 59, no. 69, no. 129; Sardinia, etc.: *GS*, I, no. 98, no. 100, no. 141.
[43] *GS*, I, no. 97.

Table 3. *Genoese trade by first place of destination,*
November 1155 – October 1156

Destination	Number of contracts	Total investment in £	Average investment	% of total
SICILY	8 (11)	1,182.54	131.39	20.14
Alexandria	6 (8)	1,075.68	179.28	18.32
Syria	2	545.00	—	9.28
Romania	1	527.75	—	8.99
Spain and Balearics	3	470.62	—	8.01
Attalia	2	396.00	—	6.74
Sardinia	2	252.50	—	4.30
North Africa	1	200.00	—	3.41
SALERNO	2 (3)	57.50	—	0.98
Provence	1	53.00	—	—
Maremma	1	15.00	—	—
No stated destination	3	1,096.25	—	18.67
Grand Total		5,871.84		

NOTE: numbers in brackets in the column 'Number of contracts' indicate the total number of contracts expressed in pounds Genoese, foreign gold and merchandise of unspecified worth. The pound totals and other figures refer solely to figures in pounds Genoese cited in the contracts. Such figures are, of course, easily overturned by the accident of the investors' choice of notary; two contracts for Syria would hardly make a voyage there worthwhile (though perhaps pilgrims provided the ballast), and many other contracts must have been recorded by other notaries. Nonetheless, the pre-eminence of the *Regno*, with many contracts and much money to its name, is striking.

and, in any case, Ingo gave his partner the right to carry some of this money beyond Sicily. On 1 September Conrado Bottaio sent £203 16s 11d in *accomendacio* to Sicily with Guglielmo Licio; and on 8 September Guglielmo added a further £160 of his own money – the act of 8 September, but not its predecessor, is un-cancelled, but since it placed no special obligation on Conrado Bottaio, failure to cancel cannot be taken to mean that Guglielmo did not take his £160 abroad. The second act was simply an act of recognition, and the total export of £363 16s 11d can be taken seriously.[44] By comparison with other destinations, the *Regno* stood very high in Scriba's registrations for 1156, as shown in Table 3.

[44] GS, I, no. 132, no. 137.

IV

Late winter and early spring of 1157 was a quiet period during which only a few trade contracts were drawn up – a perfectly normal winter phenomenon – but Giovanni Scriba's notes hint at considerable activity among the Genoese in Sicily. On 17 February 1157 Aimerico and Pietro Bono came together before the notary to settle their past business and to arrange further ventures in Messina. First, Pietro declared that he had received from Aimerico all the profit and capital of the *societas* earlier formed between him and Aimerico. A second contract shows Aimerico promising Pietro and a certain Bovono that within fifteen days of his arrival in Messina he will give Bovono 30 oz of gold at the Messina standard (16⅓ carats), and promising to restore any residue from an earlier *societas* with Bovono above the minimal sum of 20 tari. Finally Aimerico quit Pietro of his debt of £46 incurred at an earlier date. None of these characters can be definitely identified elsewhere in the notarial registers – they could even be Sicilians, but, whether Genoese or foreign, they bear witness to an elaborate network of commercial ties built on exchanges of silver for gold in the Kingdom of Sicily.[45]

June saw a return to activity as the merchants tried to arrange sailings before the onset of winter; factors were sent to Sicily in several instances until the next summer. A wide range of markets in the *Regno* was exploited: on 3 July £6 was sent to Naples (never again mentioned in the cartulary), and the same day the high-born Oberto Spinola sent £100 in *accomendacio* to Salerno, and thence to Alexandria. For the moment at least Salerno was the principal port of call in the mainland part of the Norman kingdom, ceding first place to Naples by the end of the century.[46]

Several shipping contractors, interrelated by blood or business, dominated Giovanni Scriba's summer registrations for Sicily; they themselves placed investments, as well as operating the vessels. On 7 June Merlo Guaraco sent £3 to Palermo in the form of a sea-loan; his factor was to return with £4. He had to travel out in the ship of Gionata Ciriole. On 11 July Merlo sent £32 (anticipating a return of £40) to Palermo in the ship of Gandolfo de Gotizone and Guglielmoto Ciriole. On 17 August Bonogiovanni Malfigliastro

[45] *GS*, I, no. 168, no. 169, no. 170.   [46] *GS*, I, no. 212 (Naples), no. 213 (Salerno).

entrusted £10 to Merlo's relative Graziano Guaraco, against an expected return of £12½; this too was to be carried in the ship of Gandolfo and Guglielmoto but the factor was to return to Genoa within a month of his arrival, still in the same ship. Gandolfo too was prepared to act as factor, receiving merchandise worth £298 10s 0d from Boiamonte di Giovanni Cristiani in September 1157, for carriage to Palermo. On 12 September Gandolfo made his will, leaving most of his money, said to be £40, to his wife and daughters; but he is known from subsequent documents to have returned safely from Sicily. The same day Gionata Ciriole engaged himself as factor to Bonogiovanni Malfigliastro in a *societas* of £33 9s 3d for trade in Palermo; in addition to this sum, he was to carry £140 worth of his own goods and £23 worth of linen cloth provided by Malfigliastro. That shipowners or ship's captains carried their own property overseas for sale is hardly surprising; such items come to notice only where they entered into partnership with a second party and had to declare their assets, to avoid confusion of funds or merchandise. That individual factors were entrusted to the care of captains is hardly surprising either: Graziano Guaraco was sent with a small investment for a limited period of time most probably because he was still young and inexperienced; instruction in the ways of trade was considered essential.[47]

The evidence for August and September shows how massive the response to the opportunities offered by the treaty of the previous autumn in fact was:

August   (1) £24 (Palermo, via Fréjus), uncancelled
            (2) £100 (Sicily, plus a further £200 sent to Syria), cancelled
            (3) £4 (Palermo), cancelled
            (4) £10 (Palermo), cancelled
            (5) £7 5s 3d (Sicily), cancelled
            (6) £58 (Sicily), cancelled
            (7) £80 (Sicily), cancelled
            (8) £78 (Sicily), cancelled
            (9) £20 (Palermo), cancelled
          (10) £30 (Palermo), cancelled

[47] *GS*, I, no. 191, no. 218, no. 240, no. 287, no. 286, no. 285. For a sea-loan by Ingo della Volta (£12 expecting £15 in return), see no. 298.

September (11) £89 (Palermo), uncancelled
          (12) £355 (or possibly £469; implying a visit
                to Palermo), cancelled
          (13) £4 8s (Sicily), cancelled
          (14) £7 2s (Sicily), cancelled
          (15) £100 (Sicily), cancelled
          (16) £196 9s 3d including merchandise
                (Sicily), cancelled

Total: £1,164 0s 6d, plus the merchandise in (16) and the goods contained in an inventory of 10 September, valued at £298 10s 0d, making a grand total of £1,462 10s 6d. A further contract worth £43 plus 22 bezants to be sent *apud Masale* might mean a ship was being sent to Marsala in Sicily.[48]

This compares very favourably with other destinations, as is shown in Table 4. Owing to the presence of a number of small investments in Sicily it would be unwise to offer an average figure for investment in each region – the more so as evidence for trade in Sicily outnumbers, in terms of contracts registered, evidence from all other destinations put together. Yet it is a fact that apart from one contract for Valencia, recorded overseas business in September 1157 was completely taken up with contracts for Sicily. Even those sceptical of these figures must make further notional allowance for stop-overs in Sicily by shipping bound to or from Romania, Syria and Alexandria. Vessels sent to Valencia might often make a leisurely return through Sicilian waters to Genoa. Thus the response to the 1156 treaty was enthusiastic indeed.[49]

V

For a brief period the Genoese beneficiaries of the privilege of 1156 were able to trade in Norman Africa – until the fall of Tripoli to the Almohads in 1158, and the complete eclipse of the African

48 *GS*, I, no. 225, no. 236, no. 239, no. 240, no. 245, no. 257, no. 258, no. 259, no. 260, no. 274, no. 276, no. 280, no. 282, no. 283, no. 284, no. 285; also no. 249 (*apud Masale*).
49 Valencia: *GS*, I, no. 290. There were formal negotiations with 'Lupus', ruler of Valencia, in 1160 – *Ann. Ian.* I, 60.

Table 4. *Genoese trade in August and September 1157*

Destination	Number of contracts	Investment in £
Alexandria	4 (plus 1 in bezants)	882.65
Syria	6	677.65
Provence	1	276.00
Constantinople	3	210.00
Spain	1	209.30
Tunis	1	10.00

empire with the surrender of al-Mahdiyyah in 1160.[50] Before then the Norman rulers had done much to aid the economic recovery of the devastated towns of North Africa. Ibn al-Athir was explicit about the advantages of Norman rule in Tripoli:

[Then] things went well in this city of Tripoli. The Sicilians and the Rûm [i.e., north Italians and Greeks] frequented it [for the sake of commerce (Amari's interpolation)], with the result that it rapidly became repopulated, and prospered.[51]

The geographer Idrisi talked of commercial links between Tripoli and Sciacca in southern Sicily; and he wrote at the time when Tripoli was under King Roger's sway. In addition, the Normans took trouble to mint an African coinage at al-Mahdiyyah.[52] The financial benefits that would accrue to the crown by the resurgence of commercial activity in North Africa are clear enough: port dues, access to the Saharan gold supply, a larger poll-tax following re-population. Interestingly, too, ibn al-Athir's picture of visits by north Italian merchants is confirmed by a notarial entry of 6 June 1157 in the cartulary of Giovanni Scriba. Here Albertone de Custode, Oberto Corso and Enrico Fledemerio are found forming a *societas* of £63, which Enrico was to carry first to Tripoli and 'then where

[50] For what follows, see Abulafia, 'L'Attività commerciale genovese nell'Africa normanna'. (References there are to the octavo edition of *BAS*.)

[51] Ibn al-Athir, *BAS, versione italiana*, folio ed., 119.

[52] Idrisi, ed. Amari–Schiaparelli, 37; H. H. Abdul-Wahab, 'Deux dinars normands de Mahdia', *Revue tunisienne*, n.s., 1 (1930), 215–18; K. Belkhodja, 'Roger II en Ifriqiya', *Africa* (Institut national d'Archéologie et d'Art, Tunis, 1966), fasc. 1, 111–17.

he wishes throughout this and the following summer'. In addition Enrico took £9 *de suo*; but to the total investment of £72 must no doubt be added the sums recorded by different notaries who acted as intermediaries between other merchants investing in a ship bound for Tripoli. Enrico Fledemerio, a Genoese, next appears setting his financial affairs in order with his wife Giula prior to his departure.[53] Albertone de Custode also reappears in Giovanni Scriba's cartulary; on 28 July 1158 he established a *societas* with Alberto Clerico worth £34 1s 0d, to be carried to Messina and beyond for up to three years. In addition Albertone sent some Picard cloth worth £5 15s 0d. This contract was presumably drawn up while Enrico Fledemerio was still overseas – his second summer had not quite elapsed; it may suggest a particular interest in trade with the *Regno* and its dependencies.[54]

Later contracts for Tripoli, dating to the period of Almohad rule, show that the Genoese were involved in trade between Africa and Sicily and that they brought copper as well as Genoese money to the town. They had close links, too, with native businessmen such as a certain Xecha Bohahia de Tripoli, and with 'Roxaldinus', probably a Saracen from Sicily or Tripolitania with the Arabic name Rashid-ad-din. To some extent the activity of the Genoese in Tripoli in the post-Norman period is further credit to the Sicilian overlords of the city; for the evidence of Giovanni Scriba seems to prove that the 'Rûm' as well as native Sicilians did indeed help the cities of Africa on their way to economic recovery. By 1164, certainly, the Genoese were close enough to the bosom of the Almohad sultan to be able to trade in Tripoli once again as favoured merchants. Here was one destination that remained open irrespective of the change of rulers.[55]

VI

The general characteristics of Genoese investment in Sicilian trade that can be established from the data for 1157 apply to subsequent years. Sicily and southern Italy remained numerically the most popular destinations for individual partnerships recorded by Giovanni

---

53 *GS*, I, no. 187–8 (and plate iv, p. 98).   54 *GS*, I, no. 415.

55 For contracts later than the fall of Tripoli (1158) see *GS*, I, no. 770, II, no. 1238, II, no. 1245 (Xecha Bohahia); Abulafia, 'Attività commerciale', 399–400. Privilege of 1164: *Ann. Ian.*, I, 62.

Table 5. *Genoese trade by first place of destination,*
1158 sailing season

Destination	Number of contracts	Total investment in £	Average investment	% of total
SICILY	20 (22)★	1,849.49	92.47	28.68
Syria	6	1,137.25	189.54	17.64
Alexandria	8	844.27	105.53	13.09
Provence	7	544.13	77.73	8.44
SALERNO	8	298.16	37.27	·4.62
Tunis and Gabes	4	199.60	49.90	3.10
Bougie	4	195.32	48.83	3.03
apud Arcem	2	135.00	—	2.09
apud Feriam	1	106.00	—	1.64
Balearics	1	23.00	—	—
Sardinia	1	16.00	—	—
Romania	2	12.00	—	—
No stated destination	8	1087.50	135.94	16.87
Grand Total		6,447.72		

★ Two out of 22 contracts do not supply figures in £ Genoese.

Scriba; but, once again, neither the quantities invested in the majority of deals nor the annual total invested in the *Regno* were especially high. For the season 1158 (see Table 5) Giovanni Scriba provides thirty contracts for trade in the *Regno*, of which eight concern Salerno in the first place, and of which only three are uncancelled – one of £7½ for Messina, one of £24 for Salerno and one of £65 for Messina.[56] Values range from £4 to £331 (in that instance with merchandise to add to the money); but only ten contracts are worth £100 or more. Nevertheless this was a far greater response than other destinations evoked, as the table shows. Unfortunately the high total value of contracts without a precise destination throws these figures off balance. The minuscule amount of business in the Byzantine empire – contracts of £9 and of £4 – may reflect a temporary set-back in the establishment of the Genoese colony there, unless the contracts with unspecified destination were aimed in quantity at Greek ports.[57] Furthermore, the balance of these figures is slightly disturbed by the existence of a hand-

[56] *GS*, I, no. 329, no. 353, no. 464.   [57] *GS*, I, no. 438, no. 468.

ful of contracts that refer to the carriage overseas of merchandise, or to the collection in Sicily or Alexandria of local currency; it is also disturbed, for the present purpose to the advantage of Sicily, by a group of contracts for trade in Spain, North Africa and as possible last resort the *Regno*, should the captain and passengers of the vessel wish. For the rôle of the Genoese in Spanish trade with Sicily must not be ignored.

Unfortunately, much of the evidence for trade in 1159 has been lost, since Giovanni Scriba was appointed early that year as notary responsible for affairs relating to the construction of new city walls; his attention was diverted from commercial contracts.[58] Since 1158 and 1160 were healthy years for Genoese trade in Sicily there is no reason to suppose 1159 was much different. Only one contract survives from the first six months of 1159 for trade in Sicily (a mere £10), and only one for the rest of the sailing season (£100, for Trapani, in the ship 'in which the Savonese are coming').[59] Table 6 shows the picture for 1160; it is more substantial, though the presence of an increased number of contracts that do not specify any destination makes an accurate assessment of Giovanni's evidence more precarious than ever. And, once again, total pound-figures do not include the small numbers of contracts expressed wholly or partly in bezants or tari which are already on deposit overseas, or expressed in merchandise. The pound-figures in Table 6 can be calculated for the period from mid-October 1159 to mid-October 1160. Here some of the contracts without precise destination may refer to Syria, which is under-represented in the number of contracts recorded, compared to the high average investment indicated by the sample available. They may also refer to Constantinople, since the principal expedition sent there in 1160 was given the option of delaying or stopping at the Sicilian royal court if prospects in Romania, both political and commercial, seemed unfavourable. £781 10s 0d out of a total Constantinople investment of £1,193 was invested in contracts which allowed for a Sicilian halt. It is therefore reasonably certain that a share of the £6,605 for trade

---

[58] *Ann. Ian.*, I, 74. GS, I, no. 520–38 are all the contracts we have for the first six months of the year.

[59] GS, I, no. 533 (sea-loan); no. 543 – the mention of Trapani in this contract is unique prior to the thirteenth century.

Table 6. *Genoese trade by first place of destination,*
1160 sailing season

Destination	Number of contracts	Total investment in £	Average investment	% of total	% of named destinations*
Romania	8	1,193.25	149.16	9.32	(19.25)
SICILY	16	1,017.77	63.61	7.95	(16.42)
Syria	3	853.00	284.33	6.66	(13.76)
Bougie	7	728.81	104.12	5.69	(11.56)
Alexandria	7 (8)	715.50	102.21	5.59	(11.54)
Provence	2	378.00	—	2.95	(6.10)
Ceuta	4	355.00	88.75	2.77	(5.73)
Spain	6	306.00	51.00	2.39	(4.94)
Sardinia	4	295.00	73.75	2.30	(4.76)
SALERNO	2	188.50	—	1.47	(3.04)
Tripoli	1	66.00	—	—	—
Tunis	1	60.00	—	—	—
Pisa	1	26.50	—	—	—
Maremma	1	16.00	—	—	—
No stated destination	23	6,604.92	287.17	51.58	—
Grand Total		12,804.25 (6,199.33)*			

* The column '% of named destinations' has been included since very many contracts specify no destination; this column is intended to show the ratio between contracts for individual ports of call. One contract for Alexandria gives no £ total and has not been included in the total £ figures and averages.

'anywhere' and of the £781 for trade in Constantinople was in fact spent in the *Regno*: goods purchased there could then be carried to the next point of call. Similarly, one of the Provençal contracts, a partnership of £450 between Guglielmo Filardo and Ugo Mallone, old hands at Mediterranean trade, describes a route to St Gilles and thence to Sicily or Alexandria or Syria or simply back to Genoa, or to any combination of destinations – a route which the travelling partner was to work for two years.[60] Even though Sicily remained an attractive and welcoming trading partner, the Genoese now began to explore other markets such as Bougie and Constantinople on a grand scale, and access to the former did not involve passage through Sicilian waters. Bougie would, indeed,

[60] *GS*, I, no. 606.

prove an important trade outlet when the situation in the central and eastern Mediterranean was uncertain. Was there in fact any pressure to move the emphasis of Genoese trade to less politically compromising markets than those of the *Regno*? Or did the success of the treaty with Sicily and of the grant from Constantinople merely encourage the Genoese Commune to try to make the whole Mediterranean its market?

After Conrad III's death in 1152, his successor, Frederick I of Hohenstaufen, descended into Lombardy, terrorising the communes. Caffaro described Lombardy and Tuscany as 'terrore comoti', but he spoke too for Genoa, as the construction of new city walls, those that still stand, testifies.[61] The Genoese came to Frederick to ask for confirmation of their right to trade within the empire free of tolls, since they were imperial subjects. They came too in the hope that their struggle with the Pisans over control of Sardinia would be resolved in their favour. But they did not want, in return, to receive a summons to fight for the emperor; as Caffaro says, 'fidelitatem igitur solam debent habitatores Ianue, et non possunt de reliquo appellari'.[62] The Genoese did not feel that they deserved to make concessions to Frederick, even though he was expected to accede to their wishes over commercial tolls and the lordship of Sardinia. Moreover, it was obvious that Barbarossa had in mind a military solution to the Sicilian problem that had irritated Lothar and Conrad before him; and an invasion of the Norman lands might reasonably be preceded by an attack on the allies of Sicily. The disputed papal election of 1159 provided further excuses for Barbarossa to move against the friends of his accumulated foes; and the Genoese staunchly favoured, and were favoured by, Alexander III, Frederick's papal antagonist. Furthermore the internal squabbles of the Lombard towns gave Barbarossa additional opportunities to interfere in their affairs. In 1159 he destroyed Crema.[63] In these circumstances it is not surprising that the Genoese began to look beyond Sicily, to Romania and Spain, for alternative or additional markets that would save them from being left high and dry should their links with the *Regno* become excessively embarrassing. Enrico Guercio was sent as ambassador to

---

[61] *Ann. Ian.*, I, 41 (*anno* 1155).   [62] *Ann. Ian.*, I, 51 (1158).
[63] Alexander III: *Ann. Ian.*, I, 55–9; *CDG*, I, 384–95; Crema: *Ann. Ian.*, I, 54.

Emperor Manuel, Oberto Spinola as ambassador to 'Lupus king of Spain', ibn-Mardanish of Valencia – missions described by Caffaro with the give-away phrase 'pro comuni utilitate'. In 1161 Genoese visitors to Morocco secured from the Almohad sultan a trading privilege in North Africa, together with confirmation of their existing rights at Bougie.[64]

These years of frantic diplomatic activity, of continuing uncertainty rather than direct danger, seem to be reflected in Giovanni Scriba's registrations. On 9 March 1160 Marchione della Volta entered into a sea-loan of £100 with his patrician colleague Bisacia, anticipating a return of 375 hyperpers – quite a high rate, in fact, since in 1157 a rate of 3 hyperpers per pound was cited in a sea-loan. Bisacia was to travel by galley to Romania, or wherever Marchione should choose in advance of departure, unless Marchione himself travelled east. Bisacia's primary target was to be Constantinople, or wherever the imperial court might be; but if, instead, 'I should agree to remain with the king of Sicily, I shall give you 33 oz of gold at the Messina standard, within two months [of my return]'. On 26 May Bisacia received a further £200 from Adalardo de Curia, to be repaid at the same rate of 3¾ hyperpers per pound. Once again this was to be taken in Bisacia's galleys to the Greek court, or alternatively to the island of Sicily. Should Bisacia's galleys remain in Sicily, Adalardo was to receive 33 oz of gold per pound Genoese. On 3 June 1160 a number of Genoese patricians placed further sums, totalling £181 10s 0d, in an expedition overseas 'in the galleys of Bisacia', without specifying a destination. Guglielmo Burone, Simone Auria and Guglielmo della Volta each contributed a basic £50, while della Volta and the factor – not in this case Bisacia – entered into a further *societas* of £31 10s 0d. But the della Volta interest extended further still. Three days later two princes of that clan, Ingo della Volta and Guglielmo Burone, declared their assets in various partnerships, referring *inter alia* to one between Guglielmo Piperate and Guglielmo Malocello that was backed by their finance and worth at the outset £300, to be carried 'in the galleys

---

64 Valencia: *Ann. Ian.*, I, 60 (1160) – a confirmation of an earlier treaty of 1149, printed in *CDG*, I, 248–9 and by M. Amari, *I diplomi arabi del R. Archivio fiorentino* (Florence, 1863), 239–40. A further embassy to 'Lupus' was sent in 1161 – *Ann. Ian.*, I, 61–2. North Africa: *Ann. Ian.*, I, 62.

of Bisacia'. Of these contracts the first and third, those of £100 and £181 10s 0d, are uncancelled, while in the second there is a stipulation that the original capital sum alone need be returned should Bisacia's galleys fail to depart.[65] Such a stipulation was normally felt to be unnecessary, to judge from its rarity; and it may indicate, along with the notary's failure to cancel two of these acts, that there was serious doubt whether the expedition would reach either the Greek or the Sicilian court. Not that the reason for a call on the Basileus is unclear: the promised concessions to the Genoese had still not been given practical form. But the possible delay at the court of King William throws a more elusive element into these deals. It is possible that Bisacia and the Genoese legates to Manuel were asked first to sound out opinion in Sicily on their negotiations with the Greek emperor. After all, a clause had been inserted in the communal oath of 1157, stating that no Genoese citizen was to enter the service of the Basileus in order to fight the King of Sicily; and, although the Siculo–Byzantine war was at an end, peace was not sealed by mutual trust.[66] The fear that Genoa would enter the Greek fold was compounded by continuing ambiguity in Manuel's relations with Barbarossa. A grand anti-Sicilian alliance remained a possibility; and, to judge from the notarial acts, the Genoese too were aware that William and Maio had these fears and that the fears must be placated even if this meant that the expedition proceeded no further on its way to Manuel than the court of Sicily. A further consideration in Genoa must have been that Genoese rights in Sicily were effectively unique – there are no signs that Venice had such extensive exemptions nor such extensive interest, in island Sicily at least – whereas any rights the Genoese might gain at Constantinople would clearly be overshadowed by the fuller concessions awarded to Venice and, on a more limited scale, to Pisa. The *Regno* was an asset that could not be squandered lightly. Some headway was, nevertheless, made in Constantinople in 1160 or 1161: in 1162 a Genoese colony did exist in the city, for that year it was destroyed by the Pisans, Venetians and others.[67]

The year 1160 was important in Genoese trade with Sicily for other reasons too. In May Messina received a major commercial privilege from William the Bad; in November the Sicilian towns

---

[65] *GS*, I, no. 615, no. 666, no. 673.   [66] *CDG*, I, 345.   [67] *Ann. Ian.*, I, 67–8.

rose against the King's ministers and against the Muslims in Palermo and elsewhere.[68] Maio himself was assassinated; the king's palace was ransacked; William was briefly imprisoned. An attempt has, indeed, been made to relate the Messina privilege to the rebellion, and to argue that the tight diplomatic position of the *Regno* allied with this sudden attack of internal instability adversely affected Messina's trade with continental Europe and the Near East. Only by a 'series of palliatives', Trasselli argues, could Messina's confidence in the crown and its commercial activity be restored to the *status quo ante*:

For Messina, a city which lived from the sea and from trade, this situation [rebellion] was the source of enormous damage: commerce ceased; provisioning became difficult and irregular (in view of the rebellion of the fiefs and barons); contact with the Levant was broken; the people who lived from a thousand marginal trades connected to the port and to trade, were afflicted by an increase in the price of vital commodities...Messina, which grew in exceptional circumstances, would have to return to being a little town, but for the intervention of the government, as usual in the interests of all the kingdom.[69]

The first criticism of this rousingly expressed view must surely be that the November rebellion can hardly have caused the May charter; moreover, the initial form this rebellion took was that of a conspiracy among the magnates which culminated in the assassination of Maio; urban unrest cannot be proved the first cause. Thus the Messina privilege was all the more generous in that it came out of the blue. 'All the Christians' of Messina were granted a reduction of the *commercium* to 3 per cent; free carriage of food into and out of Messina ('indice di carestia e miseria popolare', says Trasselli);

---

[68] For the Messina privilege, cf. *infra*, 117–18. An account of the revolt in Chalandon, *Hist.*, II, 270–3; cf. H. Falc., 46; Rom. Sal., 244–9. There is a detailed description by the Pisan annalist Maragone, *Ann. Pis.*, 23. In an Italian translation of the Latin original (MS of seventeenth century), further details of the revolt are offered, including the fact that 'Li pisani che erano in Palermo con altra gente corseno al palazo in aiuto de Re, et difeseno il re et il palazo'. This makes reasonable sense, since foreign merchants often encountered hostility among the native townsmen of Sicily – the Messina privilege does hint at such resentment. For Pisans and Genoese alike, the loss of royal protection could be a disaster; cf. Chapter 8, 193–9 *infra*, for the influence of such loss on the development of insurance contracts. Pisan merchants would still, in 1160, have been operating under that *fedus pacis* formed in 1137 (*Ann. Pis.*, 11–12), which survived until 1162 (*Ann. Pis.*, 28).

[69] C. Trasselli, *I Privilegi di Messina e di Trapani* (Palermo, 1949), 13. Cf. also 16.

freedom from the requisition of livestock, especially horses, by the crown bailiffs; an end to the obligation to buy serfs and chattels through government agents; freedom from the obligation to provide food and lodging for ambassadors sent to or from the royal court; and recognition of the right of inheritance to fiefs from father to son, without interference by the king's ministers.[70]

One important characteristic of William's charter is that only some of the provisions were commercial in scope. The right to carry goods back and forth free of tolls not merely facilitated regional trade in north-west Sicily, and trade between Messina and Calabria; the main effect and aim was probably a reduction in the price of food put on sale in Messina itself. Thus the Palermitans were granted the same right by King William at the end of the rebellion, when palliatives were most certainly in order: tolls charged on food passing through the city gates were to be abolished in response to public demands. Both at Messina and Palermo the sight of Genoese merchants paying lower taxes on foodstuffs purchased for export may have been irksome to the natives; and the overall reduction in the *commercium* to the Genoese level may have been inspired by the northern visitors' example.[71] However, the majority of the rights conceded in the Messina charter were what might be called status privileges. Messina, or rather its Greek and Latin majority, were being won over to Maio and the crown by a flattering but inexpensive grant of urban immunities that brought the town no autonomy or genuine freedom of action; nor, in the end, did it bring the Messinese over to Maio's side in the rebellion.

The Genoese evidence sheds light on the question whether Messina's trade was in peril. Years of rebellion and collapse might be reflected in the contracts by a diminution of interest in Palermo and Messina by Genoese merchants. Even the privilege of 1160 might perhaps find reflection in the deviation of business away from Messina during 1160 and 1161, with consequent effects on business further afield too, in Acre and Alexandria, shipping bound for which

[70] Text in C. Giardina, *Capitoli e Privilegi di Messina* (Palermo, 1937), 15–16.
[71] H. Falc., 62, describes the Palermo privilege as follows: 'ut autem illorum sibi plenius conciliaret gratiam, portarum eis immunitatem concessit, ut omnes cives panormitani victualia sua, vel empta vel ex agris et vineis suis collecta, libere possent inferre, nichilque ab ipsis eo nomine quis exigeret'. Trade between Messina and Calabria: *Doc. ined.*, no. 82 (Santa Maria della Valle Josaphat).

Table 7. *Genoese trade by first place of destination,*
1161 sailing season

Destination	Number of contracts	Total investment in £	Average investment	% of total
Syria	7 (8)	1,782.40	254.62	21.65
Alexandria	14 (15)	1,641.87	117.28	19.95
Provence	4	1,102.77	—	13.40
SICILY	12	944.24	78.69	11.47
Romania	3	481.12	—	5.85
Ceuta	5 (6)	389.90	77.98	4.74
SALERNO	3	191.80	—	2.33
Bougie	3 (4)	188.00	—	2.28
Spain	1	153.62	—	1.87
Gabes	2	103.57	—	1.26
Sardinia	3	33.06	—	—
No stated destination	9	1,218.84	135.43	14.81
Grand Total		8,231.19		

NOTE: figures in brackets in the column 'Number of contracts' indicate the total number of contracts expressed in pounds Genoese, foreign gold and merchandise of unspecified worth. The pound totals and other figures refer solely to figures in pounds Genoese cited in the contracts. For a rather different set of results see V. Slessarev, cited in n. 72 below.

tended to stop over in Messina on the way out or back. The total figures drawn from Giovanni Scriba for the 1161 sailing season are shown in Table 7. There are large numbers of uncancelled contracts for Sicily and southern Italy – both of the Salerno contracts and six of the Sicilian are not cancelled. So too ten out of fourteen Alexandrian contracts remained uncancelled. With such a proportion involved, failure to cancel can reasonably be ascribed to commercial uncertainty rather than to the notary's carelessness. When one ship renounced its sailing plans, several contracts would be made void at once. Equally,

72 V. Slessarev, 'The pound-value of Genoa's maritime trade in 1161', *Reynolds Essays*, 102. Here Slessarev uses evidence for the total value of all Genoese assets in Constantinople to calculate the total value of trade elsewhere in the same year. This involves the arbitrary use of a constant multiplier, for there is no guarantee that Giovanni Scriba records trade with each destination in exact proportion. Besides, the actual ratio, if not the level, of Scriba's figures remains quite undisturbed.

a limited response to the news that a ship was about to sail to Messina or Palermo might make the captain or lessee cancel his sailing. With so many contracts avoiding reference to a destination, there are signs that merchants had these difficulties in mind wherever their preferences really lay. The value of the uncancelled contracts for the *Regno* is as follows.

(i) £60 9s 0d for Sicily, *societas*

(ii) £94 10s 0d for Palermo, where a further £13 is waiting, *accomendacio*

(iii) £42 15s 0d for Sicily, *societas*

(iv) £32 4s 0d for Salerno and Sicily, *societas*

(v) £11 0s 0d for Sicily in the ship of Ismael, sea-loan

(vi) £152 18s 0d for Salerno, Palermo and the rest of Sicily, *societas*

(vii) £12 0s 0d for Sicily, sea-loan

(viii) £250 0s 0d for Sicily, *societas*[73]

The names of the investors in the *Regno* during 1161 are most familiar from earlier deals – many, indeed, are Byrne's 'easterners': Eliadar, Bonogiovanni Malfigliastro, Blancardo. Some of the contracts make provision for the collection of deposits of money or merchandise in Sicily. There is a backward-looking continuity: old business is being drawn to a close, profits tied in the *Regno* are being released. But a forward-looking continuity is lacking: there are no more contracts sending factors out for several years rather than for a single season. An atmosphere of closing up shop prevails.[74]

In a contract of 14 September 1161, a *societas* of £150, Vassallo Maniavacca was sent to Palermo and the rest of Sicily, with the proviso that, 'should the land present such obstacles that Vassallo cannot conveniently trade there, he may go and do business wherever seems to him to be to the best advantage of the *societas*'. On 20 September Eliadar sent Donato to Sicily with £72 in *societas*, and instructed Donato to collect in the island a further 102 tari, part of the proceeds of an earlier *societas* with Eliadar. And on 18 July 1161 Angelerio de Camilla made a *societas* of £150 18s 0d with Rolando Dordona, of which £50 6s 0d was to be handed over to Angelerio in Messina by Rolando's brother. This sum represented the proceeds

---

[73] *GS*, II, no. 806, no. 829, no. 836, no. 841, no. 875, no. 914, nos. 917–18.

[74] *GS*, II, no. 909 (Eliadar), no. 829 (Malfigliastro), no. 806 (Blancardo).

of the sale of silk, iron and tin goods in Messina or (the syntax is unclear) in Genoa. But should Angelerio fail to make contact in Messina, Rolando's brother may spend the £50 for the benefit of Rolando's partnership. Thus here too there is uncertainty about trading conditions, expressed in the idea that Angelerio and Rolando's brother may not manage to meet as arranged. It would not be totally wild to speculate that the iron goods might represent arms for export to war-torn Messina; for the export of arms and armour is indicated by later Genoese contracts for Sicilian trade. In 1191, if not in 1161, Genoese exporters may have had the disturbances within the *Regno* in mind.[75]

The autumn of 1161 saw a more marked decline in Sicilian trade. An uncancelled contract of 20 November for £80 involved the carriage of half directly to Salerno, and half to Lombardy and thence to Salerno. It was apparently a deal based on investment in Lombard textiles, for one of the partners was Roberto 'the Mercer'. Similarly on 10 January 1162 Blancardo promised to send seven pieces of woollen cloth to Palermo. Although during 1162 Giovanni Scriba provides some further documents relating to Sicily and southern Italy, only one of these is a commercial contract, an *accomendacio* for £142 16s 2d, aimed at Salerno, to which is appended a sea-loan for £11 4s od repayable as 6 oz of gold at the Salerno standard (14 carats). Blancardo's woollen cloth was also given a price in Salerno gold – 30 oz – even though the merchandise was to be sent to Sicily. Thus no record survives of any investment in Genoese pounds in the island of Sicily; no total investment for Salerno can be offered since there are exchange rates and merchandise to take into account. In fact business generally was very poor this year. Only Bougie, Ceuta and Spain received detailed attention.[76]

Whether all this confirms, or detracts from, Trasselli's views is another matter. The evidence for 1160 and 1161 shows increasing loss of confidence in Sicily that reached a peak in 1162. There is, however, a time lag that makes it hard to lay the blame on the Messina privilege or the Sicilian rebellion. That the rebellion had

---

[75] *GS*, II, no. 905 (cf. also no. 904), no. 909, no. 857. In 1190–1 exports to Sicily of *osberga*, breast-plates, and of other armour, became quite frequent – *infra*, 184–5.
[76] *GS*, II, no. 922 (Roberto), no. 937 (Blancardo), no. 935a and *b* (Salerno, 6 Jan. 1162).

some disruptive effect seems plain from the qualifications of instructions in the later Sicilian contracts, and Genoese merchants may have come to doubt the internal stability of the *Regno*. However, this decline in interest coincides also with another series of events, the repercussions of which were deeply felt both in Genoa and Palermo. The year 1162 was one in which the Genoese simply had no hope of conducting extensive overseas trade. In the summer the Genoese colony at Constantinople suffered infanticide at Pisan hands. Fighting over Corsica and Sardinia broke out between Pisans and Genoese, viciously and extensively – the two Communes' ships were committed to arts other than commerce. At the same time, what the Genoese had been hoping to avoid came about. Frederick Barbarossa triumphed in Lombardy and summoned representatives of Genoa to his court. Guglielmo Vento, Marchione della Volta, Oberto Spinola and other illustrious Genoese travelled to the German camp, pitched at Pavia on the road to the great city of Milan that the Germans had razed to the ground.[77]

In 1156 the Genoese had made an alliance with a Sicilian kingdom that had triumphed majestically over internal and external enemies; Maio had quelled his foes and Frederick's Sicilian campaign was far from realisation. In 1162 this situation was turned topsy-turvy: civil conflict in Sicily and the threat of invasion of the *Regno* by Barbarossa made it appear unlikely that William I's reign would be long or peaceful. In 1156 the Genoese had recognised in King William the current master of the central Mediterranean; in 1162 there was something to be said for recognising in Frederick Barbarossa the future master.

[77] *Ann. Ian.*, I, 67–8 (Constantinople), 68–72 (Corsica, Sardinia), 64–5 (Barbarossa). Cf. Slessarev, 'Pound-value', 96.

Chapter 5

CRISIS AND RECOVERY, 1162–79

I

Although Genoa had been scared by Barbarossa's moves in northern Italy, the Emperor could not take for granted the Republic's accession to an alliance against Sicily. Frederick clearly did not hope for much from Genoa, since in April 1162 he won the support of the Pisans with extravagant promises that included help against Genoese pretensions at Portovenere, the coastal village where the Genoese land empire met the Pisan *contado*. But even without Genoese participation, the Emperor was in a strong position to begin his Sicilian war. He had pacified northern Italy by terror and the sword; he had bought himself a fleet at Pisa; he stood to profit from the internal troubles that beset King William from 1160 onwards. All this pressed Genoa into an ever tighter position, and the Commune began to wonder whether the Norman kingdom did in fact have much chance of survival, and what penalty it might have to pay for its refusal to co-operate with Barbarossa. In addition the Genoese knew that legitimacy of control over Sardinia would be determined by the imperial nod (though the papacy too kept its pretensions on the boil here); Frederick's friendship with the Pisans might encourage him to back their claim to the island. Sardinia counted all the more since it, like Sicily, was a grain producer; if, in compensation for abandoning Sicily, the Genoese secured a tighter hold over the Sardinian estates, they need not go hungry. In the long term, too, they could hope to recover their Sicilian interests with a massive bonus, providing that Frederick achieved his aim of conquering the entire *Regno*. Thus, once again but for new reasons, the Tyrrhenian rivals were united in an assault on the Kingdom of Sicily. The privileges that each city was to receive were in direct ratio to the enthusiasm and help that they showed in 1162; but they can also be taken to indicate some of the commercial ideals of the moneyed patriciate of Pisa and Genoa. Precisely because the treaties were so sweepingly generous, they express what the north Italians regarded as a desirable and beneficial set of privileges. To that extent they can be used as approximate measures of economic intentions, as well as of political pressures.

II

Not surprisingly, the imperial privilege to Pisa (6 April 1162) begins with fulsome praise of Pisan loyalty in past years. The city was confirmed in the feudal possessions it already held from the Emperor. There was no question of an attempt by Frederick to enforce the regalian rights he had fought to recover in Lombardy. Pisan merchants were given complete freedom of travel by land and sea throughout the empire, and throughout what Frederick described (with due attention to German protocol) as 'Sicily and Calabria and Apulia and the Principality'. In all these territories, stretching from the Baltic Sea to Malta, the Pisans were to be free of *pedagium* and of other commercial taxes; nor were they to be subject to local or royal limitations on the right to buy and sell in any place or at any time and on any commodity – a right that some local lords such as the Lucchesi or indeed the Genoese must have regarded with scorn. The coast from Civitavecchia to Portovenere would be held by the Pisans in fief from the Emperor – papal rights over southern Etruria, let alone those of the Maremma towns, were conveniently ignored. Further fiefs were to be established in the so-called *Regno*: half of Palermo and Messina and Naples and Salerno, together with half of their *contado* and half the revenue from the port installations, the land, or other sources; plus all of Gaeta, Mazara and Trapani (*Trapoli*), with all the fields lying round about; and in every city at present held by William, other than these, the Pisans could have one street with houses suitable for Pisan merchants. All this brings to mind the massive promises made to the north Italians by the early Latin rulers in the east, normally well prior to the actual conquest of the region under attack – after such a conquest the ruler might think better of his extravagance. Frederick's grants were, however, formally effected at the time of issue of the treaty by investiture with a banner. In addition, one third of the Sicilian royal treasure was promised to Pisa. For their part, the Pisans promised aid not merely

against William, but against any of his successors, on behalf of
Frederick and any of his heirs. The Pisans were to be notified by
Pentecost if the army which Frederick had raised would invade
southern Italy before September of that year; if delays did occur,
a reserve time of August 1163 was set, or later still by arrangement.
Moreover, the Emperor's army was to enter Apulia before the Pisans
were expected to move. Meanwhile, should Pisa need help against
local foes – the Welfs in Tuscany, or indeed the Genoese – Frederick
was to send support. It was particularly envisaged in the privilege
that Portovenere might be a point of contention between Pisa
and Genoa. And, of course, if Frederick decided to attack Genoa in
his own right, the Pisans would happily send reinforcements.[1]

Although these promises were never put into effect, they remained
throughout the century the principle of Pisan diplomatic activity
against Sicily. When Henry VI brought Pisan help against Tancred
of Sicily he did so by the reissue of Barbarossa's treaty.[2] The completeness of the promises is, nonetheless, highly suggestive. It is
suggestive, first, of the bargaining power of Pisa: the Pisans remained
loyal to the empire in the sense that they did not wish to compromise
themselves by a lasting alliance with Frederick's foes in north and
south Italy; but the price they could exact for positive help, rather
than benevolent neutrality, remained extremely steep. It is suggestive,
too, of how the Pisans had aimed too high in certain respects. The
rights which they demanded were so extensive that their implementation can never seriously have been considered by Barbarossa.
Once he had conquered Sicily, he would be in a position of
strength sufficient to baulk all Pisan grumbles. This was exactly how
Henry VI behaved to the Pisans when he seized the Kingdom of
Sicily.

The selection of towns which the Pisans coveted is interesting.
Palermo and Messina had long been the obvious commercial
centres at which to aim – witness Robert Guiscard's reservation to
himself of these towns.[3] But Pisan interest in Amalfi had clearly
waned after a quarter of a century; and so too had Amalfi waned in

---

[1] MGH. *Const.*, 1, 282–7. For the effect of the privilege on Pisa's Tuscan interests,
see G. Volpe, *Studi sulle Istituzioni comunali a Pisa* (2nd ed., edited by C. Violante,
Florence, 1970), 166–72.
[2] See Chapter 7, 180, *infra*.
[3] Chalandon, *Hist.*, 1, 209. Strictly, all Palermo and half Messina.

the relative scale of its commercial competition. Thus the treaty emphasises Salerno instead – the city that the Genoese still frequented, and that the Pisans had earlier had a hand in capturing. Gaeta, unlike Amalfi, remained very active in Mediterranean and especially Tyrrhenian trade; at the end of the century its merchants appeared often in Genoa, and, quite apart from their trading activities, the Gaetans appear to have been doughty pirates. As lord of Gaeta, Pisa could hope to benefit from south Italian trade with Sicily and Sardinia too, which was certainly active by the end of the twelfth century; indeed, the Pisans aimed to make themselves the dominant maritime force in the whole Tyrrhenian triangle. Commercial access to, and outlets from, the south Italian hinterland would be controlled by Pisan or Pisan-protected shipping. A further zone in which the Pisans showed interest was the Tunisia–western Sicily 'circuit', access to which was through Mazara and Trapani, the latter a growing centre. The Pisan interest in the fields round these towns is especially revealing, for Mazara was agriculturally very well placed, in a wide and fertile valley. So Mazara presented two advantageous fronts, mercantile and agricultural, comprising a coherent economic unit. Lack of reference to Girgenti in the Pisan or Genoese privileges of Barbarossa is perplexing, given its prominent standing in William's grant of 1156; but there, as has been seen, signs exist that the crown might have been trying to build up the commercial importance and reputation of Girgenti, conceivably without success in the eyes of the north Italians.[4]

The promise of a third of the royal treasure was also extremely generous. Whatever damage the rioters did in 1160 when they broke into the royal palace and discovered vast quantities of precious metals and gems, not to mention silk vestments and slave girls, their actions may only have served to spread still further the reputation of the Norman kings for exceptional wealth.[5] And here, indeed, is part of the key to Barbarossa's interest in the *Regno*: capital for the taking, plus a fat income ever after from the towns and fields, as well as ships and men-at-arms.[6]

---

[4] Chapter 2, 43, *supra* (Mazara, Trapani); Chapter 4, 93–4 (Girgenti).

[5] H. Falc. 56: 'gemmas, anulosque…purpuras vestesque regias…aurea argenteaque vasis tarenis implentes…tarenos habundantissime', and so on.

[6] Cf. the comments of C.-R. Brühl, 'La politica finanziaria di Federico Barbarossa in Italia', *PSIFB*, 197–208.

III

Despite the threats uttered in Barbarossa's privilege to Pisa, Genoa steered clear of war with the Emperor and his allies, a war which Frederick well knew would distract him from his business in Rome, southern Italy and Sicily. Distraction apart, such a war would involve waste. Each republic possessed a fleet that had to be mobilised against the Norman realm, rather than one against the other. So when Genoese ambassadors came to Frederick at Pavia in the spring of 1162, Barbarossa treated them kindly and asked them to join him in alliance. The ambassadors returned to Genoa for consultations, but the benefits of friendship with Frederick and the dangers of alliance with William were by now clear. So the Commune sent a second embassy which accepted the terms that had, presumably, been the principal topic of discussion at the earlier meeting.[7]

Genoa was granted control of the whole littoral from Monaco to Portovenere, in fee from the empire; the right to elect its own consuls according to custom; and the confirmation of all its 'forts, ports, *regalia*, possessions, rights and other things, held here or overseas'. In addition Frederick promised the Genoese as a fief the whole city of Syracuse with all its appurtenances, plus 250 *caballariae* at Noto (like Mazara, a fertile region), calculated at the Sicilian measure of a knight's fee. If the lands of Count Simon at Noto were in all less than 250 knight's fees in size, the amount would be made up elsewhere.[8] In each town by the sea taken by Frederick's forces, Genoa would receive one street with a church, bath, warehouse and oven. In any land whatsoever conquered with their help, the Genoese would be free of *pedaticum* (that is *pedagium*) and other taxes that would normally be imposed. Going even further than William I's promise, the Genoese were granted the right to expel all Provençal and French merchants going or coming to Sicily, Apulia, Calabria or the Maremma on business. Such merchants travelling to Venice – but not the Venetians themselves – could also be stopped unless Venice were to come to terms with the Emperor.

---

[7] *Ann. Ian.*, 1, 65–6; *CDG*, 1, 396–401 and MGH. *Const.*, 1, 292–5, for the text of the agreement.
[8] For Count Simon, *supra*, Chapter 2, 39, n. 22. The 1191 reissue even contains an anachronistic reference to Simon: 191 *infra*.

Wherever the Genoese might trade, they could have 'one or two or more Genoese to deal justice among them' – in other words, overseas consuls such as seem possibly to have existed at Messina. They could use their own weights and measures among themselves. If any suit were brought against a Genoese resident overseas, the case could be tried before a Genoese court. After the conquest the booty of gold, silver, coins and silk was to be divided between Genoa and Frederick; and a quarter of the actual palace treasure would fall to the Republic – excluding the jewels, which were due to the Emperor (presumably the crown and royal vestments came in this category). Should William or anyone else lay hands on Genoese money in Sicily from the next Easter onwards, Frederick would compensate the Commune with one-twentieth of all the money he seized, or proportionately less if the damage were less. And Genoese property was defended henceforth by imperial ban. All these were to be the rewards of one expedition and the subsequent occupation, for the Genoese were not to be obliged to campaign outside the so-called *Regno*. Nor were Frederick's other allies to cause the Genoese offence during the expedition: no doubt the Genoese had the Pisans in mind here. Finally, Frederick would not make peace with Sicily in the meanwhile except with the consent of the Genoese.

The text of the oath sworn by the consuls and citizens of Genoa is appended to the treaty.[9] They swore loyalty to the Emperor and promised to fulfil their side of the agreement by sending forces against the *Regno* at a time to be determined by the Emperor. They would not leave the expedition without the Emperor's permission, or until the conquest of the *Regno* was complete. Even after the Genoese fleet had withdrawn, the Commune would retain certain obligations to defend the conquered territories: 'and if Sicily or Apulia or Calabria or the principality of Capua are seized, the Genoese will help keep what has been taken, but in such a way that they are not compelled to remain behind'. And should the Emperor actually lose his southern conquests – for the practical Genoese were not above doubt on this matter! – the Commune would help him recover his recent possessions from 'William the Sicilian' and his successors, with whom, in any case, they were not to make peace without imperial mandate. All citizens aged from

---

[9] *CDG*, I, 401–4, and MGH. *Const.*, I, 295–6.

16 to 70 were to swear the oath, which was to be renewed every four years (though no record of such renewals survives).

In a final section the consuls are found repeating their solemn assurances to the Emperor; in addition they promised to help imperial designs against Almoravid Majorca once the Commune's treaty with the sultan had expired – an interesting contrast to their past agreement with the king of Sicily, where a more binding oath for permanent peace with a king of the Roman faith had been suddenly sundered under imperial pressure.

The Genoese privilege provides many interesting points of comparison with the Pisan predecessor. The structure of the commercial demands made by the Genoese is very different. The Genoese were concerned to establish not control over towns, but warehouses, ovens, consulates and other institutions and services that would give a tight identity to the Genoese merchant visitors, and, in particular, a position of complete autonomy. They were less interested in taking under their wing the merchant class of Gaeta or Salerno. Indeed, it would be fair to say that the Genoese insisted more heavily upon advantages for their own merchants trading in the *Regno*, whereas the emphasis in the Pisan privilege lay on territorial lordship as well. The Pisans saw an opportunity to make money out of the existing state of affairs; the Genoese saw an opportunity to develop trade from roots they hoped to lay in the future. Too much should not be made of this difference in emphasis, since Genoese reluctance to come to terms may have affected the concessions that Frederick made. Indeed, the Genoese knew that the privilege greatly endangered their current commitments in the *Regno*, and Barbarossa's agreement to indemnify Genoa against loss must have been a major point in favour of the new alliance. Although Genoa could not hope to maintain its previous high level of trade in the *Regno* just at present, there would be no irreplaceable material loss so long as the conquest was carried through. All the more incentive, Frederick was aware, for the Genoese to accept so generous a bait as a short-term free insurance policy. The imperial promise to return up to one-twentieth of all 'captured money' must be taken to mean that, even allowing for deliberate over-estimation of their total investment, the Genoese had placed enormous sums in Sicilian trade, far beyond the figures preserved in Giovanni Scriba's acts. Quite apart from contracts recorded by other, lost notaries, it is certain that Genoese funds were held over on deposit in the *Regno* between trading seasons, often in tari; such sums might not return to Genoa for years – and then in the form of commodities as well as cash.

Genoese interest in Syracuse is, as has been seen, difficult to trace prior to the seizure of the city by Alamanno da Costa in 1205. But Barbarossa had one especially good reason for dispensing with Syracuse: Roger I had appointed his relative Tancred de Hauteville Count of Syracuse, and Tancred's descendant Simon still held sway there in 1162. Syracuse was, indeed, one of the few counties established by the Normans in the island of Sicily. It is clear too that Count Simon's lands extended behind Syracuse into the fertile Val di Noto, for here the Genoese were to receive their 250 knight's fees. The reasons for Genoese interest in the Val di Noto are not far to seek: a desire to exploit its food-producing potential. And the reasons for Frederick's generosity are not far to seek either: only Count Simon stood to suffer from the loss of his city and of his estates.

The negotiations of 1162 were led by two of the Genoese consuls, Ingo della Volta and Nuvolone de Albericis. The other consuls for the year were Guglielmo Burone (brother to Ingo), Rubaldo Bisacia (who has already appeared bound for Constantinople via Sicily) and Grimaldo. It is, therefore, impossible to attribute the change of policy towards Sicily to a change of government. The clauses confirming to Genoa, and earlier still to Pisa, free exercise of the city's regalian rights established the two republics as autonomous, sovereign entities that derived their authority, certainly, from the Emperor; but they derived their government from the citizens. Genoa was elevated to the status of a feudal person, with the right to raise troops and to invest its own feudatories. The treaty thus constituted a major accretion to the power and position of the della Volta clique that continued to control the city's affairs.[10] All this was quite against the spirit of Frederick's Roncaglia decrees, as Barbarossa well knew – their purpose had been to bring the Italian states more firmly under imperial sovereignty.[11] Nevertheless,

[10] Olivieri, *ASLSP*, 1, 305, for the names of the consuls.
[11] MGH, *Const.*, 1, 244–9 (Roncaglia decrees, November 1158); cf. Frederick I's stern treatment of conquered Milan (*ibid.* 241–3, September 1158), and of Piacenza (*ibid.* 238–9, June 1158).

there were elements of risk, too, that the della Volta clique had to take into account. The Almeria expedition of 1147–9 had shown that a campaign, however successful, and however great the commercial promise, could prove prohibitively expensive.[12] If Genoa were to break even on the new Sicilian war it must either put its full force behind Frederick, or it must try to postpone the war, and its involvement in the war, as long as possible. It might even be able to show William of Sicily that it did not aim at the conquest of his kingdom so much as at the security from conquest of Liguria; in other words, that the oath to Frederick I was lip-service. It is partly in the light of this dilemma that the evidence for slight but real continuation of Genoese trade with Sicily must be viewed.

Trade with Sicily did not break down entirely; but as far as can be seen it fell into Sicilian rather than Genoese hands. The only contracts relating to the *Regno* that survive for 1163 and 1164 concern Solomon of Salerno, never in a very big way, and a certain Xecha Bohahia, a Tripolitanian sheikh with Sicilian links. On 22 September 1163 Solomon was able to place £70 in a contract worth £100, the whole to be carried overseas by his long-standing partner Donato. No destination is stated in the contract, but a supplementary act refers to the assets of either party in an earlier *societas*, assets that included 200 tari at present in Sicily, as well as leather and textiles in Fréjus, another of Donato's favourite haunts. Presumably these items were to be collected on Donato's voyage round the Mediterranean.[13] Also striking is the absence of trade between Genoa and Alexandria or Syria during 1163, and the emphasis on trade with Bougie or nearer ports instead. One reason may have been that access to Bougie involved no danger of entering Sicilian waters. Partly, too, the campaigns of King Amaury of Jerusalem in Egypt, and the current struggle of the Genoese for recognition of their rights in Latin Syria, may have made prospects in the Near East highly uncertain. Finally, the Commune may have been reluctant to let its ships spend very long away while preparations for the invasion of Sicily were in hand. As well as Bougie, Sardinia became

12 See Chapter 9, 232, *infra*; also H. C. Krueger, 'Post-war collapse and rehabilitation in Genoa, 1149–1162', *Studi in onore di Gino Luzzatto*, vol. 1 (Milan 1949), 123–6.
13 *GS*, II, nos. 1,109–10 (Solomon and Donato); no. 1,245 (Xecha Bohahia) and Abulafia, 'L'Attività commerciale genovese nell'Africa normanna', 399–400.

a more popular market by 1164, though the Pisans still hoped for gains there and preyed on Genoese shipping in the Tyrrhenian Sea. Overall it is obvious that there was a broad shift from traditional Genoese markets for luxury and basic goods in the central and eastern Mediterranean, to alternative sources of food and exotica in the western Mediterranean. Treaties with Spanish and African rulers, Latin and Muslim, made this alternative viable, the more so as Genoese puppet rulers entrenched themselves in Sardinia. But the loss of ready access to Messina and other ports in the *Regno* had made itself felt: the route to the east became more fragile, and a positive effort was needed to build up commercial interests in regions previously of secondary importance.[14] Another answer was to let the *regnicoli* resident in Genoa take over trade with southern Italy and Sicily, on the grounds that they should be immune from seizure of goods and persons; if the limited evidence carries any weight, this transfer of interest did indeed occur.

The situation was tempered further by the failure of Frederick's Sicilian campaign even to begin. Alexander III had managed to find support in France and among many of the German bishops (not to mention Sicily and Genoa) against his rival, Victor IV, whom Frederick was actively supporting. Frederick decided to insert an attack on Rome in his Sicilian expedition. This would obviously delay Pisan and Genoese participation under the terms of the alliances, since Frederick must enter the realms of William before their aid would arrive. His need to quell opposition in Germany meant that 1162 and then 1163 passed without his entering southern Italy. He did not forget his Sicilian ambitions, however, for the imperial chancellor, Rainald von Dassel, was authorised to negotiate the support of other communes than the maritime towns in the campaign against King William. Lucca, which was commercially active in its own right and as a close partner to Genoa, won the right to elect its consuls and to keep its regalian possessions with only limited reference to imperial authority. In July 1162 the Lucchesi promised the Emperor that they would send twenty knights 'towards Rome and Apulia and Calabria'; the rights which

---

[14] Bougie: *GS*, II, no. 1,111, no. 1,119 (both 1163); no. 1,219 (to Bougie via Sardinia 1164); no. 1,222 (1164), etc. Sardinia: *GS*, II, no. 1,068 (1163), no. 1,180 (1164), etc. Treaties with North African and Spanish rulers: *Ann. Ian.*, I, 61–2.

these knights earned for the Commune were evidently won cheaply. The same year Piacenza, Cremona and Ravenna entered into similar agreements (though, interestingly, the privileges that these towns received do not explicitly mention southern Italy, let alone Sicily). Gubbio was won over to the Apulian expedition in November 1163; while in 1164 Mantua was exempted from its earlier promise, now lost, to send troops in the imperial army to Sicily and Calabria. But where Frederick failed was Venice, as he had feared all along.[15]

IV

During the early 1160s Venice, together with Verona, became the centre of opposition to Frederick's Lombard policy. For Venice feared that the German ruler might demand the appropriation of his regalian rights in the Veneto and in Istria.[16] The Venetians recognised Alexander's papal election; and they offered financial support to the Lombard towns, encouraging them to rise against their master. Most of all, Venice was aware that Frederick's Sicilian campaign might destroy the *modus vivendi* the Republic had reached with King William on one side of the Adriatic and Manuel on the other. In fact, Venice did not believe that Frederick's ambitions were confined to the conquest of southern Italy and Sicily – if he had his way, the whole Adriatic and much else would come under his sway: 'minabatur etiam imperator ille, quod totam destrueret Greciam et Grecos suo supponeret dominio'.[17] The Doge therefore hastened to reaffirm good relations with the Byzantine emperor and the king of Sicily. The triangle was completed at base by increasingly friendly approaches by Manuel to the court at Palermo, culminating in 1166/7 in a plan to elevate the King of Sicily to the status of heir to the imperial throne. During these years Greek troops were occupying Ancona, to symbolise the Byzantine view that Italy belonged to the one and true empire, and not to the ruler of Germany.[18] Thus an Adriatic alliance came into being, an alliance

15 MGH. *Const.*, I, 302–4 (Lucca), 287–9 (Piacenza), 297–9 (Cremona), 299–301 (Ravenna), 309–10 (Gubbio), 313 (Mantua).   16 Cf. *supra*, 76.
17 *Hist. ducum venet.*, 77, adding that the Doge moved into closer alliance with King William.
18 J. S. F. Parker, 'The attempted Byzantine alliance with the Norman Kingdom (1166–7)', *Papers of the British School at Rome*, XXIV (1956), 86–93. A treaty of

of expediency to be sure, but a defensive front that threatened to neutralise Frederick's advantages obtained by the elimination of Milan and by the alliance with Genoa. In the end, Frederick's hope of conquering Sicily was ruined by the effect of plague on his army camped at Rome; but the fact that Venice continued to agitate in his rear, rousing much of Lombardy in the process, prevented the Sicilian campaign from ever being revived by Barbarossa.

The open friendship of the Doge to King William paid off, literally. Venetian trade with Apulia and Sicily had flourished ever since King Roger had made his peace with the Republic. Contracts survive for trade in Apulia in 1159, and in Sicily in 1160 (for £375 of Venice, a large sum).[19] Most interesting of all is a contract of December 1169, a sea-loan in hyperpers to be carried 'in isto primo taxegio cum nave de Longobardis in qua nauclerus vadit Paganus de Missina et de hinc in Constantinopoli'. The term 'Longobardi' normally referred to south Italian Lombards; they are often met in Venetian business deals. This in itself suggests that south Italian shipping was continuing to penetrate the extremities of the Mediterranean, from the top of the Adriatic to the Golden Horn. And the ship's captain was also a *regnicolus*, though from Messina. He was not a stranger to north Italian trade, for he appears once before, in a Genoese act registered by Giovanni Scriba in 1158, but preserved apart from the main body of his cartulary. Here he is found in the company of distinguished Genoese merchants, witnessing a sea-loan in merchandise between Guillaume de Tours, a Frenchman, and a certain Embrone. The goods were to be carried to Palermo in the ship of Guglielmo Ciriole and Gandolfo de Gotizone, which has already been encountered; and the loan was to be repaid in Sicily in gold tari.[20] (So much, then for French exclusion from Sicilian trade at the hands of the Genoese!) Clearly 'Paganus Messane' or 'de Missina' was a Sicilian shipping entrepreneur, one of the island's elusive native merchants – though, to judge from his name, his ancestry could have been French or Italian. His presence first in Genoa and then in Venice suggests how, during the 1160s, Sicilian com-

---

1158 between Manuel and William I had put an end to hostilities that began eleven years earlier: Chalandon, *Jean II Comnène et Manuel Comnène*, 379. Ancona: *ibid.* 380, 573.

[19] *DCV*, I, no. 136, no. 141.   [20] *DCV*, I, no. 217; *GS*, II, p. 315, no. xxvi.

merce was redirected from one side of northern Italy to the other. Venice became Sicily's prime Latin trade partner, both because it was a political ally and because the *Regno* needed trading partners prepared to carry away its agrarian and pastoral products – food for hungry northerners, fibres for the factories of the Lombard plain. Grain, certainly, did not normally lack buyers, but the political collapse in Africa after the Almohad conquest may have meant that, outside friendly Tunis, the Sicilian crown no longer had assured markets. Not surprisingly, Venetian shipping began more often to call at Messina on its way from northern Italy to Acre. Evidence to be examined shortly shows that in the 1170s both Messina and Calabria received visits from Venetian vessels bound for the Latin east. For, now that Pisa and Genoa had joined Sicily's enemies, only Venice could seriously claim privileged status in the ports of the *Regno*.

Palermo too was not neglected by the Venetians. It is interesting that the majority of the charters relating to the church of San Marco in Palermo, which consitute the only evidence for Venetian ties with the city, date to the period when the Republic was closest to the Norman rulers. A charter of April 1165 shows how Venetian merchants based in Palermo radiated in all directions: the widow Filiberta is found stating that she wishes to be buried 'in the church of San Marco of the Venetians in the quarter of Seralkadi, where the bodies of my husband and of my father Rainaldo are buried'. At the moment, however, her relatives were far away – some of her nephews were in Gerba, the island in Tunisia that the Normans had long coveted, while others were in Dalmatia. In February 1172 the well-born Venetian Marco Canale endowed the same church with an orchard on the edge of Palermo, referring in his grant to the 'licence and assent' granted by the great King Roger for the construction of the church of San Marco. A further grant by a Venetian merchant to this church dates from the year 1186, when relations between the Doge and the King were turning more sour.[21]

Presumably the Venetians exploited to the full the chance to build a thriving trade between Constantinople (where their days were, however, numbered) and the Kingdom of Sicily. The fact that

---

[21] *Doc. ined.*, no. 39 (1165), no. 60 (1172), no. 86 (1186). Cf. Roger II's privilege of 1144 (*Doc. ined.*, no. 18) and Henry VI's privilege of 1197 (T. Toeche, *Heinrich VI.*, Jahrbücher der deutschen Geschichte; Leipzig, 1867, 630); Schaube, 457.

Paganus of Messina was bound for Constantinople provides fragmentary reinforcement for the view that Siculo–Byzantine trade went through a healthy phase in the 1160s. Whether in addition many Greek craftsmen were coming to work in Sicily at this period is a question on which art historians continue to differ.[22]

V

For a time the Genoese remained earnest in their interest in the Sicilian campaign. In February 1164 the Commune sent Frederick an embassy to ask 'whether or when' the Emperor wished to invade William's kingdom and to invoke Genoese aid.[23] But later that year the city lost its capacity to fight. The assassination of Marchione della Volta, one of that year's consuls, was the signal for the outbreak of violent civil strife, lasting till the 1170s, between the della Volta clique and their patrician rivals. It is impossible to say whether the financial pressures imposed on the mercantile classes by the redirection of trade to non-Sicilian markets fanned discontent, especially among those who were unable to determine the direction of diplomacy while the della Volta party held on to power.[24] In any case, the consuls lost the authority to enforce their decisions; although diplomatic activity against Sicily continued, it became confined to treaties of mutual benefit, for instance with the Roman Commune; meanwhile the military effort was diverted to the war against Pisa that Barbarossa had always feared. In its Roman treaties the Genoese permitted the Romans to bring their wares to Genoa for sale 'as long as the war between us and the Pisans [over Sardinia] and between us and the king of Sicily shall last, and for three years beyond...' This could be taken to imply that the Genoese were having such difficulty in obtaining supplies from the *Regno* that they had to turn – temporarily, of course – to intermediaries; in any case the fighting between Pisans and Genoese must have led to a recession in Tyrrhenian trade.[25]

The collapse of any real initiative in Genoa may explain the lack

---

[22] For an impressive exercise in dating visits of Greek craftsmen to Sicily, see O. Demus, *The mosaics of Norman Sicily* (London, 1949/50), 18, 55, 58 and, in particular, 148.   [23] Oberto Cancellario, *Ann. Ian.*, I, 157–8.   [24] *Ann. Ian.*, I, 168.
[25] Pisan war: *Ann. Ian.*, I, 183 – but trouble began earlier: 158–62. The Roman treaty is printed in *CDG*, II, 17–27, 29–39. Cf. Abulafia, 'Corneto-Tarquinia', 225, 227, for the significance of Maremma grain.

of response to an offer by King Sancho of Navarre to intercede between the Republic and the new King of Sicily, William II, whose
mother, the regent, was sister to Sancho. When Sancho wrote to
Genoa in 1166 he had already sent representatives to William re-
commending that Sicily make peace with the Republic. Such an
offer by Sicily to Genoa certainly stood every chance of realisation.
It does seem that it was the Normans who made the first substantial
moves towards reconciliation. In 1168 the consuls received a message
from King William's court, stating that Sicily was indeed anxious
to make peace. So the consuls (among whom was Nuvolone de
Albericis, formerly involved in the negotiations with Barbarossa),
sent an embassy of high-ranking citizens, who sailed south finely
prepared 'cum galee nimiis expensis bene et honeste preparata', only
to fail to come to terms.[26] Perhaps they wanted not just to return
to the situation established in 1156, but to gain further ground already
suggested in their bargain with Barbarossa. By this time Sicily no
longer had reason to fear a German invasion, nor, by extension,
Genoese participation; Sicilian approaches to the Genoese may
have been prompted by other than purely defensive considerations.
Once again the desire to keep markets buoyant and to sell wheat,
leather and other products from the royal estates, provides an
additional explanation for Sicilian readiness to negotiate with the
Genoese. In the event peace did not come until 1174, when William II
reissued his father's charter of protection and confirmed Genoese
rights in the *Regno* as they had existed in his father's reign.[27] Why
then the Genoese reluctance to come to terms? First, though Sicily
had less immediate reason to fear Barbarossa, Genoa could not
adopt the same argument. The situation in Lombardy remained
precarious: during the year of the treaty with William II, Barbarossa
was to be found campaigning on the other side of the Ligurian Alps,
against the papalist city of Alessandria. Secondly, the Normans do
not seem actually to have severed Genoese access to the east Mediterranean; the Genoese remained free to pass through Sicilian waters,
but, doubtless, if they stopped in the royal ports they had to pay
higher taxes. Genoese land in Sicily was not apparently confiscated.
Thirdly, and most importantly, the Genoese were exploring in

[26] *CDG*, II, 61–2 (Sancho); *Ann. Ian.*, I, 213 (Genoese embassy).
[27] *CDG*, II, 202–4; Otobono Scriba, *Ann. Ian.*, II, 5.

greater earnestness a wide variety of west Mediterranean markets, the most distant far away in North Africa, the nearest in Corsica and Sardinia, where Genoa still hoped to set up a dynasty of Ligurian puppet-kings. The loss of their special rights in Sicily merely suggested new opportunities elsewhere.[28]

VI

During the 1160s the Pisans were forced out of Sicilian commerce; but that did not stop them from interfering with the trade of Sicily. In October 1162 King William seized the persons and goods of all the Pisans within his domains – despite, Maragone complains, the long-standing *fedus pacis* that existed between Sicily and Pisa.[29] This probably refers back to the events of 1137, when the Pisans withdrew from the German invasion of southern Italy to avoid seizure of their property in the kingdom by Roger II, and made peace with King Roger. The *fedus* probably took the form of a promise of royal protection, without any tax concessions. Following the Pisan alliance with Barbarossa it looks as if the Commune rather than the King had broken faith.[30] Meanwhile Pisan sailors were exploiting the maritime trade of Sicily in the only way open to them. In July 1162 Pisan corsairs seized a Genoese ship on its way

---

[28] *Ann. Ian.*, II, 6; evidence that the Genoese retained their Sicilian estates is provided by GS, II, no. 950 (discussed *infra*, 230), a document of 1162 – though repercussions might have been delayed; for further west Mediterranean treaties, *Ann. Ian.*, I, 229 (Morocco, 1169) and I, 228 (Sardinia, 1169).

[29] *Ann. Pis.*, 28. A ship returning from Constantinople via Sicily was also seized. As has been seen, the Pisans supported the Sicilian crown as late as the riots of 1160. But another incident may have created ill-feeling in this period: in 1157 (1158 *stile pisano*) the Sicilian fleet had a final attempt at the invasion of Manuel's empire. In June King William sent a large fleet to Negropont, storming the town; thence the fleet moved to Almyra, a favourite Greek base for Pisans and Venetians. There they stormed and sacked both the city and 'Sanctum Iacobum Pisanorum cum turre'; this may have been the Pisan church around which a merchant colony had gathered. If the Pisans even resisted, which is not certain, the grounds for doing so were much the same as the grounds for supporting William I in 1160: it was essential to show loyalty to the emperor in Greece, as to the king in Sicily. The risk of being caught in the crossfire was stoically accepted. *Ann. Pis.*, 17, provides an account of the Almyra episode that shows more wonder at the daring of the Sicilian fleet than it shows ire at the fate of the Pisan settlement.

[30] So Maragone freely admits: 'Pisanos enim suspectos [Rex] habebat propter affectionem et fidelitatem quam ergo Imperatorem habebant' – *Ann. Pis.*, 28.

from Sicily to Elba; apparently this was a very rich prize, for together with some Genoese vessels seized earlier in the month, one from Constantinople, and one from Syria, the booty was worth over £20,000.[31] The Pisans were more concerned to bolster their position in Constantinople than to recover their possessions in Sicily, aiming to capitalise on the growing unpopularity of the Venetian Republic at Manuel Komnenos' court. But here too they suffered uncertainty and agony, for the Pisan alliance with Frederick of Germany aroused Manuel's mistrust, and he forced the Pisan merchants to transfer their colony outside the walls of Constantinople itself.[32]

The pattern of violence continued throughout the 1160s. In July 1165, the Pisan Commune armed seven galleys, to be sent to Sicily 'pro Ianuensibus capiendis', and hardly had they entered Sicilian waters when they found a Genoese galley and small ships off Ischia; these they seized. Similarly in 1166 Pisan galleys seized a small Genoese ship coming from Sicily through Sardinian waters; and all the time they continued to hope for a large-scale German invasion of the papal state and the Kingdom of Sicily.[33] Hoping and planning brought no gains; and piracy against the Genoese, for all the arrogance of the Pisan Annals, showed no impressive results. Maragone boasts of victories against rather small ships by fleets of Pisan galleys, and it is not clear that Genoese trade with Sicily and beyond was seriously disrupted by Pisan agency, nor that in these years Genoese trade with Sicily was very well developed. In these circumstances, the Pisan consuls decided to face realities and to attempt to re-establish their *fedus* with William of Sicily. In November 1167, the Commune sent Bulgarino Anfosso, one of the consuls, with Uguiccio, son of Lamberto, and Ildebrando Banbone, other notables, to Sicily to make peace with King William. The Pisan Annals cryptically state: 'Qui pacem sicut rex volebat, minime facere voluerunt'.[34] Clearly settlement of claims arising from the seizure of Pisan goods five years earlier, and, perhaps, the nature of Pisan links with Barbarossa continued to present stumbling-blocks.

---

[31] *Ann. Pis.*, 27.

[32] C. M. Brand, *Byzantium confronts the West, 1180–1204* (Cambridge, Mass., 1968), 207.

[33] *Ann. Pis.*, 36, 38 (piracy); 41–4 (hopes for invasion).   [34] *Ann. Pis.*, 44.

At any rate, when the Pisans next sent an embassy to King William, in June 1169, they entrusted it to different representatives: Gerardo Cortevecchia, a consul, and Gerardo Barattule and Guidone Gallo. Once again the King was keen – 'cum honore magno recepit' – and this time the Pisans responded, and made their peace with Sicily.[35]

Of course, piracy against Genoese vessels did not cease after the Pisan treaty with King William; but the Pisans seem to have been more careful to avoid acts of piracy off the coast of Sicily and southern Italy. Thus in 1170 three Pisan galleys standing off Sardinia seized a ship returning from Sicily jointly owned or hired by Genoese and Lucchese merchants – a double blow against Pisa's traditional foes. Again, in 1171, the Pisans seized a Genoese ship off Elba as a Pisan company was returning from Gaeta.[36] Nevertheless, the Pisans were not entirely immune from Sicilian attack. In 1174 a Pisan ship loitering in the harbour at Alexandria, where it had come from Venice, was pounced upon by an invading force of Sicilians and seized. But that, of course, was one of the risks of the trade. The north Italian communes were reminded throughout the 1160s and 1170s that their alliances bought security in one port at the price of insecurity in a dozen others.[37]

---

[35] *Ann. Pis.*, 50. An act of 26 June 1169 in the Archivio di Stato, Pisa – Pergamene Coletti, 1170 (*stile pisano*) June 26 *corta* – may be connected to the Pisan embassy to King William. Uguiccio Boccone, 'paratus ire in itinere Sicilie', appoints his relative Raffaione as executor, and commissions him to sell half of a house on his behalf. Uguiccio and Raffaione reappear in two judicial acts of 1170 and 1171 (Pergamene Coletti, 2 September 1171 *corta*, and 23 November 1172 *corta*). In the former document Uguiccio secures judgement against a recalcitrant debtor; but in the latter Raffaione's wife, as representative of Uguiccio's heir, is obliged to re-fund one of Uguiccio's partners who provided naval equipment for a galley that Uguiccio fitted out, without paying his partner for the items he obtained. Although Uguiccio and Raffaione do not appear in the 1171 document, it seems they are absent from Pisa rather than deceased. Thus Uguiccio left Pisa in June 1169, when Gerardo Cortevecchia sailed south; he was back by late summer of 1170 and gone again a year later. For further details, see my article 'Pisan commercial colonies and consulates in twelfth-century Sicily', *English Historical Review* (forthcoming).

[36] *Ann. Pis.*, 50, 53. The continued interest of Pisan sailors in Gaeta is no cause for surprise – cf. the treaty of April 1162.

[37] *Ann. Pis.*, 61, at the point where Maragone's text breaks off entirely. For a general account of the Sicilian expedition to Alexandria, see Chalandon, *Hist.*, II, 394–7. The Pisan ship is not mentioned directly in the Arabic sources: ibn al-Athir, *BAS*, folio ed., 126; ibn Khaldun, *ibid.* 205; al-Maqrisi, *ibid.* 211; Imad-ad-Din, *Recueil des historiens des croisades: Historiens orientaux* (Paris, 1872–1906), IV, 167, 177–8;

VII

The Venice–Sicily–Byzantium alliance was betrayed in a short
time by the opportunism that had brought it into existence. The
Normans seem to have regarded the Greeks as a temporary ally,
who could be used to counter-balance the threat from Barbarossa;
but that attitude proved very different to Manuel's. Manuel's
approaches to the papacy, as well as to King William, signalled the
beginning of a new diplomatic campaign to achieve East Roman
sovereignty over Italy and maybe over the papacy too. In the
context of Manuel's overall strategy, the future of the Norman
dynasty in southern Italy looked none too secure. Hence the reluctance of the Norman court to complete arrangements for a marriage
alliance between Sicily and Constantinople. The initiation of the
scheme reflected Manuel's hopes and aims as much as its suspension
reflected the Normans' doubts and fears. Moreover, the débâcle had
a direct effect on Norman–Venetian and Venetian–Byzantine
relations. This is how Dandolo describes events:

> Emanuel imperator Constantinopolitanus, suis nunciis, cum Vilielmo
> [II] rege pacem conposuit: et vinculo iuramenti, Mariam eius genitam
> regi in uxorem tradere promisit; sed, cum desisteret, scisma inter eos
> denuo reviviscit. Tunc Emanuel tres legatos, cum imperii tutela, mictere
> vellit. Dux autem, pacem cum Vilielmo conservare cupiens, et maxime
> intuitu Ecclesie, id facere recusavit; quod Emanuel grave ferens, erge
> Venetos modum in corde concepit; de hoc dux providens, Venetis, ne in
> Romaniam pergerent, universaliter interdixit.[38]

This account, though an attractive explanation, does telescope events;
the marriage negotiations of 1166/7 are separated by several years
from the expulsion of Venetians and confiscation of their goods by
the Byzantine emperor in 1171. It may be true, as most historians
have assumed, that the rôle of the Venetians in Byzantine commer-

Abu Shamah, *ibid.* IV, 164–7; Baha-ad-Din, *ibid.* III, 56–7. In the letters of Saladin's vizier al-Fadil, cited by Imad-ad-Din, 178, there is a reference to north Italian
participation in the expedition against Alexandria, be that help private or official:
'Parmi nos ennemis il y avait aussi les soldats de Venise, de Pise et de Gênes, mais
tous se comportaient tantôt comme des guerriers exerçant de sérieux dommages
et brûlant d'une haine inextinguable, tantôt comme des voyageurs qui s'impo-
saient à l'Islam par le commerce et échappaient à la rigueur des règlements.' All
this, al-Fadil explains, despite the good relations that had been built up in recent
years with the north Italians. [38] A. Dandolo, 249.

cial life was generally resented, and that Manuel responded to public feeling and to the immediate diplomatic needs of the empire when he banned the parasites; but the increasing closeness of Venice and Sicily, jointly financing and encouraging the north Italian resistance to Barbarossa, clearly made Manuel feel that the alliances of the 1160s had gradually become weighted against him; and so this very closeness of his recent allies became a major motive in turning against the Venetian colonies in the Greek empire. Nor was Venice irreplaceable: Manuel I succeeded in drawing Genoa and Pisa to his side with inferior tax concessions, knowing that they would value any concession at all, and that Pisa had long hoped for Greek friendship, and feared Sicilian wrath less than did its rivals.[39]

After 1171 the Venetians continued to hope that their dismissal from Byzantium was only temporary; and for four years they made no overt display of friendliness towards Sicily. The common aims of the Doge and of the King were plain enough, and for the moment Venetian merchants need not fear expropriation by the Norman government. The year 1175 marked a crucial stage in the Venetian alliance with Sicily. That year the Venetians sent ambassadors both to Manuel and to William; first, to Manuel to patch up peace, and then, since no news came, to William of Sicily 'pro unione erge imperatorem', apparently the Greek rather than German emperor. The Sicilian embassy was in the care of Giovanni Badoer and Enrico Dandolo, the latter of whom was to prove in 1204 how little love he felt for the Byzantine empire. Travelling down the Dalmatian coast, Badoer and Dandolo encountered their colleagues who had been sent to Manuel and were now returning with a Byzantine embassy to Venice. So back they all went to Venice, to see what arrangements could be made with the Basileus; but no progress was made, and the Doge once again decided to try the Sicilian court. He sent back Manuel's representatives with two of his own; but they would doubtless have carried news of the Venetian mission to Sicily, and thereby have dampened yet further Manuel's interest in a new deal for the Republic.[40]

King William did not hesitate to come to terms with Aureo Mas-

---

[39] J. Herrin, 'The collapse of the Byzantine Empire in the twelfth century: a study of a medieval economy', *University of Birmingham Historical Journal*, XII (1970), 200–3; Brand, 207.   [40] A. Dandolo, 260–2.

tropetro and Aureo Dauro, the Venetian ambassadors, when they
arrived in Palermo in September 1175. Two documents survive. In
the first the Venetians were promised protection by land and sea
throughout the Norman kingdom; as usual, pirates were excepted
from this immunity, but the treaty went on to mention as well
'those who act against our kingdom and those who are in the
service of the emperor at Constantinople to defend his empire'.[41]
Unusual in the series of Sicilian–north Italian treaties is the next
main clause, a promise not to attack the lands held by Venice, 'that
is to say, from Ragusa as far as Venice', for the Venetians remained
sensitive about the security of the Adriatic and could see how likely
it was that the Normans would attempt to gain a foothold in
Dalmatia (and, by extension, a stranglehold on themselves) as the
first stage in a campaign against Constantinople. The treaty then
mentioned the machinery for settlement of legal disputes between
Venetians and Sicilians or south Italians, and finally stipulated a limit
of twenty years, 'or more'. The second document represents the
business side of the deal.[42] Here William granted, in the first place,
a confirmation of the special privileges operating in the time of
King Roger, with the exception that they were to pay half what they
were accustomed to pay then; and in Messina, Palermo and Sicily
as a whole (that is, in the island) they would pay half what they
paid under Roger and William I. The documents are brief and do
not lead us to suppose that the Venetians had such wide-ranging
and complex commercial interests in Sicily as the Genoese. Thus
there was no mention of commodities. Of course, the lost charters
of Roger II and William I may have provided the details. The
mention of Sicily brings to mind Venetian contracts for trade at
Messina, which was, indeed, referred to specifically; and the
reference to Palermo is backed by the evidence that the Venetian

[41] 'defendendum eius imperium', Liber Pactorum i, f. 86v and 76v; Tafel-Thomas,
I, 172, and Carabellese-Zambler, I, 47–8, printed 'eius auxilium' from Dandolo's
Liber Blancus, f.272v, the MS from which they gleaned their text. 'Auxilium' is,
however, clearly a copyist's error after the 'auxilio' six words earlier: 'exceptis
illis qui fuerint in auxilio imperatoris constantinopolitani (Blancus, 'constantinopoli') ad defendendum eius imperium'. Blancus omits 'venerabilis' in the
name 'Gualterii venerabilis panormitani archiepiscopi', and shows minor differences in spelling. The Pactorum text must be assumed closer to the lost original.
Cf. the chronicle by A. Dandolo, 262.
[42] Pactorum i, f.85r–v; Blancus, f.273r–v.

community had an active church in the Norman capital from 1144.

Around the time of the Venetian negotiations with William of Sicily, evidence for mercantile activity in the *Regno* is ample. In November 1173 one of the da Molin clan financed an expedition from Venice to Pescara, in the Abruzzi; the total sum carried was £40 of Verona.[43] Business was brisk in Apulia too: in May 1177 Marsilia, widow of Leonardo Zimarco, announced settlement of two deals made by her husband with Giovanni Nonno di Mazzorbo at Brindisi three years earlier; these were sea-loans of 12 hyperpers each, to be carried abroad for a year. The sum involved may not have been large, but the presence of Venetians at Brindisi is more suggestive.[44] More substantial was some business through Messina. In March 1176 Domenico Bello da Murano drew up a quittance, cancelling an earlier contract made in Acre with Samuel Mairano six months before, according to which Mairano was to carry 400 bezants to Messina 'and no other destination'. In return Mairano was to deliver 500 hyperpers of 'old gold' at the weight standard 'of that land' (apparently Sicily), or the equivalent in tari ('tari aureos de rege').[45] Similarly, the other surviving document from 1176 that refers to trade in Messina also consists in a quittance for a loan made at the time of the Venetian–Sicilian treaty. In September 1176 Obertino, son of Guglielmo de la Cazaira of Verona, and Pietro Paradiso of Cannaregio, a Venetian, met to settle a business deal made between them, with the added help of Bellardo de Felsorago of Verona, in August 1175. This was expressed in goods rather than money, and no details of the cargo are given, except that after their sale £100 of Verona are to be returned to the two Veronese investors in the deal. The factor, Pietro Paradiso, is to sail to Messina and then back to Venice.[46] In both instances we have business deals of moderate size; taken together they reveal some of the wider links of Venetian trade in the twelfth century: the importance of the sea link between southern Italy or Sicily and the Holy Land, which depended on the Latin west for many of its

---

[43] Archivio di Stato, Venice, S. Zaccaria pergamene, Busta 34 (formerly B.40), 'in taxegio depiscaria'; printed in *DCV*, I, no. 251, as a contract for Peschiera, not Pescara. But Peschiera is an inland town of little importance.

[44] *DCV*, I, no. 282–3.　　　[45] *DCV*, I, no. 278.　　　[46] *DCV*, I, no. 279.

essential supplies, such as grain and armaments, and which could offer Sicilian buyers a tempting range of spices and rare textiles brought via Damascus to Acre; and, at the other end of the Venetian trade routes, the importance of the merchants of Verona above all other cities in the plain, linked to the Adriatic by the Adige water-way, minting coinage in current use in Venice and, as we see plainly, using Venice as a maritime outlet where its own citizens could do business indirectly with Norman Sicily. Not that they were unwelcome themselves at that moment, for Verona was active along-side Venice against Barbarossa. But for them, less preoccupied than the Venetians with the strategic problems of keeping the Adriatic open, the treaty of 1175 was a welcome blessing, since they could continue to trade profitably in Sicily through friendly Venetian agents.

The Venetian–Sicilian treaty was the prolegomenon to more considerable diplomatic achievements. In September 1177 the Venetians and Sicilians together helped to organise the peace treaties between Frederick Barbarossa and his enemies, Pope Alexan-der, the Lombard League and William II, treaties signed at Venice in the presence of the historian Romuald, Archbishop of Salerno and ambassador of the Sicilians. Significant in the long term was the dynastic alliance of Sicily and Germany, creating a Hohenstaufen claim to the Norman throne; the marriage of Henry to Constance had more immediate effects on Byzantine relations with Sicily. Judging all common ground to have been eroded by now, Manuel resumed his accustomed hostility to the Sicilian τυραννοί.[47] As far as the history of Venetian commerce in the *Regno* is concerned, it is events during the negotiation of the Peace of Venice, not the Peace itself, that carry weight, and suggest how fragile the promises of 1175 might yet prove to be. The Sicilians were very anxious to prevent Barbarossa from landing in Venice itself before negotiations were complete. Romuald saw that dissident factions inside Venice were ready to use Frederick's presence as a lever to remove or to neutralise the Doge; and, in any case, the Emperor's arrival threatened to undermine all the progress made by the Pope and by the Sicilian ambassadors on wider diplomatic issues. According to Romuald – the sole source for these events – the *populares* of Venice

---

[47] Brand, 18–20, emphasising the importance of the battle at Myriokephalon in the context of the Peace of Venice.

stormed the Ducal Palace and forced the Doge to promise to admit Frederick to the city immediately: then they pounced on the Pope, demanding that he make peace on Barbarossa's terms. Romuald made it known that he had four royal galleys prepared, and that he wished to carry the Pope away from Venice without delay, for negotiations could not continue under the new conditions. Moreover, Romuald seems to have threatened to cast aside the treaty of 1175:

Quod factum postquam fuit per Venetias divulgatum, timor maximus Venetos occupavit. Timebant enim, ne si Regis Nuncii indignati recederent, hac occasione Rex Venetos, qui in terra sua erant, capi faceret, et in custodia detineri. Qua de causa magna multitudo virorum et mulierum, quorum parentes in Apuliam iverant, ad Ducem properans....

These Venetians asked him to revoke his agreement with Barbarossa and the *populares*.[48] It has been thought that Romuald exaggerated the whole affair, simply to show what a major rôle Sicily was playing in the negotiations. It has also been said that the real reason the Sicilian legates prepared to leave was fear of capture, not the hope of alarming Venice nor the desire to ditch the Doge. In fact Romuald's own account shows very clearly what considerations weighed with the Norman court. The Sicilians had leverage on the Venetians, through threats against the Republic's financial interests in Apulia and the island. And they could see that if Venice fell into the hands of a pro-Barbarossa faction, there was no immediate prospect of the Lombard towns and the Pope agreeing to an overall peace that included Germany and Sicily. Hence the desire to spirit Alexander III away, and to report at once to the Sicilian King.[49]

The identity of the populist party is not clear. Romuald seems to juxtapose the *populares* against the families of the merchants, as if they belonged to separate cliques, but that is not necessarily the

48 Rom. Sal., 279–81.
49 Attitudes sceptical towards Romuald's account, none of them conclusive nor convincing, are rife: W. von Giesebrecht, *Geschichte der deutschen Kaiserzeit*, v (Leipzig, 1888), 834; however I have not been able to see Fechner's dissertation *Beiträge zum Friede von Venedig* (Berlin, 1886). In my own view, Romuald's account rings true: there are sufficient points of comparison between the fear of expropriation shown by Venetian merchants in 1177 and the actual expropriation of north Italian merchants in the *Regno* to make such fears highly authentic. Moreover, Boso, in *Liber Pontificalis*, ed. L. Duchesne (Paris, 1886–92), II, 439, makes it plain that there were dissident elements urging Frederick against peace while he was waiting at Chioggia.

case. Merchants whose traditional interests had been in Romania might not concur with those who used Apulian or Syrian ports; but it does appear from the commercial contracts that trade between Venice and the Norman kingdom was dominated by a group of very well-placed and well-born Venetians – members of such clans as the Ziani, Michiel and others who were *dogabile*. Romuald implies that the *populares* were a faction in, rather than outside, government; that is, a group of nobles who relied on popular support among small traders, perhaps, or among artisans.[50]

Following the Peace of Venice, Venetian sailors were able confidently to embark on visits to various parts of the Norman kingdom. The first expedition on record was very special: in October 1177 Venetian ships carried Pope Alexander to Siponto, in northern Apulia, whence he travelled overland through Norman territory to Benevento and Anagni.[51] Meanwhile merchants too passed through the Norman kingdom without fear of molestation. In March 1178 Pietro Ziani, son of Doge Sebastian Ziani (who had commissioned the treaty of 1175), established a sea-loan for trade in Acre with a certain Maçaroto Zorzani, who bound himself to travel in the same ship as Pancrazio Stagnaro first to Squillace or Crotone in Calabria, and thence to Acre. There he was to return to Pietro Ziani or his *missus* the sum of 50 gold bezants; but the original amount or goods invested are not specified.[52] The same

---

50 The identity of the *popolani* is discussed by G. Cracco, *Società e Stato nel Medioevo veneziano (secoli XII–XIV)* (Florence–Venice, 1967), 48–52. Cracco argues that the *Grandi* gained power at Venice in 1172 and that the succeeding years saw 'la naturale tensione tra Grandi e Piccoli', with the Doge ranged decisively on the side of the nobility, even though his power was technically derived from the *populus*: 'il popolo infatti non ambiva ancora al potere, voleva solo un potere che rispettasse le sue esigenze vitali'. Cracco points out how dependent were the *Piccoli* on business with and supplies from the *Regno* and elsewhere, but he does not explain why it was they who pressed the Doge to abandon his Sicilian allies and to admit Barbarossa. Romuald does not actually state that the popular party changed its mind after he threatened Venetian commercial interests in the *Regno*; rather he says that a third element, overlapping no doubt with popular and grandee factions alike, took alarm at the threat, and that it was the *multitudo* of those with relatives in Apulia and Sicily who asked the Doge to reaffirm his pact with the Sicilians. In other words, Romuald switches from discussing the *populares* and begins to refer to the Venetians at large.   51 Boso, 443.

52 This survives in two copies, *DCV*, I, no. 289 and no. 290. The latter is of 1193, the former is the original charter of 1178; no reason for drawing up the 1193 version is stated: Archivio di Stato, Venice, S. Zaccaria pergamene, Busta 34.

month Pietro Ziani arranged similar deals for business in Calabria and Acre with Badoer Matonno of Murano, worth 50 bezants; with Pietro Ieremia, worth 100 bezants; and with Pietro Zancairolo of Murano, again worth 50 bezants.[53] That is, he expected a return of 250 bezants on four sea-loans. In May 1178 he commissioned Pancrazio Stagnaro, with whom the four were travelling, to act as his agent at Squillace or Crotone and at Acre, apparently because he did not expect to be in Acre himself when the merchants arrived. Copies of his contracts were handed to Pancrazio. In addition, Pietro Ziani established a sea-loan with Pancrazio, under the terms of which the latter was to repay £300 of Verona (without specification of the original sum or value invested); as well as Squillace, Crotone and Acre, Pancrazio was given the option to visit Alexandria and Damietta 'si tibi placuerit et pax inter Veneciam et dominum Babilonie [Saladin] fuisset'. Business was carried out successfully. In March 1179, at the Rialto, Badoer declared to Pancrazio that he had received back the charter drawn up between himself and Pietro Ziani in March 1178, entrusted to Pancrazio under the terms of Ziani's contract of May 1178; and Badoer therefore renounced all claims. The same month, March 1179, Pancrazio formally declared to Maçaroto Zorzani that he had fulfilled his side of the arrangements, and Pietro Ziani declared to Pancrazio that the latter was quit of all debts arising from his commission of May 1178, including the refund of the sea-loan.[54] This remarkably complete series of documents illustrates the great importance to the north Italian traders of the dependence of the crusader states on supplies from Sicily and southern Italy. The commitment to stop in Calabria is suggestive: there is no talk of the settlement of outstanding business there (one common reason for compelling a *socius negocians* to break his journey); it seems that a cargo is to be collected instead, and taken to Acre for sale and conversion into bezants of the crusader kingdom. In that case – bearing in mind the evidence of the *Registrum curiae* of Genoa for a Calabrian grain trade – it would not be over-imaginative to identify this cargo as wheat.[55] Squillace is so close to Messina that, if an exchange of commodities were being

---

[53] These copies do not survive, except in summary in *DCV*, I, no. 292.
[54] *DCV*, I, no. 292, no. 301 (Pietro Ziani's sea-loan), no. 298, no. 300, no. 301 (Pietro Ziani's quittance). [55] Belgrano, *Reg. Curiae*, 10, 366; *supra*, 72.

contemplated, we should expect the Venetians to head straight for the port where they held particularly generous rights of exemption. But instead they make for open country – agricultural country.

Moreover, the same period provides evidence for Venetian shipping moving in the opposte direction, this time from Alexandria to Messina. A contract of March 1179 quits Pietro da Muggia of all obligation to Giacomo and Filippo da Molin in respect of a deal worth £65 of Verona, to be carried from Venice to Alexandria, 'deinceps de vero cum eadem nave vel cum alia et cum suprascripto habere cum mudua ipsius estatis que tunc prius expectabatur per suprascriptam indicionem aut cum mudua ipsius primi venturi yberni in Venecia debebas redire, aut in Missina, et deinde cum iamdicta mudua ipsius yberni in Venecia debebas redire'.[56] Finally, a sea-loan between Romano Mairano and Filippo Falier survives, worth £116 of Verona on the return of Romano from a voyage to Acre and thence either back to Venice, or through Alexandria to Apulia and back in one of the winter convoys.[57] This insistence on convoys seems to reflect anxiety at the situation in Egypt rather than in the Norman kingdom. Venice's troubles with Saladin apart, it is plain that the new accord with Norman Sicily benefited both the south Italian trade of the Republic and its commerce with the east Mediterranean, for there were no problems in passing through the profitable markets of south-western Italy and Sicily on the way to and from the Near East. And, in the light of the popular revolt of 1177 in Venice, it is striking that the merchants most deeply involved in this long-distance trade through Norman ports were from the most aristocratic families – the Ziani, da Molin, Falier. Whatever the overall proportion of south Italian trade compared with Venice's trade elsewhere, the treaty of 1175 and the peace of 1177 boosted Venetian commerce everywhere.

VIII

It has been seen that signs of possible discord between Venice and Sicily appeared, paradoxically, in the treaty of 1175, when the

[56] *DCV*, I, no. 299.
[57] *DCV*, I, no. 306. Romano Mairano is one of the most celebrated twelfth-century Venetian merchants, following Heynen's study of him, *Zur Entstehung des Kapitalismus*, 86–120. See also Y. Renouard, *Les hommes d'affaires italiens du moyen âge* (2nd ed., Paris, 1968), 77–80. It must be recalled that Mairano was not a member of the patriciate.

tenimentum of the Doge was said to end at Ragusa (Dubrovnik) in Dalmatia. Ragusa had long-standing commercial links with Venice on the one hand, and with south Italian ports such as Molfetta on the other.[58] Moreover, Venetian merchants resident in Palermo appear to have travelled to the Dalmatian coast as well as to Africa and around the *Regno*. In 1169 the Ragusans made a pact with Pisa too; but this agreement must probably be seen in the context of Pisan attempts to protect lines of access to the Byzantine empire.[59] For Ragusa was nominally a Byzantine city, though Latin in its church and Latinate or Slav in its population; it was a small town typical of the series of Dalmatian ports that drew their wealth from commerce between the Adriatic coast and the Greek and Croatian hinterland. Ragusa, however, was more fortunate in resisting Venetian commercial and political domination than its northern neighbours such as Traù and Zara. Its long established loyalty to the Basileus enabled Ragusa to pose as the subject of Venice's most potent ally, the Greek empire; while its remoteness from the Byzantine heartlands enabled Ragusa to shake its fist at Venice when occasion offered itself. Thus in the 1080s the Ragusans fought on Guiscard's side against the Greeks and the Venetians, in the belief that Norman power in Apulia and the Adriatic would displace Byzantine and Venetian authority in Dalmatia.[60] Such considerations carried weight ninety years later as well, though in the 1170s Byzantium, Venice and the Normans were differently aligned. In particular, it was the expulsion of the Venetians from Constantinople in 1171 that posed a problem. The Venetians judged Ragusa to be a legitimate target in attacks they planned to make against Byzantine territory. According to Venetian sources, the Doge's fleet seized Ragusa in 1171, on its way to maraud against Byzantine lands; but the town refused to stay under Venetian control and had to be stormed a second time, on the return of the Venetian fleet from the Aegean. After that Ragusa once again renounced Venetian

---

[58] J. Radonić, *Acta et diplomata ragusina*, vol. 1 (Belgrade, 1934), 17–18; Abulafia, 'Dalmatian Ragusa', 414–15, 422 and note 45.

[59] *Doc. ined.*, no. 39, for Venetian merchants travelling from Palermo to Dalmatia; Radonić, 5–6, for the Pisan agreement with Ragusa, with comment by Abulafia, 415.

[60] M. Spremić, 'La Repubblica di Ragusa e il Regno di Sicilia', *Atti CISSN*, 301; Abulafia, 419.

suzerainty.[61] Later Ragusan sources do, however, suggest that at some stage the citizens of Dubrovnik appealed to an outside protector, the King of Sicily. 'And I imagine the cause of this change was solely to guarantee protection from Venetian vexation,' wrote Restić in the eighteenth century; and he went on to argue that 'the Venetians were continually at war with the Greek empire, and as a result of their action the Ragusans were not considered by the Venetians to be dependents of that empire, but to depend on the kings of Sicily, with whom Venice at that time cultivated good relations'.[62] In other words, Ragusa was a legitimate target for the Venetians only so long as it was a Byzantine town; by changing to Sicilian allegiance, the Ragusans ingeniously held off further Venetian assaults. It may be that it was only after one or several such attacks that Ragusa declared itself a vassal of King William; but King William's promise of protection seems to have guaranteed the Ragusans their freedom from Venetian or Byzantine control. In 1182, at any rate, it is clear that Ragusa was not regarded by Venetian businessmen as an integral part of the Greek empire; a *collegancia* of £60 drawn up between members of the Tiepolo family stipulated a journey to Ragusa 'and then to wherever the ship's company shall agree, except to places forbidden of access by the Doge our Lord and his council', which must be taken to mean Byzantine territory.[63]

In 1186 there is decisive evidence that Ragusa owed its allegiance not to Constantinople nor to Venice but to the King of Sicily: the treaty made that year between the Ragusan Commune and Stefan Nemanja, ruler of Serbia, emanated from the '*curia* of the most glorious Lord King William in the presence of lord Tribunus the archbishop, of Tasiligard the king's chamberlain and of Gervasius the count'. In 1190, also, a Ragusan treaty with the Serbs made reference to 'our lord king Tancred'; and all along Count Gervasius continued to function as Ragusan representative of the Sicilian crown.[64] It was only in 1192, with Tancred's realm in disorder, that the Ragusans returned to Greek overlordship and re-established

[61] *Hist. ducum venet.*, 79.
[62] Junio Restić (Giunio Resti), *Chronica Ragusina*, ed. S. Nodilo (Zagreb, 1893), 58.
[63] *DCV*, I, no. 334.
[64] Radonić, 7–9, 12; Restić, 64. Abulafia, 423–5, for Gervasius.

their trading rights in the Byzantine empire. In subsequent years the commercial ties between Dubrovnik and the south Italian ports became closer, but the Venetian threat did not recede. In 1205, while Constantinople and Palermo were incapacitated, the Venetians at last took Ragusa in fee.[65]

The case of Ragusa is certainly instructive. Like Savona in Liguria, its freedom of action was limited, both because of its limited resources and because of its obligations to powerful overlords; unlike Savona, its geographical position was sufficiently isolated for the Commune to play off against one another a series of candidate conquerors. Byzantines, Venetians and, indeed, Serbs were balanced adroitly against the Norman kingdom across the water; and although it would be difficult to argue that the problem of Ragusa seriously affected Venetian relations with Sicily, it is important to recall the existence of minor, local interests that suffered or prospered in the wake of mightier contests.

IX

The 1160s and 1170s were, then, a period of collapse and re-establishment for all the north Italian republics, so far as their relations with Norman Sicily were concerned. Late in 1179 the series of Genoese contracts resumes, and adds a major dimension to the picture presented by the Venetian contracts for 1178 and early 1179. At this stage it is worth reflecting whether the political rivalries generated by Barbarossa, Komnenos and others were alone responsible for the coming together of Sicilian and north Italian interests – for the Genoese treaty of 1174, the Venetian treaty of 1175 and the Pisan pact of 1169. The *Annales Pisani* talk of a severe famine that began in 1173 and lasted into 1174. Moreover, Maragone cites some prices: a *sextarium* of grain rose from 6 *solidi* to 8 and then 18; millet rose from 1 to 7 and later 12; oats from 4 to 10; wine from 4 to 8, then 15; oil from 3 to 5; 1 pound of silver became worth 7 (whatever this means); the price of rabbit skins, 'scarlet' cloth, pepper, wax all rose. These figures include several items that the Genoese, if not the Pisans, were certainly exporting from Sicily; and if, as is likely, the shortage extended up the Ligurian coast as

---

[65] Restić, 65; Abulafia, 423, 413–19 (treaties with Bari, Bisceglie, Termoli, Molfetta).

well, the Genoese must have felt sorely the lack of secure commercial rights in Sicily. Hence, perhaps, their keenness to negotiate in 1174.[66]

[66] *Ann. Pis.*, 59-60. Extensive famine in 1176: Salem's continuation of Maragone, *Ann. Pis.*, 64; 1181, 71; 1191, 74. Rabbit skins and fine cloths, whether or not Sicilian by origin, were eminently saleable at Pisa too, to judge from an inventory of the possessions of a Venetian merchant who died at Pisa in 1176 (1177 *stile pisano*), Biblioteca Nazionale Marciana, Venice, MS Lat. XIV-71 (coll. 2803), no. viii. The eruption of Etna in 1168 had no noticeable effect on Sicilian trade, though Catania was destroyed, Syracuse shaken, and the port of Messina disturbed – *Ann. Pis.*, 47; Rom. Sal., 258. The account of Maragone stems from genuine wonderment at the 'miranda et stupenda miracula', unknown 'a temporibus Sodome et Gomorree', rather than from any effect on Pisa, except for the involvement of visiting eyewitnesses. Etna's reputation was great indeed: the volcano was talked of as far away as China: Chau Ju-kua, *Chu-fan-chi*, ed. and trans. F. Hirth and W. W. Rockhill (St Petersburg, 1911), 153-4.

Chapter 6

AN AGE OF PEACEFUL COMPETITION,
1179–89

I

The earliest fragments of the cartulary of Oberto Scriba de Mercato, dating from August 1179, present a picture that accords with diplomatic developments during the 1170s. The caution of the later contracts of Giovanni Scriba has evaporated; not just Genoese but Pisans, Luccans, Flemings and native *regnicoli* are shown working together in Sicilian trade, in the atmosphere of confidence generated by Barbarossa's withdrawal from Italy. This climate extended further afield too: the earliest fragments of Oberto's work show Lucchese cloth being sent to Ceuta, and, remarkably, a Pisan and a Genoese merchant agreeing to a joint venture to Sardinia, anciently disputed territory.[1] It is, however, necessary to reserve judgement on some details of this material. Oberto provides solely a month's contracts – from 3 August to 5 September 1179 – and it would be meaningless to compare the total investment of merchants in different Mediterranean ports, and to deduce from these figures the proportionate rôle of Sicily and other markets in the overall trade of Genoa that year. (This will prove a recurring problem.) In August and early September 1179, Oberto registered nine contracts for Sicily, six for Sardinia, six for Ceuta, five for Bougie, five for Syria, four for Constantinople, one for Provence, one for the Maremma and one for Naples and the Maremma together. In the light of developments in the early 1160s, none of these destinations need occasion surprise.[2]

The relative prominence of Sicily in August 1179 can be attributed to chance clustering – the tendency for a group of contracts for trade in the same convoy to be registered together.

[1] Archivio di Stato, Genoa, MS Diversorum 102, f.1r, no. 1; f.20v, no. 2.
[2] MS 102, f.1r–21v.

9 August, £70 *societas* for Sicily 'et in…nullo alio itinere'
19 August, £20 *accomendacio* for Sicily and back
20 August, £21 *societas* for 'the Maremma as far as Naples'
31 August, £6 of cloth in *accomendacio*, for sale in Sicily
31 August, £13 sea-loan, in goods to be carried to Sicily
1 September, £60 *societas* for Sicily and back
1 September, £135 *societas* for Sicily, to which is added an *accomendacio* worth £28 5s 0d
4 September, £130 *accomendacio* for Sicily

A ninth contract shows Pietro Bretone declaring that he has received from Raimondo de Reco the capital and profit from a deal made between them at an unstated date in Messina. Pietro invested the modest sum of 50 tari. De Reco returned to Genoa via Pisa, and did further business there: a rare indication of Pisan links with Messina.[3]

Excluding this document, the contracts for the *Regno* indicate over £478 worth of business for one month. To judge from Giovanni Scriba's entries, August and September had normally been very busy months for the arrangement of expeditions to Sicily, and not representative of the year as a whole. Nevertheless, the evidence for 1179 seems to show stability in Genoese–Sicilian trade, at the very least.

II

Oberto Scriba's contracts for 1180 consist in a small block accidentally bound with Giovanni Scriba's cartulary after the fire of 1684; they are all contracts for the west Mediterranean, six for Bougie and two for Sardinia, all for modest sums.[4] But other Ligurians were thinking of visiting the *Regno* that year, to judge from an entry in the Savonese cartulary of Arnaldo da Cumano. During April 1180 Michael Montis, Guglielmo Bursella and Guglielmo Trumallio engaged to carry £40 Genoese, the property of one Rainaldo, 'in terra Mussemuti…ibi ubi faciemus portum', that is, to the Almohad Maghrib. The investment was to be repaid to Rainaldo at the rate

---

[3] MS 102, f.2v, no. 3; f.8r, no. 2 (cited in full, 16 n. *supra*); f.9r, no. 2; f.18r, no. 2; f.19r, no. 3 (datable from f.19r, no. 1); f.18v, no. 2; f.18v, no. 4; f.21v, no. 2 (£124 plus £6 owed by the *socius negocians*); f.18r, no. 3 (31 August).
[4] Archivio di Stato, Genoa, Cart. 1, f.175a, r – 175b, v; GS, II, 278–83.

of 5 Moroccan bezants for every pound; however, 'si ibimus in terra Regis Sicilie idem promittimus aut de tarenis aut de bisantiis'. In other words, the Savonese foresaw the possibility that they might reinvest the African bezants in Sicily on their way back from the Maghrib; and the wording of the document implies that a Sicilian landfall would be an unexceptional event on their way home.[5] Later Savonese registers provide ample evidence for roundabout voyages taking in Sicilian, African and even Spanish ports together; so too does Giovanni Scriba hint at a Genoese rôle in the carrying trade between Sicily and North Africa.[6] The auguries were good in the 1180s. About 1180 the Sicilian navy captured an Almohad vessel carrying the daughter of the Sultan of Tunis; King William, however, treated the girl well and sent her back to her father with apologies for the outrage. In gratitude the Sultan offered to re-establish the lapsed treaties between the Normans and the North African rulers. A ten-year truce was signed, and Sicilian merchants were given a quarter or special rights at al-Mahdiyyah and Zawila, such as they had possessed in the days before Roger II became King of Africa.[7] Good auguries in other respects too: Pisa had signed a treaty with the Sultan not long before; and north Italians, Sicilians and North Africans shared distaste for events in Egypt, where Saladin was guiding a political and religious revolution of uncertain scope.[8]

In 1181 William II carried his Saracen wars west, against Almoravid Majorca, a move that his new Almohad allies may even have appreciated, given their own enmity towards their Almoravid predecessors. Late in 1180 or early in 1181 the Norman fleet sailed to Genoa, under the command of the king's admiral, Walter de Moac.

[5] Archivio di Stato, Savona, Cartolare Arnaldo da Cumano, f.77r.

[6] e.g. Archivio di Stato, Savona, Cartolare Martinus, f.83r (of 1203).

[7] L. de Mas Latrie, *Traités de paix et de commerce et documents divers concernant les relations des Chrétiens avec les Arabes de l'Afrique septentrionale au Moyen Age*, 2 vols. (Paris, 1866), I, 52. Compare Boccaccio, *Decameron*, Night IV, story iv, a tale that shows remarkable affinities to actual events; this is not entirely surprising, for Boccaccio knew the court of Naples, if not necessarily that of Palermo, very well.

[8] Mas Latrie, I, 51. Cf. the suggestive article by C. M. Brand, 'The Byzantines and Saladin, 1185–1192: opponents of the Third Crusade', *Speculum*, XXXVII (1962), 167–81, which when considered in conjunction with Saladin's Tripolitanian campaigns, William's Byzantine campaigns and the Sicilian attacks on Alexandria from as early as 1174, shows how isolated the Normans feared they might become.

The Genoese annalist was suitably impressed: Walter came 'cum maximo stolo de galeis et plurimis uxeriis cum militibus', and these ships remained the whole winter at Vado in Liguria. Perhaps Walter hoped to enlist Genoese naval aid, but none came, and in the face of pestilence his expedition to Majorca proved disastrous.[9] Indeed, in June or July 1181 the Genoese Commune confirmed its past truces with the Sultan of Majorca. Whether this had been under consideration for some time, or whether the failure of Walter's invasion determined Genoese policy, it is impossible to be sure.[10] These events are all the more cryptic in view of a stray entry in the cartulary of Arnaldo da Cumano, at the end of a series of acts of April 1182:

Nomen archiepiscopi panormi Gualterius et nomen vicecancellerii Matheus et nomen episcopi Siracuse Riccardus et nomen camerarii Goffredus et alius frater admirati Rainaldus, nomen admirati Gualterius de Moach.

After these two lines the folio comes to a finish. This list may be a rough note to help Arnaldo draw up a lost charter commissioned by one of the Sicilians and witnessed by them during the long winter in Liguria, but the placing and context of this text remain highly mysterious.[11]

III

Later in 1182, on 16 September, the series of contracts registered by Oberto de Mercato resumes, running without interruption until 30 January 1183.[12] Most of the contracts were intended for the autumn passage; but the latest, drawn up in late autumn and early winter, must anticipate the spring sailings of 1183. On this basis it seems advisable to divide the September and October contracts

---

9 For the Majorcan campaign, see *Ann. Ian.*, II, 15–16; *Ann. Pis.*, 72–3, a long account by Maragone's son Salem – Pisa had good relations with Majorca and hence the annalist's interest in the Sicilian campaign. Also Amari, *Storia dei Musulmani*, III, 527–9, speculating that the plague 'distolse i Genovesi da mandare lor navi insieme con le siciliane, come par fosse già fermato tra le due parti'. This is to exceed the limits of the evidence. Pistarino, 259, follows Amari's line.

10 *Ann. Ian.* is silent on this point, but cf. Amari, *Storia*, III, 528–9; M. Amari, *Nuovi ricordi arabici su la storia di Genova*, 45–52 (= *ASLSP*, V (1873), 593–600).

11 Archivio di Stato, Savona, Cartolare Arnaldo da Cumano, f.168v. For Richard of Syracuse, cf. 97 *supra*; 1182 was not his first visit to Genoa.

12 Archivio di Stato, Genoa, Cartolare 2, f.1r–34v.

Table 8. *Genoese contracts registered by Oberto de Mercato,*
autumn, 1182

Destination	Number of contracts	Total value (£)	Average investment	% of total
Ceuta	23	2,071.85	90.10	29.0
SICILY	13	1,893.30	145.70	26.5
Majorca	10	850.86	85.10	11.9
Sardinia	7	766.40	109.50	10.7
Bougie	5	406.25	—	5.7
Alexandria	3	392.60	71.30	5.5
SALERNO	2	221.00	—	3.1
Syria	2	127.00 plus an illegible sum	—	—
Tunis	1	150.00	—	2.1
Provence	2	115.00	—	1.6
Maremma	6 (but see text below)	83.90	14.00	1.2
Rome	6	68.70	11.50	1.0
Grand total		7,146.86		

from later documents, with the rider that November contracts for the Maremma may reflect imminent short-range sailings, not seasonal passages. The characteristics of the autumn figures, shown in Table 8, partial though such figures must be, are in line with those presented by Giovanni Scriba's cartulary. The high total investment in Sicily is countered by a low average investment in all destinations, though there are signs of a general rise in the investment average. The list of destinations is in keeping with the developments signalled by Giovanni Scriba; the addition of a heavy Majorcan interest comes as no surprise after the treaty of 1181. Noting by contrast the absence of contracts for trade in Majorca during better documented years – 1186, 1190, 1191 – it is clear that the upsurge in 1182 was a temporary response.

A detailed breakdown of the Sicilian trade total shows that massive single investments were the exception rather than the rule; much of the £1,800 was composed of rather small sums. On 28 September Elia di Palazoglio agreed to carry £15 in *accomendacio* to Sicily 'in the ships of Adalardo'; a larger investment of £131, in *societas* with Guglielmoto Ciriole, was recorded on Elia's behalf about the same date. Here he is described as bound for Sicily and then Alexandria or Constantinople. Similarly a contract of £16 dated 2 October involved a journey to Sicily with the option to visit Alexandria; and in late September one of the Embriaci sent merchandise to Sicily against a promise to receive 45 *messemutini* back in Barbary, where his factor intended to move on leaving the *Regno*. Here it is worth recalling the Savonese contract that shows movement by Ligurian merchants in a reverse direction, from North Africa to Sicily.[13] But other investors were more conservative in their selection of trade routes: in early October a certain Guido was sent to Sicily with £200 in *accomendacio*, and 'if Guido should change his route back [to Genoa] on leaving Sicily, he must consign his share' to a co-factor bound for home. The disparity between great and small contracts is particularly clear from the case of Salerno, which attracted one partnership of £200 and one of £21.[14]

For professional factors in particular small investments were nonetheless profitable ventures, for they took care to join a wide range of partnerships of varying types. Thus late in September 1182 Guglielmo Tarasco contributed £10 to a £20 *societas* with Alcherio *bancherius*, and agreed to carry this money to Sicily and beyond. Early in October his brother Enrico Tarasco placed £10 in a £30 *societas* aimed at Sicily. On 11 October Guglielmo Tarasco put £76½ in a *societas* of £229½ for Sicily, and the next day Enrico was engaged as factor in an *accomendacio* of £68, again for Sicily. Both these contracts were backed ultimately by one person, Nicola Caito, through his own intermediaries. On 15 October Guglielmo was appointed factor in an *accomendacio* of £11 aimed at Sicily. The same day his brother Enrico engaged to take a further £60 in *societas* to Sicily and beyond, at the behest of his father Giovanni Tarasco. Giovanni Tarasco was apparently well linked to Nicola Caito, for they both witnessed yet another contract for Sicily, worth £37, a *societas* between Guglielmo Fornario and Bonogiovanni Tremesens. Altogether the Tarasco family contributed £116½ to

[13] Cart. 2, f.4v, no. 46; Cart. 2, f.5v, no. 60; f.6v, no. 71; f.5r, no. 50 – cf. Cart. Arnaldo da Cumano, f.77r.
[14] Cart. 2, f.9r, no. 98; f.11r, no. 123 (£200), no. 119 (£21).

partnerships aimed at Sicilian trade, themselves worth a total of £418½.[15]

Remarkable in a different way is the accidental concentration of eleven documents around the busy day of 15 October; by contrast, the evidence for Sicilian trade in the 1183 sailing season is stark indeed: a few contracts from December 1182 and January 1183, followed by a total lacuna in the notarial cartularies until March 1184. So it is hardly surprising that the picture for 1183 does not range beyond nearby west or central Mediterranean ports; the most distant destination was Bougie, mentioned in a single contract for £24.[16] It is a picture of quiet winter recession; indeed, of the three contracts that mention Sicily during these months, one refers back to time unknown. On 5 December 1182 Ogerio Guercio de Quinto declared to Pietro Ferrari and Pietro's brother that he had received from them £20; this he took to Sicily on their behalf, returning to Genoa with £27 capital and profit. He then placed this increased sum at their behest in a contract with his relative Ansaldo de Strula, on the understanding that any profit from his deal with Ansaldo was due to the Ferrari, and not to himself. Profit of one pound in three, though respectable, does not appear to have been very exceptional.[17]

Two contracts from early 1183 show that, amid the crowd of middle-rank, middle-class investors, some outstandingly eminent Genoese continued to invest heavily in Sicily. On 26 January 1183 a group of merchants agreed to despatch £300 to Sicily, composed as follows: £66 13s 4d from Oglerio Vento, the sleeping partner; £33 6s 8d from Oglerio Arloto, the travelling partner; and £200 in *accomendacio* from Giovanni di Bonbello, at whose *bancus* or money-table the contract was drawn up. On 31 January Arloto received a further £10 from the widow Videlia, at Oglerio Vento's behest. There are grounds for thinking that the money was spent on Sicilian grain.[18]

A Venetian quittance of January 1183 refers to business completed in Messina on behalf of the active merchant Michele Simite-

---

[15] Cart. 2, f.5r, no. 52; f.6v, no. 68; f.9v, no. 102; f.10r, no. 105; f.11v, no. 126; f.12r, no. 132; f.12r, no. 131.

[16] Cart. 2, f.22r, no. 239 (1 Dec. 1182).   [17] Cart. 2, f.23r, no. 249.

[18] Cart. 2, f.31r, no. 336; f.33v, no. 364. For an extended discussion, see Chapter 10, 274–5, *infra*.

Table 9. *Genoese contracts by destination, 1184,*
registered by Oberto de Mercato[19]

Destination	Number of spring contracts	Late summer contracts
Ceuta	4	1
Bougie	2	1
Tunis	5	—
Alexandria	1	6
Syria	3	15
SICILY	6	4
S. ITALY	1	2
Rome	1	—
Maremma	4	12
Sardinia	9	—
Corsica	6	1
Majorca	—	1
Spain	2	—
Destination unknown	—	1

colo, presumably during 1182. Meanwhile Venetians and Genoese alike remained wary of trade in Constantinople. In spring 1182 a Venetian ship sailing to Constantinople met *en route* others of the Republic's vessels, whose crew hailed the merchants with the words: 'Why do you stop here? If you do not flee you will all be dead, for we and all the Latins have been exiled from Constantinople!' In the aftermath of the Latin massacre at Constantinople, Venetian merchants had to pay closer attention to their non-Byzantine interests; while the Genoese and Pisans suffered very heavy loss of life and property in their colonies on the Bosphoros.[20]

The year 1184 is better documented than 1182 or 1183, but a head-count of contracts by destination shows that gaps in the cartulary have seriously distorted the balance of the material (see Table 9). The series of contracts begins on March 13, runs uninterruptedly until May 22, and then breaks off until August 17, when

19 Cart. 2, f.183; f.144r–153v; f.184r–193v; f.154; and then f.81r–87v and f.137r–143v; also Cart. 1, f.180r (12–19 May).
20 *DCV*, I, no. 337, no. 331; cf. no. 336, no. 338.

fourteen wandering folios make their appearance, to carry events up to September 10. The concentration of business for Syria and Alexandria in September is clearly the result of haphazard survival of evidence; no comparative totals can be offered for 1184, and the Sicilian evidence must stand by itself.

Ships were aimed at Alexandria via Sicily or at Sicily via Spain. Marino de Quinto sent goods on the former route, against a promised return of £2 16s 0d, and £3 on the latter course, against a return of £4. Contracts for £6 or even less are common, though Nicola Embriaco contributed £62 to a *societas* worth a total of £172 aimed at Sicily, and sent a ship to Sicily for sale there. He was joint owner of this boat, the value of which was estimated at £50 at the time of its departure. Giovanni Tarasco had lost none of his interest in Sicilian trade in the meanwhile; a contract of August 1184 names him as factor in an *accomendacio* of £49, invested by a number of merchants in business in Sicily.[21] And to judge from three notarial acts, trade with southern Italy remained vigorous if not in scale of investment, at least in the variety of destinations. £4 were sent to the 'Principatum' – to the Principality of Capua in general – along with a further 7 bezants of North Africa; £6 were conveyed to Naples itself; and Salerno, to judge from a partnership of £8 9s 0d, was not neglected either.[22] Excluding bezants and merchandise a respectable £483 are recorded for investment in the *Regno* during a total period of about three months – months that only partially cover the main annual investment period.

In addition, the continuing variety of trade-routes and enterprises, linking the *Regno* to more distant destinations, suggests that in 1184 it was still possible to trade in the Mediterranean without excessive fear of interruption. The main source of disturbance would have been hostile Constantinople, which was studiously avoided. Mean-

[21] Cart. 2, f.152v, no. 2; f.143r, no. 3. £6 contracts: f.148r, no. 3; f.149v, no. 4. Nicola Embriaco: Cart. 2, f.153v, no. 6 – partially cancelled only, by four parallel strokes through one line. Ship for sale: f.189v, no. 2. Tarasco: f.137v, no. 5.

[22] Cart. 2, f.153r, no. 6; f.137r, no. 1; f.140r, no. 1. The article of R. di Tucci, 'Relazioni commerciali fra Amalfi e Genova', *Studi sulla Repubblica marinara di Amalfi*, claims that many notarial entries concern Amalfitan trade with Genoa, and cites two documents that he dates 5 May and 17 May 1184, in what would now be called Cartolare 2 of the Archivio di Stato, Genoa. I have not, however, found these texts. The epithet *de Malfi* need not, in any case, necessarily indicate Amalfitans.

while, other means of access to the wealth of the Greeks were being investigated by Sicilians and north Italians together.[23]

IV

The loss of information about the trade of Genoa in 1185 is less inconvenient than for other years, since it is known that King William imposed an embargo on ships leaving Sicily, in operation by January – even though the Genoese owners of ibn Jubayr's ship managed to sneak out of Trapani bound for Spain. But the Genoese themselves were playing a major rôle in the circumstances that caused the embargo. Manuel Komnenos' failure to implement the marriage alliance between Constantinople and Palermo, and the Sicilian treaty with Barbarossa, inflamed long-standing Norman ambitions aimed at the Byzantine empire – ambitions that, in any case, could only fully have been satisfied by a dynastic alliance, leading to a Norman succession to the imperial throne.[24] Military means were the alternative. And William had ample excuse. The disappearance of Manuel's son Alexios II after his father's death and the single-handed rule of Manuel's cousin Andronikos divided the Komnenoi and their supporters; fugitive nobles arrived at the Sicilian court, followed in due course by an impostor who claimed to be the Emperor Alexios II himself. These claims were magnanimously supported by a group of Genoese merchants present at William's court: they claimed to have seen the deposed Basileus during a visit to Constantinople, and the Norman king found it convenient to accept their testimony. Eustathios insists, probably justly, that William wanted the imperial throne for himself, not for the pseudo-Alexios.[25] And what the Genoese wanted is clear too:

---

23 The only evidence concerning Pisan trade in Sicilian waters during 1184 is provided by an African merchant's plea to the Commune of Pisa after his property had been seized by Pisan pirates off Malta. As a gesture of goodwill, compensation was paid: 'Cum cognovissemus', state the Pisan consuls, 'per litteras Abdeloe filii Abdella rectoris Tunissi et per quemdam saracenum mercatorem eius nomine Boamarum capsensem ipsarum latorem, Magiulinum quondam Petri in eumdem saracenum et socios maleficium commisisse, videlicet de navi eorum apud Maltam eos in mari periecisse eisque navem et bona eorum abstulisse et cum eis aufugisse' – Archivio di Stato, Pisa, Atti Pubblici, 1185 (*stile pisano*), February 9, *lunga*; formerly preserved in Florence, where Amari, *I diplomi arabi*, 271–2, found it; registered by Casini, no. 50; cf. Abulafia, 'Henry, Count of Malta', 107.
24 Brand, 160.   25 Ibn Jubayr, 354; Eustathios, *Espugnazione*, 60–2.

the Latin massacre of 1182 had more than decimated the Genoese
and Pisan communities of Constantinople, at the behest of the tyrant
Andronikos. To gain revenge, to gain compensation, to gain new
and enlarged privileges, the best hope lay with Andronikos' enemies.
Thus after the fall of Andronikos in 1186 a Genoese embassy hastened to the new Basileus Isaac. Whether the Genoese hoped for or
expected there to be a Norman ruler in Byzantium is a deeper
question; the merchants who testified to King William were not
necessarily officials of the Commune nor accredited by the
Commune; and indeed Genoa was torn by factional strife and the
Commune was in financial straits.[26] Eustathios' statement that the
Italian merchants held a grudge against Andronikos has, indeed,
been magnified into Genoese and Pisan participation in William's
Byzantine war. Pistarino talks of participation, but Vitale goes
further and talks of Genoese prompting. However, what Eustathios
says refers to events prior to 1185 (above all to 1182); private, pirate
aid to the Sicilians is likely, but there is no clear proof that
north Italians played a major rôle in the great naval attack of
1185:

Those who suffered losses were many, from many lands and speaking
many tongues, coming from all ends of the earth, some natives of Pisa,
others of Genoa, others Tuscan and Lombard by origin; nor were Longobards [south Italians] lacking, and others too.[27]

The embargo imposed by King William, aimed against the spread
of news and gossip, must have affected trade seriously, for the
Norman fleet did not sail east until June. Until then, rumour was
rife in the ports of Sicily that Constantinople, or maybe Alexandria
or Majorca, was the target of the planned expedition. And the
embargo was decidedly one-way: ships were welcomed into the
Sicilian ports, partly, it is clear, because the voyagers might bring
the latest news from the east, partly, perhaps, because some ships
might be commandeered (say, Greek ships) and partly because
some level of commercial activity could be maintained by closing
exits alone. As a result, the Sicilians did achieve a surprise attack on

[26] Embassy to the Emperor Isaac: *Ann. Ian.*, II, 21. For the Latin massacre, Brand,
41–2. Strife in Genoa: *Ann. Ian.*, II, 20 (1185–6 was more peaceful, *ibid.* 22).
[27] Eustathios, 57–8; Pistarino, 259–60; Vitale, 'Relazioni commerciali', 23.

Durazzo and Thessalonika; and although they held the latter for only three months, the Ionian Islands were captured for good, Andronikos was toppled – largely by the spectacle of Count Tancred's fleet parading in the Golden Horn – and Saladin, ally of the Greeks, trembled momentarily.[28] Moreover, the Genoese were able to edge back into Byzantine commerce under the new Basileus Isaac. Quite apart from diplomatic moves in 1186, the Genoese made sound financial gestures too, investing over £2,000 in trade with Constantinople by way of sixteen contracts, fifteen of which date from 23, 24 and 25 September 1186. Rufo della Volta placed £307, Nicola Mallone £300. As far as Genoa was concerned, King William had achieved the most desirable of results: Andronikos had gone from Constantinople, but William had not managed to move from Palermo to excessively mighty glories.[29]

V

Between 22 September and 24 December 1186 Genoese business throughout the Mediterranean flourished greatly; as is shown in Table 10, the more remote the destination, the higher the investment level – with the reasonable exception of Alexandria. The internal peculiarity of these figures is that the contracts for Syria, Constantinople and Alexandria all, with one exception, date from 22 to 25 September; those for North Africa date from October, with one earlier exception, as do those for Naples, while the Sicilian material is more widely spread throughout September and October. In keeping with this broader spread is the lower average figure for investment in Sicily, which continued to attract the more modest, less bold ventures along with very heavy commitments.

Names familiar from 1184 reappear, suggesting that the embargo of 1185 had no long-term effects. Thus on 23 September 1186 Oto the furrier (*pelliparius*) declared himself to have received £90, which

[28] Ibn Jubayr, 353–4; Niketas Choniates, 411; the Sicilian land army arrived at Thessalonika on 6 August, 1185 – Eustathios, 66. For Tancred's exploits, M. Scarlata, 'Sul Declino del Regno normanno e l'assunzione al trono di Tancredi', *Atti CISSN*, 488.

[29] *Ann. Ian.*, II, 20 (1186). Brand, 208–9, refers to an 'interim agreement' between Genoa and Constantinople. Contracts for trade there: *OSM* (*1186*), no. 26, no. 40. Nicola Mallone is mentioned in *Ann. Ian.*, II, 21, as one of the Genoese ambassadors sent to Constantinople.

Table 10. *Genoese contracts throughout the Mediterranean, September–December 1186, registered by Oberto de Mercato*

Destination	Number of contracts	Total value (£s)	Average investment (£s)	% of total
Syria	14	3,552.00	253.71	29.20
SICILY	24	2,159.80	90.00	17.75
Constantinople	16	2,118.00	132.37	17.41
Ceuta	20	1,983.10	99.15	16.30
NAPLES	9	672.50	74.72	5.52
Maghrib	10	630.40	63.04	5.18
Maremma	7	266.00	38.00	2.19
Alexandria	5	246.60	49.32	2.02
Provence	6	207.90	34.65	1.71
Sardinia	4	188.20	—	1.55
Rome	3	140.60	—	1.16
Grand total		£12,165.10		

he had lent to Nicola Embriaco and his nephews 'pro servientibus regis Sicilie', an unusual phrase that the notary inserted above the line as an addition. Oto's agent Giovanni de Dominico had recovered the sum, and the record of loan had therefore to be anulled by the issue of the charter Oberto has preserved. Clearly, much depends here on the interpretation of 'servientibus', whether the word be held to mean 'services' or 'servants'. In the former case it could be assumed that Nicola Embriaco had given armed service to the King of Sicily during the Byzantine war, and had raised money from Oto to cover his immediate expenses. Since he had sent a ship, in the ownership of which he held a share, south to Sicily in 1184, it is reasonable to suggest that he remained ready and willing to supply King William with military and naval equipment, or with other suitable services. As early as 1184 it might have been known that ships were in demand in the *Regno*, to be fitted for a campaign against an unnamed foe – whom the Genoese, at least, might be able to identify. Equally, of course, the placing of this unusual document in 1186 might be coincidence, or only of indirect relevance to the campaign: the Embriaci may have supplied the Sicilian crown with a loan backed by Oto, for example; and, to judge from the way in which Genoese at court identified the pseudo-Alexios, it was not uncommon for northern merchants to move in William II's entourage.[30]

Others less eminent than the Embriaci return to light in 1186. Giovanni Tarasco returned £182 16s 6d to Fredenzone Xamitario which he had taken to Sicily in the ship of Bonovassallo Nevitella. An earlier contract between the same two partners is known from 11 October 1182, a *societas* of £229 10s 0d, apparently a separate deal. Of course there is no knowing when the Nevitella vessel set out, given the effects of the embargo of early 1185. Giovanni Tarasco had certainly lost none of his enthusiasm for Sicilian trade, since in late September 1186 he agreed to take £15, the property of Pietro Lombardo, to Sicily in *accomendacio*; and two days later Ricadona Boterico engaged him to convey 3 oz of Sicilian gold tari, valued at a low £6 8s 0d, to Sicily for sale or investment – the low rate is partly explained by the fact that this seems to be the estimated value of the gold at the time of the ship's departure, rather than a *cambium* rate involving commission on the real value. Ricadona could hope, in this case, to increase the value of his investment by the normal processes of purchase and retail. Ricadona also sent £7 to Sicily on 27 September; otherwise he is known from small investments in Majorca in 1182.[31]

Bonovassallo Nevitella was another Genoese merchant who agreed to return to Sicily for the winter. On 3 October 1186 he engaged to take £40 belonging to the widow Sophia to Sicily and then 'wherever I go with the goods of Enrico Nevitella my uncle' – though no contracts directly between uncle and nephew exist in surviving material. Another middle-class citizen who invested in Sicily this year was Oberto Scriba himself. On 18 October Filippo de Castello agreed to take £50 in *accomendacio* to Sicily, followed by a further £67 1s 0d entrusted to him by Ugo de Reco and £52 18s 0d from Idone de Pallo. Attached to the three documents recording these partnerships is a statement that runs, in its fullest form, 'I [Filippo] have permission to order and to act in respect to this contract in such a way as may seem good to me and for the good of the *accomendacio*, at the wish of Guglielmo Longo

---

[30] *OSM (1186)*, no. 10; cf. Bach, 113 and Cart. 2, f.189v, no. 2.
[31] *OSM (1186)*, no. 22 and Cart. 2, f.9v, no. 102; *OSM (1186)*, no. 43, no. 53, no. 54; and for Majorca, Cart. 2, f.11v, no. 128; f.137r, no. 1.

[a witness] and of Oberto the notary and of their partners.' Now, this indicates that Filippo was carrying money invested by other Genoese and registered in other notaries' books, for Oberto Scriba could not register his own commercial transactions, and he and Longo clearly went to one or more other notaries to record their Sicilian business interests. But it is impossible to know whether, simply because he invested in Sicily, Oberto attracted an especially high level of Sicilian business from those who were both clients and shareholders.[32]

Two-figure investments in Sicily are the rule: £40, £48 plus a further £6, £74, £15 9s 0d (in the form of a bale of fustian), £50, £17 8s 0d; Ogerio Pallio's *societates* of £101 and £31 15s 0d, the latter partly in tari, show a relatively steep investment on his part.[33] Naples, however, flowered: on 8 October a total of £510 was invested in trade with that city, partly funded by Otone Mallone; a week earlier £165 15s 0d is known to have been directed there; and following news of the massive investments of 8 October, £41, £18, £6, £85 and £27 were engaged there in the next three days. It is clear from later notaries that trade with Naples was very highly developed in the 1190s, while Salerno fared ill.[34] But enormous investments in Sicily are also recorded, channelled into the hands of one factor, Ansaldo Sardena. Ansaldo was a relative of consul Guglielmo Sardena of 1177 and of consul Rainaldo Sardena of 1127, who negotiated with Roger II and Savona. In autumn 1186 he carried a recorded £850 to Sicily. Ingo de Flexo or de Frexia placed £400 in his hands, against which Ansaldo placed a further £200 of his own, promising to travel to Sicily and wherever else may please him. Ingo gave Ansaldo formal permission to engage in *accommendaciones* with other persons, and to carry a further £50 of his own – though it is unclear whether Ansaldo actually did so. So, that day and the next, Ansaldo received £100 from Guglielmo Burone, £100 from Nicola Capra, and £50 from the wife of Guglielmo Longo.[35]

32 *OSM (1186)*, no. 80; no. 151 – cf. no. 170, no. 185.
33 *OSM (1186)*, no. 80, no. 49 and no. 83, no. 61, no. 145, no. 151, no. 74; no. 68 and no. 81 (Oglerio Pallio).
34 *OSM (1186)*, no. 69, no. 70; cf. no. 71. I suggest that 'Aseragne' in the third of these contracts should read 'Aragno', as in no. 69, where Aragno is *socius stans*: see also no. 108, no. 113, no. 119, no. 118, no. 125.
35 *OSM (1186)*, no. 164, no. 169, no. 177, no. 181. Guglielmo Sardena: Olivieri, *ASLSP*, I, 353; Rainaldo Sardena: 171 *infra*.

Two of these backers were closely related: Ingo de Flexo was Ingo della Volta's son, and Guglielmo Burone was nephew to Ingo and son of another eminent Guglielmo Burone. Erik Bach described Guglielmo junior as 'le fils moins grand d'un père trop grand'; this was somewhat unfair, for, as Bach admitted, there is simply little evidence in surviving cartularies for his commercial activity. In other spheres he certainly carried some weight: he was consul in 1192 and 1194. Ingo de Flexo was consul more often – in 1177, 1180, 1182, 1185 and 1188; but he too was an infrequent visitor to Oberto Scriba's stall – many of his financial interests were purely local, for he was a major landowner in Liguria. So perhaps was Ansaldo Sardena, to judge from evidence to be considered very shortly. Nor was Ansaldo quite alone in attracting big business, for on 20 and 21 October £149 was invested in these plans by Guglielmo Malfigliastro, a scion of the Genoese moneyed classes.[36]

November saw the return of ships and the settlement of outstanding debts; soon after the Sardena contracts were drawn up the Sicilian convoy appears to have set sail. On 15 November Ugo de Reco, already encountered in partnership with Filippo de Castello, was declared quit of debts to Sozobono, to whom he owed 50 oz of tari, borrowed for trade in Sicily – how much he actually borrowed, or alternatively actually returned, it might not be polite to ask. And the same day Giovanni Smerigio received £19 11s od from Giovanni Balisterio, representing the profit from trade in Sicily. Smerigio had originally invested £29 in *accomendacio*, and the capital would presumably have been returned separately. With this record of a handsome profit ends the purely Genoese evidence for the trade of Sicily in the reign of William the Good.[37]

VI

Its fine port, its developed notariate and its proximity to Genoa promised Savona some share in the rise to commercial greatness of Liguria. But the Genoese, as seigneurs of Savona, began to feel that their own prosperity might suffer if Savonese trade were not placed

---

36 Bach, 111; Olivieri, 392, 394 (Burone); ibid. 353, 357, 359, 363, 367 (de Frexia)·
Ansaldo's landed interests: 171 *infra*. Malfigliastri: *OSM* (*1186*), no. 184.

37 *OSM* (*1186*), no. 262, no. 266. Another big deal is indicated in the £200 contract
of 20 October: no. 174.

under stringent controls. In March 1181 the consuls of Savona, present in Genoa, were forced to accept humiliating terms of qualified autonomy for their Commune:

lignum exinde de Saona non ibit in pelagus ultra Sardineam aut Barchinoniam, nisi prius iverit in portum Ianue, et ex eo portu non exhibit nisi cum maiori parte hominum Ianue, qui in ligno illo causa negotiandi ire debeant, et in eodem portu ad discarricandum redibit.[38]

So Savonese ships were excluded from direct trade with Sicily; Savona became a Genoese naval reserve, invaluable when, as often, the merchants of Genoa required a foreign ship because none of their own vessels was to hand, but a coolie nonetheless. Up to 1180 the Savonese cartulary of Arnaldo da Cumano shows local merchants penetrating as far as Constantinople; but there are no signs after 1181 of Savonese activity beyond the limits which the Genoese had now drawn.[39]

Except, in fact, for piracy against south Italian vessels. Gaeta was a fond target of Savonese aggression. The treaty-book of the Commune of Savona, the *Registrum a catena*, contains a 'Carta finis transactionis et refutacionis' of October 1181 – that is, not long after the Savonese submission to Genoa. Leo Demato and Simeon de Lontaci, both of Gaeta, declare Bonogiovanni Feldrato and Poncio Guasco free of further obligation to them after an attack made by men of Savona and of Noli, nearby, on some ships of Gaeta. 'And we make this refutation following the payment of £56 0s 2d and the consignment to us of 111 *minae* of wheat, and we declare ourselves duly paid. Given in front of the house of Ansaldo Sardena.'[40] The wheat, and money or goods valued at £56, must have been aboard the Gaetan ship. Since the date of the attack is unknown it is just possible that the Savonese pirates were beyond the maritime limits set that year by Genoa; the outrage could have occurred off Sardinia or Corsica, or off the mainland. But a little is known of some of the individuals involved. Bonogiovanni Feldrato and Abo Scriba came together in Savona in June 1187 to dissolve a partnership, composed of shares in a ship – conceivably the very pirate ship from

---

[38] *CDG*, II, 263–5.
[39] Cartolare Arnaldo da Cumano, f.26r (9 Feb. 1179, armed galley bound for Provence and Constantinople, with Genoese backing); f.90r (18 Feb. 1179, testaments prior to voyage to Constantinople).
[40] Archivio di Stato, Savona, Registro a catena piccolo, f.10v.

which they had launched their attack on the Gaetans.[41] The appearance of the house of Ansaldo Sardena is of interest too. Some members of the Sardena family were Genoese citizens, and consuls; but Genoese tutelage over Savona makes the appearance of resident Genoese in Savona unremarkable. For one thing, this probably facilitated the hire and purchase of ships. For another, Ansaldo's relative Rainaldo had been involved in negotiations with Roger II sixty years earlier, when the Savonese complained that a ship of theirs had been seized. Strictly, the Savonese attack on ships from Gaeta had been in breach of the agreement made in 1127 under which the *regnicoli* had the right to demand prompt justice in Savona or Genoa. And the case was evidently taken very seriously; perhaps it was owing to its connection with the treaty of 1127 that the agreement between the pirates and the Gaetans was solemnly registered in the Commune's treaty-book. However, later cases of Gaetan attacks on Savonese ships, and of Savonese attacks on Gaetan citizens, suggest that a long-standing rivalry in west Mediterranean trade existed between these two ports.[42]

In many respects the reign of William II enshrined the greatest achievements, administrative and artistic, of Norman Sicily. In diplomacy as in commerce the end of the reign was marked by confidence and security – though no commercial contracts survive from 1187, 1188 or 1189; military threats to the survival of the *Regno* had waned, and William turned his attention to ever-greater overseas expeditions on his own account. Greece he stormed, Dalmatia he took in fee, Syria he promised to protect. His death without child in 1189 revealed how thin was the security of the 1180s. Internal strife tore the *Regno* apart. For the north Italians, it was an opportunity to mould not merely the future of distant lands but their own commercial future as well; and it was a moment too of fearful uncertainty and of acute rivalry. There were takings in plenty for everybody, but everybody – of course – aimed at all the takings.[43]

[41] Cart. Arnaldo da Cumano, f.180v. The shares were equal except for a £3 16s od discrepancy, paid by Bonogiovanni to Abo.

[42] Archivio di Stato, Savona, Cart. Martinus, f.115r (March 1203), f.146v–149r (late 1203).

[43] Strictly, it would not be correct to say that all of the 1189 contracts have vanished, since a notarial act of 2 March 1190, *OSM (1190)*, no. 207, refers to an earlier partnership drawn up in Messina in 1189 or earlier.

Chapter 7

THE LAST PHASE OF ALLIANCES, 1189-91

I

King Tancred of Sicily was elected ruler by the majority of his barons, but he was not a unanimous choice; nor, internationally, could he be sure that old alliances would remain in force.[1] In particular, the Sicilian break with Germany forced Pisa to reconsider its diplomatic position, caught between its oft-asserted loyalty to the Hohenstaufen and its commercial interests in Liguria. Were the two necessarily contradictory? The Pisans reflected on their past deal with Barbarossa and decided that the reactivation of their Hohenstaufen alliance might, in the long term, bring unprecedented commercial rights in the *Regno*; moreover, the question of legitimacy, of whether the bastard Tancred or Henry and Constance was by right ruler of Sicily, was more clear-cut than in earlier reigns; no longer was the existence of the kingdom in doubt, but only the right to rule it. So, not surprisingly, Pisa began its negotiations with Henry VI well before any signs of a move by Genoa can be identified. Henry was still in Germany, at Kaiserslautern, when he promised, on 28 August 1190, to exempt Pisan merchants from 'omni theloneo sive dreitura' in the Kingdom of Sicily, Duchy of Apulia and Principality of Capua; that is, to give the Pisans the right to trade free from the majority of tolls in the kingdom.[2] At whose initiative the grant was made is, however, unclear. Against the generosity of the Kaiserslautern grant it is necessary to place its extreme emptiness at a time when no firm military plans had been drawn up; the privilege derived its real value from the renewal of Pisan trading

---

[1] D. Clementi, 'The circumstances of Count Tancred's accession to the Kingdom of Sicily, Duchy of Apulia and the Principality of Capua', *Mélanges Antonio Marongiu* (Studies presented to the international commission for the history of representative and parliamentary institutions, xxiv; Palermo–Agrigento, 1967), 57–80.

[2] J. Lami, *Deliciae eruditorum seu veterum anecdoton opusculorum collectanea* (Florence, 1736, 1769), 193; Clementi, *Cal.*, no. 1.

rights in the German empire. There was no attempt, unless tacit, to secure the allegiance of the Pisan fleet for an invasion of the *Regno* by the issue of this privilege. A fuller privilege, embodying promises by both parties, would have to await the correct diplomatic moment six months later.

And as for Tancred, he tried to protect his sea flank by alliances with Constantinople and the crusaders, and, more practical here, by means of generous privileges to a wide variety of south Italian towns. His method was to cede certain regalian rights in the towns in return for promises of fidelity; since it was nominally in consideration of the past loyalty of these towns that the grants were made, there is something ironic in the need to buy their future loyalty too. Tancred's series of privileges began in April 1190 with a privilege for Barletta in Apulia; a concession to the archbishops of Salerno, of June of the same year, involved rights over the dyeing industry, and falls into a similar category. His privilege to the citizens of Naples, also issued in June 1190, aimed directly at the root of his problems: he attempted to win the hearts of the Neapolitans by confirming and extending their control over the affairs of the city. Naples was exempted from feudal service in the royal fleet and its citizens were to be free from the payment of commercial dues throughout the kingdom. The risk was clear but calculated: Naples would have to resist Henry VI of its own volition, yet the Neapolitans might consider that they had something worthwhile for which to fight. By summer 1191, as German plans grew blatant, Trani and Gaeta (May and July 1191) were rewarded for their 'faithfulness'. Gaeta extended its territorial domain on the north-west sea frontier of the *Regno* and was permitted to export wheat from Sicily free from tolls.[3]

II

Pisa's great rival neither hesitated nor turned to Henry during 1190; in so far as Genoa continued to trade and deal in Sicily as it had

---

[3] P. F. Palumbo, 'Gli Atti di Tancredi e di Guglielmo III di Sicilia', *Atti del Convegno internazionale di studi ruggeriani* (Palermo, 1955), II, 514, no. 2 (i), no. 2 (iii), no. 2 (iv), no. 2 (xi); Gaeta: Minieri–Riccio, I, 285–7 and Palumbo, no. 2 (xii). Cf. for Naples: M. Fuiano, 'Napoli dalla fine dello stato autonomo alla sua elevazione a capitale del *Regnum Siciliae*', *Archivio storico per le provincie napoletane*, LXXVI (1956), 241–55 – reprinted as M. Fuiano, *Napoli nel Medioevo* (Naples, 1972). For Constantinople: Brand, 190.

Table 11. *Genoese trade, January–April 1190,*
registered by Oberto Scriba

Destination	Number of contracts	Total value (£)	Average investment (£)	% of total
SICILY	23	1,981.80	86.20	49.8
Sardinia	30	1,186.10	39.50	29.8
Rome and Naples	1	240.00	—	6.0
Maremma	15	217.30	14.50	5.5
Majorca	3	119.00	—	3.0
Maghrib	1	86.00	—	2.2
Pisa	1	51.20	—	1.3
Marseilles	3	23.20	—	0.6
Corsica	3	19.90	—	0.5
Syria	1	2.50	—	—
Unstated	1	50.00	—	1.3
Grand total		£3,977.00		

under William II, the Republic implicitly renounced Henry and his schemes. Oberto Scriba's contracts resume in January 1190, and leave no doubt that Tancred's kingdom remained a very valued and valuable trading partner; for the period January to April the surviving investment figures are shown in Table 11. Recent treaties with Majorca (1188) and with the *iudex* of Arborea in Sardinia (1189), and a fragile improvement of relations with Pisa as a result of papal intervention (February 1188) explain several characteristics of these figures.[4] Business with Syria held back until the departure of the crusaders from Genoa, when it boomed again. Of course, the correlation between the treaties and these figures inspires added confidence in Oberto Scriba's evidence; and, in these circumstances, the strength of emphasis on Sicily in early 1190 is very significant. Genoese exclusion from the turbulent east Mediterranean left Sicily the most desirable trading partner overseas.

This 'exclusion' from the eastern Mediterranean was not complete, but the Genoese remained wary of most infidel lands. Thus on

4 Majorca: *Ann. Ian.*, II, 26; *CDG*, II, 341–4; Amari, *Nuovi ricordi arabici*, 52–8 (600–6). Sardinia: *CDG*, II, 348–53, 355–61. Pisa: *CDG*, II, 321–41, *Ann. Ian.*, II, 26–9.

16 January 1190 Berardo Ricio made an agreement with two men from Camogli, just outside Genoa; all three were travel 'from Genoa to Gaeta and then to Sardinia and from Sardinia to Syria [*Ultramare*] and from Syria they are to return to whatever Christian land Berardo and his colleagues may choose'. As payment for their services, Berardo would pay his colleagues 14 Syrian bezants, and in Sardinia he would purchase for each of them 10 *minae* of wheat or barley. Later, Berardo hired another sailor, Ansaldo da Sori, as cook, and allowed him 20 *minae* of grain 'from where Ansaldo wishes', that is, Genoa or Gaeta or Sardinia. A different route to southern Italy was exploited the same year by Villano Asaxino, who carried £90 in *societas* and £140 *super societatem*, the property of Guglielmo Rataldo, to Rome and then 'per terram regis', into the *Regno* (15 February 1190).[5]

These specific routes apart, it was Sicily itself that continued to be the prime attraction for visitors to the *Regno*; 'continued', certainly, for on 2 March 1190 Ogerio Pallio declared the existence of a *societas* made at Messina between Anselmo Carmaino and Pasquale Baltigato, and backed by his own funds and those of his brother. The original Messinese contract must have been drawn up in winter 1189/90 at latest, and, since Ogerio Pallio was an old hand in Sicilian trade, this document suggests that business had, not unnaturally, flourished in the last year of King William's life too.[6]

Certain factors attracted business from a wide variety of sleeping partners, indicating something of a 'mass movement' of investment in Sicily. Roger de Çura, for instance, had a good record as *socius negocians*:

14 March   £36 *accomendacio* for Sicily;
17 March   £50 *accomendacio*;
8 April   £50 *accomendacio*.[7]

Better connected still was Bufaro Sarago:

1 February   £24 *accomendacio* from Bonifacio della Volta, a figure
    of importance;
27 March   £24 *accomendacio* to be carried jointly with Roger Elia;
5 April   £10 *accomendacio* on behalf of Ugo Ismael's sister;

[5] *OSM* (1190), no. 17, no. 49; no. 146.
[6] *OSM* (1190), no. 207 – cf. *OSM* (1186), no. 68, no. 81 (reading 'Oglerio' for 'Aglerio').   [7] *OSM* (1190), no. 252, no. 267, no. 354.

5 April £8 *accomendacio* on behalf of Alcherio *bancherius*;

8 April £138 *accomendacio*;

8 April £24 *accomendacio*;

8 April Bufaro declares he has £88 12s od in *accomendacio* from Rubaldo Belfoglio, for which [*pro eo*] he is to receive 3 oz of tari per pound Genoese from Rainaldo de Maica in Sicily;

19 April £222 *accomendacio* from the wife of Guglielmo Burone; this includes a £5 *accomendacio* from a secondary investor, plus a quantity of pepper and alum;

19 April Bufaro states he has in *accomendacio* from Maria, wife of Alamanno Quartano, £61 16s 6d, in the form of proceeds from the (recent or anticipated?) sale of pepper and alum, for investment in Sicily.[8]

The Genoese nobility expressed quite heavy interest in Sicilian trade this season: on 8 April Oglerio Vento invested £57 in Sicily, to be carried by his patrician colleague Nicola Squarçaficio. The same day Idone Mallone and his wife sent £97 17s od and a robe to Sicily; and Guglielmo Malfigliastro provided the same factor with £214 7s od. This factor also carried £3 6s od of his own, apart from one-third of his *societas* with Malfigliastro, and a purple cloth and other merchandise worth a total of £5. Meanwhile Anselmo Rondana declared he was carrying £172 to Sicily on behalf of Guglielmo Malfigliastro, a sum that represented the proceeds of an earlier *societas* 'which I have with you Guglielmo Malfigliastro, of which a charter was made by the hand of Oberto the notary'. Idone de Pallo, known for long-standing Sicilian interests, invested £129 12s 6d in gold and cloths aimed at the *Regno*; Guglielmo Malocello, a well-born Genoese, sent £72 to Sicily. Both appear in a declaration of commercial interests made by the factor Ugo Polexino, listing contracts for trade in Sicily. Alongside their £200 odd are found numerous investments by a certain Oglerio – not specifically named as Oglerio Vento, or any other Oglerio known to have had Sicilian connections. Oglerio or his nephews and colleagues placed four partnerships in Ugo Polexino's hands, worth a total of £337.[9]

[8] *OSM (1190)*, no. 85, no. 288, nos. 341–2, nos. 368–9, no. 365, no. 404, no. 406.
[9] *OSM (1190)*, nos. 362–4, no. 366, nos. 358–9, no. 357.

Table 12. *Genoese trade, July–August 1190,*
registered by Oberto Scriba

Destination	Number of contracts	Total value (£)	Average investment (£)	% of total
Syria	19	1,718.90	90.50	54.3
SICILY	18	1,182.40	65.70	37.4
Marseilles	1	87.00	—	2.7
Maremma	4	83.50	—	2.6
Sardinia	2	40.00	—	1.3
Provence	1	36.00	—	1.1
NAPLES	1	10.00	—	0.3
Corsica	1	6.40	—	0.2
		on return		
Grand total		£3,164.20		

III

The closeness of the relationship between the main investors early
in 1190 is emphasised once again in the folios that survive from late
July and early August of that year. Now, Genoa was torn in the 1180s
by civil strife between long-standing rivals, in particular the Grillo
and Vento cliques.[10] In the late 1180s trouble did not die away, but
the Vento–della Volta interest became paramount, to judge from
the consul lists. To recapitulate the names of some of Genoa's public
officials during this time is to repeat names familiar from their investments in trade: Ingo de Frexia was consul in 1188, Raimondo
de Frexia in 1190; Oglerio Vento was consul in 1188, Guglielmo
Vento in 1189, Simone Vento in 1190; Guglielmo Embriaco was
consul in 1189; Ugo Mallone was judge of pleas (*consul de placitis*)
in 1188.[11] These names carry extra weight in view of the accession
of Tancred. By spring 1190 his coronation was in the news and Pisa

[10] *Ann. Ian.*, II, 19: 'hoc anno multa odia atque dissensiones fuerunt in civitate'
(1183); II, 26 (1188). Cf. Bach, 154–6, who talks of the 'caractère très temporaire'
of these quarrels with the Genoese aristocracy. That may be true of individual
rivalries, but the existence of long-standing tension is suggested by *Ann. Ian.*,
with its insistence that certain consuls brought peace to the Commune amid the
discord of factions – II, 18, 20, 22, 25. That is to say, factious elements persisted;
it was simply the expression of factiousness that was tempered.
[11] Olivieri, 367, 387–8.

had made its first moves into the Hohenstaufen camp. But in late summer 1190 the Genoese took courage from Tancred's installation, rather than taking hope in Henry's crystal-gazing.[12] However, the fragment of Oberto's cartulary terminates before the autumn investments would normally be fully under way. That the Syrian figure is to be explained by the Third Crusade is clear enough. Philip Augustus hired his ships at Genoa, and Genoese businessmen responded to his appeal in every possible way. A group of factors was sent to find profit amid the slaughter, backed by Ingo de Frexia, Ansaldo Mallone and other nobles.[13]

Not that the della Volta group neglected Sicily. On 20 July Ingo de Frexia sent Ogerio di San Lorenzo to Sicily with £45 in *accomendacio*; Ogerio was to carry this sum 'where I shall go with the *societas* I have with Marchesio della Volta', himself a relative of Ingo. An *accomendacio* with Marchesio, but not a *societas*, is also recorded by Oberto de Mercato; this was for £123 7s 0d of which £20 belonged to Bonifacio, son of the late Giacomo della Volta, in whose house the contract had been drawn up. This was followed by a further £38 13s 2d invested directly by Bonifacio in Sicilian trade; and the same day Ogerio also received £28 in *accomendacio* from Idone Mallone. Whether an additional *societas* did indeed exist between Marchesio della Volta and Ogerio, as the first of this group of contracts states, it is hard to say: the term '*societas*' could be an error, or signify nothing more than looseness of expression. '*Societas*' could mean 'partnership' in a general sense as well as a particular form of commercial arrangement.[14]

The Grillo clique is less prominent generally in the commercial records, but in 1190 some Sicilian business came its way. On 7 August Bonogiovanni Calla received in *accomendacio* a twenty-fourth part of a ship, in which Rubaldo Grillo also had a share. This

---

[12] Clementi, 'Accession', 60, for the date of Tancred's coronation.

[13] Roger of Howden, *Gesta Regis Henrici secundi*, ed. W. Stubbs, 2 vols. (Rolls Series; London, 1867), III, 37, 39–40. Philip travelled via Messina. Thus the Syrian contracts worth £1,719 have some meaning in the context of Sicilian trade – providing the quarrels of King Philip of France and King Richard of England did not entirely disrupt the commercial life of Messina, as very possibly they did: see Richard of Devizes, *Chronicle*, ed. J. T. Appleby (London, 1963), 19–25. For investment in Syria, *OSM* (*1190*), no. 569 (Ansaldo Mallone); no. 655 (Ingo de Frexia).   [14] *OSM* (*1190*), no. 526, nos. 528–30.

[15] *OSM* (*1190*), no. 602.

ship was to sail to Syria, and thence back to 'Sicily or Genoa or Apulia or the Principality [of Capua]', or wherever the shareholders agreed, and it could be sold *en route*. Expenses were to be paid in bezants of Acre.[15] Another familiar name is that of Ugo de Reco, who had a partnership with a certain Pietro de Teierono for trade in Sicily; on 13 July Ugo gave his assent to an *accomendacio* between Pietro and a third party, worth £20 and aimed at Sicily. This third party, Giovanni Mazamorro, was joint sleeping partner with Ugo in a further *societas* of £34 13s 0d for Sicily recorded a few days later. His acquaintances included *regnicoli* as well as Ligurians, for in a charter of quittance of late July 1190 drawn up on his behalf two Gaetans – Petrus de Leo Gaietanus and Bonus Manganella Gaiete – stood witness. Other Gaetans too were active in Genoa at this moment: on 16 August Johannes Gaietanus and Ricardus Bonus Fides Gaiete engaged to travel to Syria in the ship of Lanfranco Malfigliastro and Ansaldo Mallone, apparently as crewmen.[16]

Though Naples attracted a single recorded contract – a mere £10 from the widow of Enrico Trencherio – contact with the *Regno* as a whole seems to have been substantial.[17] The Grillo–Calla contract, with its unusual reference to Apulia, and the presence of Gaetans in Genoa, suggest continuing contact with the Norman mainland. A £21 *societas* of July 1190 was aimed at Sicily and then 'quo michi videbitur per terram regis et nullo alio alio [*sic*] itinere', which seems to suggest further travel in the island or a return via the mainland of the *Regno*.[18] That, perhaps, is to end on a note of sound co-operation; but a sour note also existed, to judge from the sale of a slave on 10 August 1190. Enrico di Buonfantello sold a Saracen slave named Busso to Rubaldo Mallone for £5. For his part, Enrico promised to protect Busso from violence, 'except by the king of Sicily'. 'And if I cannot defend him from his force' [namely, that of the king], the sale will be cancelled and the money refunded. What is strange is not the continuing liability of the seller to goods already sold, for sales on deferred payment, or loans against securities, were quite common – the *cambium maritimum* contract in its fullest form involved this device – it is the personal reference to Tancred,

---

[16] *OSM* (*1190*), no. 492, no. 512, no. 574, no. 640.
[17] *OSM* (*1190*), no. 617 (Naples).   [18] *OSM* (*1190*), no. 520.

King of Sicily that is unique, prior to the Genoese–Hohenstaufen alliance of 1191, and it does suggest that even the Malloni could not say for sure how relations with the new King of Sicily might develop.[19]

IV

Henry VI followed Barbarossa in believing that only by a combined land and sea attack could the *Regno* be domesticated; and, as has been seen, Tancred was wise to this strategy and had made early moves to secure the allegiance of the Campanian and Apulian ports. Unlike Tancred, Henry could not dismiss part of his fleet in the hope that loyalty would outweigh obligation, for he had no fleet at all and no existing rights in the *Regno* to cede; ships must be won by material promises set in the future. Tancred placed his trust in the ports of the *Regno*; Henry, by contrast, asked Pisa and Genoa to place their trust in him. In February 1191 he went in person to Pisa to negotiate a renewal of the grant made by his father in 1162. His new privilege, of 1 March, added little to Barbarossa's text. The same towns were promised to Pisa – half Palermo, Messina, Salerno and Naples; all Gaeta, Mazara and Trapani. There was the same limitation of date, so that Henry was allowed three months within which to notify Pisa if he required the city's help that year; and there was a generously spaced timetable to permit Pisa to arm for invasion in subsequent years, should the campaign be deferred. The Pisans were not, in any case, expected to move south until the German army had entered the *Regno*. The new privilege leaves the impression that Pisa was not just ready but keen to negotiate with Henry; past agreements between Pisa and the Normans were held to be no more than temporary truces in the imperial war on Sicily, while Barbarossa's remained the ideal programme.[20]

Once more Genoa was obliged to spin itself a tight-rope; and by 1191 the Republic had clearly learnt some balancing tricks. The astonishingly high level of Genoese trade with Sicily during 1191 has been noticed already; and it has given rise to a variety of explanations. Erik Bach, looking at the political history of Genoa, argued

---

[19] *OSM* (*1190*), no. 612. Cf. de Roover, 'Cambium Maritimum', 15–33. See 194–9 *infra*, for evidence that genuine insurance contracts were being drawn up once Genoa had abandoned Tancred for Henry of Hohenstaufen.

[20] MGH. *Const.*, I, 472–7; Clementi, *Cal.*, no. 2.

that from the start of the year the Genoese were well aware that they would be attacking Sicily, and that the merchants sent out their ships to the *Regno* ahead of the imperial fleet 'escomptant de gros profits'; but it will soon be obvious that so neat an explanation does not accord with the internal evidence of the contracts. Vito Vitale, who skimmed the surface of Guglielmo Cassinese's cartulary less thoroughly than Bach, was nevertheless nearer the truth when he said that Genoa was reluctant to commit itself to the imperial cause early in 1191.[21] Meanwhile, too, a major change in the government of the city had occurred with the appointment of the first *podestà* in Genoa, Manegold of Brescia. His reign was limited to the single year 1191, and he was assisted by eight judicial officers representing the established nobility – two of them, Bellobruno de Castello and Rolando de Carmadino, in due course commanded the war fleet sent to Naples.[22] But Manegold's aim was the reconstruction of the civic life of strife-torn Genoa, and not, apparently, a diplomatic turnabout vis-à-vis Genoa's maritime neighbours. There is no evidence that he immediately established contact with the Emperor – rather, indeed, are there signs that the Commune held back from commitment until late in the campaigning season. The presence of two *consules de placitis* as naval commanders must be taken to indicate how seriously the Genoese took their obligations once the fleet was being prepared; but it does not mean that these individuals were actually behind the move to negotiate with Henry VI.[23]

More significantly, Genoese businessmen, and northerners trading through Genoa, began to invest large sums in Sicilian trade months before Henry visited Pisa and sent letters to Genoa (in mid-February), months, too, before any decision on Genoa's alignment was made.[24]

---

[21] Bach, 67, arguing that from the start of the year the Genoese were well aware that they would be attacking Sicily – which is quite untrue; Vitale, 24.

[22] *Podestà*: *Ann. Ian.*, II, 37; Bach, 157. *Consules de placitis*: *Ann. Ian.*, II, 37–9; Olivieri, 391. For evidence that Bellobruno was investing in Sicilian trade shortly after his return from the attempted invasion, cf. Chapter 8, 196, *infra*.

[23] Thus *Ann. Ian.*, II, 41–2, states: 'bene et egregie rexit et gubernavit civitas Ianue; et consules etiam supradicti civitatis et civium negotia decenter tractaverunt'. Bach, 157–9, does not seem justified in saying that 'Manegoldus se mit tout de suite en rapports avec l'empereur', for the Genoese continued to hold back from the campaign until the last moment.

[24] Henry's visit to Pisa and his letters to Genoa are discussed in Clementi, 'Unnoticed aspects', 339–40.

Table 13. *Genoese trade, 1191, registered*
by Guglielmo Cassinese

Destination	Value (£), spring and summer	Value (£), autumn	Total value (£)
Syria	133.00	8,652.10	8,785.10
SICILY	5,351.70	2,464.00	7,815.70
Constantinople	10.00	7,486.00	7,496.00
Ceuta	2,228.10	2,443.30	4,671.40
NAPLES	3,585.90	None	3,585.90
Sardinia	839.60	2,107.40	2,947.00
Maghrib (general)	1,019.90	1,638.00	2,657.90
Bougie	1,672.70	408.70	2,081.40
Tunis	1,461.10	None	1,461.10
Catalonia	608.50	299.30	907.80
France, Midi	547.70	63.50	611.20
Pisa	None	471.80	471.80
Rome	44.00	185.00	229.00
Maremma	191.50	None	191.50
Majorca	None	43.80	43.80
Corsica	22.50	9.00	31.50
'Quo ierit'	23.30	None	23.30

Guglielmo Cassinese's register runs from the end of December 1190 to the end of April 1192, spanning the first German invasion of the *Regno* and the Genoese agreement with Henry VI. Table 13 shows the distribution of business for 1191. Such figures are not to be taken to indicate that the total pound value of Genoese trade in 1191 was necessarily very much higher than in 1190, nor that the range of markets had dramatically increased. With forty-two contracts registered for Sicily (plus twenty-two for Naples), Sicily as a whole attracted more partnerships than any other region, for only Ceuta (fifty-three) and Sardinia (fifty-two contracts) were more favoured than the island of Sicily, while if southern Italy is brought into the scales the *Regno* stands a head higher than rival destinations in terms of the number of contracts registered. But the average investment in Sicily has not greatly altered (it is £186.09 in 1191).[25] Above all, it is necessary to take into account the different character of Cassinese's cartulary. The notary drew much of his business from the Genoese middle class and from visiting northern merchants; the character of his clientèle was rather different from that of Oberto de Mercato's clientèle, though the emphasis did remain on maritime trade (whereas his contemporary Oberto de Placentia had even closer links with the merchants of Champagne and Flanders). Erik Bach went so far as to say 'dans son minutier, le groupe de Volta–Buronus–de Flexo–Mallonus brille par son absence ou joue en tout cas un rôle tout à fait effacé', but this should not be taken to indicate a decline in their fortunes.[26] The presence of an active political faction in the trade contracts of Oberto and Giovanni Scriba has made it possible to see more clearly how the ruling class regarded the Norman kingdom. Guglielmo obscures this side of the picture, but handsomely compensates in information about the structure of trade, such as the movement of alien merchants through Genoa, and the flow of cash.[27]

The spread of destinations is familiar in all respects, except in the case of Naples. To be sure, individual contracts for Naples are recorded by Oberto Scriba; these themselves may represent a fraction of the sum invested in a ship or convoy bound for Naples. But during 1191 Naples was important not solely in the commercial sphere, for the city had received King Tancred's blessing and would soon receive King Henry's battering rams. By contrast, the absence of Salerno, an ancient favourite much patronised by Giovanni Scriba's clients, is very remarkable. Salerno remained more securely under the archbishop's thumb, and a creeping commercial anaesthesia seems to have overtaken the ports on the Amalfitan side of the Sorrentine peninsula. The Amalfitans themselves had set up

[25] As against the following averages for other major ports of call:
Syria: £209.17 (42 contracts);
Constantinople: £202.59 (37);
Ceuta: £88.14 (53);
NAPLES: £162.99 (22);
Sardinia: £56.67 (52);
Bougie: £109.54 (19)
As usual, it is the very distant eastern destinations that tend to attract the greatest single investments: compare Giovanni Scriba's figures for the 1150s and 1160s.
[26] Bach, 72.
[27] For which see my Chapter 10, 255–73.

money-tables in Naples, and perhaps transferred much of their own financial business there.[28]

January 1191 was dominated by large Neapolitan investments. The earliest record is of a *societas* of 29 December 1190 (1191 *stile genovese*) in which Pietro de Silo agreed to take £524 to Naples, the property of his relatives and of other business colleagues. The latter included Giovanni Parvo de Canneto, known also as a colleague of Jean de Liège.[29] Still in December, Gionata Cavarunco and Imberto Vezastello agreed on a partnership for trade in Naples and elsewhere excluding Romania; the investment totalled £401, mostly in *societas*. Imberto added a further £150 to this sum a few days later, bringing in Odo de Melazo as third partner. Odo himself contributed a sapphire ring, valued at £2 10s 0d. Imberto's fellow sleeping partner also increased his investment, adding, with the help of Odo and his factor, £109 to an existing contract for £300; and Odo added further diversity by contributing a breast-plate for sale overseas. Imberto himself agreed to take four pieces of cloth valued at £68 4s 0d or 32 oz of tari to Naples.[30] Odo de Melazo also appears as witness to a Neapolitan *societas* of £114 9s 6d and to an *accomendacio* of £15. The factor in this *accomendacio*, like Odo, may be a Sicilian: he is Guglielmo de Meleto, perhaps Mileto in Calabria, just as Melazo may be Milazzo in Sicily.[31] On 8 January 1191 another familiar name appears, known from her investment of £10 in Naples recorded by Oberto Scriba in 1190: in 1191 the widow of Enrico Trencherio is seen sending a more substantial £100 to the same city.[32]

Although Guglielmo Cassinese offers no Neapolitan contracts from mid-January, this is not because interest in Naples evaporated. By chance a handful of folios from another notary, Guglielmo da

[28] R. Filangieri, 'Note al *Privilegium Libertatis* concesso dai Napoletani agli Amalfitani nel 1190', *Papers of the British School at Rome*, XXIV (1956), 116. Cf. Palumbo, no. 2 (iv).

[29] *G. Cass.*, I, no. 12. For Jean de Liège, *infra*, 200, 219, 255, 262, and, in this context, *G. Cass.*, I, no. 8, where Lambert de Besançon made a *societas* for Naples worth £360 with Jean de Liège and Gautier de Besançon.

[30] *G. Cass.*, I, no. 19 (damage to the MS at this point makes the text difficult to read – see *G. Cass.*, plate I); *G. Cass.*, nos. 20–2.

[31] *G. Cass.*, I, no. 36, no. 41. To be fair, Odo's Sicilian origin seems unlikely; he appears to be a resident in Genoa.

[32] *G. Cass.*, I, no. 43; cf. *OSM* (*1190*), no. 617.

Sori, survive from January 1191; these are the earliest fragments of his registers. On 15 January Pietro de Castaneto da Sori, Ado Mangiavacca and Bernardo Scutarius came together to place £20 each in a *societas* for Naples. By the standards of other notaries, this was an unusual partnership: only Bernardo was to stay at home. Moreover, the contract states that in another (lost) contract a certain Boniaudus had agreed to take a further £5 7s 6d in *accomendacio*, also apparently to Naples. So this contract probably constitutes part of a longer series of Neapolitan investments recorded by Guglielmo Cassinese's colleagues. For a merchant of Sori such as Pietro de Castaneto, the use of a notary from the same home town must have seemed very logical.[33]

Guglielmo Cassinese bears witness to a further buzz of Neapolitan activity – much of it backed by one merchant, Guglielmo Fornario – on 23 and 24 January. Fornario's wife joined a *societas* of £67 10s 0d and his son declared that he was carrying £300 from a *societas* with Ogerio Scoto, both partnerships being for trade in Naples. The same day Fornario gave his son £100 from the patrimony of his wife – presumably this accounts for the fact that the son placed £100 in the £300 deal with Ogerio Scoto, as was required under the terms of the *societas* type of contract. Also on 23 January, the son received £193 17s 0d from his father, as well as one *osbergum* (breast-plate) and two *gamberas* (greaves) for sale in Naples: further evidence for the demand for arms in Naples on the eve of the German attack.[34] Guglielmo Malfigliastro was another Genoese merchant who gave Neapolitan business heavy priority. He placed £231 in a £346 10s 0d *societas* for trade in Naples. Of this, £115 10s 0d – the remainder – came from the property of the sons of Baldezone Visconte, placed in a *societas* at the behest of the consuls. These would be the governing consuls of 1190 or, more likely, the judges of pleas (*consules de placitis*) of 1191, who would no doubt have been acting on behalf of noble orphans; and the fact that the communal officials still placed trust in Naples is striking, given that within a few months the Genoese would be participating in an attack on Campania.[35] Similarly, an *accomendacio* of £124 stands as testimony to confidence in Naples. The basic sum in this contract was swelled

---

[33] Archivio di Stato, Genoa, MS Diversorum 102, f.142r, no. 2.
[34] *G. Cass.*, I, nos. 116–19.   [35] *G. Cass.*, I, no. 123; cf. no. 124.

by a further £300 *extra accomendacionem*, of which £200 belonged to the factor Marchesio Zurlo. Another contract of the same day shows Marchesio Zurlo selling a half share in a house for £90, so he was deliberately transferring funds from property to commercial investment in Naples. Impressive too is an *accomendacio* of £481, invested by Giordano Ricerio for trade not merely in Naples but 'throughout the land of the king of Sicily as well', and to be carried by a junior member of the della Volta family.[36]

Ships and men arrived from southern Italy as well as sailed there; on 24 January Guglielmo Visconte stated he had received in *accomendacio* from Guglielmo Malfigliastro two and a quarter shares (*loca*) in a ship containing forty *loca*, which he and Ugo de Figar, apparently a Provençal, had recently sailed from Gaeta to Marseilles. On 15 February Oto *iudex de Castello* declared Rubaldo Pezulla quit of debts after Rubaldo had paid him £19 2s 9d, the proceeds of an *accomendacio* of one and a half *loca* in a ship, drawn up between them in Naples and valued at 8½ oz of tari. And, to join the ranks of Gaetans in Genoa, there is clear evidence that Salernitan merchants continued to travel north to Liguria for business. Two of them came before Guglielmo Cassinese on 8 January 1191 in order to form a *societas* for business within Genoa – the only mention of Salerno in Guglielmo's cartulary, and rather upside-down, at that.[37]

The last few days of January and the first two weeks of February saw only a little more Neapolitan trade – a £60 *societas* on 26 January, a £2 *accomendacio* on 14 February. After that, the sequence of contracts for trade in the mainland part of the *Regno* came to an abrupt halt. The latest German moves help to explain why. Some time after 12 February 1191, William, archbishop-elect of Ravenna, and Arnaldo Stricto of Piacenza arrived in Genoa, sent by Henry to negotiate an alliance between the Hohenstaufen and the Commune. They brought letters addressed to the *podestà*, Manegold, which no doubt offered Genoa a renewal of the lapsed agreement with Barbarossa.[38] During early spring the Genoese made

---

[36] *G. Cass.*, I, nos. 134–7 (Zurlo); no. 138 (Ricerio). For Giordano Ricerio's involvement in an insurance agreement, see Chapter 10, 197–8.

[37] *G. Cass.*, I, no. 124, no. 217, no. 47.

[38] *Ann. Ian.*, II, 38; Clementi, 'Unnoticed aspects', 340 and n. 2.

no obvious attempt to come to terms, but by now they had some idea of Henry's proposed time-table, and they could see that further investment in Naples might collide with the promised invasion of Campania. However, there are no signs that the ships in which so many businessmen had placed such trust failed to sail. Very few of the contracts for Naples are uncancelled, nor do the factors engaged for trade in Naples reappear later in the season in other Genoese contracts. It is clear, then, that the Naples convoy sailed early in the spring – say, in the first days of March at latest – while the German king's ambassadors reached the Republic at about the same time. Doubtless their failure to come to a rapid agreement with Genoa was as much the result of Genoese concern for the sons of the Republic, and for the sums of money in Naples, as it was the result of pique at the fact that Henry had merely sent ambassadors to Genoa, but had gone in person to Pisa.[39] By mid-March news must have arrived of the Pisan accord with Henry VI. Despite all this, interest in the commerce of the *Regno* did not evaporate; it was merely displaced, moving from Naples to Sicily. Before the end of February, commercial interest in the island of Sicily had been limited: £35 early in January, and possibly a further £40 from the same investor; and one large placement of £210 in Sicilian trade, dated 7 January.[40]

Otherwise, the series of Sicilian contracts does not begin to flow until the last day of February. Giovanni Usura joined a £300 *societas* that day with Ruggero Noxenzio and Giovanni Mazamorro, and a second *societas* the same day, worth £108, with Guglielmo Ponzio. On 13 March Ruggero Noxenzio and Giovanni Mazamorro joined a further *societas*, of £112 10s 0d, with a second factor; still unsatisfied, Ruggero placed £150 with a third factor, Guido Bonaventura, on 20 March. Guido was to take Ruggero's pounds and £75 of his own to Sicily and beyond – specifically to Syria, for in a codicil Ruggero provided £186 extra in *accomendacio*, of which £20 may be given over to 'the service of God and of Outremer', that is, the Anglo-French crusade. So too did Guido receive sums of £57 4s 3d from Guglielmo Barbavaira, £35 from Amico 'the

---

[39] Pique was Clementi's explanation – 'Unnoticed aspects', 339–40 – but the notarial evidence sheds further light.
[40] *G. Cass.*, I, no. 30, no. 29 (probably for Sicily to judge from no. 30), no. 38.

draper', and £18 6s 7d from one of the de Castello family, for trade in Sicily and the Near East.[41] Another persistent merchant with Sicilian interests was Ogerio Scoto, who added £28 to a *societas* totalling £238 that Ogerio Porco was to take to Sicily, and sent £200 in *accomendacio* to Sicily with Rubaldo Detesalvo. Ogerio Porco had a number of backers apart from Ogerio Scoto; and a relative of the latter, Balduino Scoto, placed £300 in a £450 *societas* with Rubaldo Detesalvo. The chain extends further, for Balduino helped finance Rubaldo's contribution to the *societas*, by giving him £96 out of £150 as dowry for his daughter, whom Rubaldo had married. This group of contracts emphasises two stages in the career of Genoese travelling merchants. Ogerio Porco appears as an experienced factor, who collects *societates* and builds his new partnerships on the residue of older ones – the source of much of the £238 total lay in the balance of old *societates*. But in Rubaldo Detesalvo is epitomised the group of less experienced factors who drew for financial support not on accumulated profits but on relatives and fathers-in-law.[42]

In truth Naples is mentioned as well in the March contracts, but not in the context of the February convoy. The city is mentioned more as a geographical limit than as a port of call in its own right. On 16 March Urso de Arenzano took £48 in *societas* 'a Ianua usque ad Montempessulanum et usque ad Napolim'. This does not necessarily mean a journey to Naples via Montpellier, though that was the longest possible voyage permitted by the partnership agreement; rather is the contract a licence to trade in the entire region between these ports – Provence, Liguria, Tuscany, the Maremma, Campania, and possibly Corsica or Sardinia too. Indeed, Urso's backers had explicit interests in Rome the same season; and on 20 March another 'de Arenzano' was sent similarly 'from Genoa as far as Montpellier and as far as Naples'. A contract of 15 March does, however, suggest that in other merchants' eyes the Tyrrhenian Sea was still relatively untroubled: it is a £29 *societas* for trade in the Maremma 'and as far as Sicily', which could, obviously, include Campania too if the factor judged this appropriate.[43]

[41] *G. Cass.*, I, nos. 248–9, no. 286, no. 320, no. 322.
[42] *G. Cass.*, I, no. 316, nos. 327–9.
[43] *G. Cass.*, I, no. 307, no. 330, no. 319, no. 296.

Towards the end of March the merchants began specifically to mention Palermo, which does not appear in the late winter registrations. On 29 March £8 6s 0d was sent to Palermo and beyond. The same day a number of business partners came together to regulate their outstanding contracts, some of which concerned Palermo or Sicily in general. Enrico Detesalvo declared he had £231 and Pietro da Porta £155½, the basis of a *societas* between them. Enrico also placed £209 'ultra societatem' with Pietro. Of all this, Pietro was to carry £354 16s 10d to Palermo, and Enrico was to conserve the remainder in Genoa along with the balance of his other *societates* (£82); he would invest a further £40 in a venture to Bougie.[44] Such diversification characterised other Genoese merchants: Ansuisso de Sancto Genesio sent £150 with Giacomo Bonbello to Ceuta, while he himself agreed to travel to Sicily with £100 belonging to Angeloto de Caffara. Meanwhile Odo de Melazo placed £100 in a voyage to Ceuta, the Maghrib and Spain.[45] Do all these multiple investments indicate a desire to protect funds by parcelling them out, sending part to Sicily and part to Africa, or do they indicate a degree of optimism, a belief that during 1191 Sicilian markets would remain available for exploitation jointly with those of the west Mediterranean? An answer is perhaps suggested by two further contracts, dated 20 and 24 April, for trade either in Sicily or in Barbary ('vel in Barbariam'). Since the journey to Barbary (or Tripolitania) involved passage through Sicilian waters, this contract must be taken to mean that the partners were to be guided by financial, not political, considerations. If commercial prospects in Sicily were unfavourable, they would transfer their interests to Africa. Admittedly, a document of 4 May, showing a merchant of Rapallo investing solely in Barbary, could mean that ships bound for Sicily and Barbary were now being directed solely to the latter, but even so a passage through Sicilian waters seems likely.[46]

A contract of £5 4s 0d of 23 April concludes the concentrated series of Sicilian spring contracts. Though contracts survive from May 1191 as well, the evidence is complicated by the decision of

---

[44] *G. Cass.*, I, no. 383, no. 386, no. 387 (Bougie).
[45] *G. Cass.*, I, nos. 425–6; cf. no. 422; no. 460.
[46] *G. Cass.*, I, no. 482, no. 502, no. 548 (Barbary). Cf. I, no. 580 (Tripoli), no. 581 (Barbary), no. 601.

the Commune of Genoa to reopen negotiations with Henry VI. An exact time-table of moves cannot be drawn up. The same month that Henry's army crossed the frontiers of the *Regno* and approached Naples, the envoys of Genoa arrived in his presence.[47] It is, however, unclear when they left their home city or, more to the point, when the *podestà* decided to abandon Tancred for Henry. Arguably the Genoese had banked on the forecast that Henry would never manage to depart on his mission of conquest according to the announced schedule – as had been the case with Barbarossa; and they had banked too on the probable failure of Henry ever to conquer Sicily. But, once Henry had made initial minatory moves against Tancred, the Genoese hurried to adopt their reserve plan: far from banking on probable failure, they would now cash in on possible success. Yet the contracts continued to be registered, with interesting flavours. For 9 May an *accomendacio* of £150 15s 0d is recorded, aimed at Sicily and beyond. On 3 May Guido da Lodi stated that he held in *accomendacio* from Guglielmo and Simone Malocello seven shares (*loca*) in a ship, which Ansaldo Malocello had taken with other items to Naples – the past tense, 'portavit', suggests that Ansaldo had left for Naples that spring at the very latest. The value of these *loca* was £13 6s 8d; and Guido was to be allowed to travel with a further £20 of his own, making a grand total of £113 odd. For accounting purposes this was to be reckoned at an exchange rate of 3⅓ bezants per pound Genoese in Syria; 'and if he should not go to *Ultramare*, in Sicily he shall receive...for every 40 solidi, one ounce of gold'. This seems to have been a credit transaction, according to which Guido provided the ready cash against the security of the *loca* taken by Ansaldo Malocello to Naples. As the price of his credit, he was offered by Guglielmo and Simone a very favourable exchange rate against the Sicilian tari. Thus there is no direct proof that Guido would visit Naples nor, indeed, that the ship was still there, but the contract certainly suggests a recent ship sale in Naples or the *Regno* in general.[48]

On 10 May Bonadu di San Damiano received £127 in *societas*

---

[47] Contract of 23 April: G. *Cass.*, I, no. 495. Henry VI: Clementi, 'Unnoticed aspects', 340; *Ann. Ian.*, II, 38. A further account of the attack on Naples is provided by Pietro da Eboli, *Liber ad honorem Augusti*, ed. G. B. Siragusa (FSI; Rome, 1905), and ed. E. Rota (RISS, ser. 2, XXXI, part 1), lines 306–77.

[48] G. *Cass.*, I, no. 546, and Chiaudano, 'Contratti commerciali', no. 65, no. xvi.

from Oliviero Marzoco, £127 from Baiamonte Barlaira, and contributed £127 of his own. He was to take this money to Tripoli in Africa, thence if he wished to Sicily and from Sicily anywhere except enemy Egypt. Other individuals added a further £84. So it seems that discretion extended as far as Egypt, but not as near as Sicily.[49] The common characteristic of the May contracts, excluding the straightforward partnership of 9 May, is the lessening of emphasis on Sicily itself. This was achieved either by diversion, as perhaps in the Barbary contracts, or by addition – the mention of further or alternative destinations. Against this, there is the simple fact that the spring convoys to Sicily had probably departed before mid-May: these are stray contracts in any case.

V

On 30 May, 1191, outside Naples, the Emperor Henry VI granted to the Commune of Genoa, represented by its envoys, a renewal and extension of Barbarossa's privilege of nearly thirty years earlier. The policy of the Commune towards the *Regno* had come full circle, the more so as Henry's grant added little to his father's, apart from some minor concessions of rights in Liguria and the German empire. As far as Sicily was concerned, there was no change; even the reference to Count Simon's lands in Sicily was preserved. Otherwise, the names of Tancred, the *podestà* and certain Ligurian barons were simply substituted for out-of-date names.[50]

As often, the climate of the *Regno* struck its invaders before ever they could entrench themselves. Before Genoese naval aid arrived in the kingdom, in the second half of August, the German army had withdrawn from the Phlegrean fields and retreated north. Tancred's admiral Margarito was blockading the Pisan fleet in the mouth of the Volturno River as the Genoese sailed south, and the Ligurians were unable to do more than parade in the Bay of Naples and to overrun Ischia.[51] The Emperor wrote to the Genoese at Civita-

[49] G. *Cass.*, I, no. 601; cf. Vitale, 25. 9 May saw a £150 15s od contract for Sicily: G. *Cass.*, I, no. 576.

[50] *CDG*, III, 4–12; MGH. *Const.*, 479–83; cf. Clementi, Cal., no. 7. Material results of the agreement are evinced in *CDG*, III, 17–18, the cession of Monaco to Genoa as an imperial fief.

[51] *Ann. Ian.*, II, 39–40; Clementi, 'Unnoticed aspects', 340–3, providing a detailed account of the Genoese campaign in Sicilian waters.

vecchia giving them permission to return home; the treaty was to be held in abeyance until better prospects arose another year.[52] Henry for his part well knew from his recent experiences that, unless both Pisa and Genoa provided full naval support, his hope of striking at the cities of the *Regno* was vain. By reason of lengthy delays, as Genoa negotiated its terms and fitted its fleet, Henry's failure on land had been mirrored by a poor showing at sea. So he promised Genoa that he would come to the city in person to arrange the next stage in the campaign, and in November he passed via Pisa to Genoa full of martial resolve. Arguably, this was one of the few promises he made to Genoa that he ever found it worthwhile to keep.

[52] *Ann. Ian.*, II, 41; Clementi, *Cal.*, no. 15. For an examination of Venetian attitudes to Henry VI between 1189 and 1197, see 204 *infra*.

Chapter 8

'QUID PLURA?' 1191–5

I

After the Genoese agreement with Henry VI interest in trade with Sicily evaporated. The contracts concerned with Sicily that survive from the summer of 1191 look back to a period when trade prospects were good; they do not look forward to future financial ventures aimed at the *Regno*. On 30 June 1191 the Lucchese merchant Buonesegno, son of Amigueto, received back £67 that he had invested on an earlier occasion in a partnership aimed at Sicily. It seems that the planned expedition never departed, and so Buonesegno recalled his investment. On 11 September three Genoese, Ugone Busca, Vassallo Straleira and Giovanni Grita, came together to reapportion capital and profits following an expedition to Sicily which seems to have ended in financial disarray.[1] From late August onwards, factors sent earlier to Sicily and Tunis appeared before Guglielmo Cassinese to have their partnerships augmented by further investment; but, significantly, they were now bound for east Mediterranean destinations.[2]

As early as 25 August 1191 Giovanni Mazatorta had announced his intention of travelling to Sicily that coming winter, and had received £2 on loan, promising to repay 50s. In the loan contract Mazatorta refers to the 'maiori parte rerum navium euntis et venientis'; whether by this he meant a primarily military expedition, planned as a reinforcement of existing Genoese forces, or a primarily financial expedition, is not clear.[3] It was not until late September, with news of Henry VI's withdrawal, that hopes of trade in Sicily were renewed. Balduino Scoto received £19 2s 0d on loan

---

[1] *G. Cass.*, I, no. 792, no. 976 (fragment preserved in *Notai Ignoti*, Busta 1, and not in Cart. 6).

[2] *G. Cass.*, I, no. 905, no. 906, no. 1,109 (Odo de Melazo and others).

[3] *G. Cass.*, I, no. 907.

from Ogerio Porco, promising to return him 2¾ hyperpers of Constantinople per pound Genoese, or 'if they [the merchants as a whole] put in at a port in Sicily, one ounce of gold for every 42s'. There was also an option of visiting Syria. Some were less sure that Sicily had anything to offer. Odo de Melazo and Gionata Cavarunco, old investors in Sicily, turned their attention to the Maghrib and the east Mediterranean.[4] There was no knowing whether funds and merchandise sent to the *Regno* would be secure from seizure. On 12 January 1192, Guglielmo Scarpa stood before witnesses to declare that there were 1¼ oz of gold belonging to a certain Germano among the goods owned by himself and his backers that had been seized by Tancred, King of Sicily; Scarpa promised to return this sum to Germano if he managed to recover everything that had been confiscated. The seizure of goods can, therefore, be dated some time during 1191.[5]

Not surprisingly, several merchants decide to enter into insurance contracts, in the hope of protecting visitors to Sicily and their merchandise from the royal wrath. On 27 September 1191 Nicola Lecanoce, or Leccanuptias, known as *rector* in 1196 and judge of pleas in 1202, promised to guarantee the safety of Guillaume de Beders, who was apparently a French, Flemish or Provençal colleague in trade. Guillaume's person, Guillaume's property, and property entrusted to him were guaranteed by Nicola against damage 'a domino rege Trancherio Sicilie, et ab omni homine sui districtus'; 'and should he receive any damage to his person or his goods from the lord king or his court or from anyone from his lands, Nicola promises to make full restitution, either directly or through his heirs'. Similarly, should Guillaume have to pay taxes above those normally accorded the Genoese in the days when they were at peace with Sicily ('si ei foret ablatum pro dricto terre ultra consuetum ultra quam solitum est recipere ab Ianuensi in pace olim'), then too Nicola would make appropriate restitution. Interestingly, this does suggest that non-Genoese merchants trading through Genoa were able to claim the same reductions in taxes as their Ligurian patrons. Should Guillaume decide to remain in Sicily longer than Nicola wished to stay there himself, Guillaume must

4 *G. Cass.*, II, no. 1,134; cf. I, no. 905.
5 *G. Cass.*, II, no. 1,485.

obtain from the king a *cartam securitatis* stating that he and his possessions would be safe – such *cartae* are well attested over a hundred
years later, when the Peruzzi of Florence were given special trading
rights by the Aragonese kings of Sicily, even though Florence gave
its political support to the Angevins of Naples. This insurance contract is followed by an uncancelled act in which Nicola is seen promising to lend ('prestare', a rare word) Guillaume de Beders the
hefty sum of £400, to be taken to Sicily. Guillaume replied by
promising to repay Nicola 1 oz of gold tari for every 35s, either in
Messina or in Palermo. This exchange rate was to be altered to 40s
for the ounce should those ships at present bound for Constantinople
or Syria put in at Palermo or Messina – a reference, it seems, to the
vessels that Odo de Melazo and others were so extensively patronis-
ing.[6] It has been seen that Balduino Scoto promised a rate of 1 oz
for 42s should these ships go to Sicily. The variation in rates, both
within Nicola's contract and between Nicola's and Balduino's, is
revealing. It seems that Nicola believed that the more Genoese there
were in port, the more the price of gold would rise. Conversely, if
the eastern-bound ships did not make for Sicilian ports, Nicola's
agent would have a much freer hand in the bullion market. Nicola
was, then, banking on the existence of a recession in Sicilian trade,
or on the existence of a buyer's market. It was precisely because
Sicily was not a favoured destination that Nicola hoped to draw
especial profits from business there.

Nicola was to travel to Sicily as well as, if not necessarily with, his
partner Guillaume, and to be repaid in gold in the Sicilian ports.
Other investors expected repayment in Genoa, not in gold of Sicily
but in silver of their own city. On 9 October 1191 Guillaume agreed
to take £100 in *accomendacio* to Sicily 'et per terram regis', on behalf
of Raimondo Unaldo. Moreover, Raimondo sent seven and a half
pieces of scarlet cloth, priced at £151 13s 0d; the profit or loss on

---

[6] G. *Cass.*, II, nos. 1,144–5. Nicola Lecanoce: *Ann. Ian.*, II, 60, 82; also 210 *infra*,
for his activities in Sicily on 1 January 1195. See also A. Lattes, 'L'Assicurazione
e la voce "securare" in documenti genovesi del 1191 e 1192', *Rivista del diritto
commerciale e del diritto generale delle obbligazioni*, xxv (1927), 64–73; G. P. Bognetti,
Note per la storia del passaporto e del salvacondotto (Pavia, 1933), 353; Vitale, 'Relazioni commerciali', 25–6; Vitale, 'Genova ed Enrico VI', 92–4; also, *ASLSP*,
IV, 224. For Florentine *cartae securitatis*, C. Trasselli, 'Nuovi documenti sui Peruzzi,
Bardi e Acciaiuoli in Sicilia', *Economia e Storia*, III (1956), 188–9.

this was to be calculated in Genoese money, at the rate of 35s per ounce of gold in the instance of loss.[7] Nicola too had his backers: the same day Bellobruno de Castello entered into a *societas* with him, composed of £300 of Nicola's money and £605 invested by Bellobruno. Of the latter sum, £200 came from an earlier *societas* with a third individual, Guglielmo Figal, who assented to its use on this venture. Bellobruno was *consul pro iustitiis*, judge of pleas, in 1191; indeed, he had recently returned from the waters of the *Regno*, for he and Rolando de Carmadino had jointly commanded the fleet of thirty-three galleys sent to aid Henry VI's invasion. This change of attitude to Sicily seems to provide the clearest indication that, in the eyes of the Genoese patriciate, the invasion of 1191 had only been an interlude in their continuing commercial activities in the *Regno*.[8]

Later, on 9 October, Guillaume received £600 on loan from Nicola Lecanoce; Nicola thereby fulfilled his promise of 27 September that he would lend Guillaume £400, augmenting that sum substantially as a result of his success in finding further backers of his own. On this occasion Guillaume promised to repay his partner 1 oz of tari for every 35s 6d invested, within forty days of the arrival of Guillaume and Nicola in Palermo or Messina (the same clause is inserted stipulating a higher rate of *solidi* should the long-distance ships arrive). At 1 oz per 35s 6d, this would signify a total repayment of 338⅓ oz, or a little over 21 pounds of Sicilian gold. But, in fact, direct repayment was not necessarily envisaged. Guillaume entrusted to Nicola, as warrant for his intention to repay, a large quantity of expensive northern cloths: three pieces of the green cloth of Ghent, six pieces of brown cloth of Ypres, and other green, red and brown cloths of Le Mans and Flanders, as well as one 'Stanfort' cloth from Flanders or England. All this was to be carried to Sicily by Nicola; he was to sell sufficient of these items to compensate for any failure by Guillaume to repay him at the rate stipulated in the loan. The final section of the agreement is that which reveals the underlying truth: 'and what shall be left over, he promises to return to Guillaume, in such a way, however, that Nicola must have handed back this guarantee in merchandise (*pig-*

---

[7] *G. Cass.*, II, no. 1,201.
[8] *G. Cass.*, II, no. 1,202; *Ann. Ian.*, II, 39.

nus), both in order that it may be sold and in order to make the said repayment'.[9] There was, of course, little point in carrying cloth to Sicily without the intention of selling it; and hopes for selling it must have been very high when imports of northern products had probably fallen rather low. These were, in any case, luxury manufactures of top quality. Fifty-nine items are mentioned in the contract; an average sale price of £10 per item – a very crude average, considering variations in size, quantity and quality – does not seem ridiculous. Unaldo's cloth, sent with Guillaume de Beders, averaged about £20 an item.[10] On the basis of Unaldo's agreement, as well as those between Nicola and Guillaume, a joint venture in cloths and money, valued at £1,450, is indicated – a massive investment considering that the travelling partners ran especial risks of capture of goods and persons, and considering that the tax exemptions of the Genoese in Sicily were now, as Nicola conceded, very much in doubt. The later fortunes of Nicola and Guillaume cannot be traced from Cassinese's cartulary; but evidence to be reviewed shortly will show that Lecanoce, like Bellobruno de Castello, played a double game, for in 1195 Nicola Lecanoce is found in Sicily helping the Genoese Commune to pay war expenses incurred during the conquest of the *Regno*.

Certain other connections resurface in a document of 7 March 1192, drawn up by Guglielmo Cassinese. Guglielmo Barca declared he had received a loan of £800 from Giordano Ricerio, in return for which he promised to give Raimondo Unaldo 410¼ oz of tari 'free of all tax'; this was to be paid within two months of their arrival in Messina or Palermo, at the ounce-weight of either city – given, as usual, the safe arrival of the ship (*'nave'*, singular) bound for Sicily. Guglielmo Barca placed as security – apparently in Genoa – goods and money to the value of £900. 'Moreover he [Barca] promises to make safe (*securare*) Raimondo and the said £800 from the lord king of Sicily and from all men of his district, both on the way out and on the way back, other than from pirates and robbers. And if the king or anyone from his district should make any seizure, Guglielmo Barca promises to restore all the damage, subject to the penalty of otherwise paying double [that is, the standard penalty].

9 *G. Cass.*, II, no. 1,203.
10 *G. Cass.*, II, no. 1,201.

And if a pirate or robber shall take away from him the said goods, or part thereof, with any of the goods of Guglielmo Barca, and Barca shall recover some of his own property, he promises to restore to him [Ricerio] proportionately (per libram)' part of Unaldo's property – by which is meant that he will restore to Ricerio the same proportion of Ricerio's goods as he has recovered of his own goods, whether or not an equal proportion of Ricerio's goods has also been recovered. This guarded Ricerio from the possibility that, in the event of loss, Barca would concentrate entirely on the recovery of his own merchandise. In addition Barca promised to pay Ricerio 50s per ounce remaining, should he have returned to Genoa without handing Raimondo his due. He promised too to provide food both for Raimondo and his servant until the money had been paid. Finally, Nicoloso de Oria, or Doria, promised to serve as proxy for Guglielmo Barca, by taking responsibility for up to half the sum named – that is, £400 – since this share of the total had been placed by him with Barca.[11]

Here there appears to be a disparity between the rate of repayment in Sicily, 1 oz of gold per 39s, and that in Genoa, 1 oz of gold being quoted at 50s. That, of course, would make sense both in the context of the imposition of a penalty on a dilatory Barca; and it would allow for the fact that Barca, but not Unaldo, had been able to use the money for trade in Sicily, and draw further profits from it. In many respects, however, the similarity between this and the earlier insurance contract of Nicola Lecanoce is very striking; here, too, there is £900 worth of goods in *pignus* as guarantee, and here too it may have been expected that Unaldo would indeed sell these goods or part of them, in Sicily, and that repayment would only be demanded to compensate for the failure of these goods to fetch an adequate price. Unaldo has, of course, been seen as a backer who stayed behind in Genoa; and to find that, five months later, he was preparing to travel or had already travelled to Sicily suggests the extent of his commercial interests in the *Regno*. Whoever he may have been, his close links with the Ricerio and Doria families suggest he had good connections either by business or by birth.

The Lecanoce–Beders and Ricerio–Barca contracts are of interest for other reasons than the attitudes to King Tancred that they dis-

11 *G. Cass.*, II, no. 1,701; Lattes, 65–9.

play. The use of insurance techniques, however simple, had long been concealed in the way that risks were apportioned in commercial contracts. If the factor lost goods or money 'honestly', through no fault of his own, the backer would normally have to bear the loss; but if the factor failed to fulfil his legal obligations, the *pena dupli* or other forms of distraint could be brought into play. The issue of specific insurance contracts is, however, a novelty – so far as the evidence allows it to be seen. There seems to have been no premium involved; the insuring party would hope to make a profit from the commercial employment of the funds entrusted to him. Many points are unclear in these texts; but one point can confidently be made. The need to continue to trade in Sicily and to purchase its produce, even in the face of King Tancred's hostility, led to further developments in the range of commercial techniques and services available in Genoa. Where peace prevailed, the Commune would press for privileges of protection and of tax exemption; and the protection promised by the Sicilian crown, with the judicial machinery thereby established, would provide sufficient guarantee of security to Genoese merchants trading in the *Regno*. Conversely, the withdrawal of privileges, or the threat of withdrawal, led merchants to formulate private pacts of protection, since the need for safe access became all the greater as the lack of privileges was made plain.[12]

Very large sums needed to be insured all the more; contracts for middling and low amounts of money continued to be registered without such complex controls being stipulated. On 23 January 1192 Oto *iudex* agreed to take £36 in *accomendacio* not merely to Sicily but to the *Principatum*, to Campania; thus danger was thought to have receded with the failure of Henry's invasion plans, and even southern Italy was considered a viable destination.[13] However, no

---

[12] Bognetti, *Passaporto e salvacondotto*, 353, emphasised the significance of these documents as early examples of the *laisser-passer*; but Lattes, 71–3, laid greater stress on their rôle in the development of insurance techniques – without, however, arguing that they were straightforward insurance contracts. His view that they must be seen in the light of the maritime loans they mention, and that they are midway between insurance contracts and loan agreements, seems confirmed by the way in which earlier Genoese contracts took care to apportion blame in the event of loss or carelessness. Thus prior to 1191 insurance was limited in scale and entirely dependent on the nature of the trade partnership negotiated; but it was not nonexistent.   [13] *G. Cass.*, II, no. 1,511.

other contracts for south Italian destinations are available from 1192. More significant still of the recovery of Sicilian trade, from the Genoese angle at least, is a group of contracts that show specialists in the *Regno* known from 1191 and earlier resuming their Sicilian investments. On 3 March 1192, Jean de Liège and Gautier and Lambert de Besançon together committed £250 10s 0d to trade in Sicily and wherever next the factor might choose to go. The same factor, Giacomo de Bombel – perhaps a relative of the banker Giovanni Bonbello – also received shares in three ships and, rather strangely, a *carrico grani*, for carriage to the 'terram Regis Sicilie', a phrase which could suggest a south Italian halt. The value of these items was £280, and his backer was Lanfranco Ricerio, a relative of Guglielmo Barca's backer. From the *Regno* he was to travel to Marseilles, or alternatively to Nice, to continue business there. Indeed, it is stated that he had already formed an earlier partnership with Lanfranco Ricerio, which had been drawn up at Marseilles; subsequently the Pisans had seized some of his goods, and the earlier contract was now cancelled. On 4 March Jean de Liège engaged another factor, Giovanni Guercio, to take £152 10s 0d to Sicily, and Gautier de Besançon entered a further *societas* with Giovanni, worth £300. Giovanni Boleto and Bonovassallo of Cartagena, in Spain, sent £150 to 'Siciliam terram regis' and beyond, on behalf of the wealthy financier Ansuisso de Sancto Genesio.[14]

Investment in Sicily continued to gather pace in March. Enrico Mazala promised to take £166, the property of Ugone Fornario, to Sicily. Several other contracts were drawn up on his behalf for unstated destinations, which must clearly have included Sicily. From Bonogiovanni di Caffaro he received £50; Amico the draper and two colleagues sent two cloths with him, priced at £33 15s 0d in all; from a merchant of Savona he received £20; from Giovanni di Marino, £35 16s 0d.[15] Guglielmo Rataldo sent £43 12s 0d to Sicily with the experienced factor Ogerio di San Lorenzo; Ruggero Noxenzio sent £63 7s 0d with Ogerio; Michele Vozicanto entrusted

[14] *G. Cass.*, II, no. 1,659, no. 1,668, no. 1,659 (cf. also no. 1,667); no. 1,672, no. 1,674, no. 1,676. That the *carrico grani* contained the red dye called *grana* rather than wheat or barley seems confirmed by *G. Cass.*, II, no. 1,700, where one Lucchese merchant agrees with another to take 8½ *centenarii* of Spanish *grana* to their home city.

[15] *G. Cass.*, II, no. 1,710; also no. 1,708, no. 1,709, no. 1,711, no. 1,712.

to him a breast-plate valued at £7 12s 0d. And Paxio of Lucca placed
£213 in his hands, in the form of textiles; these were part of a consignment worth £426 that was owned by Paxio of Lucca, Ansaldo
Buferio and a second factor, Matteo, son of Trancherio de Platea
Longa, in proportions of one-half, one-third and one-sixth. Matteo's
contract with Ansaldo is, in fact, slightly more specific: Matteo was
to call at Messina, not simply in 'Sicily' in general. Meanwhile
Paxio sent a further three pieces of green cloth to Sicily for sale
there ('causa vendendi in Siciliam'); Ogerio promised to refund
22½ oz of tari, against the estimated value of £42. Marchesio della
Volta sent £66 in *accomendacio*, again employing Ogerio as his
factor. Ogerio was to work '*gratis*': for some reason no profit was
promised him. Michele Bergognono, however, promised Ogerio
the normal quarter share of the profit if he would take belts
(*cincturis*) to Sicily on his behalf; these, which were no doubt for
military use, were valued at £4. On 20 March Ogerio and Ruggero
Noxenzio added a further £8 to their pre-existing contract worth
£63 7s 0d.[16]

Particularly important this year were the activities of non-Genoese
merchants trading with Sicily. Paxio of Lucca and Jean de Liège
have been encountered already. Lesser names, however, also appear;
and the employment of non-Genoese factors, as well as the existence
of non-Genoese backers, may be significant. A Lucchese merchant,
Bodono, took one piece of scarlet cloth of Lyons and one piece of
red cloth of Lucca to Sicily on behalf of another Lucchese, Corso
Raimondino of Lucca. The price of these items is given in Lucchese
denarii, as £35½ of Lucca; moreover, Bodono was given the choice
of returning from Sicily either to Genoa or to Lucca. The money
men of Asti are found too. On 4 February 1192 Rolando Calcagno
of Asti stated that he was carrying a quantity of cloth to Sicily on
behalf of the Genoese Rufino de Canneto and of the dyer Widoto.
The textiles included cloth of Ypres, Lyons and Maastricht, for sale
in Sicily for an estimated 149 oz of tari, that is, over 9 pounds of
gold.[17] In view of the difficulties they had been encountering in

[16] G. *Cass.*, II, no. 1,692, no. 1,713, no. 1,722, no. 1,723 and no. 1,721, no. 1,724,
no. 1,725, no. 1,726, no. 1,770. See also II, no. 1,757, a £600 partnership for trade
in Sicily, invested by Enrico Alfer (£200), Belardo Belardengo (£240), Giacomo
di Cortemiglia and Pietro de Rodei (£140 together).
[17] G. *Cass.*, II, no. 1,753, no. 1,565.

Sicily, with seizure of goods and, possibly, loss of tax rights, the Genoese took more interest in the employment of non-Ligurian factors; even so, Guillaume de Beders, a non-Genoese, had still required insurance cover. Of course, the Genoese also had access to information about Henry VI's future invasion plans; their awareness that no immediate invasion was possible may have encouraged investment in their old Sicilian trading bases. Naples, however, may have seemed too exposed to merit concentrated attention; and the north Italians may not have been very popular in those towns that had been within sight of the German army and of the north Italian fleets. In addition, the probable depression of Sicilian economic activity during the invasion months may have prompted a rush by the Genoese to fulfil anticipated demand during 1192. And, finally, the Genoese did not want to lose any further ground in Sicily – they did not want the King of Sicily to conclude that they had withdrawn all their Sicilian interests, and to favour their rivals; by continuing to invest the Genoese might appear to be remaining friendly. Indeed, some Genoese came to suspect that Tancred secretly favoured the Pisans; but the feeling in Pisa may well have been that he favoured the Genoese.[18] The intensity of rivalry distorted political judgement. It is possible, in fact, that Genoese slowness to act in accordance with Henry's invasion plans was a considered ploy, by which Genoa hoped to demonstrate that it had been coerced into the invasion against its will. In the presence of German emissaries the Genoese could insist that they had fulfilled their promise to send aid; while in the presence of Sicilian officials they could argue that they had been of no strategic use in Henry's campaign, and had deliberately tried to ensure that his successes were not pressed too far.

II

Ample evidence survives to show that the Venetians continued to visit the *Regno* for commercial purposes during Tancred's reign; less well documented is the rôle of the *Regno* in Venetian diplomacy. In 1187 a Venetian *rapprochement* with Constantinople indicated how fully the Republic's fears over Norman domination of the Adriatic had been reawakened, after the assault on Thessalonika

[18] *Ann. Ian.*, II, 50.

and the submission of Ragusa to the Sicilian crown. On the other hand, Tancred maintained a friendly attitude to the Greeks, despite his earlier career as admiral in the fleet sent to Thessalonika and beyond.[19] These varied strands are brought together in a contract of October 1189, in which Leonardo de Bocasso is found making a *collegancia* in Constantinople with Filippo d'Albiola. Leonardo placed 72 hyperpers of old gold against Filippo's 36; the total was to be taken by Filippo in the ship of Samaricus 'Longobardus' to Apulia, or to Ancona, and thence back to Constantinople. This agreement is, in fact, known only from a quittance drawn up by Giovanni Barastro and Filippo d'Albiola at Venice in July 1192. Leonardo, although a Venetian, was a 'habitator in Constantino-poli', and he deputed Barastro to quit Filippo of further obligation and to collect his share of the profits. The *collegancia* of Filippo and Leonardo stands in several ways as testimony to the Italian carrying-trade between Constantinople and southern Italy. First, there is the route prescribed, with its insistence that the factor return to Con-stantinople even before he has reached Venice; secondly, there is the description of the ship's master as 'Longobardus', commonly an epithet for south Italian Latins.[20]

From Venice, too, merchants set out for destinations in the *Regno*. In March 1190, Pietro Tiepolo and Marco Tiepolo agreed to form a *collegancia* worth £150; Pietro's son Giacomo was to carry this sum from Venice 'to Messina as well as overseas beyond the *Regno*'. In November 1190, Domenico Corner received £374 from his brother-in-law Michele Simitecolo, to be taken to Apulia and thence where he chose by sea and by land. The same month Domenico Corner sent £150 jointly with Andrea Donato to Apulia for trade there; the quittance, which is all that survives, is dated April 1191, indicating that Andrea was only away for a single winter season. And in June 1192 Giovanni, son of Romano Mairano, took a similar sum in *collegancia* to Apulia, 'in such a way that you must not stop anywhere else'. Giovanni was back very soon indeed: the quittance that survives is dated September of the same year. Thus both nobly born Venetians, such as the Tiepolo and Corner investors, and the wealthy middle class, such as Mairano,

---

[19] Tafel-Thomas, I, 179–203; Brand, 190; Scarlata, *Atti CISSN*, 488; Abulafia, 'Dalmatian Ragusa', 422–3.   [20] *DCV*, I, no. 409.

continued to place money in south Italian and Sicilian trade even during the critical years of Henry VI's first assault on the *Regno*.[21]

Nor did Venice suffer for its neutrality. In January 1195 Henry VI confirmed Venetian rights over the church of San Marco in Palermo; this church remained very active in the 1180s and 1190s – thus a Venetian merchant resident in Palermo asked in his will of March 1186 to be buried there.[22] Henry also confirmed Venetian tax rights throughout the German empire and any lands additionally attached to it.[23] This was in effect a reissue of Barbarossa's grant made at the time of the Peace of Venice. Indeed, Clementi has argued that, since the Sicilian chancellor did not authenticate the 1197 reissue, it was solely an 'imperial concern'; 'the presumption is that the relations between the kingdom and the Venetian Republic remained subject to the agreement concluded in 1175 by William II'. Of course, the main achievement of Venice lay in the fact that royal favour had been conferred without the Republic suffering any military or diplomatic expense.

III

Henry of Hohenstaufen remained anxious to conquer the *Regno*. In 1191 Tancred had captured his wife Constance – through whom, indeed, Henry's claim to the *Regno* existed. On 30 May 1193 the Emperor issued from Gelnhausen a confirmation, word for word, of the privilege granted the Pisans in 1191; one reason for the reissue may have been that he had by now been crowned emperor and could substitute imperial for royal titles, but another was probably that he wished to encourage the Pisans in their support.[24] The campaign would continue; the setbacks of 1191 would not affect the award of

---

[21] *DCV*, I, no. 377, no. 391, no. 397, no. 410.

[22] Henry VI and the Venetian church: Toeche, 630; Clementi, Cal., no. 44. Toeche cites a personal letter from Huillard-Bréholles: '...doit se trouver aussi dans les libri pactorum aux arch. de Venise'; but no copy is known to me from Pactorum or Blancus. Document of 1186: Garufi, *Doc. ined.*, no. 86.

[23] Archivio di Stato, Venice, Liber Pactorum i, f.12r–15r; MGH. *Const.*, I, 526–30; Clementi, Cal., no. 115, listing further MS texts and pointing to its connection with Barbarossa's privilege of 1177 (Pactorum I, f.8v–11v; MGH. *Const.*, I, 374–7), which added to previous privileges the promise of exemption in lands conqered in the future.

[24] F. dal Borgo, *Raccolta di scelti diplomi pisani* (Pisa, 1765), 24; but see Clementi, Cal., no. 18.

prizes to his loyal allies. The Pisans responded as he had hoped, sending Bulgarino Visconti and Suavizio Orlandi to him with loyal greetings. Henry promised to set out for the *Regno* in May 1194; once again he reminded the Pisans that they could be sure of great rewards.[25]

Unfortunately there is no Pisan (nor, for that matter, Venetian) account of the Hohenstaufen conquest of the *Regno*; the *Carmen* of Pietro da Eboli says nothing about the north Italians; and only the Genoese account by Ottobono Scriba provides details of Pisan participation in the expedition to Sicily.[26] This source is extremely hostile to the Pisans, for reasons that will be plain enough; it is also very hostile to Emperor Henry. This does not necessarily mean that Henry and the Pisans were in close alliance; indeed, there are signs that the Pisans lost interest in the campaign a month after it had begun. It would, in consequence, be dangerous to suppose that, following Henry's coldness towards the Genoese, Pisa acquired what Heywood called 'commercial hegemony' in the Sicilian kingdom.[27] The only commercial document available is a letter of 1198 sent by Alberto Celone, a Pisan resident in Messina, to Baratterio Congiario in Pisa asking Baratterio to pay a third person, Villano, for a breast-plate, and appointing Baratterio his agent in the transaction. Alberto had the document drawn up in the presence of several witnesses, who were possibly Pisan; and, in particular, the notary he employed appears to have been Pisan, since he described himself as notary of Emperor Henry, without any reference to Henry as king of Sicily. But the existence of a Pisan settlement in Messina is certainly not evidence for a Pisan hegemony in Sicilian trade.[28]

---

25 R. Roncioni, 'Delle istorie pisane', *Archivio storico italiano*, VI (1844), 429, for an Italian version; see Clementi, Cal., no. 20 for critical comment and dating.

26 For Pietro da Eboli's account of the conquest of Campania, see *Liber ad honorem Augusti* ed. by Siragusa, and ed. by Rota, lines 1,119–1,226.

27 *Ann. Ian.*, II, 51: after Henry VI arrived in Sicily, 'Pisani vero nec per mare nec per terram amoverunt se Messana'. Commercial hegemony: Heywood, 227, against Manfroni, *Storia della Marina*, 294–6.

28 Archivio di Stato, Pisa, R. Acquisto Roncioni, no. 136 (1199 corta); cf. Archivio di Calci, 9 Oct. 1190 for further evidence of a Pisan colony in Messina, and 280 *infra*. For the effect of the invasion of Sicily on developments in Pisa and its contado, Volpe, 307–14. Cf. my article 'Pisan commercial colonies and consulates', *English Historical Review* (forthcoming) document iii.

IV

No Genoese contracts survive from 1193 or 1194; but the activities of the Genoese in Sicily are well documented for the latter year. Their home city was torn by internal strife, and only after a visit from Markward von Anweiler, Henry VI's seneschal, was it possible to concentrate on preparing a fleet for the invasion of the *Regno*. In June Emperor Henry came in person to Genoa, full of encouragement; 'if with your aid and by God's will', he said, 'I shall acquire the kingdom of Sicily, the honour will be mine (meus erit honor), but the profit will be yours; for I am unable to remain there with my Germans, but you and your heirs shall remain there; thus that kingdom will not be mine but yours'. So, at least, the Genoese annalist Ottobono narrates.[29] Certainly there were generous actions to accompany his exhortations: a confirmation of Conrad II's grant of minting rights, and a grant of the fief of Naso in Sicily to Rubaldo son of Bonifacio de Platea Longa, made on 20 June.[30] The rapid surrender of Gaeta to the combined fleet of Genoa and Pisa under Markward's command was witnessed by the Genoese *podestà* and by Ottobono the annalist; together they entered Gaeta to receive an oath of fidelity to the conqueror Henry. Since Gaeta had been promised in fee to Pisa, the Genoese probably wished to keep an eye on events there. (Of course, Ottobono takes care to attribute as much of the Gaetan success as possible to the Genoese, leaving an impression, deliberately no doubt, that Gaeta swore its oath to the Genoese.) Naples too put up no resistance to Henry's army, and the combined fleets rapidly received the surrender of the islands nearby – Ischia, Capri, Procida. Then, while the army was held up at Salerno, which had resolved to resist, the Pisans and the Genoese headed south to Messina, arriving there on 1 September 1194.[31] Here too opposition was negligible. One reason for these rapid successes was certainly the lack of central authority following King Tancred's death in February 1194; his elder son, already crowned Roger III,

[29] *Ann. Ian.*, II, 46. Markward: *ibid.* 45.
[30] *CDG*, III, 108 (minting rights); J. F. Böhmer, *Acta imperii selecta*, ed. J. Ficker (Innsbruck, 1870), no. 191 (Rubaldo's fief); see also, for both grants, Clementi, *Cal.*, no. 21 and *Ann. Ian.*, II, 46, n.1.
[31] *Ann. Ian.*, II, 47–8; cf. Pietro da Eboli, lines 1,151–1,226, dwelling on the capture of Salerno.

shortly predeceased Tancred; and the government came into the hands of Queen Sibylla and her young son William III.

Indeed, the fighting for spoils began even before the fall of Palermo. The Pisans and the Genoese fell out in Messina; there was fierce fighting in the streets and harbour. Ottobono states that thirteen Pisan galleys were seized by his fellow citizens, which may be untrue, since he also reports a little earlier that the Pisans sent only twelve galleys to help conquer Sicily. Not to be outdone, the Pisans seized the 'fundicum sancti Iohannis', the warehouse of St John, one of the Genoese warehouses in Messina, as well as houses inhabited by Genoese citizens. They held many Genoese citizens prisoner in the palace of Margarito, apparently Admiral Margarito of Brindisi, Count of Malta; this later became a Genoese possession, and was granted to the Genoese by Frederick II, who then took it back in 1221. It seems to have come to the Genoese, along with the County of Malta, in Henry VI's reign or in Frederick II's youth, and there are no grounds for asserting, as some have done, that it was the building erected in 1116 as a result of Roger II's privilege to Ogerio the consul.[32]

After further fighting (and the seizure of another thirteen Pisan galleys!) Markward von Anweiler came to impose order. The Genoese agreed to restore to the Pisans 1,000 silver marks and the shells (*corpora*) of their galleys – but not, apparently, the contents. The list of what the Pisans handed back to the Genoese is valuable evidence for the commodity market in 1194, and may be held to reflect the contents of the warehouses that the Pisans had seized from the Genoese. For the presence of large numbers of Genoese in Messina, living in houses and carrying on trade there on the eve of the invasion, is clearly attested by the Genoese annalist. Those already there had to hope that the war would wash over them gently, without drowning them; and what risks this involved have already been suggested in the insurance agreements. The Pisans took a shield, an oven for boiling pitch, ten bundles of flax, some cinnamon and galingal, armour, silk clothes, a silver vase, gold and other goods; and, Ottobono grumbles, they did not return all of these items

---

[32] *Ann. Ian.*, II, 48. Margarito's palace: *ibid.* n.1, 81, n.1, 132, 171; J. Huillard-Bréholles, *Historia diplomatica Frederici Secundi*, 5 vols. (Paris, 1859–61), I, part 1, 65; Abulafia, 'Henry, Count of Malta', 120.

despite their promises to do so.[33] A further emergency threatened to break out on the sudden death of Oberto de Olivano, the *podestà* of Genoa. The Pisans hoped to exploit his funeral and to trap Markward von Anweiler, Boniface of Montferrat and other notables who were to be in the cortège. News leaked out, and Markward ordered the royal palace and castle to be fortified against attack. The Pisans then cancelled their plans, for the element of surprise had vanished. The plot against Markward may have been the ultimate reason for the Seneschal's favours to Genoa in subsequent years. In 1200 he gave the Genoese extensive trading rights, and fell out with Genoa only in 1201. It was even suspected that the Pisan plot had been motivated by a desire to help Tancred's wife and son; thus Ottobono says, for what the statement is worth, 'the Seneschal's *fideles* and friends, who were aware of the secret designs of the Pisans, told him that the Pisans favoured the wife and son of the late King Tancred, and that they had letters and promises from them'.[34] The existence of such letters is not impossible; Sibylla may have offered many attractive rights in the hope of saving Sicily; but the outcome of the invasion was little in doubt by now, and the Pisans are very unlikely to have wished to come to terms – particularly after the signs of Pisan enthusiasm in 1193.

After the destruction of Salerno Henry came south to Messina, and, with Genoese help, took Catania and Syracuse, long the focus of Genoese territorial ambitions. The Genoese annalist insists that disaffected Pisans were inside Syracuse defending the city against Henry; certainly, the Pisans seem to have absented themselves from Henry's forces at this stage, but large-scale aid to the Normans seems very unlikely. And after Syracuse, the other Sicilian towns rapidly surrendered, so that the Genoese were able to enrich themselves with booty. Meanwhile the Genoese had appointed a new *podestà*, Ottone di Carreto, a Ligurian, and the *podestà* took the opportunity of asking the Emperor when the ancient promises to Genoa would be fulfilled: 'Lord Emperor, it pleased your Excellency to make peace with the city of Genoa, and you promised us Syracuse and the

33 *Ann. Ian.*, II, 49. Heywood, 224, aptly remarks that 'the only naval battle of the war was fought between the Pisans and Genoese in the waters of Messina'.
34 *Ann. Ian.*, II, 50; T. C. van Cleve, *Markward of Anweiler and the Sicilian Regency* (Princeton, 1937), 44–5.

Val di Noto: here we are, who by God's grace and a happy omen seized and obtained that city by the sword, in your name; if it please you we ask that you give it to us, since God has given it into your power'. The Emperor replied: '…we do not yet hold the palace of Palermo; once I have it, you shall be given Syracuse and the Val di Noto and whatever we promised'.[35] Palermo too fell rapidly, once Henry had promised Sibylla and William III favourable terms of surrender; though, like most of his promises, he failed to keep them. And, soon after the conquest of Palermo, the Genoese once again decided to press for the fulfilment of the promises Henry had made to them. The representatives of the Commune found the new King of Sicily walking in one of the palace gardens, and pleaded with him: 'Lord, all is complete through God's grace…' But Henry replied, 'Your *podestà* is dead…when I see for sure him or them who represent your community, I shall indeed do what I promised.' Thus he refused to recognise Ottone di Carreto as Genoese representative.

The Genoese annalist accuses Henry of 'playing Nero' ('nerozavit'). Deftly recalling that Henry was, as King of Sicily, heir to Roger II and to William I and II, Ottobono contrasts the obstinacy of the new king with the generosity of his predecessors. Of course, another line – suggested by the privileges of Barbarossa and of Henry – was that Henry had swept away the works of usurpers; but Henry himself took care to recognise the legitimacy of his predecessors up to William II, claiming the crown, as he did, not as Emperor of the Romans and lord of all Italy, but as King of Sicily in right of his wife Constance and her father Roger. If indeed he forbade the Genoese to appoint officers within the *Regno*, he drove home the point made in his speech in the palace garden at Palermo. The Genoese had no representative; and he would do his best to ensure that none was created. The Genoese, he said, were nothing more than men of the sea, but he with his army could raze their city to the ground.[36]

Pirate attacks by the Pisans on Genoese shipping became more and more frequent. With the conquest of Sicily the danger to merchants bound for the *Regno* no longer lay so much in the towns of Sicily and southern Italy as on the high seas. There was intense fighting in Corsica; and the Genoese replied to Pisan assaults by seizing a

---

[35] *Ann. Ian.*, II, 51.   [36] *Ann. Ian.*, II, 52–3.

Pisan grain ship off Corneto.[37] To some degree, Emperor Henry may have exploited these quarrels; at any rate, they diverted the attention of the Genoese and Pisans from their Sicilian ambitions.

There were as late as January 1195 still large numbers of the Genoese patriciate in Sicily. To abandon the island might have meant abandoning the chance to press Ligurian claims to territories in Sicily, especially after Henry left the kingdom to travel north. Ottobono, the annalist, had also rejoined the Genoese in Sicily by now, after his short detour to Gaeta; and two acts survive from his hand, drawn up in Palermo on 1 January 1195. In the first, Guglielmo Bucca, Ugone Lercario and Lamberto Cane declared that the Commune of Genoa owed Nicola Lecanoce – whose activities in late 1191 have been witnessed aready – the sum of 11 oz and 13 tari, paid by him on behalf of the Commune of Genoa; this was part of a larger sum of 114⅓ oz that Nicola had lent, on behalf of Lamberto Cane, to the commune's *podestà*, Ottone di Carreto, 'pro armandis galeis ad conquistandum regnum Sicilie'. Guglielmo, Ugone and Lamberto, 'speciales missi predicti Otonis potestatis', promised to pay Nicola 56s for every ounce outstanding, by the end of August 1195. And by late August, to judge from a scribbled note at the foot of Ottobono's charter, Nicola had returned to Genoa and been repaid. Also on 1 January 1195, Ugolino Mallone came before Ottobono to declare that he had received on loan from Nicola Mallone 26½ oz of gold; this he had borrowed in order to repay Oberto Usodimare, Ugone Lercario and Lamberto Cane part of the 114⅓ oz that Lamberto had lent in Messina to Podestà Ottone, and to repay Oberto and Ugone part of the 1,250 tari that they had lent the Commune towards the expenses of the invasion of Sicily. Ugolino promised to repay Nicola Mallone £74 4s 0d by the end of August 1195. Clearly, then, the creditors Lamberto, Oberto and Ugone had decided to reclaim the sums owed to them by the Commune – possibly because they were shortly returning to Genoa, possibly because their original contracts with the Commune had set 1 January 1195 as the date for repayment. It then became necessary for the Commune to find other creditors who could support at least part of the debts incurred, and, in small measure, Nicola Lecanoce and Nicola Mallone were able to help. Ottobono's

[37] *Ann. Ian.*, II, 54–8; Abulafia, 'Corneto-Tarquinia', 231.

charters were then taken to the communal archive and preserved there as a record of the city's debts to the two Nicolas.[38]

Other Genoese in Palermo included Rolando de Armandino, Mauro de Platea Longa, Rubaldo Taxio, Guglielmo Alfachino, Oberto de Nigro, Rolando Mallone; and their bases in the city included the *ecclesia sancti Iacobi*, possibly a Genoese foundation. Ottobono was at the church to draw up the first contract, but had moved 'ante domum Presteconti' to compose the second; this house was 'in alza', in the Khalsa quarter adjoining the harbour, and so probably was the church.[39]

None of the patrician Genoese mentioned in the loan contracts was actually a consul or judge of pleas in 1194 or 1195, though they had close family ties with officials in both years; and in 1196 Nicola Lecanoce himself became consul in company with Guglielmo Fornario, Belmosto Lercario, Ingo Longo and others.[40] But some of the figures mentioned in Ottobono's contracts of January 1195 were, as has been seen, 'speciales missi' of the new *podestà* Ottone di Carreto, who had replaced his dead predecessor in Sicily during 1194. They, indeed, were probably those who spoke with Henry VI in the palace gardens at Palermo, in an attempt to extract from him confirmation of his earlier promises. In 1195, however, Henry moved north to Pavia, and a different set of ambassadors was appointed by the Commune and sent directly from Genoa to the imperial court; the Genoese were mindful of Henry's insistence that either the *podestà* or his accredited agent should be sent, and that an *ad hoc* mission elected in Sicily would not suffice. Bonifacio, Archbishop of Genoa, Giacomo Manerio, *podestà* of Genoa, Ansaldo Buferio and other eminent citizens took with them the Genoese

---

38 Archivio di Stato, Genoa, archivio segreto, materie politiche, (2721) Busta 2, nos. 45 and 46. Printed by Olivieri, 'Serie dei consoli', *ASLSP*, I, 396–8, from modern copies of the surviving originals; the edition is incomplete and contains errors – the scribbled notice of repayment at the foot of no. 45 is omitted. Registered by Lisciandrelli, *ASLSP*, n.s., I, nos. 163–4.

39 The witnesses and location are cited in the charters described in n.38 *supra*. The church of S. Giorgio dei Genovesi in Palermo dates no further back than 1576.

40 *Ann. Ian.*, II, 60. Ingo Longo seems to have been a betting man: on 2 October 1191 he promised his mother Sibilia that he would not lose more than 3s a day *ad ludum*; his debts would be secured against his Sicilian fief (*feudo Sicilie*) and other property, *G. Cass.*, I, no. 1,167. In 1195 he won fame by helping lead the war of attrition against the Pisan fleet in the Tyrrhenian Sea – *Ann. Ian.*, II, 55–8.

copy of the privilege granted by Henry in 1191, and offered to read it to the Emperor. But Henry forbade them to read out the contents, saying, according to Ottobono: 'I have one myself and I know well what is contained in it. Do you wish to please me? I shall make a bargain with you. But you must truly know that I shall not give you [Syracuse] in the kingdom of Sicily, nor will you share in my gains; nor should you expect to have land in common with me; but, if you want to make an expedition, I shall help you capture another kingdom, the whole of which shall be yours. If you want to send an army against the King of Aragon, I shall be with you.'[41]

'Quid plura?' Ottobono plaintively asks. Individual acts of favour or enterprise enabled the Genoese to install themselves in Sicilian bases. However, it is not clear from the cartularies of Guglielmo da Sori and Oberto de Placentia that commercial activity in the *Regno* continued during 1195, 1196 and 1197. Other Genoese involved themselves in Sicilian affairs by entering imperial circles. As early as June 1194 Rubaldo de Platea Longa had received his Sicilian fief from the Emperor; but Sicily had still to be conquered and there is no guarantee he entered into possession of it. On 25 September 1197, at Messina, two loyal Genoese, Marino and Matteo di Marino, received lands in the Val Demona from the Emperor; this was in gratitude for their loyalty in coming to Sicily and bringing with them troops armed at their own expense.[42] Another grant in favour of a Genoese citizen, Porcio de Catonibus, dated 4 August 1197, seems to be a forgery.[43] There is also a record of a grant to Buonaccorso Cicogna, *civis Pisanus*, made in January 1197 at Gioia del Colle in Apulia. This, however, was for construction rights in the city of Pisa, and did not affect the status of the Pisans in the *Regno*.[44] The most significant case of imperial favour was that

---

[41] *Ann. Ian.*, II, 58–9.
[42] Rubaldo: see 206, *supra*. Marino: G. Paolucci, 'Il parlamento di Foggia del 1240', *Atti della R. Accademia di Scienze Lettere e Arti di Palermo*, ser. 3, IV (1896), 29; Clementi, Cal., no. 132. Cf. Frederick II's confirmation (1212), Paolucci, 33; G. L. Barberi, *Capibrevi*, vol. II, ed. G. Silvestri (Palermo, 1886), 178–80. Also: P. Scheffer-Boichorst, *Zur Geschichte des XII. und XIII. Jahrhunderts* (Berlin, 1897), 393–4.
[43] C. Gallo, *Annali della Città di Messina*, 2 vols. (Messina, 1758), II, 74; Clementi, Cal., no. 126.
[44] K. F. Stumpf-Brentano, 'Acta imperii ab Henrico I ad Henricum VI usque', *Die Reichskanzler vornehmlich des X., XI., XII. Jahrhunderts*, vol. III (Innsbruck,

shown towards a practised corsair of Genoese origin, Guglielmo
Grasso. Grasso was appointed admiral of the Sicilian fleet in
succession to Margarito of Brindisi, whose home was now a German
prison; and the appointment also brought Grasso lands that had
not been mentioned in Henry VI's grant to Genoa: the County of
Malta – lands, moreover, which had been part of the royal demesne
until Tancred created the county for Margarito. There is no great
surprise in Henry's decision to appoint a Genoese to the admiralcy;
if the Emperor were to find a marine commander anywhere, he
could not do better than look to Genoa.[45] But it was only after
Henry VI's death that the Genoese were able to add Syracuse to their
possessions in the *Regno*, using Malta as a base to expel the Pisans
from Syracuse, in defiance of Pisan, let alone royal, claims to
possess the town. Like Corsica and Sardinia, Sicily became the object
of direct competition between the Pisans and the Genoese, and royal
rights of taxation passed unnoticed.

Thus in Genoa and Sicily there were accounts to settle and debts
to reclaim, with ample interest. In the *Regno*, the charge the north
Italians wished to make for their patience in awaiting German
victory was heavy indeed: tax exemptions, towns, rural areas too.
For, as ever, the north Italians insisted that they had favoured the
invasion all along; and, though they were indispensable in achieving
the conquest, they failed to realise how very dispensable they would
become thereafter.[46]

1881), no. 205; Clementi, Cal., no. 99. Cf. also J. Heers, *Le clan familial au moyen
âge* (Paris, 1974), 47–8.

[45] Abulafia, 'Henry Count of Malta', 108–9; L. R. Ménager, *Amiratus-'Αμηρᾶς:
l'Emirat et les origines de l'Amirauté* (Paris, 1960) 111-12.

[46] For later developments, see Abulafia, 'Henry Count of Malta'; Vitale, 'Genova
ed Enrico VI', 97–102; V. Vitale, 'Genovesi colonizzatori in Sicilia nel secolo
XIII', *Giornale storico e letterario della Liguria*, n.s., v (1929), 1–9; C. Imperiale di
Sant'Angelo, *Genova e le sue relazioni con Federico II* (Venice, 1923), and the
works by H. Chone, P. Nardone and A. Schaube cited in Chapter 1. For later
centuries, C. Trasselli, 'Genovesi in Sicilia', *ASLSP*, n.s., IX (1969), 155–78, and
G. Yver, *Le Commerce et les marchands dans l'Italie méridionale au XIIIe et au XIVe
Siècle* (Paris, 1903).

PART III

THE STRUCTURE OF TRADE

Chapter 9

THE STRUCTURE OF GENOESE TRADE
WITH SICILY, 1155-64

I

Giovanni Scriba's registrations stand out for their internal variety. Later notaries provide a greater quantity of contracts per year for Sicily and elsewhere, as business blossomed, but most of these are reduced to simple formulae. The more consistent the material the better, from a statistical point of view; but, given the lacunae in the notarial registers, even a stable set of statistics does not take matters very far. Giovanni Scriba comes to the rescue with information about trade routes, commodities and profits; and, in addition, he provides a wide enough spread of contracts to illustrate the mercantile careers of many Genoese citizens and denizens. For, at a time when Genoese trade was still edging forward into new areas of influence, and expanding its contacts with existing markets, the notaries did not regard commercial acts as so commonplace that they could easily be standardised. Moreover, Giovanni's evidence gains added proportion from its unique antiquity. It provides a starting point for the study of several phenomena, such as the rôle played by the aristocracy in overseas trade. In these circumstances it seems appropriate to ask a rather different series of questions of the earliest evidence from the questions that will be asked of late-twelfth-century notaries. On the basis of Giovanni Scriba's registrations it will be possible to identify elements of continuity – elements strictly commonplace in the 1180s and 1190s, or elements that underwent changes in emphasis and scale as the century progressed.

Among economic historians of this period there has been a tendency to catalogue items of merchandise, and to lay emphasis on the wide variety of luxury goods that came in small quantities under exotic names to Genoa and Sicily. Items exported in bulk, such as primary foodstuffs and fibres, have been neglected in favour of relatively limited imports of exotic items such as drugs and spices, greater, no doubt in the number of varieties available, but strictly limited in the number of tons carried. Moreover, there has been a tendency to ignore chronological development in the scale of imports and exports. Thus it is far from clear that the 1150s saw imports of Flemish woollens into Sicily on the scale that such imports can be witnessed at the end of the twelfth century. Recent work on the expansion of the textile industry of northern Italy makes it clear that Lombard, if not Flemish, textiles only began to be mass-produced in the late twelfth and thirteenth centuries.[1]

Now, the Sicilian–Genoese agreement of 1156 makes one point very clear: that Sicilian raw cotton was being exported to Genoa in the 1150s. Girgenti and Mazara produced cotton; from Palermo and the lands round about the Genoese were permitted to export raw cotton, wool and lambs' fleeces. Only in the case of Messina is there any indication that cloth rather than raw fibres may be in the Genoese suitcases; and in that instance the text of the privilege is simply ambiguous.[2] Moreover, the commercial contracts refer to *bombax*, raw cotton, from the *Regno*. The Genoese merchant Guglielmo Scarsaria had in his possession in 1164 raw cotton from Malta, 'medietatem unius sacci bombacis de Malta', which was to be put up for sale in Genoa or elsewhere in northern Italy. Against this, there is plentiful evidence that the north Italians were selling finished cloth in the *Regno* – often, no doubt, made of Sicilian or south Italian fibres. On 3 May 1156 Guglielmo Vento sent eight pieces of *sagie et volgia* to Salerno, with the option of carrying the cloth to Alexandria if they wished. On 30 June 1156 Ribaldo Castagna received in *accomendacio* seventy-eight pieces of fustian and forty *cannas de nativis*, together with one *cultram de pallio*, all to be taken to Salerno for sale. These were obviously Lombard cloths, since Lombard towns took sufficient pride in their linen and cotton weave to name it after the exotic Egyptian cloths of Fustat. Other linen cloth found its way south, to judge from a contract of 12 September

---

[1] R. L. Reynolds, 'The market for northern textiles in Genoa, 1179–1200', *Revue belge de philologie et d'histoire*, VIII (1929), 831–51, in certan respects takes this static view; he refers to the 'large and steady volume of northern textiles shipped to the City', without comparing the position in 1179 to that in 1155. See now M. Mazzaoui, 'The cotton industry of northern Italy in the late Middle Ages', *Journal of Economic History*, XXXII (1972).

[2] *CDG*, I, 339.

1157. Here Bonogiovanni Malfigliastro is found sending £23 worth of linen cloth to Palermo in the hands of Gionata Ciriole. A contract of 18 July 1161 may indicate the sale of silk goods, along with iron and tin, in Sicily by Genoese merchants; but there is no guarantee in this particular text that the silk was not Sicilian. Not that there was anything wrong with sending coals to Newcastle; at any rate, Solomon of Salerno sent cotton in raw form from Genoa to Sicily. This may have been Egyptian cotton, to judge from Solomon's extensive interests in Alexandria, another overseas source of cotton for north Italian looms.[3]

Northern textiles of Flemish or north French origin are significantly rare in Giovanni Scriba's cartulary. On 28 July 1158 Alberto Clerico agreed to take £34 1s 0d plus some cloth of St Riquier in Picardy to Sicily for sale. He was to travel to Messina and then to stay abroad for the rather long period of three years.[4] Certainly it would be difficult to describe Flemish cloth as part of the regular stock-in-trade of Genoese businessmen of the mid-twelfth century. Milan and Piacenza were the principal producers of cloths exported to Sicily, whereas the Flemings had to await the 1180s and 1190s before their products, urged on by their own merchants, broke into the southern Mediterranean. With the arrival in Genoa of Jean de Liège, and indeed of the Lucchesi, the market for northern textiles in the Tyrrhenian region was dramatically enlarged. But the implications go deeper, too: in the 1150s and 1160s the Genoese could not apparently pay for their imports from Sicily and elsewhere with industrial products of northern Italy and Europe; the majority of payments had, rather, to be made in silver.[5]

An inventory of goods to be imported into Sicily does, however, survive, and it shows that Ligurian businessmen also managed to pay for foreign items with their stocks of imported spices and miscellanea. Inventories, or even barren references to 'goods worth so much', are the exception, compared to payments in Genoese

---

[3] *GS*, II, no. 1,212; I, no. 73; I, no. 89 (uncancelled); I, no. 285; II, no. 857. Solomon's cotton: *GS*, I, no. 420, no. 482.

[4] *GS*, I, no. 415; cf. Abulafia, 'L'Attività commerciale genovese nell'Africa normanna', 339.

[5] Milan and Piacenza: *GS*, I, no. 678. For Jean de Liège and the Lucchesi, see 255–64 *infra*.

cash; and it is not be be expected that the more irregular businessmen were as agile as their professional colleagues in holding stocks
over on deposit, or at transferring their assets as chance allowed.
Thus this inventory must be taken to indicate not the normal means
by which Genoese merchants paid for Sicilian produce, but the range
of items available to them in instances where they did not pay directly
in Genoese silver. On 10 September 1157 Gandolfo de Gotizone was
preparing to travel to Sicily with the following stock.

(1) One eightieth share in the ownership of the vessel in
which he was to sail
(2) 'Saracen books' – sold, presumably, because demand
was high, not because they were select texts of particular
authors
(3) A barrel of spices, containing euphorbium worth £16,
sandalwood worth £2½, white pepper worth £5,
myrobalan worth £4½ and a further substance
(*Ansaroti*) worth £18
(4) A second barrel, containing sal ammoniac, valued at
£92
(5) A mantle from Huesca in Spain, worth £5
(6) £2 worth of myrrh
(7) £65 worth of caps – clearly a very large consignment
of mass-produced textiles
(8) £2 worth of 'best caps', presumably better in quality
or colour than the mass-made articles
(9) £3 worth of myrobalan, described as 'diebuli'
(10) Four *virgae* of copper, worth a total of £5, as well as
thirteen rods and eighteen *centenaria* of copper, price
unstated
(11) A variety of other commodities, unspecified, worth
£72½ – all adding up to a grand total of £292½,
excluding the unknown value of the share in the ship, the
books and the rods of copper[6]

---

[6] *GS*, I, no. 287. The 'euphorbium' (spurge) was a member of the spurge family,
Euphorbia is the plant, euphorbium the dried latex obtained therefrom, and
would have been used pharmacologically – C. Chicheley Plowden, *A manual of
plant names* (London, 1972), 236; O. Polunin, *The flowers of Europe* (London,
1969), nos. 669–84.

It may appear surprising to find evidence for the transport of eastern spices from Genoa to Sicily, since these would very probably have been brought to Liguria via the Norman ports in Sicily and Africa; but it was only natural for the Genoese merchants to keep stocks and to try to control the release of surplus merchandise. What they could not sell, or preferred to hold back, while they were in northern Italy, they could carry back to other foreign markets, such as Sicily, Sardinia, Provence and Andalusia, to find buyers there. For all the active exchange centres in the Mediterranean had to obtain their drugs and spices from visiting merchants; ultimately even Acre and Alexandria were dependent on such visitors, though there a different price régime existed, freed from the cost of Mediterranean transport. By holding back their release of goods, the Genoese might even manage to break into the market when local supplies of exotic goods were low, and prices favourable to the seller – a phenomenon displayed in the Geniza documents. It is unlikely, however, that Gandolfo stood to gain from this, unless he intended to sell very fast, for when Gandolfo's ship arrived in Palermo the autumn sailings from Egypt and Syria would also be due there. It is worth adding that in Salerno, seat of a famous medical school, there would have been substantial demand for drugs, though it is unknown to what degree the Genoese took advantage of this opportunity.

A second document, of 7 September 1157, presents a picture of exports from Sicily. Rainaldo Albiçola, clearly a native of Albissola near Savona, declared in the presence of the great aristocrat Ingo della Volta that he held the following sums and articles in *societas* with Ingo's son Guglielmo and with Ingo himself:

(1) £355 in money, for investment in trade
(2) £48 capital, held in Palermo
(3) 11½ sacks and 16 *cantaria* of cotton
(4) Two rabbit-skins
(5) A further sack of cotton worth 40 *solidi* or £2[7]

Judging from the evidence that part of the *societas* was tied up in Palermo, it seems that this document exposes a midway stage in the history of the partnership. Because of the complex nature and long

[7] *GS*, I, no. 280.

duration of the triangular deal between Rainaldo on the one hand and Ingo and his son on the other, Ingo demanded a statement of account on Rainaldo's return to Genoa, prior to Rainaldo's next trade tour. How much was originally invested canot be said – nor, indeed, is it clear whether the itemised goods were the sole imports from Sicily or merely part of a larger consignment, much of it sold within Genoa in order to raise the hefty £355 that Rainaldo still bore. As for the goods mentioned, they are decidedly unexceptional. Raw cotton was evidently one of the most sought-after products of Sicily, while rabbit-skins served proxy for more expensive furs gentlemen might wear. The Norman and Hohenstaufen kings permitted the daughter house of the monastery of Santa Maria Latina in Jerusalem to export from Messina to Syria 4,000 rabbit-skins per annum – as well as 200 hams, 100 lamb-skins, 30 ox-hides, linen, wool and hemp. All these items appear either in the Genoese contracts for Sicilian trade or in the Genoese–Sicilian treaty, with the exception of ox-hides and hemp; but here the Geniza further confirms the picture.[8]

The picture is, indeed, a remarkably consistent one. It would be foolhardy to insist that any particular product of Sicilian and south Italian estates took priority in exports to Genoa. That wheat was the paramount purchase of the North Africans from Sicily is clear; and that the north Italians bought Sicilian and south Italian wheat is also apparent. Raw cotton is mentioned with impressive consistency; and, whatever the distinction in quality, Sicilian cotton was cheaper in terms of transport costs than Egyptian, its main rival in Giovanni Scriba's cartulary. Moreover, the Sicilian customs tariffs seem to have been far less elaborate than the Egyptian from 1156; and the length of voyages to Alexandria involved a decision to tie up capital for very lengthy periods that could, at times, have been unwelcome to the averagely endowed Genoese businessman.[9] The weightiest

---

[8] *Doc. ined.*, no. 82. Cf. Goitein, 'Sicily and southern Italy', 19; Idrisi, ed. Amari–Schiaparelli, 30.

[9] For the Egyptian tariffs, see C. Cahen, 'Douanes et commerce dans les ports méditerranéens de l'Egypte médiévale d'après le Minhadj d'al-Makhzumi', *Journal of the Economic and Social History of the Orient*, VIII (1964); also H. Rabie, *The financial system of Egypt, A.H.564–741/A.D.1169–1341* (London, 1972), and J. Riley-Smith's stimulating 'Government in Latin Syria and the commercial privileges of foreign merchants', in D. Baker (ed.), *Relations between East and West in the Middle Ages* (Edinburgh, 1973), 109–32.

question, in this context, is surely how rapidly the north Italian purchasers of Sicilian cotton were able to expand industrial production, and when they began to sell back to the *regnicoli* the processed products of the Norman kingdom. From the references available in Giovanni Scriba's cartulary, it does seem that the Genoese were performing this rôle by the middle of the twelfth century; though, equally, it seems that the main market for their cloth was in Syria and not in Sicily. For the moment, it may be, Sicily managed to produce a variety of styles of cotton cloth and of woollens, made for sale within the *Regno* rather than in northern Italy or the east Mediterranean; and, of course, a silk workshop also existed, its scale now uncertain. However, it would be niggardly to deny the north Italians credit for one of their greatest commercial achievements: the ability to create and to sustain demand for the merchandise they manufactured or carried.

II

These considerations raise once again the problem of the balance of payments – whether Sicilian gold was flowing out of the *Regno* at a greater rate than north Italian silver was flowing in. Certain aspects of this question are more fully illuminated by the acts of later notaries and Giovanni Scriba has relatively little to say about banking techniques and connected themes. Discussion of banks and of gold deposits must therefore be reserved for a later chapter. Less elusive, on the basis of the mid-twelfth-century evidence, is the question what profits individual merchants made in Sicilian business. In analysing the overall profitability of Sicilian trade to the Genoese this question provides an obvious first approach. And, by good fortune, there does survive a group of acts and accounts concerning an *accomendacio* between Ingo della Volta (*socius stans*) and Ansaldo Baialardo (*socius negocians*), bound with the main part of Giovanni's cartulary and written in his hand. Originally, however, these folios formed a separate dossier provided for the merchants at their request. Interestingly, too, this is not the only occasion when Ingo is known to have demanded a statement of account – the inventory of goods and funds held by Rainaldo Albiçola has already been discussed. It is evident from the Baialardo accounts that profits of 100 per cent were feasible; but it is as well to enter a *caveat* that other evidence for profits, such as the sea-loans with their fixed returns, seems to show that such high returns were the exception.[10]

Giovanni Scriba does not furnish a copy of the original contract in the main cartulary which may indeed have lost a few folios here (between f.11 and f.12, contracts for mid-1156, which are rather sparse). The contract is preserved only in the midst of the accounts, and then in a partial and highly summarised form that probably represents part of the first redaction:

III. die augusti, testes Lambertus Guercius, Dragus Fraimundus, Petrus Ferrar. In capitulo. Ultramare et Damascum si velet, in Sciciliam si voluerit, vel Ianuam, vel Alexandriam, inde Ianuam et a Scicilia. Quarta superflui in proficuum societatis.
Si ei Ingo voluerit demandare de expensis quas ante istud iter fecerit ipse Ansaldus ei debet inde respondere racionabiliter et componere que racio erit.[11]

So Ansaldo Baialardo provided a list of goods brought back from the east 'in nave de Ospitale', apparently aboard a ship of the Order of St John of Jerusalem. He had indigo, wax and the proceeds from the sale of silk (20 *solidi*); he had £245 6s 0d worth of grain, out of which he had to pay £4 in taxes, apparently in Liguria. It is unlikely that this grain came from Syria, especially in the light of Ansaldo's permitted Sicilian halt; nor indeed can it have come from Alexandria. It may even be that the minimal taxes recorded – less than 2 per cent – were so low because they were paid in Sicily not in Liguria, but this is dangerous ground, considering that the 1156 privilege had not yet been granted to the Genoese. Other commodities too occur in the Baialardo accounts – brazilwood, cardamom and pepper from the east, and sugar, cotton and a silver cup, which could have had a Sicilian origin. The pepper and brazil were together worth £475, over twice the value of the grain, but of course this is no reflection of the relative bulk of the exotic goods against the foodstuffs. It is interesting too to find that it was not apparently the Commune but individual merchants who made sure that supplies

[10] *GS*, II, p. 248–57, and G. Astuti, *Rendiconti mercantili inediti del Cartolare di Giovanni Scriba* (Turin, 1933), with facsimiles; cf. *GS*, I, no. 280 (Rainaldo Albiçola). Ingo's profits are summarised as follows (*GS*, II, p. 257):
capitale,   CCLXXIII. s. IIII. d. I
proficuum lb. CCXLVIII. s. XVI minus d. I.
[11] *GS*, II, p. 250.

of grain were to be had in Genoa – and even then the decision whether to hoard or to sell seems to have been theirs. Guglielmo Scarsaria also had grain in his store when he died.[12] Now, the grain, spices, dyes and drugs were the means available to Ligurian and other merchants to obtain silver for their overseas investments. The crucial factor was that, by selling their imports in their home town to residents or northern visitors, or by travelling in person to the French fairs, the Italian merchants were able to fund their future investments. The statement that the balance of trade was unfavourable to the west must not be taken to mean that it was unfavourable to the western linkmen in Genoa, Venice and Pisa who carried the bullion back and forth. In some instances capital would be raised in Genoa by the mortgage of a house or the release of a dowry, but always with a view to amassing further funds and profits following an overseas venture.[13]

By far the greater number of contracts were expressed in *librae denariorum ianuensium*, but there are also, here and there, references to exchanges of Genoese *denarii* against foreign gold – bezants of Syria or Alexandria, hyperpers of Constantinople and tari of Sicily. In October 1158 Elia, possibly an emissary of the Sicilian government, made a sea-loan of £155 18s 6d, paid in Genoese silver; in return he was to receive in Palermo 81 oz of tari and 66 oz of purer *paiole* gold.[14] Solomon of Salerno seems to have had deposits of tari in Sicily while he himself was based in Genoa and planned to travel to Alexandria. His colleague Donato was sent to Sicily in 1161, partly to collect 102 tari outstanding from a partnership with Solomon's wife Eliadar. The use of native currency in Sicily made ample sense if merchants were to avoid extortionate exchange rates and problems of comparability in the purchasing power of gold and silver. The fewer conversions the better and the cheaper. Signs do, however, exist that Sicilian gold was used within Genoa for repayments of debts. On 13 September 1156 Bonogiovanni Tigna received from Ferro de Campo goods of unnamed value, and promised to return him 5 oz of gold at the Palermo standard, following his forthcoming voyage to Palermo. Bonogiovanni also owed Ribaldo Sarafia 5½ oz of gold. Similarly Solomon of Salerno is

---

[12] *GS*, II, no. 1,212. [13] *GS*, II, p. 310, no. xviii.
[14] *GS*, II, no. 909.

found in the summer of 1156 trying to extract some of his tari from the hands of his agent in Sicily – the exact sum seems garbled, but it may have been over 200 oz. In both instances, those of Bonogiovanni Tigna and of Solomon of Salerno, it is clear that the creditor is prepared to accept payment in Genoa in Sicilian gold. More categorical is the group of documents of March, May and June 1160 that refer to a diplomatic and commercial venture to the Greek court via that of William of Sicily. Here the sleeping partners stipulated repayment at the rate of 33 oz for £100 of Genoa, should part of the Genoese fleet proceed no further than Sicily, with the result that their funds would have to be used in Sicilian rather than Greek commercial business.[15] All this is very different from the groups of contracts in the 1180s and 1190s that insist on repayment of sea-loans and *cambia* actually in Sicily; in the 1180s, it is clear, the sleeping partner would very often spend part of the sailing season travelling with his own funds and those of his partners, while his own agent went ahead to earn funds on his behalf in a stipulated destination or region. There was, too, less reason to carry back a large part of the profits at the end of a merchant's tour of duty; as credit techniques and deposit banking gained in scope and popularity, money was carried over from one season to the next without being transported back from Palermo to Genoa or other ports. By contrast, the 1150s and 1160s show less sophistication in techniques of long-term investment – in the existence of deposit facilities or of legal instruments such as the *cambium maritimum* which aided credit and currency exchange. Just as the volume of business recorded per annum by Giovanni Scriba constitutes only a small fraction of the sums registered by late-twelfth-century notaries, so too do the later notaries reveal an elaboration of commercial methods that far outdistanced the range of techniques available in the 1150s.[16]

Certain merchants did, it is true, make efforts to sell western merchandise overseas. Solomon of Salerno, whose career demands detailed examination, seems to have encouraged his partners to supply goods rather than Genoese silver; but his principal preoccupation in this respect was Alexandria rather than the *Regno*. No lists of these goods survive, though lists of the luxury goods brought back

---

[15] *GS*, I, no. 137, no. 112, no. 615, no. 666.
[16] See diagrams, 258, 273 *infra*.

do exist. Certainly merchants were only too glad to put ships up for sale in Egypt, despite papal prohibitions against the export of timber and military equipment to Saracen lands. How far Sicily participated in all this and how many merchants followed Solomon's lead after his retirement cannot be said.[17]

III

Genoa attracted foreign visitors just as its own citizens travelled to other commercial centres. Men of Toulouse, Pavia, Piacenza, Milan, as well as Jews and Arabs can be identified in Giovanni Scriba's documents. The Toulousains had interests in Salerno and Sicily in 1155; others, such as the Pavians and Lucchesi, may as yet have used Genoa as a trading-post at which they could obtain the produce of the southern Mediterranean against the sale of their own cloths or services. Flemings too were not unknown. On 29 June 1157 Olivier de Verdun made a *societas* of £80 on behalf of his nephew Hospinel, who was to carry the money to Salerno. On his return Hospinel was to hand the profit either to his uncle or to Blancardo, who was a well-known specialist in trade with both Syria and continental Europe. This contract adds dimension to the picture, already drawn in outline, of the import of northern cloth into Sicily and southern Italy. The picture is additionally illuminated by the frequent references in south Italian charters to coins of Anjou and Champagne, proof positive that the funnel linking the *Regno* to northern Europe functioned regularly and brought south to Italy the silver of France and Flanders. Some middlemen, such as Olivier de Verdun and Blancardo, may have known both extremities of the funnel, but more generally the movement of goods and bullion must have been in a series of independent stages.[18]

In addition to northerners with Sicilian bases in Genoa, Giovanni Scriba shows how Genoese would travel to Sicily to base themselves there for periods of several years. When, on 28 July 1158, Alberto Clerico agreed to travel to Messina with £34 1s 0d and a piece of Picard cloth, he was given licence to stay abroad for up to

[17] Solomon is discussed 237–54 *infra*. Sales of ships: *GS*, I, no. 240 (possible sale in Palermo), no. 578 and no. 610 (Alexandria). Cf. E. H. Byrne, *Genoese shipping in the twelfth and thirteenth centuries* (Cambridge, Mass., 1930).

[18] *GS*, I, no. 11 (Toulouse), no. 500 (Pavia), no. 951 (Lucca), no. 970 (Arabs), no. 436 (Jews), etc. Olivier de Verdun: I, no. 210; cf. Gattola, *Accessiones*, I, 257.

three years. Of course, part of this period would have been spent
beyond Messina, but contracts stipulating a winter stay in Sicily
(and nowhere else) also occur. Thus on 16 August 1157 Guglielmo
Filardo and Ugo Mallone, both eminent Genoese businessmen,
came together to form a *societas* of £300, to which the latter contributed £100 and the former the remainder. Fusion of funds was
followed by further fission: Ribaldo, son of Ugo, was to take two-
thirds of the total, plus some cloth, to Syria, while Otone, his brother,
was to carry £100 to Sicily, whence he was to return the next summer. This complex deal expresses clearly the higher investment
potential of the east Mediterranean ports in the eyes of major Genoese
business families. Later that summer Guglielmo Filardo's Sicilian
interests were reawakened, and he invested £7 5s 3d in one
accomendacio for Sicily plus £30 in a similar contract aimed more
specifically at Palermo.[19] Short-term investments, anticipating
returns within the sailing season or, in any case, at the end of the
winter, were still the rule; only the richest investors could afford,
now and again, to commit their money to a long-term expedition
around the Mediterranean, with all the risks and temporary loss of
capital that this involved. Thus even Guglielmo Malfigliastro, a
man of evident wealth, insisted that his factor Graziano Guaraco
travel 'in the ship of Guglielmoto Ciriole and of Gandolfo de
Gotizone...to Palermo, and back from there the month afterwards'. Not surprisingly, Malfigliastro only required a small profit
– £2½ – on his sea-loan of £10; but, given that Graziano Guaraco
would also be in search of profit, it seems that a months' business in
Palermo in 1157 was sufficient to guarantee both backer and factor
financial gain rather above 25 per cent.[20]

The records of the notaries are rich in evidence about trade routes
as well as about the variety of individual destinations visited by the
Genoese. Here Sicily and southern Italy can be seen in the
context of wider commercial links, such as the Genoese carrying-
trade in the east and central Mediterranean. In addition, the evidence
for trade routes and destinations helps to illuminate the effects of individual commercial treaties between Genoa and other mercantile
centres such as Almohad Africa, Majorca or the *Regno*. So it would
be unwise to presume that the same routes were being worked

[19] GS, I, no. 415, no. 236, no. 245, no. 274.   [20] GS, I, no. 240.

throughout the century, regardless of the commercial growth of new centres in Africa or Spain and regardless of the diplomatic exigencies of the year in question. In the 1150s and early 1160s, a period of comparative peace in the west Mediterranean, the Genoese are seen linking Spain to Sicily. Thus on 7 September 1158 an un-cancelled contract was composed on behalf of Giordano the notary and a certain Maraxi, perhaps a Saracen, for trade 'at Denia, then at Majorca if he [Maraxi] wishes and from Denia or Majorca to Sicily if it shall be his will and the greater part of his colleagues shall go thither'. On 26 September of the same year Solomon of Salerno entrusted £103 in *accomendacio* to Oliverio da Pavia, for trade in Spain in the ship of Enrico Nevitella, 'but if I [Oliverio] shall go to Sicily, I must then return to Genoa, wherever Enrico may go after-wards'. Enrico Nevitella's ship is met six days earlier in another of Solomon's contracts, for £45 'wherever he may go, and then to Genoa or to Sicily and thence to Genoa'; and on 26 September Solomon and Enrico themselves entered into a partnership for £210 'laboratum quo velit' – all these must be ascribed to the same route from Genoa to Spain and back via Sicily.[21]

Another contract of the same day is far more complicated: Guidone da Lodi and Odone made a *societas* of £39 18s 0d, the route of which was very carefully specified: 'to Spain, then to Sicily, or Provence or Genoa, from Provence to Genoa or Sicily, and if so desired from Sicily to Romania and thence to Genoa, or from Sicily to Genoa'. It would not be inexcusably anachronistic to refer in this context to ibn Jubayr's voyage in a Genoese ship from Trapani via Favignana, southern Sardinia, the Balearics and the port of Denia to Cartagena; here is evidence, from 1185, of movement from Sicily to Spain rather than from Spain to Sicily.[22] Indeed, Genoese trade with Sicily and southern Italy must not be seen as a maritime funnel linking Genoa to Sicilian markets without reference to the Republic's commitments in other parts of the Mediterranean. Trade with Syria and Alexandria demanded access to Sicilian waters, given Sicily's favourable geographical position astride the eastward-bound trade routes. Merchants were often sent to Sicily to begin business there before moving on to their main destination in Syria or

---

[21] *GS*, I, no. 487, no. 500, no. 495, no. 499 – cf. no. 497, no. 498.
[22] *GS*, I, no. 501; ibn Jubayr, 361–5.

Alexandria. Messina in particular received much mention as first port of call on the way east. No less striking are the diversions of route from Spain to Genoa via Sicily. For Genoese trade in Spain was enhanced in value by the opportunity to work a wider circuit that brought in the Mediterranean islands, not least Sicily where the Norman kings made the Genoese so decidedly welcome. After 1162, it is true, these visits to Sicily became less frequent and the Genoese had increasingly to confine their west Mediterranean trade to Spain and the Maghrib – if the surviving records are at all representative of events.

Moreover, the Genoese merchants do not seem to have hesitated to move inland on their arrival at a particular destination and to buy what they were after at its point of production. To this extent a map of trade routes that links ports but not hinterlands, country towns and river routes is incomplete. One of the main advantages of the 1156 treaty was just this, that it gave the Genoese exceptional freedom to move beyond the city markets with few financial re-strictions; it brought them directly to the estates round Girgenti and behind Palermo; and if these were royal estates, the King could only argue that this was all to the good.[23] However, by the end of the century some of the estates behind Palermo were not the King of Sicily's lands, but those of Genoa. The evidence that in the mid-twelfth century also the Genoese had lands in Sicily needs therefore to be considered.

IV

The will of Guglielmo Scarsaria, drawn up in 1162, refers to the land and vineyard held by Guglielmo in Sicily: 'vinea et terra quam Scicilie habeo'.[24] Guglielmo had major commercial interests in the *Regno* – his Maltese cotton has already been encountered. However, the will gives no indication of the extent of his holdings in Sicily; rather than extensive estates they may have been a small group of gardens and vineyards in one of the major towns. Not until the 1180s is it apparent that the Genoese had estates in the less populated parts of the island, whereas the urban property they gained

---

[23] Apart from *CDG*, I, 338–41, see the late-twelfth-century contracts for trade *per terram regis*, eg. *OSM (1190)*, no. 146, *G. Cass.*, II, no. 1,201.

[24] *GS*, II, no. 950; cf. II, no. 1,212.

in 1116 does not seem to have been fit for the cultivation of any sort of produce. Given that some Ligurians did settle for lengthy periods in the *Regno* it is hardly surprising that they, along with others who visited Sicily at all regularly, should have acquired their own cultivable property as well as the houses and shops they owned inside the towns.[25] Indeed, the Venetian analogy is instructive here: the church of San Marco in Palermo had landed assets, partly composed of legacies from wealthy Venetian merchants; and so, even if the greater part of Genoese lands in Sicily may have been church lands, or lands owned by the Commune, a number of private estates may have existed by the middle of the twelfth century.[26] Interestingly, too, Genoese abandonment of the Normans in 1162 promised to be amply compensated with a major grant of towns and estates when Barbarossa conquered Sicily. Clearly, then, the establishment and extension of Genoese estates in the *Regno* was only partly a dream; future hopes for landed wealth were built upon past realities.

V

Guglielmo Scarsaria's testament, along with the inventory of his possessions drawn up after his death, provides valuable information about the nature of mercantile links with Sicily; and yet Scarsaria did not belong to the political aristocracy, despite his evident wealth. A pecking order is soon apparent among the Genoese merchants who invested in Sicily, related partly, of course, to their assets and to their interests in particular trading regions, but partly too to their family connections. The Genoese aristocracy formed an enclosed merchant group that was highly selective in its choice of travelling partners or other commercial colleagues – selective, but not socially exclusive, for wealthy non-patricians might be brought in for gain. Moreover, the Genoese patriciate was not politically united, nor did all patricians indulge in commercial activity. By chance, Giovanni Scriba's connections were primarily with the one patrician group, the della Volta clique, that dominated Genoese political activity in the twelfth century. On the basis of his evidence, and of that of Oberto Scriba in the 1180s, it is easy to assume that the political dominance of the della Volta clique was mirrored in commercial

[25] See 279–82 *infra* and *Doc. ined.*, 184, 185, 210, 211; also *Doc. ined.*, no. 76, 188–90.
[26] *Doc. ined.*, no. 18, no. 39, no. 60, no. 86; Toeche, 630; and 135 *supra*.

dominance too. To the extent that the della Volta clique was able to engineer treaties and concessions in selected ports, both as representatives of the Commune and as practising tradesmen, this image may be historically valid. In any case, the bias towards an eminent patrician faction, once recognised, has compensations at this period.

The years preceding the treaty with William the Bad were difficult ones for the Genoese Commune. The consuls had sent a naval expedition to Almeria and Tortosa (1147-9), and though the Genoese took the towns from the Moors, the Commune was left very short of money. It became necessary to mortgage out the right to collect various taxes – trade tolls, taxes on weights and measures, minting rights and so on. This overseas venture was one investment that did not pay off – all the more so since there were political repercussions at home. The della Volta family, which, with its friends and relations, had controlled the consulate throughout the century, was pushed out of office for a few years, though it recovered its position by 1154, when the friendly Auria (Doria), Spinola and Ususmaris families provided public officials.[27] At the same time a series of diplomatic initiatives in Palermo and Constantinople enabled the Republic to recover its mercantile position overseas. This did not involve the enrichment of the Commune itself – its overseas interests were still being diverted to private exploitation, as the leasing of Gibelet in Syria to the Embriaci in 1154 shows.[28] But it did lead to the enrichment of members of the communal government. Power had returned to the moneyed class, and this group used its status to push for greater commercial opportunities – a situation that it is tempting to describe as an alliance of capital and political authority.

When the Commune sent its embassy to William I, the consuls included Guglielmo Burone, brother of Ingo della Volta who placed £323 in a contract for Sicilian trade that season. Confidence was maintained in the *Regno* among the consular families, for the

---

[27] *Ann. Ian.*, I, 34-8; *CDG*, I, 254-5, 276; H. C. Krueger, 'Postwar collapse and rehabilitation in Genoa, 1149-1162', *Studi Luzzatto*, I, 123-6. Caffaro, *Ann. Ian.*, 37-8, remarks that the communal government was only aroused from its lethargy in 1154. So too was he – his remarks from 1149 to 1153 are sparse indeed, a sign of his exclusion from ruling circles.

[28] *CDG*, I, 296-9.

next year, 1157, Oberto Spinola was elected consul and sent £100 to Salerno and Alexandria. Other consular families, friendly to the della Volta clan, had big commercial interests in the *Regno*: the Mallone family, for instance, or the Guercio clique, one of the latter of whom was Rubaldo Bisacia, consul in 1159, 1162 and 1167, and several times in the 1170s.[29] Nevertheless it is impossible to say that the della Volta clique actually dominated trade with Sicily, even on Giovanni Scriba's showing. The scale of its investments in the *Regno* was disproportionately large, but in view of their established wealth members of the faction were able to take even greater risks in more distant markets that promised more substantial profits. Their interest in Sicily consisted to some extent in maintaining the right of access to the island so that their ships could travel safely to Syria and Alexandria; and it is just this group of merchants that presents most examples of combined contracts involving complex routes that took in Sicily among many other lucrative markets.[30]

Leaving aside the patricians, much of the trade with Sicily fell into the hands of people whose social standing in Genoa cannot clearly be established. Their lives are known exclusively from the cartularies, though where their wills survive it is sometimes possible to point to considerable reserves of wealth. Guglielmo Scarsaria invested the following sums during 1158:

£91 17s 6d in an *accomendacio* for trade in Sicily only
£16 in a *societas* of £24 for trade in Salerno
£3 in a *societas* of £5 for trade at St Gilles
£21 8s 0d in a *societas* of £32 2s 0d for trade in Tunis
£156 3s 0d in a *societas* of £331 plus merchandise for Sicily only
£12 0s 0d in a *societas* of £18 for Salerno
£30 in an *accomendacio* for Montpellier,

making a total of £330 8s 6d in one season, five-sixths of which was for trade in the *Regno*, and all of it for trade in the west and central Mediterranean.[31] His will makes it quite clear he was Genoese. He

---

[29] *Ann. Ian.*, I, 45, 53, 64, 201; Olivieri, *ASLSP*, I, 289, 302, 305, 331; *GS*, I, no. 71, no. 213.

[30] *GS*, I, no. 385 (14 May 1158) – Marchione della Volta invests money and cloth in a venture to Sicily and Egypt.

[31] *GS*, I, no. 327, no. 353, no. 366, no. 378, no. 383, no. 402, no. 494.

left his wife £50, his daughter £100, his nephews the 'vineyard and land that I have in Sicily', and he left several sums to the churches of Genoa. But much of his wealth was kept on active service: he had over £400 in *societates* with other merchants during 1162. Two years later, on 17 June 1164, an inventory of his possessions was drawn up, for he had just died. It included a vast assortment of objects from the *Regno*, Spain and elsewhere.[32]

Another family that was not admitted to consular status was the Filardo clan, of whom two, Guglielmo and Giovanni, are known in detail. Their activities were less concentrated on Sicily than those of Scarsaria. On 21 August 1156, with the financial support of their nephews, they collected together a *societas* of £680, to be carried for one year to Alexandria. A year later Guglielmo was sending *baldinelli*, eastern cloth or a western imitation, to an unnamed destination. But the real indication of this merchant's rôle lies in a contract cited already, for £300, of which £100 was to be provided by Ugo Mallone, a member of a newly elevated patrician family; this sum was to be carried to Syria, Sicily and back to Genoa along with £84 worth of textiles.[33] A nod must also be made in the direction of the very many other Genoese citizens whose individual rôle in overseas trade never rivalled that of the great families, however great the total volume. For those who wanted a quick profit on a legacy of £4 or £10 there were many worse ways of investing the money than an *accomendacio* or *societas* for Palermo.

It might, in addition, be useful to slice the cake a different way. There were evidently major interest groups, such as the della Volta family, for whom commercial activity was a highly valued means to wealth and the accumulation of resources; but among these patricians other financial operations promised to bear fruit, such as investment in town property or involvement in the land market in Liguria. The Avvocato and Gavi families, for instance, concentrated their attention on rural estates above all else, though land was scarce and, with so much money circulating in Genoa and Savona, the price of an estate in Liguria may have been extremely steep.[34]

[32] *GS*, I, no. 950, no. 1,212.

[33] *GS*, I, no. 121, no. 186, no. 236. For the elevation of the Mallone family, Bach, 62.

[34] A study of the land-market in twelfth-century Liguria would certainly be feasible, on the basis of notarial records.

Similarly, most of those who made only spasmodic investments in commercial enterprises must have had other sources of wealth and other professional activities. Thus notaries and priests were not averse to overseas investments now and again; and there are many instances of wives and widows who hoped to increase a legacy in this manner. The professional merchants comprised a smaller group – full-time merchants who acted both as backers to factors sent overseas and as travelling partners in their own right, as well as shippers and professional sailors. They were not politicians nor patricians; were they even Genoese? Some, such as Guglielmo Scarsaria, seem certainly to have been; others, known for their connection with a particular town such as Pavia or Verdun, were possibly birds of passage. But certainly some of the most eminent commercial figures are also the most elusive on this matter of their origins.

Both casual visitors and denizens who had taken up residence in Genoa appear in the cartularies. Thus there is a Joseph the Jew who was almost certainly a foreigner, since very few Jews lived in Genoa at this period, and one of the two principal ones is known by name.[35] Flemings and Pavians have already been encountered; there were a few Muslims too. This basic knowledge has been taken much further in the works of Eugene Byrne, who maintained that until the 1160s Genoese trade was dominated by a group not of native patricians, but of Greeks, Jews and Syrians; these 'easterners' gave way to native Genoese competition only after a series of financial crashes and even, Byrne argued, crises of conscience. The candidates for oriental origin are Blancardo, on no evidence whatsoever, Ribaldo di Sarafia, because his name might recall Saffuriyya in Syria, the Malfigliastro clan and Solomon of Salerno. All these had business in Sicily on some occasion during the 1150s and 1160s; one, indeed, apparently came from the *Regno*. Since Byrne wrote, others have shown that few if any of this group were Jews or Syrians. Blancardo, whom Byrne transmogrified into 'Solimanus Blancardus Iudeus', was never described as Solomon nor as a Jew. Given his involvement in the northern European textile trade it is tempting to regard him as French or Flemish – witness, for example, his contact with Olivier de Verdun – and the recent attempt to locate his origin in southern France makes sense, though at the cost of being more specific than

---

[35] *GS*, I, no. 436; Benjamin of Tudela, ed. Adler, 5.

the evidence confidently allows. Similarly Ribaldo di Sarafia may have been a native of southern France or, indeed, Liguria; and the Filardo family have also been classified as men of Languedoc. And as for Byrne's argument that the Malfigliastro family were Greeks, on the grounds that one of them held lands from the Byzantine emperor, it has already been established that Genoese merchants often held land from foreign lords – the case of Guglielmo Scarsaria can be placed alongside the larger instance of the Embriaco clan at Gibelet in Syria.[36]

Bonogiovanni Malfigliastro was one of Giovanni Scriba's most active commercial clients.

> August 1156, £33 sea-loan for trade in Salerno and Sicily
>
> June 1157, £48 in a *societas* for Sicily
>
> August 1157, £4 sea-loan for Palermo and back
>
> August 1157, £10 sea-loan for Palermo and back
>
> February 1158, £24 *cambium maritimum* for Salerno, repayable there to Bonogiovanni's son Guglielmo as 12 oz of gold at the Salerno standard
>
> August 1158, 10 *centenarii* of pepper for Sicily, to be repaid as £57½ Genoese
>
> August 1158, £36 in a *societas* of £108 for Salerno and Sicily
>
> October 1158, £69 in an *accomendacio* for Sicily[37]

All along, too, he was investing sea-loans and other deals in trade in Alexandria, Syria, Sardinia and North Africa. What is particularly interesting is the emphasis he placed on sea-loans, deals with exact, predetermined returns. On the £33 he would receive £41 back, on the £4 loan £5, on the £10 loan £12½. Probably he was primarily a banker, accepting money on deposit and sending out small portions on a variety of different expeditions with clearly defined risks. His profits and part of his capital might later be reinvested in

---

[36] E. H. Byrne, 'Easterners in Genoa', *Journal of the American Oriental Society*, XXXVIII (1918), 176–87; B. Nelson, 'Blancardo (the Jew?) of Genoa and the restitution of usury in medieval Italy', *Studi Luzzatto*, I, 99–108; V. Slessarev, 'Die sogennanten Orientalen im mittelalterlichen Genua. Einwänderer aus Südfrankreich in der ligurischen Metropole', *Vierteljahrschrift für Sozial- und Wirtschaftsgeschichte*, LI (1964), 22–65, especially 43–4.

[37] GS, I, no. 106, no. 196, no. 239, no. 240, no. 348, no. 461, no. 471, no. 504.

a more ambitious *societas* or *accomendacio*, where a greater risk fell on his shoulders but less of a limit was set on the profit he could hope to draw from a successful venture. He did not 'dominate' Genoese trade any more than most of the so-called easterners; he shows no signs of being other than a north Italian – indeed, his family remained in Genoa, and was still active in Sicilian trade in the last decades of the century.[38]

VI

There were, however, some foreigners who lived and worked in Genoa even though they can only vaguely be described as 'easterners': the Salernitans, whom Byrne also regarded as Jews. Not more than three can be identified: Solomon (Solimanus), Eliadar his wife, and a certain Sergius, who has not so far received attention. Now, Salerno had two distinct reputations by the late twelfth century: it was a commercial centre, and it possessed a famous medical school. In the acts of an unnamed notary, meagre fragments of whose work are bound with Giovanni's cartulary, there survives a contract of July 1156 between 'Sergium de Salerno medicum filium Ursi Scarsi et Symonem medicum filius Leonis de Regimundo', worth £8 15s 0d (£5 9s 0d plus £3 6s 0d), which was to be the basis of a two-year partnership.[39] The same notary shows that in January 1155 another contract involving a 'Sergius medicus' was drawn up. This time there is no mention of Salerno after Sergius' name; but 'Sergius' was a very common name in Campania, whereas it was as yet unknown in Genoa, and the two medical Sergii can be assumed identical. On this occasion, Sergius took into his service a certain Romaudus, for a period of four years, promising to feed and to clothe him. Possibly Romaudus was to be trained as his medical assistant.[40] In any case, the presence of doctors from Salerno, dabbling on occasion in business enterprises, should hardly occasion any great surprise.

'Sergius' at least was a good Christian name, but 'Solomon' is

---

[38] The Malfigliastro family took a long time to achieve consular status: Bach, 116–19.

[39] Archivio di Stato, Genoa, Cart. I, f.169r, no. 2. *GS*, II, p. 262, no. 7, erroneously prints a comma between 'Salerno' and 'Medicum', with the result that 'Medicum' appears to be a separate individual, rather than a doctor of Salerno.

[40] *GS*, II, p. 259, no. 3.

much more ambiguous, and could certainly have belonged to a Jew. Nevertheless, the evidence that Solomon of Salerno was Jewish is very slight indeed. He was prepared to marry his daughter into the Christian Mallone family; and so, even if he was Jewish, he was ready to put his social advancement before strict Jewish observance – the fact that the Malloni were interested in a marriage with a foreign settler is, however, impressive enough indication of the financial, if not social and political, status of Solomon.[41] In any case, the Jews were not welcomed to Genoa in the twelfth century; indeed, they had to pay a tax towards the illumination of the altar in the new cathedral of San Lorenzo. Moreover, Benjamin of Tudela travelled through Genoa during Giovanni Scriba's period of activity; and the Rabbi mentions no Solomon the Jew in his book of travels, as very probably he would have done, had there been any Jews of outstanding eminence in the city. Instead he refers to two Jews who originally came from North Africa.[42] Nor does Giovanni Scriba ever refer to Solomon as *iudeus*; and, were he a convert to Christianity, his supposedly Jewish name, if Jewish alone it was, would possibly have been changed. But in fact he is not the only Solomon in the cartulary: there is a Solomon *de Langasco*, a Solomon *de Portu Veneris* and so on.[43] All the same, Solomon remains of special interest because of his connection with Salerno; if he was not an 'easterner' under one of Byrne's criteria, he may have been under another – a survivor from the time when Amalfi and its neighbours maintained commercial primacy in the Tyrrhenian Sea and, along with Venice, kept open the shipping lanes to Egypt and Constantinople.

Even Solomon has been knocked from Byrne's list of 'easterners', on the grounds that he came from Salernes or Salerno in Provence, not from Salerno in Campania. But Salernes was a tiny town; its inhabitants occur in thirteenth-century Marseilles charters, but its connections with Genoa are impossible to trace. Vsevolod Slessarev has sought to show that the general emphasis of Solomon's business, as of that of Blancardo, Ribaldo di Sarafia, and other 'easterners', lay with Provence; the 'easterners', he has argued, were (locally

---

[41] *GS*, II, no. 1,064; cf. Nelson, 100.
[42] Nelson, 105, n. 3, for the altar illumination; Benjamin of Tudela, ed. Adler, 5.
[43] *GS*, I, no. 793 (cf. I, no. 556, no. 646, no. 687, II, no. 895); II, p. 269, no. 26 (unknown notary).

speaking) westerners, neighbours to the Ligurians. Although Provençaux do appear in the cartulary of Giovanni Scriba, and had, now
and again, trading interests in Sicily, it is important to recall King
William I's promise, made at the instigation of the Genoese, to forbid the Provençaux and *Francigeni* direct access to the *Regno*. Thereby
the Genoese may have hoped to gain a monopoly over movements
between Provence and Sicily, which would henceforth have to be
made in Ligurian ships. Solomon and his colleagues certainly had
interests in precisely this connection, operating directly, as will be
seen, between Fréjus and Sicily; his Provençal business fed his
Sicilian. And, in any case, there is an act of Giovanni Scriba, dated
18 September 1162, in which the merchant is described as 'Soli-
mano ianuense fideli domini Wuilielmi regis Scicilie'. Against this
Slessarev has maintained that it was possible for Genoese merchants
to become *fideles* of a foreign ruler without being in any sense
natives of that ruler's lands; there is, for instance, the case of one of
the Malfigliastro family at Constantinople, or the case of a certain
Bubonoso who swore allegiance to the King of Sicily in 1183. There
are, however, signs that Slessarev has forced Solomon into a mould
fashioned for other figures such as Blancardo – and the grounds for
thinking Blancardo to have been southern French are more solid in
every way. Slessarev has fallen into Byrne's trap, in that he has
attempted to create a clearly defined social group out of a diverse
assortment of individuals.[44] In any case, Solomon qualifies for
attention since he was a *fidelis regis Siciliae*, if not a native Salernitan.
He was also said to be a *ianuensis*, a Genoese; and this too makes
sense, for Genoa was clearly his financial base in the 1150s and 1160s.
He does not seem to have visited Provence, leaving his agent
Donato to do that; he does not seem to have stayed in Salerno or
Sicily; his only recorded travels were to Alexandria, the continual
focus of his interest. To find that a man from Salerno was a *fidelis
regis Siciliae* and yet spent little or no time in Sicily does, if anything,
strengthen the argument that he was a native of the *Regno*, for there
would be no need to insist on his tie to King William, unless indeed
this were an accident of birth and origin. He was Sicilian as it were
by passport, but Genoese by residence and preference. His wife,
indeed, may have been entirely Genoese, since her name, Eliadar,

[44] Slessarev, 'Sogennanten Orientalen', 44. Bubonoso: *Doc. ined.*, no. 76.

was rarely known outside Liguria; and here was another reason for Solomon to treat Genoa as his home. Moreover, Solomon had a brother called Lanfranco who appears to have lived at least for a time in Genoa.[45]

Solomon's political links with the *Regno* are, therefore, beyond doubt, and his Campanian origin seems also to make reasonable sense. Eugene Byrne, however, believed that the notarial acts revealed a dramatic story of the apogee and collapse of this man's financial empire: 'for nearly ten years in full view he served his betters, aided them in the field of trade he knew so well, lost a great [marriage] alliance, and sank into obscurity'.[46] He was, Byrne said, one of a generation of eastern merchants for whom the 1160s constituted a commercial death-knell; and it will be necessary to consider how far the rich documentation confirms this argument. Over forty of Giovanni Scriba's acts concern Solomon of Salerno in some way; several of these concern trade in Sicily, but none, surprisingly, mentions Salerno except as part of Solomon's surname.

Solomon was both backer and traveller, accepting commissions from Genoese merchants with the same regularity as he entrusted commissions to his juniors. On 19 August 1156 Bonogiovanni Malfigliastro entrusted unspecified goods to him; these were to be converted into Egyptian bezants by Solomon when he arrived at Alexandria. From Alexandria he would carry this sum, set at 110 bezants, to Cairo, and purchase lac and brazilwood there on Bonogiovanni's behalf. Solomon clearly did not expect a long stop-over in Sicily, for the same day he commissioned Ogerio de Ripa to recover 1,254¾ tari owed him by Giordano de Molino; to find Giordano, Ogerio was to search in Syracuse, the royal court and elsewhere in Sicily. Ogerio de Guidone also entrusted goods to Solomon, which Solomon was to take to Alexandria. This time he was to be accompanied by Ogerio de Guidone's son, whom he was to train and to advise on commercial prospects. If the son stayed with Solomon, Solomon would repay Ogerio with £140 worth of pepper and brazilwood. (This contract is repeated, not quite verbatim, in the cartulary – presumably because Giovanni forgot he had already registered it, rather than because the partners

---

[45] Eliadar is clearly stated to be Solomon's wife: *GS*, I, no. 225, no. 733; Lanfranco: *GS*, I, no. 111.   [46] Byrne, 'Easterners', 181.

came together once again, almost immediately, to double their original investment; such an act would be recorded in a codicil to the first charter, not as an independent registration.) Not merely the Malfigliastro but also the della Volta family clearly regarded Solomon with trust; consul Ogerio Vento sent £15, to be converted in Alexandria into local gold, and he sent also a silver chain; both gold and silver were to be entrusted to Ogerio's son who was already, or would by then be, in Alexandria.[47] On the basis of these documents it is clear that Solomon had established commercial ties with Sicily, through his use of factors, well before the treaty of 1156 between William and the Genoese. His 'network' is emerging already from the sources.

Next year this network is even more eloquently expressed through an act of 1 August. Here, not Solomon but Aliadar or Eliadar, 'wife of Solomon of Salerno' (uxoris Solimina de Salerno) is found agreeing on a partnership with Garsias, brother of Petrus de Bur – possibly a Provençal or Catalan merchant. Eliadar contributed £16, and Garsias £5; the whole was to be taken to Fréjus by Garsias who would then return to Genoa. Here Eliadar would add a further £3, making a total of £24, and Garsias would add on top of this the profits gained in business at Fréjus. Then Garsias would send his own agent, Oliverio, to Palermo with all this money, to pursue the aims of the *societas* there. Eliadar, in a manner that will prove characteristic, insisted that Garsias should be insured aganst loss, the indemnity being borne by his brother Petrus de Bur.[48] Meanwhile Solomon seems to have remained abroad in Alexandria, for he does not reappear in Giovanni's acts until 2 April 1158, when he is cited as a witness to a £35 sea-loan aimed at Bougie; here he is in the company of Bonogiovanni Malfigliastro and of one of the Grillo clan, Lamberto.[49] That, all along, Solomon's financial affairs could function through his wife and other agents is one sign that Solomon's business house was continuously and profitably active; but another sign lies in the elaborate nature of Eliadar's commission to Oliverio and Garsias – it is elaborate in route, since it involves a return journey to Fréjus prior to the main trip aimed at Palermo; and it is elaborate in personnel, since Eliadar is using two travelling

[47] *GS*, I, no. 111, no. 112, nos. 113–14, no. 117.
[48] *GS*, I, no. 225.   [49] *GS*, I, no. 370.

partners, one the deputy of another, as well as a third party who will protect her against default.

In August 1158 Solomon and Eliadar are seen working in collaboration with Donato di San Donato, a favourite commercial colleague. On 5 August Solomon entrusted £40 to Donato, who placed a further £20 against this, and promised to travel to Sicily and then back to Genoa. Donato's services to the husband and wife were old ones, since the next document consists of a declaration of assets made by Donato to Eliadar, in which Donato enumerated merchandise remaining from an old *societas* with her. Thirteen loads (*carricas*) of cotton, and a further £20 worth of cotton, are mentioned; presumably this was raw cotton. Not that Solomon was afraid to diversify: as a long-term settler in Genoa he bought land too, paying £108 for a plot at Sampierdarena. Interestingly this was sold to 'you and to your heirs', so clearly Solomon's family was regarded as a settled one, whose roots, if not deep, would in time deepen.[50]

Another old partner, apart from Donato, was Marchese Castagna. In August 1158 they divided their assets, which included silver money, bezants, brazilwood, pepper and a furred cape, as well as shares in a ship. Similarly Solomon held on deposit from a certain Elione funds and merchandise which were being brought back from Alexandria on behalf of both parties. Meanwhile Solomon planned further business in Alexandria through his agent Baldo di Campo, who was to take £206 to Egypt, £126½ of which belonged to Solomon and the remainder to himself. Again, this was an old relationship being renewed rather than a new commercial venture: 'they declared also', Giovanni noted, 'that all partnerships that they had up till now should be divided'. The same statement occurs at the end of a *societas* between Solomon and another agent, Guglielmo Adricto, aimed at Alexandria and worth £484½, £323 of which was invested by Solomon.[51]

Solomon's activity in late August and September 1158 was very intensive. On 25 August he entered a partnership composed of units of £18 and £6, the purpose of which was to commission a certain Cellario to work 'in Genoa for up to one year' – an unusual task, to be sure, considering that Solomon seems to have stayed in

---

[50] *GS*, I, nos. 420–1, no. 423. [51] *GS*, I, nos. 426–7, nos. 436–7.

Genoa himself that winter.[52] On 4 September an old colleague of
Eliadar reappears; Oliverio, agent of Petrus de Bur and of Garsias,
made a *societas* worth £24 for trade in Palermo. Oliverio was to remain there until the summer of 1159 and then to return to Solomon
in Genoa. Once again Petrus and Garsias guaranteed Solomon against
the possibility that Oliverio might wantonly waste the money with
which he had been entrusted: a further attack of nerves on the part
of Solomon and his wife. Perhaps the disappearance of Giordano de
Molino in Sicily had made them suspicious of their subsequent
partners, especially those bound for the delights of the *Regno*.
Interestingly, too, Solomon also gave Oliverio a quantity of goods
– 'Oliverio declared that he carried all the goods of the said Solomon
that are mentioned in the chirograph (*papiro sisso pari*) entitled
"In the name of the Lord Amen", of which he has one copy and
Solomon the other.'[53] Three weeks later Ribaldo Dodone de Albericis was sent in Enrico Nevitella's ship to do business on Solomon's
behalf 'wherever he [Enrico] shall go, and then to Genoa, or to
Sicily and then back to Genoa'; this was a relatively modest
societas of £45. The same route was to be followed by Culorio,
whom Solomon commissioned the same day to carry £64½ in
Nevitella's vessel. The day after, 26 September, Enrico Nevitella
himself appeared in partnership with Solomon, who contributed
£142 13s 4d to a *societas* worth £210. In addition Nevitella and
Solomon agreed to divide equally the capital and profit outstanding
from earlier *societates*, including a debt of £9 of Melgueil owed to
two other merchants in exchange for 36 bezants. Responding to the
opportunities offered by Nevitella's expedition, Solomon then struck
a deal with Oliviero da Pavia, who seems a separate individual
from Garsias' agent Oliverio. He was to carry £200 in *accomendacio*
'to Spain, and I must not be separated from Enrico Nevitella; but, if
I go to Sicily, wherever Enrico goes next, I must still return to
Genoa and place in your or your agent's hands all the money,
capital and profit'. Two further contracts seem to be associated with
this group of investments. On 20 September Solomon sent £30 in
a £45 *societas* to Majorca; the factor was to return to Genoa unless
his ship moved on elsewhere. This deal does not seem to have
involved Enrico Nevitella's ship, but it signals further extensive

[52] *GS*, I, no. 440.   [53] *GS*, I, no. 482.

interest in west Mediterranean trade. And on 26 September Guido
da Lodi and Odone drew up a contract worth £139 18s 0d, the
whole to be carried to 'Spain, then to Sicily or Provence or Genoa,
from Provence to Genoa or Sicily, or if he wishes from Sicily to
Romania and then to Genoa, or from Sicily to Genoa'. There is
no specific mention of Solomon nor of Nevitella's ship, but the route
prescribed has enough similarities to make it likely that a voyage in
that vessel was being planned. Overall, Solomon had placed
£348 13s 4d in an expedition worth, on the basis of Giovanni's
figures, £404 10s 0d.[54] His stipulation to his factors that they should
not travel beyond Sicily makes sense since he had already commissioned ventures to Alexandria during August; no doubt he wished
to keep his east Mediterranean operations in a separate compart-
ment, to avoid duplication of activities – his agents in Alexandria
could be expected to return with rather different stocks from those
that other agents would purchase in Spain and Sicily. Whatever the
explanation, Solomon was financially able to maintain simultaneous
ventures to both extremities of the Mediterranean, a fact that speaks
for the diversity of his commercial interests no less than for his
wealth.

On 24 October Gionata Crispino borrowed £10, apparently free
of interest, from Solomon; this was to be returned within a fortnight
of the arrival of the first ship the following summer to come from
Alexandria; but it is not entirely clear that, so late in the year,
Crispino planned to travel to Egypt. He may, simply, have required
some ready cash while other assets were tied up with agents in
Alexandria.[55] Principally, however, Solomon spent the winter of
1159–60 tidying up affairs. On 18 October, for instance, Eliadar
commissioned Donato as her agent for up to three years, on the
basis of returns from earlier *societates* between them. And in
November Solomon had to arrange to have a ship caulked, prior to
its departure for Alexandria, where it was hoped to sell her. Three
professional caulkers promised the joint owners of this ship – Solomon, Guglielmoto Ciriole and Musso Boiachesio – that they would
service the 'navim' and the 'barcam et caravellum coopertum et
gabias eius' for £8½. Guglielmoto also appears as a shipowner in

[54] *GS*, I, nos. 497–500, no. 495, no. 501.
[55] *GS*, I, no. 514.

the contracts of summer 1157; here he is one of a group of shippers and merchants bound for Palermo, and associated with Solomon's trading colleague Bonogiovanni Malfigliastro.[56] By February 1160 Genoese merchants were investing money with factors who were due to travel in Solomon's ship. The patrician Marchione della Volta sent £80, in the form of a sea-loan, with Embrone, 'to Alexandria in the ship of Solomon and his partners...returning thence in the summer after next [1161], and, if the ship be sold or change route...in the ship in which the greater part of Genoese men and Genoese property (*pecunia ianuensium*) shall come...' But the departure of Solomon's ship – still, doubtless, being serviced – remained in doubt: 'and if Solomon's ship does not go this year, I [Embrone] shall pay you £90 in Genoese money before next Michaelmas'. During the summer, indeed, Solomon's vessel remained in Genoa, but meantime the city's merchants poured further funds into his venture to Egypt. Alessandro Nasella appointed Solomon his agent for merchandise he was sending to Alexandria, and Solomon promised to repay him in Egyptian bezants or in pepper and alum. But there was plenty of room aboard for other agents, and in August 1160 Marchione de Caffaro appointed Bonovassallo Bulferico his factor, sending a sea-loan of £20 with him in Solomon's ship. Moreover, Marchione insisted that Bonovassallo return 'in that ship in which Solomon himself shall begin to come that [next] summer from Alexandria, and which shall be loaded with the greater part of his goods', a stipulation even stronger than that made by Marchione della Volta to Embrone.[57]

Eliadar too was active, looking after the other end of the Mediterranean while Solomon laid his plans for his voyage east. On 22 August she commissioned a £5 *societas*, aimed at Sicily, whence the factor was to return early the following summer. Interestingly, the contract was drawn up 'in domum ipsius Eliadar', which could mean that she had a separate establishment from her husband; together, no doubt, they owned a large number of houses and plots of land – the Sampierdarena instance has been cited already. Solomon, however, used a variety of locations – 'in domum', even 'in camera Solime', and once 'in curia', which Byrne, with

[56] GS, I, no. 562, no. 578; Guglielmoto: I, no. 240.
[57] GS, I, no. 610, no. 658, no. 708.

245

true *incuria*, thought a reference to his palace or grand entourage, but which others might suppose a reference to the courtyard in his house.[58] Eliadar also sent £18 to Spain in April; this was her share of a £27 *societas* that her factor was to work for two years. As ever, she kept a tight control over her agent's activities: 'he must not delay there longer [than two years] unless he sees authentic letters of the said Eliadar…he must not take a wife in the meantime or become a resident in any other place'; and the penalty was fearsome indeed – 'unless he acts thus…the messenger of the said Eliadar may seize his person, along with the money he has, and place him in Eliadar's hands'.[59] A further activity in which Eliadar was presumably involved was the marriage alliance between Solomon and Ansaldo Mallone, a wealthy patrician, to be effected by the marriage of Solomon's daughter Alda to Ansaldo's son. As the first stage towards completion of formalities, Solomon gave Ansaldo £100 in dowry.[60]

On 17 July 1160 Solomon declared to his old trading partner Marchese Castagna that he still held goods entrusted to him by Marchese a year ago, as a first contribution to his Alexandrian expedition. And then Solomon disappears from view for exactly a year, to return to light on 17 July 1161, when he commissioned Guglielmo Hostaliboi to take £150 in *societas* to an unnamed destination.[61] In the meantime Solomon was almost certainly in Alexandria. But his other activities during 1161 cannot be traced in Giovanni Scriba's cartulary. Byrne argued that his disappearance from prominence in 1161 and after reflects the failure of his finances during these years; the expedition of 1160–1 ended, perhaps, in disaster, or (to adopt a view that Byrne did not actually express) the commercial problems of 1162, when Genoa lost its Sicilian links, destroyed Solomon's financial empire.[62] And yet Byrne argued precisely from the latest scraps of evidence that Solomon was a man of enormous prestige and wealth; on the basis of some documents of 1162 that show Solomon being visited by agents of a Muslim potentate, Byrne showed how widely diffused this merchant's reputation had become – and yet he also argued that this series of docu-

[58] *GS*, I, no. 733. Location: Byrne, 'Easterners', 180; *GS*, II, no. 856 ('in Curia').
[59] *GS*, I, no. 625.   [60] *GS*, I, no. 701.
[61] *GS*, I, no. 702; II, no. 856.   [62] Byrne, 'Easterners', 180.

ments illustrated Solomon's newly attained poverty. Similarly, his virtual disappearance from view in 1161 could be used to show that he was no longer a business magnate; and yet it was in the one document from 1161 that mentions Solomon that Byrne found evidence for his *curia*, as he understood the term. Now, this document refers also to Solomon's notary – 'Robertus notarius Solime', who appears as a witness to the contract.[63] That Solomon had his own scribe to help him with his financial calculations is hardly surprising, given the complexity of his operations on behalf of large numbers of eminent clients. But his disappearance from the day-to-day record may also be explained by his decision to use his own notary for commercial registrations. Possibly Robertus' cartularies were among those destroyed in 1684; there is no way of knowing. In any case, there are no grounds for assuming that Solomon's disappearance from Giovanni Scriba's cartulary meant his disappearance from other notaries' cartularies as well. And, even though Solomon did little, Eliadar and Donato continued their long-standing partnership: Eliadar and Donato made a *societas* composed of £48 and £24 for trade in Sicily (September 1161); Donato was to return directly from Sicily to Genoa – as usual, Eliadar eschewed the east Mediterranean in her investment policy. She promised Donato a further 102 tari, to be collected in Sicily, part of the profit of an earlier *societas* between these two. Other past *societates* were allowed to go into mothballs: Eliadar retained in Genoa '8 cantara 26 rotuli' of raw cotton, the property of Donato, and '6 cantara 14 rotuli', her own property. In any case there are no signs of a contrary wind as far as Eliadar's partnerships with Donato are concerned.[64]

The year 1162 was that to which Byrne pointed when he said Solomon's fortunes crashed. Three uncancelled notarial acts of that year do, it is true, place Solomon in an exotic light. He appears on 18 September 1162 among friends – his witnesses include Bonogiovanni Malfigliastro, Donato di San Donato – to settle his affairs with the emissaries of a Saracen lord, qaid Abu-l-qasim:

[i.] Witnesses: Bonogiovanni Malfigliastro, Donato di San Donato, Giovanni Cristiani and W. da Pavia. We Simon, Bombarchet and Iusuph [Jews or Muslims] agents of Caitus Bulcassem received on loan

---

[63] *GS*, II, no. 856.   [64] *GS*, II, no. 909.

from you Solomon the Genoese, *fidelis* of lord William king of Sicily,
£55 in Genoese money which we gave to Ismael for the bundles
('fardellis') of the said Caitus Bulcassem; he gave us twelve of these, for
which, at the exchange rate of 35s 10d per ounce of gold, then current
in Genoa, we shall pay within a month of our arrival in Sicily 31⅓ oz of
gold to your agent, who will be either Matteo, or Manfredo de Portinico,
or any other accredited agent – that is to say, anyone who shall show us,
or one of us, the Arabic charter ('cartulam sarracenicam') which we
leave with you, and which will be expected. I Simon swear to observe
this agreement on the holy gospels and we Bombarchet and Iusuph
swear it on [or 'by'] the law that we follow. Given in the house of
Solomon in Genoa, 1162, XIV Kal. Oct., 9th indiction. In the [Saracen]
charter however it was the month of September. [As it still was in
Genoa – *ante Kalendas Octubris*!]

[ii.] Witnesses: Filippo di Lamberto, Oto *iudex*, Ogerio de Pallo,
Donato de Clavica, and Giovanni Cristiani. Solomon gave Ismael on
deposit, for £34, two new silver cups (one larger than the other), an
ermine mantle and a grey mantle and one *xoca*, so that, unless Solomon
has repaid him the said sum by the middle of October, Ismael can
legally sell these securities, though he must return to Solomon what
excess there may be [over £34] in the sale, if anything be left behind.
Subject to the penalty of paying double [in the event of default], with the
rider that Solomon promised him restitution within three days. Given in
Solomon's house, 1162, on the said day, 9th indiction.

[iii.] Witnesses: Filippo di Lamberto, Oto *iudex*, Lamberto Filippi
[*sic*], Solomon, Bonogiovanni Malfigliastro, Ogerio de Pallo and many
others. Bombarchet and Simon, emissaries of Caitus Bulcassem, in the
presence of these and of many others, received the twelve bundles of the
said Caitus which Ismael then returned; and they declared them to be
signed and bound in the manner that he had received them and they
declared that otherwise he would have returned to them, instead of these,
another ten bundles of the same [Caitus]; now, however, there remained
with him two bundles, one the property of Almussalis, and not [in either
case] of the said Caitus. Given in the house of the said Ismael, 1162, XIV
Kal. Oct., 9th indiction.[65]

Ismael was a common name among Genoese Christians, and this
Ismael possessed a house in Genoa; he probably falls into the category
of resident Genoese merchants and was not, as Byrne assumed, a
'Saracen friend' of the easterner Solomon. But Caitus Bulcassem

[65] *GS*, II, nos. 970–2; Byrne, 'Easterners', 180.

was clearly a Muslim, and a man of distinction: his name is qaid Abu-l-qasim, metamorphosed into notarial Latin; he is clearly a man of some wealth, with agents to act on his behalf; and he seems to be based in Sicily or to have strong financial interests there. Abu-l-qasim was indeed a Sicilian Muslim of the greatest eminence, a fitting business partner for the merchant magnate Solomon. Hugo Falcandus wrote of him, ibn Jubayr even met him and described him, poets and essayists such as ibn Zafar and ibn Qalaqis dedicated their works to him. Amari claimed the blood of the family of Muhammad for him, and family links with dynasties in southern Spain and northern Morocco: the noble Idrisi may have been a distant relative. He was widely known for his wealth and generosity; ibn Zafar wrote that 'he does not give ear to slanderers, neither does he suffer his coin to rust' – and yet by 1185 he had been 'traduced with untrue stories' and had been fined 120,000 tari, or 30,000 dinars, by the crown. In Palermo and Trapani he had extensive property; after his death Frederick II's ministers gave the Genoese 'in Trapana domum que fuit Gaeti Bulcasimi', as well as property belonging to Christians in Messina and Syracuse. And indeed it was in Trapani that ibn Jubayr talked with him. The Spanish traveller called him 'leader and Lord of the Muslim community' in Sicily; 'this man belongs to that noble house on the island of which the eldest son successively assumes the Lordship [of the Muslims]'. In the light of this evidence it should occasion little surprise that his emissaries were met by some of the most eminent Genoese businessmen and city officials, nor that their transactions were recorded in such detail, nor that the merchant Solomon should be involved in the affairs of another subject of the Sicilian king. It is worth recalling, too, the agreement between Latin and Arabic sources that Muslim merchants still dominated the Palermitan business community at the end of the twelfth century.[66]

---

[66] For qaid Abu-l-qasim ibn Hammud see ibn Jubayr 358–9; H. Falc., 119; M. Amari, tr., *Solwan el Mota' ossiano conforti politici di Ibn Zafer arabo siciliano del XII secolo* (Florence, 1851), xxiv–xxvii, xxxiii, 2–4 (also English translation of Amari, *Solwan or Waters of Comfort by Ibn Zafer a Sicilian Arab of the Twelfth Century*, 2 vols. (London, 1852), I. 29, 43, 139–143); Amari, *Storia*, III, 175 n., 510, 550–3, (though Amari's editor, C. A. Nallino, doubted Amari's claim that Abu-l-qasim was a member of Muhammad's family, his claim that the Idrisids of Spain and Morocco were related and the identity between this Abu-l-qasim and the person

Byrne, on the other hand, believed the second document showed into what financial straits Solomon had fallen; but he made no attempt to interpret the other two contracts. The first document has some of the characteristics of a *cambium maritimum*; the use of merchandise as a medium to divide the loan of Genoese money from repayment in Sicilian gold was a common ruse in the late twelfth century. But the rate of repayment stipulated in the first contract was about half that cited in contemporary sea-loans recorded elsewhere in the same cartulary. The arithmetic certainly works well enough: $31\frac{1}{3}$ oz at £1 15s 10d per ounce makes a total of £56 and a few pence; and of course the rather higher exchange rates current at about the same time involved a hefty profit – if this document is to be believed, a profit of about 100 per cent, excluding the factor's own profit or share. The decline in Genoese trade in Sicily in 1162 may, to be sure, have affected the exchange rate by reducing demand in Genoa for Sicilian gold; with access to Sicily more limited by September 1162, gold may have fetched a price nearer to 'reality' and shorn of high profits.[67] Solomon does not actually seem to be the loser in the first text; it is simply that he is not the gainer either. However, his own agents in Sicily could be expected to reinvest the money there and draw profit from its use in trade. Caitus too seems to have been engaged in a *cambium maritimum* pledged against his own goods; and in the second document Solomon is seen entering into yet another contract of just this type. Whether £34 represented the real value of the items entrusted to Ismael cannot be said; but, the document says, there was a chance of profit from their sale; and in late-twelfth-century *cambia* similar language was used where a profit was reasonably certain, to hide accusations of unfair gain through unequal or usurious exchanges. Byrne used the emotive word 'pawned' of this transaction; and to place in *pignus* does mean, etymologically, to place in pawn – but with such strong overtones of long-term gain by the depositing

to whom ibn Zafar dedicated the *Sulwan*. Nallino did not, however, provide any discussion in his notes to Amari's *Storia*). Frederick's grant of 1200 is printed by Huillard-Bréholles, I, part 1, 64–7. Muslim merchants of Palermo: ibn Jubayr, 348; H. Falc., 57.

[67] A lower gold price is, similarly, indicated in the comparable year 1191; then, too, Genoa was abandoning the Normans for a German alliance, and then too the cited price of gold was rather less than it was during the 1180s – cf. *supra*, 195.

party that it would be foolhardy to suppose this text to be proof of Solomon's financial crash.

To find Solomon maintaining his Sicilian interests even after the Genoese had joined Barbarossa's side suggests that he was indeed a Salernitan from Campania. In the first place, he is described as King William's *fidelis*, who must have remained *persona grata* in Sicily even after 1162; in the second place other Genoese-based merchants did not follow his example, for trade with Sicily, outside his and his wife's hands, was sparse in 1163 and 1164. It is even possible to suggest why he is gratuitously described as 'ianuense fideli domini Wuilielmi regis Scicilie' in the first of this group of contracts. Since Abu-l-qasim was himself a Sicilian subject, the contracts concerned negotiations, through intermediaries, between two of King William's men. The commune had recently received an imperial privilege which studiously avoided all reference to William of Sicily as 'King'; perhaps, in a rather heavy-handed way, they wanted to avoid the impression that they themselves did business with residents in Sicily, though *regnicoli* resident in Genoa were not discouraged from doing so.

Nonetheless Solomon's plans did not all bear fruit in the 1160s. On 11 July 1163 Solomon declared to Ansaldo Mallone that he had received £192 10s 0d minus seventeen rolls of cotton, paid originally as the dowry of his daughter, which Ansaldo was now returning. In other words, the marriage alliance would no longer come into effect. The reason is far from clear; it may be that Ansaldo was unwilling to link his fortunes to those of a house whose loyalties were to the King of Sicily rather than to the new pact with Barbarossa. Byrne's view was that Solomon was no longer a financial giant and so no longer worth knowing, for a Genoese patrician would have to look carefully before entering so close an alliance with an 'eastern' family.[68] But Genoese merchants continued to frequent Solomon's house, and Giovanni Scriba came there on 22 September 1163 to draw up a series of acts, only two out of three of which actually mentioned Solomon. One of this series is an uncancelled contract between Solomon and Donato di San Donato, according to which the latter would take £100 (£70 of which was contributed by Solomon) to an unstated destination 'in the ship in which

[68] *GS*, II, no. 1,064 (uncancelled); Byrne, 'Easterners', 180.

Enrico Guiono is travelling'. A subsequent document enumerates goods and other assets held by Solomon and Donato at Fréjus: three hundred hides, a further hundred and thirty skins, five pieces of fustian, as well as several *cantara* of alum and wax, plus £30; moreover, there were 200 tari on deposit in Sicily – a fact which makes it likely that Donato once again intended to go to Sicily after a prior call at Fréjus. Another factor, Guglielmo Fasol, was sent to Bougie, a newly developed interest on Solomon's part. He was to carry £120 belonging to Solomon and £60 nominally contributed by himself, but in fact drawn from a partnership between himself and Solomon's old colleague Marchese Castagna. After leaving Bougie Fasol was expected to return directly to Genoa; but since, once again, the contract is uncancelled it is not certain that the voyage took place. Byrne cogently remarked that the £190 odd recovered by Solomon from his marriage pact with the Malloni had found a new use in the £190 he now sent to Fréjus, Sicily and Bougie; conceivably, therefore, this really is evidence that Solomon no longer had capital to spare. On the other hand, this coincidence does not prove that he was deeply in debt, for almost the whole of the dowry was made available within two months for overseas trade; and, since 1163 was a poor year for trade anyhow, it is worth insisting that Solomon was not much less active commercially than were his patrician counterparts.[69]

In 1164 Solomon's financial position appears once again in a strange light, with a contract of 27 March acquitting him of further obligation over a debt of £12½. This was owed in exchange for 135 tari, a quarter of which had been recovered in Sicily by the creditor's brother. After Solomon paid the creditor a further £6 the matter was considered closed. Since £12½ was rather a high exchange rate for 4½ oz of tari – a rate more in accord with commercial or usurious exchanges – the decision to reduce the exchange to £6 plus a little over 1 oz of tari may have been dictated by changes in the money market, or equally by Solomon's difficult financial position. The former seems more likely, since legally the creditor

[69] *GS*, II, no. 1,106 ('in domo solimani'), no. 1,107 ('eodem loco') – in both cases Solomon stands as witness. Donato: II, no. 1,109, no. 1,110. Fasol: no. 1,111 (uncancelled). Cf. II, no. 1,108, also 'in domo Solimani'; Byrne, 'Easterners', 180.

would have had powers of distraint, and an act of generosity aimed simply to reduce Solomon's debts cannot automatically be presumed. In any case, Eliadar possibly still had funds: on 9 August 1164 Eliadar or Aliadar sister of Giordano di Michele sent £40 for trade wherever the factor pleased; this may, however, be another Eliadar not encountered elsewhere in the cartulary. In any case, Solomon's social standing cannot have plummeted. On 16 August that year he appeared in the company of Ribaldo di Sarafia, another well-tried trader, to witness the purchase of a house worth £15 by the eminent political figure Guglielmo Vento, a leading member of the Genoese aristocracy; and so it seems that he continued to move in gracious circles. He probably died some time between 1164 and 1179, when the cartularies resume, free of reference to Solomon of Salerno or to Eliadar.[70] Similarly, Blancardo died in 1178; and the only reason that the date of his death is known is his extraordinary testament, requesting the restitution of money gained by usury.[71] Of this group of active merchants, centred on Solomon, Bonogiovanni Malfigliastro and the della Volta family, only the native Genoese seem to have survived into the 1180s; and to that extent it is possible to agree with Byrne and Slessarev that the 1150s saw the dominance of a group of non-Genoese merchants in Genoese trade. Accepting some points from the analysis of each of these authorities, it seems that both southern French and 'eastern' merchants played a major rôle in the early development of Genoese trade with Provence, Spain, Alexandria and, very possibly, with Sicily too. Although Solomon's commercial empire lacked the co-ordination of the networks established in the 1180s and 1190s, which brought northern cloth south to Sicily against tari and pound deposits, his empire was nevertheless very elaborately and carefully organised. By way of deputies and agents, specialising on his behalf in western or eastern Mediterranean affairs, he was able to operate on a financial scale in which he had few rivals. When deprived in the 1160s of his Egyptian and Sicilian outlets, he may have suffered a recession, but it would be exaggeration to suppose this was necessarily a mortal blow; and some of the texts employed to show how he had fallen into dire financial straits can be used equally to show how he was

[70] *GS*, II, no. 1,178, no. 1,275 (uncancelled), no. 1,292.
[71] Nelson, 96.

able to anticipate the complex pledging techniques of the 1180s and 1190s in order to secure the smooth operation of credit and of commercial friendships with overseas partners. His links with the crown of Sicily as *fidelis* or as native Salernitan qualify him in any case to be considered under the very special heading of *regnicoli* trading through Genoa. In the 1180s and 1190s there were others, Gaetans above all, but none of them appears to have established such close links with Genoa nor to have established so extensive a commercial empire. Solomon of Salerno was, therefore, an exceptional merchant whose importance lies in the stimulus he gave to Genoese trade in the Mediterranean, and the lessons he taught Genoese merchants on their way to and from Egypt. To that extent Byrne's picture cannot be rejected; he was indeed a merchant prince.[72]

[72] For south Italians in Genoa in the late twelfth century, see *OSM* (*1190*), no. 640 (Gaetan merchants or sailors), and, for Salernitans, *G. Cass.*, I, no. 47, a *societas* between two men of Salerno for business within Genoa (8 January 1191). For Sicilians in Genoa, see 278–9 *infra*.

Chapter 10

THE STRUCTURE OF TRADE IN THE LATE NORMAN PERIOD

I

On extracting from the lengthy sequence of Genoese contracts for the 1180s and 1190s those that refer to merchandise or to foreign merchants, several themes stand out, each closely related. In the first place, the presence of merchants from Lucca and Liège attracts attention. These were major cloth-producing centres; and, to be sure, the evidence for the career of Jean de Liège or the Lucchese merchants concerns the sale and pledging of cloth. Moreover, textile contracts directed to trade in Sicily often cite prices in ounces of tari, that is, in Sicilian gold instead of, or as well as, Genoese silver pounds. They are complex documents that range in catchment area from the North Sea to the central Mediterranean; and, equally, they reveal an institutional and financial sophistication that the evidence of the 1150s and 1160s does not appear to display. They raise the crucial issue of when, or how, the merchants of the north began to substitute, for payments in bullion, payments effected through the sale of northern industrial items imported into Sicily. Of course, this question has implications that range beyond a study of the Norman *Regno*, and concern Genoese trade with North Africa, Syria and other major markets as well. However, the case of Sicily, an exporter of agricultural items above all else, is of especial interest. This chapter is concerned not with the commercial exchange of luxury merchandise of one type for luxury merchandise of another, but with an overall change in the manner of purchase of basic foodstuffs and of raw fibres. A further dimension is provided by evidence that the northern textile merchants exported unprocessed cotton from Sicily as well as importing processed textiles into Sicily; it is, therefore, not unreasonable to suppose that the northern merchants sent back to the *Regno* products that had their ancestry in the cotton farms of southern Italy and Sicily. In addition, the *Regno* became increasingly dependent upon Flemish woollens, high-quality, high-demand items that the kingdom was unable, for a variety of reasons, to produce for itself.

II

By 1182 Lucchese merchants were using Genoa as an outlet for trade with Sicily. Both citizens of Lucca and the products of its looms travelled to Genoa on their way to the *Regno*. This double link is illustrated by two independent contracts of the same day, 15 October 1182. In the first, Paxio of Lucca lent Giovanni Faber a sum of money, which Giovanni promised to repay the Luccan in Messina, in the form of 32 tari of the Messina standard. And later that day Stefano de Clavica declared he owed Perasco 11⅛ oz of gold, which was to be paid in Sicily or Salerno in person – it is unclear whether the purer Sicilian tari was to be the medium of repayment, or the tari of Salerno. As pledge, Stefano entrusted to Perasco two pieces of Lucca 'scarlet' cloth, which Perasco was to sell in the *Regno* prior to his rendezvous with Stefano. Should the sale of the cloth raise less than 11⅛ oz, Stefano would pay Perasco £3 for every ounce outstanding; but should Perasco earn more than the stipulated sum, he in his turn would owe Stefano £3 for each excess ounce of gold.[1] On the basis of the information provided in the contract, the cloth appears to be valued at a heady £33 7s 6d; but it is essential to recall that this was a profit-oriented transaction, in which lender and borrower partially exchanged their rôles. Merchandise was cited not simply because it was to be exported and sold, as far as possible, at profit; it was cited also to conceal the charging of commission, with its usurious overtones, which would become more plainly apparent when partners expressed their loan in Genoese *denarii*. A second point is that such a *cambium* contract gave both parties opportunities for profit. Stefano had an assured selling price for the cloth, while Perasco could claim a guarantee against failure to reach that price. Moreover, any profit he drew from the sale was to be repaid not in gold but in Genoese silver; and this is highly significant, since it suggests that Perasco would repay Stefano the £3 per ounce he had promised not in the *Regno*

[1] Archivio di Stato, Genoa, Cart. 2 (Oberto Scriba de Mercato), f.11r, no. 120, no. 122.

but in Genoa. In the interval between selling the scarlet and returning to Genoa, Perasco would thus have an opportunity to invest the surplus in financial deals of his own choosing, so long as he made available to Stefano the promised excess in due time. It does, indeed, seem probable that something more than $11\frac{1}{8}$ oz was expected as the price of the cloth, and that the contract conceals a loan for an unspecified sum, to come into effect in Salerno or Sicily when that cloth had been sold. Reversal of rôles in this fashion is in fact typical of the full-scale *cambium maritimum* contract.[2]

Perasco's rôle becomes clearer as the volume of business for autumn 1182 increases. In mid-October Fulco Perasco received four rolls of cloth, worth £13, in *accomendacio* from Baldezone Curto. These rolls were in settlement of a debt of 4 oz of gold owed to Perasco by Baldezone. Thus a rate of $3\frac{1}{4}$ oz per pound Genoese is revealed, involving a concealed interest rate apparently a little higher than that demanded of Perasco by Stefano. But, once again, Perasco agreed to carry the cloth in *accomendacio* on behalf of the debtor; he did not receive it outright.[3]

Nevertheless, the full story does not revolve around Perasco alone. On 16 November 1182, Vedianus of Lucca received from Stefano de Clavica money or merchandise (*res*) and promised to return to him or his agent in Sicily the sum of 12 oz of gold. As security he gave Stefano two pieces of Lucca scarlet 'quos debes vendere in Sicilia'; should they raise a higher price than 12 oz, Stefano was to give his partner £3 for every ounce gained; similarly, the Luccan was to pay £3 for every ounce lost. Bellissimo agreed to act as guarantor.[4] Here is a contract remarkably similar to that in which Stefano handed Perasco two pieces of Lucca cloth, said to be worth $\frac{1}{8}$ oz less. In each instance the document states quite clearly who the debtor was, first Stefano, then Vedianus. And, since this document is a month later in date than Perasco's contract with Stefano, it does not seem likely that the cloth Perasco had arranged to take to the *Regno* was the same as that which Stefano arranged to take there. Rather does Stefano appear to have acted as an autonomous 'cloth exchange', selling, lending, buying and borrowing Lucchese goods

[2] R. de Roover, 'The Cambium Maritimum Contract', 17–21, 25–6; for other examples of these contracts, see Abulafia, 'Corneto-Tarquinia', 226–8.
[3] Cart. 2, f.13r, no. 143.   [4] Cart. 2, f.20r, no. 216.

with an eye to resale abroad, either in person or through his agents. A diagram, Figure 1, suggests the complexity of the transactions involved, so far as they are known from the sources; dotted lines represent loans, solid lines merchandise, but it is not, of course, possible to represent the time element very adequately.

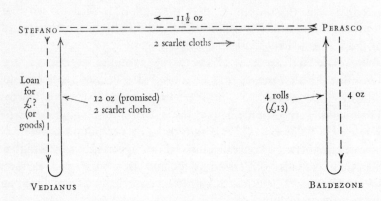

Fig. 1

But it is also evident that Sicily continued to provide cotton in a different manner, in unprocessed form. On 16 December 1186, Rustico, brother of Angelo of Lucca, received from Giovanni di Bombello, a banker of some eminence, an unnamed sum, in return for which he promised to repay him £100 during January. As security he gave fifty *cantara* of cotton from Sicily and Syria (*L cantare bonbecis de Sicilia et ultra mare*). This merchandise was entrusted to his companion Guido Bellissimo, who has already appeared as guarantor of Vedianus' deal with Stefano de Clavica. Significant is the location: 'actum in banco Iohannis Bonbelli'.[5] For this contract does not necessarily indicate an overseas expedition. Rather was the cotton sent to the textile centres of northern Italy, most probably to Lucca itself. What the contract does reveal is an interest-bearing loan from someone who was evidently a credit banker. Bombello stood to gain either the difference between the unnamed sum given in loan and the £100 expected in return, or the proceeds from the sale of the cotton. Whether Rustico had

5 *OSM* (*1186*), no. 326. For Bombello, see also 274–5 *infra*.

already arranged with Bombello that he would, in effect, default in January is not made clear, understandably enough in so suspiciously usurious a context. But a mere month between loan and repayment seems a very short time, and the cotton may have been put into employment as a matter of course. The price of £2 on average per *cantara* must also include allowance for credit, and cannot be accepted as a typical rate.

Simpler *cambium* contracts, as well as those involving pledges in merchandise, became more common in the 1180s and 1190s than Giovanni Scriba shows them to have been earlier in the century. Once again, the Lucchesi provide important fragments of evidence. Paxio of Lucca has already been encountered, lending Giovanni Faber a sum of money against the repayment of 32 tari in Messina. The money was lent in October 1182; *ergo* the repayment must have been made some time in 1183. Interestingly, too, Paxio is known from other surviving parts of Oberto Scriba's cartularies. On 20 July 1190 he received £39 15s 0d from Marchesio di San Lorenzo, promising to repay him or his agent in Sicily 'ubi navis Anfosi bancherii et sociorum fecerit portum'. Repayment was to be made in tari, to the total of 20 oz. This represents a rate of just under 2 oz to the pound Genoese. The reason for so favourable a rate, and for the reversal in Paxio's credit relationship, soon becomes clear. Later on 20 July Paxio lent £69 to Marchesio's relative Ogerio di San Lorenzo, to be carried to Sicily, 'and there I [Ogerio] must pay on your behalf 20 oz out of this' – that is, the money Paxio owed Marchesio. The remainder would be used for the purchase and sale of goods. But should 20 oz of gold cost more than £39 15s 0d Ogerio was authorised to break into the £30 residue. These two contracts reveal not a usurious transaction but an equitable one, in which Paxio and Marchesio have come together to fund an expedition overseas by a third party. Certainly, it is interesting that Paxio too planned to go to Sicily; and, to judge from the description of Ogerio's ship as 'navis Anfosi bancherii', it may be that a large expedition was being aimed at the bullion market. That would certainly fit Paxio's known activities, as well as those ascribed here to Anfoso.[6]

---

[6] *OSM* (1186), no. 530, no. 532. In no. 531 Paxio appears as witness to a Sicilian *accomendacio* of Ogerio with Bonifacio della Volta; in no. 529 he appears as witness

Another Luccan based in Genoa was Coenna *Lucensis*, whose commercial interests were restricted to the Tyrrhenian Sea region. On 4 September 1179 he sent £19 invested in silk and £16 10s 0d invested in other cloths to Sicily, with the active factor Oberto Corso; on the last day of August he stood witness to the sale of a Sardinian slave who was to be sent to Sicily. In 1184 he reappears, sending £30 to Sicily, and a total of £53 15s 0d to the Maremma; contracts of 1186 and 1191 reveal his Roman and Corsican interests. In the twelve-year period from autumn 1179 to summer 1191 Coenna has, therefore, made his appearance in four distinct years – ample testimony to the continuity and value of their Genoese connections to the merchants of Lucca.[7]

The growth of Lucchese trade with Sicily fits into several wider secular developments. In the first place, there is the increasing industrial activity of the north Tuscan towns. In the early thirteenth century Lucca expanded into the silk industry and cornered many European markets, but even before then its textile interests were booming.[8] Coenna, as has been seen, sent silk of unknown origin to Sicily in 1179. Lucca responded warmly to demand in the Latin Mediterranean for top-quality cloths; the scarlet sent to Sicily in the 1180s was the economic ancestor of the silk it sent fifty years later. A second wider development that concerns the growth of Lucchese trade with Sicily is the evidence that Luccan merchants were prepared to travel in company with Genoese colleagues to the *Regno*. Though never, for lack of a fleet, a maritime power with all the diplomatic leverage that possession of a navy gave Genoa or Pisa, Lucca did receive commercial privileges in Sicily before the end of the twelfth century. In 1197 Henry VI granted the Luccans 'idem jus quod Pisani in tholoneo per omnes portus regni Sicilie obtinent' as well as 'idem jus...in introitu et exitu quod habent

---

to a Sicilian *accomendacio* of Ogerio with Marchesio della Volta. His activities in 1192 are recorded by G. Cass., II, no. 17 and *supra* 201, where I refer to other Lucchese activities too, in the context of the breakdown of Genoese trade with Sicily.

[7] Archivio di Stato, Genoa, MS Diversorum 102 (Oberto Scriba), f.21r, no. 2; f.18r, no. 2; Cart. 2 (Oberto Scriba) f.141r, no. 2; f.82r, no. 4; f.140v, no. 1, f.143r, no. 4; *OSM* (*1186*), no. 110; G. Cass., I, no. 697. Activities in 1192: G. Cass., II, no. 1,463 (Rome), no. 1,638 (Oran), no. 1,836 (Syria).

[8] F. Edler de Roover, 'Lucchese silks', *CIBA Review*, LXXX (1950), 2902–30, especially 2907–8.

Pisani'. This privilege meant that Lucca would be able to trade free of royal imposts, though, to be sure, it is unlikely that it was ever put into effect – Henry died the same year, before he had confirmed Pisa in the rights granted in 1190 and 1191. But, political realities apart, it is interesting to find Lucca singled out as a minor competitor to Pisa.[9]

Moreover, the Lucca privilege was not confined to Lucchese merchants. It was addressed primarily to the 'consilio et communitati Lucensi' but the terms were applicable to 'fideles nostri Lucani et universi homines totius Tuscie'. Fortunately, these Tuscans are not entirely beyond identification. In 1193 Bartholomew de Lucy, Count of Paterno, granted the Cistercians of Messina 'in rua Florentinorum domum meam soleratam, quae est ante domum Zacchi'.[10] Admittedly, a street name does not necessarily infer a colony; and, given the somewhat tardy expansion of Florentine overseas trade compared to that of Pisa, the idea of a Florentine colony must be treated with caution. Equally, the presence of Florentines among the 'universi homines totius Tuscie' must be taken to have been extremely probable.

III

The entry of north European, as well as north Italian cloth, into Sicilian markets can be documented from the 1180s. A full picture of the rapid growth of this commerce would range well into the thirteenth century, for the twelfth-century evidence does not indicate a massive, nor necessarily a regular, supply.[11] The principal point here is to note the contrast between the evidence drawn from Giovanni Scriba's cartulary and that provided by the late-twelfth-century notaries. Giovanni Scriba refers often to *fustanei* and other cotton cloths that can be attributed to north Italian or even Near Eastern looms. Flemish cloth and, above all, Flemish merchants, do not often appear in his rota of business.

9 B. de la Roncière (ed.), *Les registres d'Alexandre IV* (Bibliothèque des Ecoles françaises d'Athènes et de Rome, Paris, 1902), I, 20–1, no. 77; Clementi, *Cal.*, no. 133.
10 R. Pirri, *Sicilia Sacra* (Palermo, 1733), 1288; cf. Amari, *Storia dei Musulmani*, III, 224.
11 Doehaerd, *Relations commerciales*, I and II, officially starts at 1200, but in fact includes very many documents of Oberto de Placentia from the late 1190s, all misdated '1200'.

On 20 October 1186 Ansaldo Fornario and Oberto Savono came together in an *accomendacio*. The latter, conceivably a Savonese citizen, was to carry twenty-four pieces of Ypres cloth ('panni Ipre') to Sicily for sale there. A value of £243 Genoese was placed on the goods, so £10 per piece would appear to be the price of the cloth. (The remaining £3 is catered for, 'pro labore quod in ista accomendacione sustineris' – not his share of the profits, but necessary travelling expenses.) In any case this is a very substantial investment, arguably worth its weight in silver in a particular sense that shall in due course be interpreted.[12]

Even at this early stage in the development of a major market for northern cloth in Sicily, there are signs of active participation by Flemish businessmen: north French and Flemish settlers in Genoa, analogous to the Genoese settlers in Sicily, clearly had high hopes for trade in the Norman kingdom. Thus, on 29 December 1190 (1191 *stile genovese*), Lambert of Besançon made a *societas* with Jean de Liège and with Gautier, son-in-law of Charles of Besançon. Each contributed £120, which Lambert was to carry 'to Naples and then where seems best to me...except to Alexandria and Syria (*Ultramare*)'. In addition he carried a further £59 belonging to Gautier, £14 belonging to Jean, ten pieces of sage cloth, the property of Jean, and two pieces of le Mans cloth, these to be sold in the *Regno* for at least 28½ oz of gold. Should they fetch less, Jean was to reimburse Lambert at the rate of £2 10s 0d per ounce.[13] Of course, the stipulation not to visit the east Mediterranean resulted more likely from fear that the fighting there would disrupt business, than from any frantic desire to concentrate on central Mediterranean markets. But that desire existed too, to judge from some contracts of 19 April 1191, in which Jean de Liège reappears sending £132 15s 0d in the hands of Giovanni Guercio to Palermo 'and through Sicily'. In addition, Giovanni agreed to join a *societas* with Gautier of Bescançon valued at £312. This money was to be put to use 'in Palermo and throughout Sicily and throughout all the land of the king of Sicily'. In addition to all this, Giovanni was to

---

[12] *OSM* (*1186*), no. 173.

[13] G. *Cass.*, I, no. 8. For Jean de Liège, see R. L. Reynolds, 'Genoese sources for the 12th-century history of Liège, with special attention to John of Liège', *Etudes d'histoire dediées à la mémoire de Henri Pirenne* (Brussels, 1937), 291–8. Also *supra*, 200, for his activities in 1192.

carry £123 from a separate partnership with Gautier, £125 from one of Gautier's relatives, and £248 12s od from other partners, of which £100 could be transmitted to the Maghrib instead, should Giovanni's partner so decide. The factor is thus involved in nearly £800 worth of business.[14]

More common than direct investment by northern merchants seems to have been what could be called chain investment in Sicily. A series of loans or partnerships traceable directly to north French or Flemish businessmen might end in a voyage to Sicily or beyond by a Genoese factor who had not met, nor had reason to meet, the presiding genius from the far north. A series of documents from 26 and 27 March 1191 shows how well concerted was the transmission of goods southwards from Flanders, and the refund of money northwards from Genoa and, ultimately, Sicily. On 26 March Rambaud Baratier of Nice borrowed £43 5s od from Simon de Iser, Arras-born; the debt was guaranteed by two Genoese, Guglielmo Martino and Bertramo Sicardo. On 27 March, Enrico Vitale declared that he would carry eight lengths of cloth received from Guglielmo Martino, Bertramo Sicardo and a further partner, Raimondo de Odo, to be sold at Messina for at least 100 oz of gold. But in Genoese money they were valued at £210. Enrico was clearly a well-trusted factor; a further £111 came his way in *accomendacio* later on the same day, for trade in Sicily, 'et inde quo ierit cum suis'. The next day a further £100 was placed in his hands, this time with the request that he return directly to Genoa from Sicily, or send an agent thence to Genoa with capital and profit. In any case, Enrico would be in good company in Sicily; some of his partners were bound for the *Regno* too. Raimondo Dodo, or de Odo, and Bertramo Sicardo agreed on a joint venture, investing £150 and £144 respectively, which they would take 'communiter' to Sicily.[15] Now, the links between the Genoese investors and Simon de Iser suggest very strongly that the cloth to be carried overseas was north European; the high price is, moreover, characteristic of the fine quality Flemish cloths rather than of local

---

[14] *G. Cass.*, I, no. 475.

[15] *G. Cass.*, I, no. 360, no. 362, no. 364, no. 375, no. 379. Of general interest, though unconnected, is no. 361, an £89 loan arranged between Belardo Belardengo and Ogerio Galleta, against repayment at the forthcoming Champagne fairs – a document that suggests the multiple direction of Genoese trade in the 1190s.

north Italian production, though this point should not be pressed. From the point of view of the Sicilian trade, it is evident that payment in silver was increasingly being displaced by the export of luxury cloth from the north into the *Regno*; in other words, Genoese merchants were ceasing to deal primarily in their own silver *denarii* but, in some instances, they were transferring their interests to commodities that could be exchanged in Sicily for the gold of the kingdom. Any picture of the balance of trade at this period must be impressionistic, but on the basis of these arguments a shift in favour of the west (which, for the present purpose, must exclude Sicily) can be detected.

Moreover, the sums invested in textiles were very large. Cases in hundreds of pounds have been cited. Even where the cloth cannot be identified as necessarily Flemish, its value was high. On 15 March 1191 Raimondo di Rodolfo received in *accomendacio* from Arduino de Canneto £62 worth of textiles, to be carried to Messina against a guaranteed sale price of 10 oz of Messina tari; any surplus on the sale price was to be shared four to one in Arduino's favour. Then, on 16 March 1191, Raimondo agreed to take a further £46 worth of textiles, against which he agreed to repay 16 oz in tari. During January 1191, Imberto Vezastello declared he was taking four pieces of cloth to Naples, to sell there on behalf of his near-namesake Imberto de Verzellato. Their value was set at £68 4s 0d or 32 oz of gold.[16]

These documents provide a point of transition from the study of luxury imports into Sicily to the study of the conversion of profits from their sale into Sicilian gold.

IV

The principal characteristic of monetary transactions in the late-twelfth-century contracts, as opposed to those of the 1160s, is the extent to which repayment is stipulated in an overseas port. Although profits might often be transmitted to Genoa at the end of business, as in earlier days, there is a marked increase in the incidence of deposit payment. The technique must have been that Genoese merchants would place their funds with a banker in Messina, Naples or another overseas port and extract from him a written

---

[16] G. *Cass.*, I, nos. 300–1; no. 21.

receipt. A unique document of 1205 does, however, shed important light on banking techniques in the *Regno*. This document is a complete copy of a charter originally drawn up by a Neapolitan notary, Benencasa, for several Genoese and Savonese businessmen, and recopied by the Savonese notary Martinus 'quia predictus Vivaldus Bavosus cartam secum portare volebat ut debitum lueret et ne caso aliquo perderet'.[17] It is important not merely in the present context, but also because it is one of the very few commercial contracts to survive from the *Regno* before the year of the Vespers, 1282.[18] It has never been published, and yet it is of more than ephemeral interest, since the Genoese cartularies of the 1180s and 1190s suggest, in outline, the commercial techniques which it describes in further detail, and for that reason it is fair to be anachronistic. Evidence for 1205 will be supposed valid for the previous two decades as well.

The Neapolitan contract begins by explaining 'that I, viz. Accardo of Genoa, son of the late Calvo, received in *accomendacio* ['commanditia'] from you, viz. Bibaldo of Savona, nicknamed Babuso [*sic*], 20 oz of the golden money of Sicily at the Naples standard, in such a manner that I collected it in place of you from the Neapolitans with whom you had changed it...I Accardo promise you Bibaldo ...that I shall collect the same money from the said Neapolitans' for the purpose of reinvestment and trade.[19] The notary's phrasing

---

[17] Archivio di Stato, Savona, Cartolare notarile Martinus, f.200v–201r. The text I cite is drawn from a transcription held in the Istituto di Paleografia e di Storia medievale, University of Genoa, made available to me with great kindness by Professor Geo Pistarino. In 1974 I visited the Archivio di Stato, Savona, to check these transcriptions against the original manuscript, but the staff of the archive denied all knowledge of its whereabouts.

[18] For the internal trade of the *Regno* a single contract survives, printed by S. Cusa – *I diplomi greci ed arabi di Sicilia*, 2 vols. (Palermo, 1860–82), II, 502–4, 719.

[19] Cart. Martinus, f.200v:
'Ex ac publicam litterarum serie, omnibus clareat ad quorum presentia pervenerit, sit notum et manifestum, quod ego viz: Accardus ienuensi, quondam filius Calvo adcepit in commanditia a te viz: Bibaldus Sagonensis, quid vocatur 'Babuso', idest uncias viginti quinque aureii monete Sicilie a pondus Neapolis i[n] tali ordine ut in loco tuo ipse recoligere de Neapolitanorum ad quod tum ad eis mutuastis... Et promitto ego Accardus tibi suprascripto Bibaldus ut ego ipse suprascripte untias si Deus nos salvi portaveris sicut superius legitur, ego recoligere de Neapolitanorum ad quod tum ad eis mutuastis... Et promitto ego Accardus tibi suprascripto Bibaldus ut ego ipse suprascripte untias si Deus nos salvi portaveris sicut superius legitur, ego recoligere debeas ipsa peccunia de suprascripti Neapolitanorum et mictere illas debeas insimul cum ipsa peccunia mea et ille innplicare et facere et salvare'

combines long-windedness with utter grammatical abandon; but
the tenor appears to be that the money Bibaldo owned was held on
deposit by Neapolitan colleagues – 'de Neapolitanorum', unnamed
– until the owner decided to engage in a further series of commercial ventures. Accardo would send the proceeds of the partnership
to Genoa when the whole deal had been completed to his satisfac-
tion. This document seems to add to the picture presented by
the *cambium maritimum* contracts from Genoa by showing that the
bankers in the *Regno* were not simply the officials of the Genoese
denizen community, but ordinary money changers who had close
relations with regular Genoese visitors. Now, in 1190 the Commune of Naples granted the citizens of Amalfi a 'privilegium
libertatis', under the terms of which the Amalfitans were permitted
to set up their money tables freely in the city of Naples. The economic circumstances that led to this grant are not very clear, though
Riccardo Filangieri has explained the political background.[20]
Logically we could postulate a massive increase between 1150 and
1200 in the scale and techniques of deposit banking, in which the
appearance of bullion-heavy Genoese ships played a direct rôle.
But credit techniques were much older and no less sophisticated
among the Jewish and Muslim merchants who visited Sicily from
Africa in the eleventh century.[21] Although the existence of these
facilities in earlier times is not greatly in doubt, the shift in ownership
of bullion deposits from eastern to western hands is rather more

– grammar so wild that the passage could, admittedly, be read in a variety of
ways. This is, of course, not the work of Martinus, but a copy by Martinus of a
Neapolitan notary's work; Martinus himself usually makes better sense by far,
and he may have copied the Neapolitan errors, or have had difficulty reading the
original contract presented to him in Savona for copying, and thereby have compounded the mistakes.

[20] R. Filangieri, 'Note al *Privilegium Libertatis* concesso dai Napoletani agli Amalfitani nel 1190', *Papers of the British School at Rome*, XXIV (1956), 107–15.

[21] Goitein, *Medit. society*, I, 197–200, 241–8. 'In wholesale, the deferment of payment
was paramount. When Maimonides was asked whether this procedure was not
religiously objectionable since it involved some sort of veiled interest, he replied
that without it most livelihoods would come to a standstill' (197). Cf. A.L.Udo-
vitch, *Partnership and profit in medieval Islam* (Princeton, 1970), and 'At the origins
of the western Commenda', *Speculum*, XXVII (1964), arguing that western techniques had an eastern origin. My own preference is for a functional view of
commercial techniques; economic circumstances, more than outright imitation,
must be given first place in explaining similarities between Latin and oriental
methods.

significant, for it is linked to the critical question of bullion flow in the late twelfth century.

A recent study of the Genoese evidence for the flow of silver and gold in the twelfth-century Mediterranean has been offered by Henry L. Misbach. He has paid particular attention to Norman Sicily, concluding that 'the Genoese notarial records show a steady accretion of Sicilian tari with little gold returned to Sicily as exports', from the mid-twelfth century.[22] This argument is founded on a study of notarial contracts referring to the gold tari or to *paiole* gold (the unworked gold imported from the Sahara); but it is an argument based on a serious misinterpretation of what the documents say. They do not refer to the flow of gold from Sicily, or elsewhere, to Genoa – though that can occur in certain instances. The emphasis is on the conversion of Genoese silver money or northern textiles into Sicilian bullion, and on repayment in gold in the foreign ports – such as Messina and Naples – to which the backer sent his factor. Even where the backer names an agent to collect the money, instead of travelling out himself in due time, this is not necessarily evidence that the money would be conveyed back to Genoa as gold bullion. It is only by ignoring the existence of credit institutions and of banking techniques that such a picture can be drawn, with deceptive plausibility.

Misbach fails to provide a detailed breakdown of his bullion-weight totals. In fact the figures he offers for the 1180s and 1190s bear no obvious relation to the documents available. The case of 1182 may be taken as a glaring example: Misbach refers to £102 Genoese being received in Genoa in Sicilian gold. He states that there were no gold exports that year.[23] The evidence is derived from unprinted material and is worth checking. On 21 December 1182 the sum of £100, in the form of 44 oz of gold and $13\frac{1}{3}$ tari, was entrusted to Enrico *iudex* by Giacomo Malfigliastro, member of a great Genoese trading family; this sum was to be cashed *in Sicily* before mid-Lent; otherwise, Enrico engaged to refund Malfigliastro

22 H. L. Misbach, 'Genoese commerce and the alleged flow of gold to the East, 1154–1253', *Revue internationale d'histoire de la banque*, III (1970), 67–87; 'Genoese trade and the rôle of Sicilian coinage in the Mediterranean economy, 1154–1253' *ibid*. V (1972), 305–14. Unless otherwise stated, references are to the latter of these articles.
23 Misbach, 311, Table I.

the sum of £3 for every ounce outstanding.[24] Far from an import of £102, there was a £100 export, as explicit as ever such a case could be! And, from the same year, there survive contracts such as that in which Stefano de Clavico arranged to repay Perasco 11⅛ oz of gold in Sicily or Salerno, and that in which Vedianus promised to repay Stefano 12 oz of gold in Sicily.[25]

For 1184 Misbach provides no exports again, but £316 in receipts.[26] Here is the real evidence: on 18 August Corie *iudex* took £26 7s 0d in Genoese money from Gandolfo Croce, promising to repay him one pound of gold in Palermo by the second week of January 1185. This is, in Genoese terms, neither a gold import nor a gold export; it is a sale of 'native' bullion abroad, involving a silver loss but no gold loss from Genoa.[27] There are no signs of Misbach's receipt anywhere. Wayward too is the picture for 1186. On 3 October of that year Gandolfo 'the blacksmith' accepted £25 14s 2d, in the form of 12 oz of *tarenorum novorum*, new tari, to be carried in *accomendacio* to Sicily and beyond. On 21 October Opizo the furrier accepted a sea-loan of £32 from Ansaldo, 'in return for which I promise to pay you in Sicily 15¼ oz of gold, and I give you as a pledge "duas pennas grixias et tres rusas et unam variam", [a selection of skins], to be sold to cover this debt, though whatever remains above the debt shall be mine'. On 17 December Peire Ugo de Montpellier received £8 4s 0d on loan from Rubaldo Lercario, in return for which he was to give Rubaldo or his agent 4 oz of tari, to be handed over when they met in Sicily. In surety he gave six skins ('pellicia de grixatis'), and promised to refund £2 15s 0d for every ounce not recovered from the sale of the merchandise by Rubaldo, should the skins fail to fetch their estimated price in Sicily. Yet another complex *cambium* here, with no signs of the gold moving into or out of Sicily.[28]

In 1190 a Sicilian merchant, Symon Gatto *Siculus de Plaça*, lent Oberto Mallone a sum of *denarii* against which Oberto promised to repay 3 oz of tari, to be paid in Sicily 'ubi navis qua imus fecerit portum'. Similarly, on 27 March of that year Oto *vicecomes* sent £40

[24] Archivio di Stato, Genoa, Cart. 2, f.26r, no. 277.
[25] Cart. 2, f.11r, no. 122; f.20r, no. 216.
[26] Misbach, 311, Table I.
[27] Cart. 2, f.81v, no. 2.
[28] *OSM (1186)*, no. 84, no. 178, no. 328 (uncancelled).

to Sicily, against 19 oz to be returned 'quo portum fecerit' to himself or his agent. Since Oto had recently received the dowry of
£104 due to him from Giovanni Busca after Oto married Giovanni's daughter, this investment indicates an attempt to draw profit
from the dowry.[29] Of course, Oto took care not to risk his entire
dowry capital on this single venture. Much the same is the pattern
in 1191, to which Misbach attributes 'the highest receipt figures of
tari in Genoese trade, 1415 Genoese pounds'.[30] Thus on 27 January
Anselmo Zarela declared he had received £10 from Alda, daughter
of Balduino de Campo; this he invested on her behalf, against the
recovery of 5 oz of gold in Sicily or Naples. And on 15 February
Oto *iudex* de Castello declared Rubaldo Pezulla quit of debts, having
paid Oto £19 2s 9d, the proceeds of an *accomendacio*. This partnership had been expressed in the form of one-and-a-half *loca* in a ship;
the original contract had been drawn up between Rubaldo and Oto
in Naples, and was valued there at $8\frac{1}{2}$ oz of tari.[31]

Such a divergence between this picture and Misbach's is not, in
fact, beyond explanation. After his extraordinary claims for 1191,
Dr Misbach adds a footnote: 'there are no contracts in the Genoese
collection which can be called "imports" as such. Recourse has
therefore been had to contracts which indicate that repayment will
take place in a foreign currency and at a named port... The payment
may be stated either as, in this case, [an example having been
offered], 200 ounces of tari or at the hypothetical rate of one and
three-quarters ounces of tari for each pound. Options of going to
other ports or repaying on return in Genoese money are taken as
having been intended for extreme emergency.'[32] Now, this simply
will not do. Misbach has assumed a licence to print money, or rather
to coin gold, when contracts refer solely to the export of Genoese
pounds, as many of them do. He fails to consider the wider functions
of trade in bullion: that commerce flourishes not solely by the exchange of bullion, but also by the movements of commodities.
Certainly, much of the money placed on deposit in Sicily or Naples

---

[29] *OSM (1190)*, no. 232, no. 289, no. 231. 'Symon Gattus Siculus' is among the
witnesses to the second and third documents.

[30] Misbach, 310. But cf. his note 3.

[31] G. *Cass.*, I, no. 151; I, no. 217: 'pro accomendatione unius loci et dimidii navis,
quam fecit Iohannes judex ei in Napolim, ponendo pro unciis viii$\frac{1}{2}$'.

[32] Misbach, 310, note 3. Cf. also 305, note 1, and 'Flow of gold', 84–7.

would have been converted into merchandise for the return voyage to Genoa – hence, as early as Giovanni Scriba's day, the expectation that factors would delay several days or weeks after their arrival at Genoa before repaying their backer his capital and profits. Time had to be found for the sale or transfer of merchandise, whether as units of credit in its own right (for example, pepper) or by outright reconversion into the silver of the north. Thus not 'extreme emergency' but normal practice resulted in repayment to sleeping partners in Genoese silver. There is no justification whatsoever for presuming that Genoese factors were normally, or regularly, expected to return with gold rather than with goods, though of course this *could* happen, at the backer's insistence or because the factor managed to secure gold at a good price – as he might, indeed, with pure gold (of which more in a minute) or as he might if the exchange rate between tari and silver was temporarily favourable. Often, indeed, he might be buying tari in non-Sicilian markets; North African *morabitini* and Syrian bezants were perfectly well known in Sicily – that is a commonplace well confirmed by the Ligurian contracts.[33]

The incidence of tari deposits in Sicily and Naples, without any stipulation that they be imported into Europe, does, nevertheless, indicate that some tari were flowing to Genoa. Some of the contracts discussed here were for the export of Genoese pounds, against deposits to be made in Sicilian gold: others were for the export of Sicilian tari for use in the trade of the *Regno*. Given the low number of contracts mentioning tari, relative to those referring solely to pounds of *denarii* or to merchandise, it would be foolhardy to suggest that the movement of gold out of Sicily was substantially more marked than the movement back to Sicily of temporary exports of tari. Certainly silver was sucked into the south Italian economy during this period, to judge from the frequency of references to *provesini* coins in the Campanian and Apulian charters (though some, the *provesini Senatus*, were struck at Rome as imitations); a recent find of several hundred Champagne coins dated between 1197 and about 1253 – the identification of the Count Thibault by

[33] Of course, a trade in money *did* exist, providing access to seasonal profit by speculation on the exchange markets. Foreign coins were, in addition, convenient to hold if a trading firm had recurrent interests in a particular overseas region.

whom they were struck is as yet uncertain – was made in Basilicata at Montescaglioso, and if such money reached the abbeys of the interior, its circulation in the market towns must have been quite extensive.[34] Unfortunately, references to exports of non-Genoese silver to the *Regno* cannot be offered. On 23 March 1191, Guglielmo di San Giorgio received in *societas* from Ansuisso di San Genesio £275½, to be invested in business in Sicily and beyond. This itself represented the proceeds of an older *societas*, of which Ansuisso retained part in silver marks (the exact number, 21, is deleted, for no apparent reason), but he gave Guglielmo a further £50 to carry overseas, and permitted another backer to give him another £18 in *accomendacio*. The marks, whatever their origin, do not, then, seem to have been sent on to Sicily.[35] The silver of Champagne and of the north was readily available at the fairs of Bar and Troyes, quite apart from the stalls of the money changers in Genoa. Along with the textiles they bought at the same fairs, this silver would have come south to Liguria in return for the products of the east sold in eastern France by the Genoese. Even when the balance of trade was most unfavourable to the west, it was not Genoa nor its rivals that suffered the drain; the points of efflux were shifted farther back.

The way that gold moved through Sicily to Genoa and then back to Sicily again is illustrated by the contracts of 1190 that refer to *paiole* gold. In one contract the *paiole* gold is seen moving out of Genoa; its source of origin, as is well known, was 'Sudan' or 'Ghana' – that is, the south Sahara region – and it is far from certain whether the *paiole* gold available in Genoa came directly from a North African port such as Bougie, Ceuta or Tripoli, or whether it was frequently purchased by the Genoese in Sicily. Often, this gold may have been obtained in payment for Sicilian corn. Its value, as befitted gold of up to 20½ carats, was normally higher per ounce than the 16⅓-carat coined gold of Sicily. Thus on 8 April 1190 Rufo the banker (*bancherius*) and Berardo his nephew gave Ugo Polexino 70 oz of *paiole* gold, nominally as pledge for the loan of goods

---

34 I am grateful to Mr Terry Volk of the Fitzwilliam Museum, Cambridge, for informing me of the existence of this hoard. Provesini Senatus: P. Toubert, *Les structures du Latium médiéval*, 2 vols. (Rome, 1973), I, 583–4.

35 G. *Cass.*, I, nos. 352–3, no. 359. Cf. also G. *Cass.*, II, no. 1,753, citing a price in Lucchese *denarii*; but this is the value of cloth that will be sent to Sicily, and does not represent a payment made inside Sicily in money of Lucca.

worth 70 oz of *auri tarenorum*, Sicilian money. Ugo was to carry the *paiole* gold to Sicily for sale and exchange; he was to recover the 70 oz of tari for himself there, and then to return to his partners the difference between the sale of the high-quality *paiole* gold and the value of the 70 oz of Sicilian tari: 'et si defuerit dabimus tibi cumplementum ad rationem de s.55 per untiam' (though it is hard to see how the purer uncoined gold could fail to catch the higher price). On completion of this transaction Ugo's pledged goods would be released.[36] A similar manoeuvre can be identified on 10 July 1190. On that day Giovanni Patrio received £50 from Otone Guercio and promised to refund him or his agent in Sicily 22½ oz of tari, minus 1 tari, at the ounce weight of Genoa (for from 1156 Genoa had the right to use its own scales in Messina). This is not all, for meanwhile Giovanni entrusted 20 oz of 'auri pajolie' to Otone, which Otone was to sell. In effect the debt would then have been redeemed, for if Otone sold 20 oz of pure *paiole* gold in Genoa he could recover 22½ oz of less pure tari gold at the stipulated weight standard, as well as a surplus of several ounces. This surplus was to be reinvested by Otone on Giovanni's behalf.[37] Similarities to the contract between Ugo Polexino and Rufo the banker, of 8 April 1190, are obvious, except that here the pledge consists in *paiole* gold itself. The bullion movements directly observed concern the movement of silver out of Genoa, not the movement of Sicilian gold out of Sicily; but *a priori* an import of *paiole* gold from Africa or via Sicily is inferred.

On the basis of this very varied information about the gold coinage of Sicily, the problem of its rôle in Genoese business can be resolved. From the evidence for gold deposits in Sicily and Naples, a stylised framework for Genoese trade in Sicily and southern Italy can be drawn, to show how, on the arrival of Genoese businessmen in the *Regno*, these deposits were activated; and this is shown in Figure 2.

In other terms, the merchant's business in Sicily entailed several operations: (1) Exchange, (2) Deposit, (3) Purchase, (4) Collection, each of which might overlap, depending on the speed of business and on the special conditions demanded by individual partners.

---

[36] *OSM (1190)*, no. 370. Rufo also dealt in Provençal grain – *OSM (1190)*, no. 486 (10 July).   [37] *OSM (1190)*, no. 483.

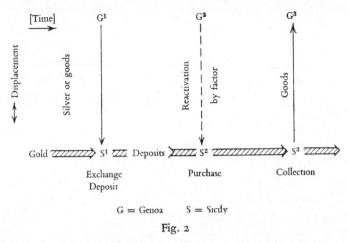

Fig. 2

At S[icily][1]: Exchange and deposit of Genoese money. S[2] (may not always occur): Purchase of merchandise. S[3] Collection of merchandise; or purchase and collection (if S[2] absent). The interval between S[2] and S[3] allows for warehousing, resale and repurchase, or advance purchase – e.g. of agricultural produce, prior to collection when ready.

According to this proposed *schema*, gold would not have moved in great measure out of the *Regno*, especially in the instance of the richer merchants with recurring investments. Of course, the gold deposits had their origin in the profits of trade and exchange; but against their function as bank accounts and as financial investments, it is important to take into account their activation for purposes of purchase. For it is clear that, on the release of funds from deposit overseas, Genoese merchants would reinvest these funds in a commercial venture even for the comparatively simple purpose of transferring the money from, say, Sicily to Genoa. By the conversion of funds into grain or luxury goods, further profit could be extracted from the funds in the course of their transfer to Genoa, through the sale of the commodities purchased. Into grain there disappeared not merely part of the gold deposits, but a steady flow of Genoese silver – bullion only gradually displaced by the import into the *Regno* of northern cloths and, presumably by the increasing rôle of the Genoese in the Sicilian carrying trade with the ends of the Mediterranean. It is time, therefore, to turn to that elusive but massive export, grain.

V

A contract of 27 September 1186, arguably one of the most significant of all the Genoese contracts for business in Sicily, ties together
many strands. 'I Oglerio Arloto promise you Giovanni Bombello
and Thomas Vento that if at any time I should recover, by my
power or by that of another person, anything out of the 65 *salmae*
of grain and of the 11 North African bezants ('besançiis marabotinis')
that I should receive in Sicily, which are the proceeds of the *societas*
that I had with Oglerio Vento and with you, Giovanni, I shall give
you or your agent your portion. Penalty: double the value, etcetera.
Given in "bancho Iohannis Bonbelli", 27 September.'[38] Now, in
this instance the original contract of *societas* may still exist. On
26 January 1183, Oglerio Arloto received £67 13s 4d from
Oglerio Vento, against which he placed £33 6s 8d of his own;
from Giovanni he received £200; from the widow Videlia, at
Oglerio Vento's behest, he received £10.[39] As has been seen, he
was treating with major figures: Oglerio or Ogerio Vento was
consul in 1176, 1179 and 1192 and a member of an outstandingly
powerful Genoese family; and Giovanni Bonbello was a major
credit banker, who extended his techniques to the purchase of
Sicilian commodities for the Genoese market.[40] Moreover, it is
clear that the quantity of grain they were trying to extract from
Sicily was not small. A *salma* of Sicily weighed about 263 lb,
but 315½ lb at the Messina measure.[41] The total weight of the grain
bought by Oglerio Arloto in Sicily, of which record survives, was
therefore between 7.7 tons and 8.4 tons. We know, too, from the
treaty of 1156 what customs duty would normally be payable by
Genoese merchants on an export of 65 *salmae*: 1 tari per 4 *salmae* of
grain exported directly from Messina to Genoa.[42] On 8.4 tons of
wheat, the King's officers at Messina would collect a mere 16¼ tari.
Fresh tari were estimated to weigh 30 to the ounce, which in the
1180s Genoese businessmen reckoned to be approximately £2 to
£3 of their own money, including interest rates or exchange commission. Rounding off figures to allow for this, it does not seem that

[38] *OSM (1186)*, no. 55.
[39] Cart. 2, f.31r, no. 336 (also by Oberto Scriba).
[40] Cf. 258–9 *supra*, and *OSM (1186)*, no. 326.
[41] Schaube, 815.   [42] *CDG*, I, 339.

the King received much more than £1 10s 0d in tax on the export of 8.4 tons of grain from Messina.[43] It is worthwhile at this point to remember that the low tax was a special right to which Genoese and, at a higher rate, Venetians were entitled; the King could expect a far higher profit from other merchants, such as North African buyers, for those without privileges would be paying their 10 per cent κομμέρκιον, and sundry additional imposts. Set against this there is the sum invested by Giovanni Bonbello and Oglerio Vento in Arloto's expedition: £300. The 11 bezants still in Sicily – of low worth, relative to the grain – suggest that the £300 sum was not entirely consecrated to grain purchases, but that wheat was the principal object of Arloto's commission. Whether the decision to invest in wheat was made from the start by Oglerio and Giovanni is more difficult to say: it does not seem unlikely. Assuming, on this basis, that the money was spent immediately on grain, we reach a price of about £4 12s 0d per *salma*, but there are serious objections to this calculation. In the first place, Arloto seems to have sailed to Sicily in spring 1183. It is possible that he returned to Genoa and took out a second, lost contract for a different sum, and then went back to Sicily late in 1184, or that he used *nuncii* to contact his Genoese partners from a base in Sicily and to send back goods or obtain more cash. In any case, he was away long enough to spread his business widely, to invest and re-invest throughout several seasons, perhaps buying his grain gradually as prices became favourable in different parts of the island of Sicily, perhaps moving temporarily to Africa or Naples. Moreover, the embargo of 1185 appears to have upset his affairs. He arrived in Genoa sometime before 27 September 1186 without the cargo he had purchased. There is no indication in the contract as to where the cargo was stored, or whether, indeed, it was a real or notional cargo – in other words, whether Arloto merely had in his hands a receipt for the advance purchase of part of the crop of 1184, 1185 or 1186. If he did have the goods in store in Sicily, events during 1185 destroyed all chances of extracting the grain before the fleet sailed to conquer Byzantium. Furthermore, it is likely that the crown commandeered grain stocks to feed the fleet bound for the Greek empire. The kings had power so to do, and

---

[43] This figure would clearly apply in other cases, even if this particular contract does not necessarily indicate a journey to Messina.

such power need not have referred solely to the alleviation of famine. The mercenaries expected their biscuits, as well as their booty.[44]

VI

Grain and raw cotton belong together in one major category, that of bulk exports of agrarian produce; but luxury items were available in Sicily and southern Italy too, and attracted Genoese investment in the 1180s and 1190s. In the context of the Geniza documents that refer to 'Sicilian coral', evidence for the movement of coral out of Sicily in the 1180s comes as no surprise. On 4 April 1190 Bufaro Sarago, one of an active group of Genoese merchants with strong Sicilian interests, declared he had received a payment from Bonovassallo de Rufino. This money represented the proceeds from the sale of one case of coral 'which I consigned to you in Sicily and which you carried to Alexandria'. Oto *vicecomes* witnessed the act. This contract does not necessarily alter the picture drawn by Goitein, according to which Sicily was a market for the purchase and sale of coral, rather than a major producer – a rôle he assigns to North Africa. This contract does, however, illustrate quite plainly how travelling merchants would accumulate merchandise for resale when they were already far from their home town. Capital placed in a venture 'for Sicily and thence where the factor shall desire' would be converted into another medium in the *Regno* and then transported to a likely oriental market.[45]

Some luxury items exported from Sicily are still in existence. Painted ivory caskets of Sicilian origin survive in many European collections; the large numbers in German and Spanish collections probably reflect patterns of conquest at least as much as patterns of trade. More germane is the appearance of a cylindrical casket in the Sicilian style in the treasury of San Marco in Venice. The date normally ascribed to these objects is the late twelfth or early thirteenth century, so the San Marco example may have arrived in the

---

[44] See 163–4 *supra* for the embargo of 1185, and 40 for the royal controls on grain movements.
[45] *OSM (1190)*, no. 333; Goitein, *Medit. society*, I, 47.

Norman or early Hohenstaufen period.[46] Another item in St Mark's treasury that may be of south Italian or Sicilian origin is an elaborate gilt and silver censer, which seems to have been in Venice by 1283 at latest, and which may have been fashioned in the years around 1200.[47]

Other luxury items exported from Sicily are not traceable. However, there are signs of demand in the *Regno* for prestige products from the north – not merely textiles, but gems and metalwork. Thus in January 1191 Odo de Melazo sent a sapphire ring worth £2 10s od from Genoa to Naples and beyond.[48] In the same few days Odo entrusted one breast-plate to another factor bound 'quo voluerit preter in Romaniam'; and on 23 January Lamberto, son of Guglielmo Fornario, received £193 17s od from his father, in addition to one *osbergum* and two *gamberas*, to be sold in Naples. The sale of these items of armour – breastplate and greaves – may be linked to increased demand for fine armour as the *Regno* placed itself on the defensive against Henry of Hohenstaufen.[49]

Another category of northern metalwork is represented by the Pisan-made doors of Monreale cathedral. The sculptor, Bonanno of Pisa, was commissioned to make these bronze doors some time before 1185. There is little doubt that the doors were made in Pisa rather than in Sicily, and shipped to Palermo complete, for Bonanno made no allowance for the ogival shape of the doorway he was supposed to fill; his doors are rectangular instead. Of course, such an import was exceptional, the more so if the doors took several years

---

[46] P. B. Cott, *Siculo-Arabic ivories* (Princeton, 1939), no. 83, and plate xxxvi; K. Erdmann, 'Opere islamiche', in H. R. Hahnloser (ed.), *Il Tesoro di San Marco: il Tesoro e il Museo* (Florence–Venice, 1971), 119, no. 130, and plate cv. See now R. H. Pinder-Wilson and C. N. L. Brooke, 'The Reliquary of St Petroc and the ivories of Norman Sicily', *Archaeologia* (Society of Antiquaries of London), CIV (1973), 261–305.

[47] A. Grabar, 'Opere bizantine', in *Il Tesoro di San Marco*, 86–8, no. 109, and plates lxxviii–lxxx: 'si suppone che la sua destinazione originaria fosse quella di bruciaprofumi di uso profano, in una dimora principesca'. Also discussed and illustrated in *Venezia e Bisanzio* (catalogue of an exhibition at the Ducal Palace and Marciana Library; Venice, 1974), no. 44. It is the first entry in the oldest inventory of the treasure of St Mark (1283): R. Gallo, *Il Tesoro di San Marco e la sua Storia* (Venice–Rome, 1967), 273.

[48] *G. Cass.*, I, no. 20.

[49] *G. Cass.*, I, no. 21 (Odo); II, no. 119 (Lamberto) – cf. nos. 117–18. Compare the document reported in note 54 *infra*.

to design and cast. Certainly it is of interest to find the patron of Monreale commissioning north Italian work, in a lively, narrative, Romanesque style, alongside the other set of bronze doors that were made for Monreale by the south Italian craftsman Barisone of Trani – these were in the Byzantine manner long associated with cathedral doors in southern Italy. At a time when the Pisans were smarting from the Constantinople massacre of 1182, the extension of Sicilian patronage to their artists makes sense; but it would be safer to suppose that William's use of Bonanno was more a tribute to that artist's calibre than it was a symbol of Pisan–Sicilian accord.[50]

VII

The continuing presence of Sicilian merchants in Genoa is ample reminder that the gold and luxury products of the *Regno* could come north in the hands of non-Ligurian merchants. Although the 1180s and 1190s show no figure to rival Solomon of Salerno, Sicilian visitors to Genoa prove to have been well connected. Thus Symon Gatto *Siciliensi de Plaça* has been encountered in the company of one of the Mallone family. But his known activities were modest in scale and in value. For instance, on 20 February 1190 he bought a Sardinian slave named Maria from the Genoese Simone Botarius, for £5 5s 0d; and on 8 March he sold the same slave to Giovanni Busca for an identical sum. To be sure, this may reveal more about Maria's domestic usefulness or uselessness than about Symon Gatto's profit ventures. Since *Plaça* would appear to be *Platea* or *Piazza* in central Sicily – Piazza Armerina, in modern usage – Symon's ancestry need not be Greek or Muslim. Piazza became a Lombard stronghold during the struggle against Maio of Bari, and the famous Roman palace there was occupied by Maio's enemies; hence its destruction by William the Bad. It is possible, therefore, that Symon's forebears were followers of the Savonese Aleramici whom Roger I brought to Sicily.[51]

---

[50] A. Boeckler, *Die Bronzetüren des Bonanus von Pisa und des Barisanus von Trani* (Berlin, 1953); W. Kroenig, *The Cathedral of Monreale and Norman architecture in Sicily* (Palermo, 1965), 17; F. Bartoloni, 'La data del portale di Bonanno', 39–41. Bonanno also made two sets of bronze doors for Pisa cathedral, a little before those of Monreale; his set in the south transept at Pisa survives.

[51] *OSM (1190)*, no. 164, no. 230. Symon's other activities: *ibid.* nos. 231–2, no. 289. For Piazza and its Lombards, see Rom. Sal., 248; H. Falc., 70; Amari, *Storia dei Musulmani*, III, 235–7; also G. V. Gentili, *La Villa Imperiale di Piazza Armerina* (7th ed., Rome, 1971), 6.

Sicilian merchants certainly combined with Genoese in recurrent business partnerships. Thus on 24 December 1186 Oberto Scriba drew up a contract on behalf of 'Iane magister de Sicilia de terra Regis Siculi', in which Iane announced he had received £5 from Oberto de Quinto. He renounced any further claims that might arise from 'all the *accomendaciones* which you once had with me', as well as £11 which the consuls of Genoa confiscated from Oberto to cover the Genoese merchant's debts. In other words, a Genoese citizen had proved unable to meet his obligations, and as a result the consuls had intervened to secure the standard 'pena dupli'. Whether Oberto was guilty of fraud is not stated; whether Iane was a merchant *sensu stricto* or, to judge from his title, a minor royal official who placed money with Oberto to secure consumer goods from Genoa and its maritime markets, is equally uncertain – the *magistri capitanei* and *magistri justitiarii* known from the Norman period were outstanding in rank and tasks, but Iane does not seem to be a disguised magnate of the realm. Rather it is necessary to emphasise the statement that many *accomendaciones*, all lost, tied the Sicilian to the Genoese. Residing in Sicily – 'de terra Regis Siculi' – Iane nevertheless used the energetic merchants of Genoa to obtain goods and profits.[52]

VIII

The larger towns, Genoa and Pisa, possessed resident representatives and their own buildings in the *Regno* – the Genoese, as has been seen, had a hospice from the start of the century. By 1194 there was a 'fonduk of St John' that seems to have been the Genoese warehouse in Messina. Pisa had its own overseas consuls at Messina, to judge from a charter of 9 October 1189.[53] This refers to an earlier, lost

---

[52] *OSM (1186)*, no. 346. For the *magistri capitanei* and *justitiarii*: Caravale, *Regno normanno*, 254–68.

[53] Archivio della Certosa di Calci, pergamene, 9 October 1190 (*stile pisano*). Volpe, 233, refers to 'una carta rogata "nell'ospizio dei Consoli dei Pisani a Messina"', dating this to 9 October; he seems to have consulted the register in Archivio di Stato, Pisa, called Carte Lupi, Fonti I, Certosa, I, 756–7, rather than the original at Calci; Nardone, 14, note 2, follows Volpe word for word. For details of the Carte Lupi see editorial comment in Volpe, p. lxii, and the first volume of a projected edition of the Calci material: S. Scalfati (ed.), *Carte dell'Archivio della Certosa di Calci*, II (1100–50), introd. by C. Violante (Thesaurus Ecclesiarum Italiae; Rome, 1971); it should be noted, however, that the eighteenth-century transcriptions by Maggi (Archivio di Stato, Pisa, Misc. MSS 67), end in 1121/2. See Abulafia, 'Pisan commercial colonies and consulates', document ii and *passim*.

document of 12 September 1189, 'scriptam a Corrigia iudice et notario domini imperatoris rogatam apud messanam in hospitio consulum pisanorum messane', in the presence of Enrico Muscerifa, Guido son of Pagano de Portamaris and Gerardo son of Sigerio. The Messina charter was a *mandatum* issued on behalf of a certain Pipindone, authorising Pipindone's nephew Bartolomeo to find Odimundo – in Pisa, apparently – and to collect 250 North African bezants that Odimundo had borrowed from Pipindone in Montpellier. (This sum was paid originally in Provençal money – 'libris quinquaginta merguliensium et ramundigorum'.) Further indication of the activity of the Pisan colony in Messina is supplied by a document of 16 March 1198. This is a letter from Alberto Celone in Messina to Baratterio Congiario in Pisa, asking him to pay a certain Villano for an *asbergum* (breast-plate); the document was drawn up 'messane in domo Bonaccursi Unguenti et consorti prope ecclesia sancti petri in canniccio', in the presence of several other Pisan witnesses. Alberto, Bonaccurso (a common Pisan name) and some of the witnesses appear to have been members of the Pisan colony in Messina.[54] This colony must, however, have undergone transformation following the conquest of Sicily by Pisa's German ally and following the break-up of central authority on Henry's death a year or two before the letter was drawn up. These colonies did not, of course, possess the exceptional rights of the north Italian settlers in the Holy Land; it was only after Henry's death that the Pisans and Genoese attempted to create autonomous units in the Sicilian towns. Rather were the north Italian colonies bases where resident northerners and visiting merchants could treat together, store goods and find religious and domestic comfort.

The maritime communes did not merely try to build up landed interests in overseas ports; the countryside also came within their colonising purview. Just as in Terra Sancta the Venetians possessed sugar estates, so too did the Genoese possess wheat estates in Sicily a dozen years before Henry VI's conquest. When in 1182 King William II consigned to the abbey of S. Maria Nuova at Monreale vast estates in the Palermitan hinterland, the King's *duana* took great

[54] Archivio di Stato, Pisa, R. Acquisto Roncioni, 16 March 1199, *corta*; Abulafia, 'Pisan commercial colonies and consulates', document iii.

care to describe in minute detail the boundaries of the abbey's lands.[55]
Even though the exact borders cannot be recovered by reference to
modern place names, it is clear that a triangle between Calatafimi,
Corleone and Palermo was the principal territory granted out by
the crown. This was wheat-bearing land – 'continent in se semina-
turum ad mille saumas' or 'ad MCCLX salmarum' – land of impressive fertility and desirability. In the 'divisions of *Summinum*',
a territorial division of this triangle, the lands of Monreale bordered
on those of the Genoese:

jungitur cum cultura ianuensis, redit directe per communes fines cum
terra ianuensis et vadit usque ad extremitatem planiciei; [and later] redit
orientaliter communi divisa cum ianuensi.[56]

The character of the abbey estates bordering on the Genoese *cultura*
is said to be both agricultural and pastoral – 'septem milium salmarum et sunt in eo pascua ducentarum salmarum' (here the *salma*
is a unit of area, not a measure of packed wheat) – with an emphasis
on the agricultural. On this basis it is difficult to imagine that the
Genoese lands were any less agricultural; their extent is far from
clear, but the impression remains of a lengthy border between the
two estates. An attempt at location might be hazarded. The neighbouring *divisa* are called *Beluin*, a name perhaps connected to Monte
Belliemi on the south-west slopes of the Conca d'Oro, the massif
that rises sharply behind Palermo, and on the north-east of which
stands Monreale. That would place the Genoese lands on the road
between Palermo and Calatafimi, a *via publica* of the crown much
used, surely, by merchants travelling overland from Trapani and
Val di Mazara. The general region of Partinico seems indicated. The
value of wheat lands to the Genoese is obvious. For a commune so
poor in cultivable land in Liguria, the opportunity to obtain estates
overseas was of unquestionable value. It is true that such lands might
revert to the crown of Sicily in the event of a dispute between king
and commune; but in 1182 relations were good, and the King did
not begrudge Genoa the right to export the produce of its own
Sicilian estates at reduced tolls.

[55] Cusa, 179–244, 730–1. For Venetian estates in Syria, see J. Prawer, 'Etudes de
quelques problèmes agraires et sociaux d'une seigneurie croisée au XIIIe siècle',
Byzantion, XXII (1952), 5–61; XXIII (1953), 143–70.
[56] Cusa, 184, 185; 210, 211.

The Genoese community in Messina shows further signs of life in January 1183, when William II issued from Capua a grant of 'casalinum unum, quod est in Magistra Ruga Messane' to Bubonoso, 'nobilis civis Ianue'. This Bubonoso may be the contentious leader of the anti-Volta faction known from the late 1180s and 1190s; equally he may have been a Genoese resident in Sicily of the same name or clan. Bubonoso became the liegeman of the King and promised to pay him a rent of a pound of gold *per annum*; he was placed under no obligation to perform any services for the crown. The high value of the house, as expressed in rent, and the fact that Bubonoso travelled to Capua and did homage for the *casalinum* there, speak for the importance and scale of the Genoese settlement in Messina.[57] Others, such as a certain Ingo Longo, known from a notarial act of October 1191, may have lived far from their *feudo Sicilie*; Ingo spent time in piracy and politics, and wasted time gambling, without settling in Sicily as far as can be seen.[58]

The activities of the Venetian church of San Marco in Palermo have already been mentioned; and the plans of the Pisans and Genoese for the complete take-over of many of the towns of Sicily and southern Italy, along with extensive tracts of countryside, are plainly to be witnessed in their agreements with Barbarossa and Henry VI. Thus there is plenty of evidence for two separate but interlocked activities: the acquisition of urban property and of urban bases for trade; and, more ambitiously, the acqusition of rural property and of control over the sources of production.

[57] *Doc. ined.*, no. 76. For Bubonoso (Bulbonosus), see *Ann. Ian.*, ii, 19, 29, 44. In 1183 and 1188 he was leader of a political faction ('illos de Curia' – 19). Opponents from the della Volta clique seized his tower in Genoa in 1193, and destroyed most of it the next year (*ibid.* 44–5).

[58] *G. Cass.*, i, no. 1,167. Sicilia was, to be sure, also a feminine name: *Bonvillano* (Notai Liguri, iii), 14, no. 103, no. 184. Thus this *feudum Sicilie* could be the fief held by or on behalf of a person called Sicilia. Such an interpretation would not, however, fit Guglielmo Scarsaria's lands: *GS*, ii, no. 950. For Ingo Longo's other activities, see *Ann. Ian.*, ii, 55–8, 60, and Chapter 8, n. 40, 211 *supra*.

CONCLUSION

The aim here has been to show that the kings and the communes together drew wealth from the resources of the *Regno* and from the commercial activity of town and countryside – from the ports most obviously, but ultimately from the fields too. An attempt has also been made to demonstrate the weight of commercial considerations in the pattern of alliances woven by the Sicilian kings and by the north Italian communes; for here, as in the commercial contracts, the special value of the *Regno* as a composite and well-endowed market is indicated. The *Regno* was a mercantile centre that belonged wholly neither to east nor to west. As an entrepôt for the sale of the precious products of the further orient it shared many of the characteristics of Acre, Alexandria or Constantinople; so too in the use of golden money and in the κομμέρκιον-based tax structure; so too in the commercial connections of its numerous and elusive Jewish and Muslim merchants. As a producer of primary produce – wheat, skins, raw cotton – the *Regno* offers points of comparison with Provence, Sardinia or the agricultural regions of northern Italy, except that the imposition of political unity seems to have enlarged the scale of central control over the exploitation and transfer of agricultural and mineral wealth.

The question whether the presence of the north Italians was, in the long term, damaging to the *Regno* must be seen in the context of the rather exceptional identity of the kingdom as both an 'oriental-type' luxury market and as an 'occidental-type' agricultural producer. A great change occurred in the course of the twelfth century with the rapid growth of northern Italian and Flemish textile production, the former of which was, moreover, partly based on exported raw cotton grown in Sicily. Increasing demand in the *Regno* for high-quality cloths appears ultimately to have shifted the balance of trade in favour of the north. How northern cottons came to supplant local products inside the market towns of the *Regno*, and how Flemish woollens established a firm and famous place on the bazaar counters of Sicily is an important but mysterious question; at any rate, the evidence from the twelfth century indicates not an answer but merely an occurrence. The failure of urban industry to develop in Sicily after the precocious commercial growth of Amalfi and Bari in the eleventh century raises the sticky question as to whether Norman central control discouraged the development of free communes in the south, and the equally sticky question as to what effect communal autonomy had on the industrial expansion of the north Italian towns, the towns that did, as it were, succeed. Certainly, the presence of north Italian merchants in southern Italy suggests that outside agents helped, if they did not engender, the industrial conservatism of the south. The increasing quantity of cloth the north Italians brought into the *Regno* helped to solve the northern problem of how to pay for the goods extracted from the south; and the more the textile trade was in north Italian hands, the more the north Italian merchants found it in their interests to deepen the dependence of southern Italy on northern cloth. The attitude was natural enough. If the south proved able to produce on the same scale, the north Italians would lose control both of their northern outlets and of their southern customers. In addition, they would lose the capacity to pay for grain with finished products, and have to revert to a situation similar to that in the mid-twelfth century, when silver flowed south at a steady rate. For those who lived by the maintenance of such supply lines between north and south, a situation developed by the late thirteenth century whose foundation was the primacy of northern cloth.

So in the very long term the north Italian presence may have had drawbacks for southern Italy. What its effects on the urban and rural population of the twelfth-century *Regno* were cannot be said, on the basis of the evidence available. Yet in the short term the presence of the north Italians was advantageous if not to the kingdom at least to the king. And the wealth of the king made sense to his subjects, in so far as it allowed him to defend his frontiers with ample resources and to protect their lives and bellies. So the king and the merchants grew very rich in partnership; for the myriad partnership contracts themselves reflect the light of a yet grander commercial partnership established in the twelfth century between the king and the communes.

BIBLIOGRAPHY

PRIMARY SOURCES

LIST OF MSS

DUBROVNIK, HISTORIJSKI ARHIV
  Acta Sanctae Mariae Majoris (classified by date)

GENOA, ARCHIVIO DI STATO
  Cartolare notarile I (Giovanni Scriba *et al.*)
  Cart. 2 (Oberto Scriba de Mercato *et al.*)
  Cart. 3/ii (Guglielmo da Sori, or de Sauri)
  Cart. 56 (Oberto de Placentia)
  MS Diversorum 102 (Oberto Scriba de Mercato, Oberto de Placentia, Guglielmo
    da Sori)
  Archivio segreto, Materie politiche, busta 1, busta 2

GENOA, BIBLIOTECA UNIVERSITARIA
  Liber Jurium Reipublicae Genuensis

PISA, ARCHIVIO DI STATO
  Atti pubblici
  Carte Lupi, Fonti I, Certosa (classified by date)
  Diplomatico, Monastero degli Olivetani (classified by date)
  Diplomatico, San Lorenzo alle Rivalte (classified by date)
  R. Acquisto Coletti (classified by date)
  R. Acquisto Roncioni (classified by date)

PISA, ARCHIVIO DELLA CERTOSA DI CALCI
  Pergamene (classified by date)

SAVONA, ARCHIVIO DI STATO
  Cartolare notarile Arnaldo da Cumano e Giovanni di Donato
  Cart. Martinus (in Genoa, Istituto di paleografia e di storia medievale)
  Cart. Saonus (*ibid.*)
  Cart. Ubertus (*ibid.*)
  Registro a catena i (piccolo)

VENICE, ARCHIVIO DI STATO
  Liber Blancus
  Liber Pactorum i
  San Zaccaria pergamene, busta 2, busta 34
  Codex diplomaticus Lanfranchi, 1000–1199 (transcriptions in chronological order)

Bibliography

VENICE, BIBLIOTECA NAZIONALE MARCIANA
MS Lat. XIV-71 (2803)
MS Lat. XIV-72 (4273)

VIENNA, ÖSTERREICHISCHE NATIONALBIBLIOTHEK
MS Lat. 2507

PRINTED WORKS

Alexander Telesinus. *De Rebus Gestis Rogerii Siciliae Regis*, ed. G. del Re, *Cronisti e Scrittori sincroni napoletani editi e inediti*, 1. I Normanni, Naples, 1845.

Amari, M. (ed.). *Biblioteca arabo-sicula, versione italiana*, folio edition. Turin–Rome, 1880–1.

Amari, M. *I diplomi arabi del R. Archivio fiorentino.* Florence, 1863.

Nuovi ricordi arabici su la storia di Genova. Genoa, 1873 (also in *ASLSP*, v, 1873).

Gli Annales Pisani di Bernardo Maragone. Ed. M. Lupo Gentile. RISS, ser. 2, VI, part 2.

Annali Genovesi di Caffaro e de' suoi continuatori. Ed. L. T. Belgrano and C. Imperiale di Sant'Angelo. FSI; Rome 1890–1929.

Aprile, F. *Della cronologia universale della Sicilia.* Palermo, 1725.

Bartoloni, F. and de Stefano, A. 'Diplomata Regum Siciliae de gente normannorum', *Archivio paleografico italiano*, XIV (1954–5).

Benjamin of Tudela, *The itinerary of Benjamin of Tudela.* Ed. M. N. Adler. London, 1907. Also ed. by A. Asher, *The itinerary of Rabbi Benjamin of Tudela.* 2 vols. London and Berlin, 1840–1.

Blancard, L. *Documents inédits sur le commerce de Marseille au moyen-âge.* 2 vols. Marseilles, 1884–5.

Böhmer, J. F. *Acta imperii selecta.* Ed. J. Ficker. Innsbruck, 1870.

Bonaini, F. 'Due carte pisano–amalfitane', *Archivio storico italiano*, ser. 3, VIII (1868).

Bonvillano. Ed. J. E. Eierman, H. C. Krueger, R. L. Reynolds. Notai Liguri del sec. XII, III; Genoa, 1939.

Boso, Cardinal, in *Liber Pontificalis.* Ed. L. Duchesne, II. Paris, 1892.

Carabellese, F. and Zambler, A. *Le Relazioni commerciali fra la Puglia e la Repubblica di Venezia dal sec. X al XV.* 2 vols. Trani, 1897–8.

Cusa, S. *I diplomi greci e arabi di Sicilia.* 2 vols. Palermo, 1860–82.

dal Borgo, F. *Raccolta di scelti diplomi pisani.* Pisa, 1765.

Dandolo, Andrea. *Cronica.* RISS, ser. 2, XII, part 1. ed. by E. Pastorello.

de Mas Latrie, L. *Traités de paix et de commerce et documents divers concernant les relations des Chrétiens avec les Arabes de l'Afrique septentrionale au Moyen Age.* Paris, 1866.

Doehaerd, R. *Les Relations commerciales entre Gênes, la Belgique et l'Outremont.* 3 vols. Brussels–Rome, 1941.

Eustathios of Thessalonika. *La Espugnazione di Tessalonica.* Ed. S. P. Kyriakidis and V. Rotolo. Palermo, 1961; German translation by H. Hunger, *Die Normannen in Thessalonike.* Graz, 1955.

Falco Beneventanus. *Chronicon.* Repr. by Del Re, *Cronisti e scrittori* (*vide* Alex. Telesinus).

Fazello, T. *De rebus Siculis decas prima.* Ed. V. M. Amico. Catania, 1749.

Filangieri di Candida, R. *Codice diplomatico amalfitano.* 2 vols. Naples, 1917; Trani, 1951.

Bibliography

Filippi, G. 'Patto di pace tra Ruggiero II normanno e la Città di Savona', *Archivio storico per le provincie napoletane*, XIV (1889), 750–7.

Freshfield, E. H. *A manual of later Roman law: the Ecloga ad Procheiron mutata...including the Rhodian maritime law.* Cambridge, 1927.

Garufi, C. A. (ed.), *I Documenti inediti dell'epoca normanna in Sicilia.* Documenti per servire alla storia di Sicilia. Ser. 1, *Diplomata*, XVIII. Palermo, 1899.

Gattola, E. *Ad historiam abbatiae cassinensis accessiones.* Venice, 1734.

Giardina, C. *Capitoli e Privilegi di Messina.* Palermo, 1937.

Il Cartolare di Giovanni Scriba. Ed. M. Chiaudano and M. Moresco. 2 vols. Rome–Turin, 1935.

Guglielmo Cassinese. Ed. M. W. Hall, H. C. Krueger, R. L. Reynolds. Notai Liguri del Sec. XII, II; Genoa, 1938.

Historia ducum Veneticorum. Ed. H. Simonsfeld, MGH. SS., XIV, 72–97.

Holtzmann, W. 'Papst-, Kaiser- und Normannenurkunden aus Unteritalien, I', *Quellen und Forschungen aus italienischen Archiven und Bibliotheken*, XXXV (1955).

'Hugo Falcandus'. *La Historia o Liber de Regno Sicilie e la Epistola ad Petrum Panormitane Ecclesie Thesaurarium.* Ed. G. B. Siragusa. FSI; Rome, 1897.

Huillard-Bréholles, J. *Historia diplomatica Friderici Secundi.* 5 vols. Paris, 1859–61.

Idrisi. *L'Italia descritta nel 'Libro del Re Ruggero' compilato da Edrisi.* Ed. and tr. M. Amari, C. Schiaparelli. Rome, 1883.

Imperiale di Sant'Angelo, C. *Codice diplomatico della Repubblica di Genova.* 3 vols. FSI; Rome, 1936–42.

Ibn Jubayr, *The travels of Ibn Jubayr.* Tr. R. J. C. Broadhurst. London, 1952; tr. M. Amari, *BAS*, versione italiana, folio ed., 35–45.

Io. Kinnamos. *Epitome rerum ab Ioanne et Alexio Comnenis gestarum.* Ed. A. Meineke. Corpus Scriptorum Historiae Byzantinae. Bonn, 1836.

Kukuljević, J. *Codex diplomaticus regni Croatiae, Dalmatiae et Slavoniae.* Zagreb, 1874–5.

Lami, J. *Deliciae eruditorum seu veterum anecdoton opusculorum collectanea.* Florence, 1736.

Ljubić, S. *Listine o odnasajih juznoga Slaventsva i mletačke republike*, I. Zagreb, 1868.

Lombardo, A. and Morozzo della Rocca, R. *Documenti del commercio veneziano nei secoli XI–XIII.* 2 vols. Rome–Turin, 1940; *id., Nuovi documenti del commercio veneto dei secoli XI–XIII.* Venice, 1953.

Minieri Riccio, C. *Saggio di Codice diplomatico, formato sulle antiche scritture dell'Archivio di Stato di Napoli.* Naples, 1878–83.

Monumenta Historiae Patriae edita iussu Regis Caroli Alberto. Chartarum, II. Turin, 1853.

Monumenta Historiae Patriae. VI and VII. *Liber Jurium Reipublicae Genuensis.*

Niketas Choniates. *Historia.* Ed. I. Bekker. Corpus Scriptorum Historiae Byzantinae. Bonn, 1835.

Oberto Scriba de Mercato, 1186. Ed. C. Jona. Notai Liguri del Sec. XII, IV; Genoa, 1940. The title-page carries only the name of M. Chiaudano, the general editor, owing to the Fascist race laws.

Oberto Scriba de Mercato, 1190. Ed. M. Chiaudano and R. Morozzo della Rocca. Notai Liguri del Sec. XII; Genoa, 1938.

Odo of Deuil. *De profectione Ludovici VII in orientem.* Ed. V. Berry. New York, 1948.

Petrus de Eboli. *Carmen de rebus Siculis.* Ed. G. B. Siragusa, FSI; Rome, 1905, and E. Rota RISS, ser. 2, XXXI, part 1.

Pirri, R. *Sicilia Sacra.* 2 vols. Palermo, 1734.

Pratesi, A. (ed.). *Carte latine di abbazie calabresi provenienti dall'Archivio Aldobrandini.* Vatican City, 1958.

Radonić, J. *Acta et diplomata ragusina.* I. Belgrade, 1934.

Recueil des Historiens des Croisades – Historiens orientaux. Paris, 1872–1906. IV (Imad-ad-din, Abu Shamah, Beha-ad-din).

Registrum curiae archiepiscopalis Janue. Ed. L. T. Belgrano. *ASLSP,* II, fasc. 2. 1870.

Resti (Restić), Giunio. *Chronica Ragusina.* Ed. S. Nodilo. Zagreb, 1893.

Roger of Howden. *Gesta Regis Henrici Secundi Benedicti Abbatis.* Ed. W. Stubbs. Rolls Series. London, 1867.

Romuald of Salerno. *Chronicon.* Ed. C. A. Garufi. RISS, ser. 2, VII, part I.

Smičiklas, T. *Codex diplomaticus regni Croatiae, Dalmatiae et Slavoniae.* II and III. Zagreb, 1904–5.

Stumpf-Brentano, F. 'Acta imperii ab Henrico I ad Henricum VI usque', *Die Reichskanzler vornehmlich des X., XI., XIII. Jahrhundert.* III. Innsbruck, 1881.

Tabularium Cassinense, Codex diplomaticus Cajetanus. 2 parts. Montecassino, 1887–91.

Tafel, G. L. F., Thomas, G. M. *Urkunden zur älteren Handels- und Staatsgeschichte der Republik Venedig.* 2 vols. *Fontes Rerum Austriacum,* section ii, vol. XII. Vienna, 1856.

Wattenbach, W. 'Iter austriacum, 1853', *Archiv für Kunde österreichischer Geschichtsquellen,* XXIV (1855).

CALENDARS OF DOCUMENTS

(a) SICILY AND SOUTHERN ITALY

All Norman kings

Behring, W. 'Sicilianische Studien', I (Roger II), II (later kings), *Programm des kgl. Gymnasiums zu Elbing,* 1882, 1887.

Enzensberger, H. *Beiträge zum Kanzlei- und Urkundenwesen der normannischen Herrscher Unteritaliens und Siziliens.* Kallmünz, 1971. 'Urkundenverzeichnis' – supplements to all previous registers.

Roger II

Caspar, E. *Roger II. (1101–1154) und die Gründung der normannisch-sicilischen Monarchie.* Innsbruck, 1904, Regesten.

Collura, P. 'Appendice al regesto dei diplomi di re Ruggero compilato da Erich Caspar', *Atti del Convegno internazionale di studi ruggeriani.* Palermo, 1955.

William I and II

See Behring, II, and Enzensberger.

Tancred and Henry VI

Palumbo, P. F. 'Gli Atti di Tancredi e di Guglielmo III di Sicilia', *Atti del Convegno internazionale di studi ruggeriani* Palermo, 1955.

Clementi, D. 'Calendar of the diplomas of the Hohenstaufen Emperor Henry VI concerning the kingdom of Sicily', *Quellen und Forschungen aus italienischen Archiven und Bibliotheken,* XXXV (1955).

(b) THE NORTH ITALIAN COMMUNES

Casini, B. *Inventario dell'Archivio del Comune di Pisa (secolo XI–1509)*. Livorno, 1969.

Lisciandrelli, P. 'Trattati e negoziazioni politiche della Repubblica di Genova, 958–1797'. *ASLSP*, n.s. I, fasc. I (1960).

(c) THE CAIRO GENIZA

S. Shaked. *A tentative bibliography of Geniza documents*. Paris–The Hague, 1964.

SECONDARY WORKS

This list comprises (a) items frequently mentioned in the text; (b) items of general significance for the understanding of this book's theme – in that respect, it is necessarily selective. For a very full bibliography, see the work of H. Enzensberger cited here.

Abulafia, D. S. H. 'L'Attività commerciale genovese nell'Africa normanna: la città di Tripoli', *Atti CISSN*.

'Corneto–Tarquinia and the Italian mercantile republics: the earliest evidence', *Papers of the British School at Rome*, XLII (1974).

'Dalmatian Ragusa and the Norman Kingdom of Sicily', *Slavonic and East European Review*, LIV (1976).

'Henry, Count of Malta, and his Mediterranean activities, 1203–1230', *Medieval Malta: Studies on Malta before the Knights* (supplementary monograph of the British School at Rome, ed. A. Luttrell, London, 1975).

'Pisan commercial colonies and consulates in twelfth-century Sicily', *English Historical Review* (forthcoming).

Ahrweiler, H. *Byzance et la mer*. Paris, 1966.

Amari, M. *Storia dei Musulmani di Sicilia*. 3 vols. in 5. 2nd ed., annotated by C. A. Nallino, Catania, 1933–9.

Ancora, A. 'Alcuni aspetti della politica di Maione da Bari', *Studi storici in onore di Gabriele Pepe*. Bari, 1969.

Antoniadis-Bibicou, H. *Recherches sur les douanes à Byzance*. Paris, 1963.

Ashtor, E. *Les métaux précieux et la balance des payements du Proche-Orient à la basse époque*. Paris, 1971.

Astuti, G. *Rendiconti mercantili inediti del Cartolare di Giovanni Scriba*. Turin, 1933.

Aymard, M., Bresc, H. 'Problemi di storia dell'Insediamento nella Sicilia medievale e moderna, 1100–1800', *Archeologia e geografia del popolamento, Quaderni storici*, XXIV, fasc. 2 (1973).

Bach, E. *La Cité de Gênes au XIIe siècle*. Copenhagen, 1955.

Bartoloni, F. 'La data del portale di Bonanno nel Duomo di Monreale'. *Studi medievali in onore di Antonino de Stefano*. Palermo, 1956.

Boeckler, A. *Die Bronzetüren des Bonanus von Pisa und des Barisanus von Trani*. Berlin, 1953.

Bognetti, G. P. *Note per la storia del passaporto e del salvacondotto*. Pavia, 1933.

Per l'edizione dei Notai Liguri. Genoa, 1938 – volume edited by M. Moresco.

Brand, C. M. 'The Byzantines and Saladin, 1185–1192: opponents of the Third Crusade', *Speculum*, XXXVII (1962).

Byzantium confronts the West, 1180–1204. Cambridge, Mass., 1968.

Bibliography

Bresc, H. 'Les jardins de Palerme', *Mélanges d'Histoire et d'Archéologie de l'Ecole Française de Rome*, LXXIV (1972).

Brett, M. 'Ifriqiya as a market for Saharan trade from the 10th to the 12th century A.D.', *Journal of African History*, X (1969).

Brooke, C. N. L., and Pinder-Wilson, R. H. 'The Reliquary of St Petroc and the Ivories of Norman Sicily', *Archaeologia* (Society of Antiquaries of London), CIV (1973).

Brühl, C.-R. 'La politica finanziaria di Federico Barbarossa in Italia', *PSIFB*.

Byrne, E. H. 'Commercial contracts of the Genoese in the Syrian trade of the XIIth century', *Quarterly Journal of Economics*, XXXI (1916/17).

'Easterners in Genoa', *Journal of the American Oriental Society*, XXXVIII (1918).

Genoese shipping in the twelfth and thirteenth centuries. Cambridge, Mass., 1930.

Cahen, C. *Le Régime féodal de l'Italie normande*. Paris, 1940.

Carabellese, F. *Bari*. Bergamo, 1909.

Il Comune pugliese durante la monarchia normanno-sveva. Bari, 1924.

Camera, M. *Memorie storico-diplomatiche dell'antica città e ducato di Amalfi*. 2 vols. (Salerno, 1876–81.)

Caravale, M. *Il Regno normanno di Sicilia*. Milan, 1966.

'La Feudalità nella Sicilia normanna', *Atti CISSN*.

Caspar, E. *Roger II. und die Gründung der normannisch-sicilischen Monarchie*. Innsbruck, 1904.

Cessi, R. 'Venezia e i normanni', *Archivio storico pugliese*, XIII (1959).

Chalandon, F. *Les Comnène: Jean II Comnène et Manuel Ier Comnène*. Paris, 1912.

Histoire de la domination normande en Italie et en Sicile. 2 vols. Paris, 1907.

Chiaudano, M. *Contratti commerciali genovesi del secolo XII*. Turin, 1925.

'Genova e i normanni', *Archivio storico pugliese*, XIII (1959).

Chone, H. *Die Handelsbeziehungen Kaiser Friedrichs II. zu den Seestädten Venedig, Pisa, Genua*. Berlin, 1902.

Ciccaglione, F. 'La vita economica siciliana nel periodo normanno-svevo', *Archivio storico per la Sicilia orientale*, X (1913)

Classen, P. 'La politica di Manuele Comneno tra Federico Barbarossa e le città italiane', *PSIFB*.

Clementi, D. 'L'Atteggiamento dell'Imperatore Federico I nella Questione del Confine terrestre nel Regno normanno di Sicilia, Puglia e Capua', *PSIFB*.

'The circumstances of Count Tancred's accession to the Kingdom of Sicily, Duchy of Apulia and the Principality of Capua', *Mélanges Antonio Marongiu*. Studies presented to the international commission for the history of representative and parliamentary institutions, XXXIV; Palermo–Agrigento, 1967.

'Notes on Norman Sicilian surveys' in V. H. Galbraith, *The making of Domesday Book*. Oxford, 1961.

'Some unnoticed aspects of the Emperor Henry VI's conquest of the Norman Kingdom of Sicily', *Bulletin of the John Rylands Library*, XXXVI (1954).

Costamagna, G. *La Triplice Redazione del Instrumentum Genovese*. Notai Liguri del Sec. XII e XIII, VIII; Genoa, 1961.

Cracco, G. *Società e Stato nel Medioevo veneziano (secoli XII–XIV)*. Florence–Venice 1967.

d'Angelo, F. 'La Ceramica normanna nella Sicilia', *Atti CISSN*.

de Boüard, N. 'Problèmes de subsistances dans un état médiéval; le marché et le prix des céréales au royaume angevin de Sicile', *Annales–H.E.S.*, X (1938).

Bibliography

de Roover, F. E. 'Lucchese silks'. *CIBA Review*, LXXX (1950).

de Roover, R. 'The Cambium Maritimum contract according to the Genoese notarial records of the XIIth and XIIIth centuries', *Reynolds Essays*.

di Tucci, R. 'Relazioni commerciali fra Amalfi e Genova', *Studi sulla Repubblica marinara di Amalfi*, a cura del comitato per la 'Celebrazione di Amalfi imperiale'. Salerno, 1935.

Engel, A. *Recherches sur la numismatique et la sigillographie des Normands de Sicile et de l'Italie*. Paris, 1882.

Enzensberger, H. *Beiträge zum Kanzlei- und Urkundenwesen der normannischen Herrscher Unteritaliens und Siziliens*. Kallmünz, 1971.

Filangieri, P. 'Note al *Privilegium Libertatis* concesso dai Napoletani agli Amalfitani nel 1190', *Papers of the British School at Rome*, XXIV (1956), *Studies in Italian medieval history presented to Miss E. M. Jamison*.

Fuiano, M. 'Napoli dalla fine dello Stato autonomo alla sua elevazione a capitale del *Regnum Siciliae*', *Archivio storico per le provincie napoletane*, LXXV–LXXVII (1955–7). Reprinted as *Napoli nel Medioevo*. Naples, 1972.

Galasso, G. 'Il Commercio amalfitano nel periodo normanno', *Studi in onore di R. Filangieri*, 3 vols. Vol. I. Naples, 1959.

Dal Comune medievale all'Unità. Bari, 1969.

Mezzogiorno medievale e moderno. Turin, 1965.

Goitein, S. D. *A Mediterranean society*. Vol. I, *Economic foundations*. Berkeley–Los Angeles, 1967.

'Sicily and southern Italy in the Cairo Geniza documents', *Archivio storico per la Sicilia orientale*, LXVII (1971).

Grierson, P. and Oddy, W. A. 'Le Titre du Tari sicilien du milieu du XIe siècle à 1278', *Revue numismatique*, ser. 6, XVI (1974).

Guillou, A. 'La Lucanie byzantine', *Byzantion*, XXXV (1965).

'Production and profits in the Byzantine province of Italy (tenth to eleventh centuries): an expanding society', *Dumbarton Oaks Papers*, XXVIII (1974).

Hahnloser, H. R. (ed.) *Il Tesoro di San Marco: il Tesoro e il Museo*. Florence–Venice, 1971.

Herlihy, D. *Pisa in the early Renaissance*. New Haven, Conn., 1958.

Herrin, J. 'The collapse of the Byzantine Empire in the twelfth century: a study of a medieval economy', *University of Birmingham Historical Journal*, XII (1970).

Heyd, W. *Histoire du commerce du Levant au Moyen Age*. Tr. F. Raynaud. 2 vols. Leipzig, 1885–6.

Heynen, R. *Zur Entstehung des Kapitalismus in Venedig*. Stuttgart, 1905.

Heywood, W. *A history of Pisa, eleventh and twelfth centuries*. Cambridge, 1921.

Hibbert, A. B. 'The economic policies of towns', *Cambridge Economic History of Europe*. III. 1963.

'The origins of the medieval town patriciate', *Past and Present*, III (1953).

Hoffman, H. 'Hugo Falcandus und Romuald von Salerno', *Deutsches Archiv*, XXIII (1967).

Hughes, D. O. 'Urban growth and family structure in medieval Genoa', *Past and Present*, LXVI (1975).

Hyde, J. K. *Society and politics in medieval Italy*. London, 1973.

Idris, H. R. *La Berbérie orientale sous les Zirides*. 2 vols. Paris–Algiers, 1962.

Jamison, E. M. *Admiral Eugenius of Sicily: his life and work and the authorship of the 'Epistola ad Petrum' and the 'Historia Hugonis Falcandi Siculi'*. London, 1957.

Bibliography

'The Norman administration of Apulia and Capua', *Papers of the British School at Rome*, VI (1913).

Jasny, N. *The wheats of classical antiquity*. Baltimore, 1944.

Jones, P. 'La storia economica dalla caduta dell'Impero romano al secolo XIV', *Storia d'Italia*. Ed. R. Romano and C. Vivanti. Vol. II, part 2. Turin, 1974.

Kehr, K. A. *Die Urkunden der normannisch-sicilischen Könige*. Innsbruck, 1902.

Krueger, H. C. 'Genoese trade with Northwest Africa in the twelfth century', *Speculum*, VIII (1933).

'Post-war collapse and rehabilitation in Genoa, 1149–1162', *Studi Luzzatto*, I, 123–6.

'Wares of exchange in twelfth-century Genoese–African trade', *Speculum*, XII (1937).

Lagumina, B. *Catalogo delle monete arabe esistenti nella Biblioteca Comunale di Palermo*. Palermo, 1892.

Lamma, P. *Comneni e Staufer: Ricerche sui rapporti fra Bisanzio e l'Occidente nel secolo XII*. 2 vols. Rome, 1955–7.

La Monte, J. L. *Feudal monarchy in the Latin kingdom of Jerusalem, 1100–1291*. Cambridge, Mass., 1932.

Lattes, A. 'L'Assicurazione e la voce "Securare" in documenti genovesi del 1191 e 1192', *Rivista del diritto commerciale e del diritto generale delle obbligazioni*, XXV (1927).

Lizier, A. *L'Economia rurale dell'età pre-normanna nell'Italia meridionale*. Palermo, 1907.

Lopez, R. S. 'The unexplored wealth of the Notarial Archives in Pisa and Lucca', *Mélanges Louis Halphen*. Paris, 1951.

Luttrell, A. T. 'Malta nel periodo normanno', *Atti CISSN*.

Luzzatto, G. *An economic history of Italy from the fall of the Roman Empire to the beginning of the sixteenth century*. London, 1961.

Storia economica di Venezia dall'XI al XVI secolo. Venice, 1961.

Studi di storia economica veneziana. Padua, 1954.

Mack Smith, D. *A history of Sicily*. Vol. II, *Medieval Sicily*. London, 1968.

Manfroni, C. *Storia della marina italiana dalle invasioni barbariche al trattato di Ninfeo (400–1261)*. Livorno, 1899.

Marongiu, A. 'A model-state in the Middle Ages: the Norman and Swabian Kingdom of Sicily', *Comparative Studies in Society and History*, VI (1964).

Maschke, E. 'Die Wirtschaftspolitik Kaiser Friedrichs II. im Königreich Sizilien', *Vierteljahrschrift für Sozial- und Wirtschaftsgeschichte*, LV (1966).

Mathieu, M. 'La Sicile normande dans la poésie byzantine', *Bollettino del Centro di studi filologici e linguistici siciliani*, II (1954).

Mayer, H. E. *Marseilles Levantehandel und ein akkonensisches Fälscheratelier des XIII. Jhdts*. Tübingen, 1972.

Mazzarese Fardella, E. *Aspetti dell'organizzazione amministrativa nello stato normanno e svevo*. Milan, 1966.

Mazzaoui, M. F. 'The cotton industry of northern Italy in the late Middle Ages', *Journal of Economic History*, XXXII (1972).

Ménager, L. R. *Amiratus – Ἀμηρᾶς: L'Emirat et les origines de l'Amirauté*. Paris, 1960.

'L'Institution monarchique dans les états normands d'Italie', *Cahiers de civilisation médiévale*, II (1959).

Milone, F. *Memoria illustrativa della Carta della utilizzazione del suolo della Sicilia*. Rome, 1959.

Bibliography

Ministero dell'Interno, Pubblicazioni degli Archivi di Stato, XXII and XLI, *Archivio di Stato di Genova: Cartolari notarili genovesi*. Rome, 1956 and 1961.

Misbach, H. 'Genoese commerce and the alleged flow of gold to the East, 1154–1253', *Revue internationale d'histoire de la banque*, III (1970).

'Genoese trade and the rôle of Sicilian coinage in the Mediterranean economy, 1154–1253', *Revue internationale d'histoire de la banque*, V (1972).

'Mostra Storica del Notariato Medievale Ligure', *ASLSP*. n.s., IV, fasc. i (1964). (Contributions by G. Borlandi, G. Costamagna, D. Pincuh, *et al.*)

Nardone, P. *Genova e Pisa nei loro rapporti commerciali col Mezzogiorno d'Italia*. Prato, 1923.

Nelson, B. 'Blancardo (the Jew?) of Genoa and the restitution of usury in medieval Italy', *Studi Luzzatto*, I, 99–108.

Noberasco, F., and Scovazzi, I. *Storia di Savona*. Vol. I. Savona, 1926.

Norwich, J. J. *The Normans in the South*. London, 1967. *The Kingdom in the sun*. London, 1970.

Olivieri, A. 'Serie dei Consoli del Comune di Genova', *ASLSP*, I (1858).

Parker, J. S. F. 'The attempted Byzantine alliance with the Norman Kingdom (1166–7)', *Papers of the British School at Rome*, XXIV (1956).

Peri, I. *Città e campagna in Sicilia*. 2 vols. Palermo 1953/6. Also published in *Atti della Accademia di Scienze Lettere e Arti di Palermo*, ser. 4, vol. XIII, part 2, fascs. 1 and 4 (1953–2).

Studi sul Comune di Genova, I. *Genesi e Formazione del Comune Consolare a Genova*, II. *Ordinamento del Comune Consolare*. Palermo, 1951. Also published in *Atti della Accademia di Scienze Lettere e Arti di Palermo*, ser. 4, vol. XI, part 2 (1951).

Il Villanaggio in Sicilia. Palermo, 1965.

Pistarino, G. 'I Normanni e le repubbliche marinare italiane', *Atti CISSN*.

Powell, J. M. 'Genoese policy and the Kingdom of Sicily, 1220–1240', *Mediaeval Studies*, XXVIII (1966).

'Medieval monarchy and trade: the economic policy of Emperor Frederick II in Sicily', *Studi medievali*, 3rd ser., III (1962).

Rabie, H. *The financial system of Egypt, A.H. 564–741/A.D. 1169–1341*. London, 1972.

Rassow, P. 'Zum byzantinisch–normannischen Krieg', *Mitteilungen des Institut für österreichisches Geschichtsforschung*, LXXII (1954).

Reif, S. C. *A guide to the Taylor–Schechter Genizah Collection*. Cambridge University Library, 1973.

Reynolds, R. L. 'Genoese sources for the twelfth-century history of Liège, with special attention to John of Liège, *Etudes d'Histoire dédiées à la mémoire de Henri Pirenne*. Brussels, 1937.

'Genoese trade in the late twelfth century, particularly in cloth from the fairs of Champagne', *Journal of Economic and Business History*, III (1931).

'The market for northern textiles in Genoa, 1179–1200', *Revue belge de philologie et d'histoire*, VIII (1929).

'Merchants of Arras and the overland trade with Genoa', *Revue belge de philologie et d'histoire*, IX (1930).

Riedmann, J. *Die Beurkundung der Verträge Friedrich Barbarossas mit italienischen Städten*. Österr. Akad. d. Wiss., phil.-klasse, Sitzungsberichte, 291. Band, 3. Abhandlung. Vienna, 1973.

Riley-Smith, J. S. C. 'Government in Latin Syria and the commercial privileges of foreign merchants', in D. Baker (ed.), *Relations between East and West in the Middle Ages*. Edinburgh, 1973.

Rossi Sabatini, G. 'Relazioni tra Pisa e Amalfi nel Medioevo'. *Studi sulla Repubblica marinara di Amalfi*, a cura del Comitato per la 'Celebrazione di Amalfi imperiale'. Salerno, 1935.

L'Espansione di Pisa nel Mediterraneo. Florence, 1935.

Sambon, A. *Le Monete del reame di Napoli e di Sicilia*. (Printed but never published.)

Sayous, A. E. *Le Commerce des Européens à Tunis depuis le XIIe siècle jusqu'à la fin du XVIe*. Paris, 1929.

Scarlata, M. 'Sul Declino del Regno normanno e l'assunzione al trono di Tancredi', *Atti CISSN*.

Schaube, A. *Handelsgeschichte der Romanischen Völker des Mittelmeergebiets bis zum Ende der Kreuzzüge*. Munich–Berlin, 1906.

Shaked, S. *A tentative bibliography of Geniza documents*. Paris–The Hague, 1964.

Sieveking, G. *Genueser Finanzwesen vom 12. bis 14. Jhdt*. Freiburg-im-Breisgau, 1898.

Slessarev, V. 'Die sogenannten Orientalen im Mittelalterlichen Genua. Einwanderer aus Südfrankreich in der ligurischen Metropole', *Vierteljahrschrift für Sozial- und Wirtschaftsgeschichte*, LI (1964).

'*Ecclesiae Mercatorum* and the rise of merchant colonies', *Business History Review*, XLI (1967).

'The pound-value of Genoa's maritime trade in 1161', *Reynolds Essays*.

Spremić, M. 'La Repubblica di Ragusa e il Regno di Sicilia', *Atti CISSN*. Also printed in *Archivio storico per la Sicilia orientale*, LXIX (1973).

Stern, S. M. 'Tari', *Studi medievali*, ser. 3, XI (1970).

Tadić, J. 'Ragusa e i normanni', *Archivio storico pugliese*, XIII (1959).

Toeche, T. *Heinrich VI*. Jahrbücher der deutschen Geschichte. Leipzig, 1867.

Toubert, P. *Les Structures du Latium médiéval: le Latium méridional et la Sabine du IXe siècle à la fin du XIIe*. 2 vols. Paris, 1973.

Trasselli, C. *I Privilegi di Messina e di Trapani, 1160–1355*. Palermo, 1949.

Venezia e Bisanzio (catalogue of an exhibition at the Ducal Palace and the Marciana Library, 8 June–30 September 1974). Venice, 1974.

Vitale, V. 'Genova ed Enrico VI di Svevia', *Miscellanea di studi storici in onore di Camillo Manfroni*. Padua, 1925.

'Le relazioni commerciali di Genova col Regno normanno–svevo', *Giornale Storico e letterario della Liguria*, n.s., III (1927).

Volpe, G. *Studi sulle istituzioni comunali a Pisa*. 2nd ed., introd. by C. Violante. Florence, 1970.

Watson, A. 'Back to Gold – and Silver', *Economic History Review*, ser. 2, XX (1967).

White, L. T. *Latin monasticism in Norman Sicily*. Cambridge, Mass., 1938.

Whitehouse, D. B. 'The medieval pottery of south Italy'. Ph.D. dissertation. Cambridge University, 1967. (revised ed. in the press, Rome).

Wieruszowski, H. 'The Norman Kingdom of Sicily and the Crusades', in *A history of the Crusades*, K. M. Setton (General Editor). Vol. II, *The later Crusades, 1189–1311*. Philadelphia, 1962; Madison, Wis., 1969.

Yver, G. *Le Commerce et les marchands dans l'Italie méridionale au XIIIe et au XIIVe siècle*. Paris, 1903.

INDEX

NOTE: where identification seemed possible, the following abbreviations have been added to personal names to indicate a person's origin: G, Genoese; P, Pisan; S, Savonese; V, Venetian. For Genoese trade with ports named in the text and tables, see under the port of destination. Only selected headings have been supplied for Sicily (island of), Sicily (kingdom of) and for Genoa. See the entry 'Treaties' for a chronological list of Genoese, Sicilian and other treaties, pacts and grants.

In accordance with custom, medieval individuals are listed under forenames, but certain large families have general entries as well.

Abruzzi, 31, 35, 144
Abu-l-qasim, Saracen of Sicily, 247–9, 251
accomendacio (commenda): legal form of, 14; liability, 15; origins, 266n
Acre: in First Crusade, 51, 53; Venetian contracts for, 135, 144, 147–9; *see also* bezants; Syria
Adelaide, Countess of Sicily, 64
Africa, Norman, 22, 31, 156: advantages of Norman rule for, 109; Genoese trade in, 108–10; invasion of, 66; loss of, 86, 91, 109–10, 135; Sicilian agents in, 40; *see also* Africa, North; Almohads; al-Mahdiyyah
Africa, North: coral of, 43, 276; Genoese contracts for, 99, 112, 162, 165, 166, 174, 189, 194, 236, 263; Genoese trade in, 71, 84, 138, 230; privileges, 91n, 228; gold of, 72; maritime trade, 22, 43, 53; Messinese trade in, 77n; Pisan trade in, 84; Savonese trade in, 155–6; Sicilian trade in, 27, 40, 77, 156; *see also* Africa, Norman; Almohads; al-Mahdiyyah; gold; *paiole*
Agrigento *see* Girgenti
Albania, 31; *see also* Durazzo
Alberto Celone, P of Messina, 205, 280
Alberto Clerico [G], 110, 219, 227
Alcherio *bancherius* [G], 159, 176
Aleramici, 39, 64–9, 278
Alexander III, pope, 114, 132: and Venice, 133, 145–7
Alexandria
Genoese contracts for, 99, 104–5, 108,

111, 112, 113, 118–19, 158, 159, 161, 166, 233, 234, 236, 253: and Solomon of Salerno, 102, 225, 226, 239–42, 244–6
Genoese trade in, 71; exclusion from, 131, 262; textiles and, 102, 219
Pisan shipping at, 140
shipping from: in Genoa, 71; in Sicily, 44, 92
Sicilian attacks on, 140, 156n, 164
Sicilian trade with, 44
trade routes and, 64, 229–30
Venetian merchants in, 54, 148–9
Alexios I Komnenos, Greek emperor, 54, 76, 80
Alexios II, pseudo-emperor, 94–5, 163
Almeria, Genoese expedition to (1147–9), 131, 232
Almohads: and Genoese, 91, 110, 115; and Normans, 86, 91, 94, 108–10, 135, 156; and Savonese, 155–6
almonds, 46–7
Almoravids, 129, 156–7; *see also* Majorca
Almyra, Pisan colony, 90n, 138n
alum, 176, 245, 252
Amalfi
merchants of, 42, 48–9: in Apulia 76; in Byzantium, 55, 81; at Durazzo, 54; at Genoa, 74, 96, 162n; at al-Mahdiyyah, 52; in Naples, 183–4, 266; in Palermo, 49
Pisa and: treaty of 1126, 59; attack on, 49, 60
Roger II and, 60
trade of, 33, 162, 238, 284

Index

Amaury, King of Jerusalem, 131
Amico, draper of G, 187-8, 200
Ancona, 133, 203
Andrea Dandolo, Doge of V, 25n, 88, 141
Andronikos Komnenos, Greek emperor, 163-5
Anjou, coins of, 227
Ansaldo Auria (Doria) noble of G: as ambassador, 90; as businessman, 101
Ansaldo Mallone, G noble, 178, 179, 246, 251; see also Mallone family
Ansaldo Sardena [G], 168-9, 170-1
Ansuisso de Sancto Genesio, (di San Genesio) [G], 189, 200, 271
Antioch, 51, 53, 77
Apulia
  Duchy of, 31, 32
  Genoese and: in Genoese-imperial treaty, 1162, 127; contract for, 179
  Pisa and: in Pisan-imperial treaty, 1162, 125
  Provençaux and French in, 127
  rebellions in: 1120s, 77; 1155, 89, 90
  Roberto di San Giovanni in, 87
  Venetians in, 55, 76-80, 81-2, 127, 134, 144, 146-7, 149, 203
Arabic writings: books, trade in, 220; charters, use of, 8n, 248, 265n; historical sources, 25
Aragon, kingdom of, 212
Aragonese kings of Sicily, 195
arms and armour, 121, 185, 207, 277: belts, 201; military equipment, 166; see also breast-plates
Arnaldo da Cumano, S notary, 23, 155, 157
arsenal, royal, 94
Asti, 201
Athens, 80-1
Attalia, 105
Avvocato, family, 51, 234

bailiff (baiulus), 39, 42n, 118
balance of payments, 219, 223, 264-73: textile trade and, 255-64
baldinelli, cloth, 234
Balduino Scoto [G], 188, 193-4, 195
Balearics, see Majorca
Banking, see deposit banking

Bar, fair of, 271
Baratterio Congiario [P], 205, 280
Barbary, 159, 189, 191; see also Tripoli
Barcelona, 42, 170
Bari: church of St Mark, 80; destruction of by William I, 90; merchants of, 33, 85, 284; seizure of by Normans, 32; shipping of, 75; see also Maio of B
Barletta, 173
barley, 91, 175
Bartholomew de Lucy, Count of Paterno, 261
Basilicata, 30n, 35-6, 271
Belardo Belardengo [G], 201n, 263n
Bellobruno de Castello [G], 181, 196
Benjamin of Tudela, 25, 42: visits Bari, 90; visits Genoa, 238; visits Greece 82n
Benevento: papal enclave, 31, 35, 147; Treaty of, 90-1
Bernardo Maragone, 25, 117n, 138n, 139, 153n: his son Salem, 25, 153n, 157n
Besançon, 184n, 200, 262
bezants, 112, 242: Egyptian, 240; Moroccan, 156, 270, 274-5, 280; Syrian, 148, 175, 179, 190, 225, 270
Bisacia, G noble, 115-16, 130, 233
Bisceglie, 69
Blancardo, Provençal or French merchant, 120, 121, 227, 235, 238, 253
Boccaccio, 156n
Bonanno [P], 30n, 277-8
Boniface of Montferrat, 208
Bonifacio, G abp, 211
Bonifacio della Volta [G], 175, 178, 259n
Bonogiovanni Malfigliastro [G], 102, 107, 120, 219, 236-7, 245, 247: and Solomon of Salerno, 240, 241, 253
Bonogiovanni Tigna, 104, 225-6
Bonvillano, G notary, 19n, 282n
Bougie: Genoese contracts for, 104, 111, 113, 115, 121, 131, 154-5, 160-1, 182-3, 189, 241, 252; gold from, 271
brazilwood, 45, 224, 240, 242
breast-plates, 121n, 184, 185, 201, 205, 277, 280

296

Index

Brindisi, 144
Bubonoso [G], 239, 282
Bufaro Sarago [G], 175-6, 276
Buonaccorso Cicogna [P], 139
Byzantium, *see* Constantinople

Caffaro, Genoese annalist, 97, 114-15, 232n
Cairo, Genoese trade in, 240; *see also* Fustat; Geniza
Caitus Bulcassem, 247-9
Calabria, 31, 32: economic life of, 36, 118; Genoese trade in, 71-2; Pisans in (970), 51; Venetian trade in, 135, 147; *see also* Crotone; Reggio C.; Squillace
Calatafimi, 281
Caltagirone, 65
cambium maritimum: advantages of, 14, 256-7; development of, 226, 250
Camogli, 175
Campania, 31, 32, 237: Genoese trade in, 22, 188, 199; Pisans and, 25, 59-62; rebels in, 59-62, 78; Roger II in, 60-2; textiles imported from, 48, 102, 184, 218; *see also* Capua; Naples; Salerno
Capua: city of, 282; principality of, 32 (Genoese trade in), 162, 179, 199; *see also* Campania; Naples; Salerno
carpets, 44
cartae securitatis, 195
Cartagena, 200, 229
cartularies, *see* Notaries
de Castello family [G], 18, 50, 67, 188
Catalonia, 96, 182
Catania, 37, 153n, 208
Cephalonia, 80; *see also* Ionian islands
Ceuta, Genoese trade in, 113, 121, 154, 158, 161, 166, 182-3, 189, 271
Champagne: coins of, 30n, 227, 270-1; French fairs in, 225, 263n, 271; Genoese and, 95, 183, 263n
cheese, 45
Civitavecchia, 124, 191-2
Coenna of Lucca, 260
coin evidence, 30; *see also* Champagne; gold; tari
commenda, see accomendacio

commercial contracts: as sources, 5, 7-24; cancellation of, 12-13; development of, 226; Genoese, 8-9, 11-16; Marseilles, 8n, 23; Neapolitan, 265; Pisan, 8n, 23-4; registration in cartulary, 11-13; Savonese, 8n, 23, 265; Sicilian, 8, 265n; use of parchment, 12n; value of, 20-2; *see also accomendacio*; *cambium maritimum*; quittance; sea-loan; *societas*
confiscation and seizure of goods (in chronological order)
  Roger II and Savona (1127), 65-6, 69
  Roger II and Pisa (1137), 61
  Roger II and Venice (*circa* 1151), 82-3
  William I and Pisa (1162), 138
  Manuel I and Venice (1171), 141, 150
  William II threatens Venice (1177), 146
  Latin massacre, Constantinople (1182), 161, 164
  Tancred and Genoese (1190s), 179, 194-9
Conrad II, German emperor, 30n, 206
Conrad III, German king, 80, 114
consuls, overseas: Genoese, at Messina, 62-4, 128-9, 279; Pisan, at Messina, 23, 63, 205, 279-80
collegancia, legal form of, 14
commercium, see κομμέρκιον
Constantinople (*also* Romania, Byzantine Empire)
  Genoa and: contracts for, 71, 89-90, 99, 105, 108, 111, 112, 113, 115, 119, 154, 159, 165, 166, 182, 183n, 194-5, 229; embassies to, (1157) 98, (1156) 104, (1160) 112, 115-16, 226; exclusion of (1190), 184; Latin massacre (1182) and, 161, 162, 164; quarter in, 89, 116, 122; shipping and, 109, 224; trade in, 20, 71, 75, 85, 111, 113-14, 170n
  Messina, merchants of, in, 42, 134
  Pisa and: Latin massacre (1182) and, 161, 164; quarter in, 89-90
  Ragusa and, 150-2
  Savona and, 170n
  Sicily and: embassies to, (1155) 89,

297

Index

Genoa (cont.)
Sancho of Navarre and, 137
Sardinia and, see Sardinia
Savona and, 22–3, 95, 152, 169–71
Sicilian admirals from, 213
Syracuse and, 127, 130, 208–9, 212, 213
Tancred and, 174, 179–80, 202, 205–8
tower of Bubonoso, 282n
treaties of, see Treaties
walls of, 49, 112, 114
William I and: treaty of 1156, 28–9, 70, 86, 90–9, 101; Rubaldo Bisacia and W., 115–16
William II and, 28–9, 137, 152, 282
George of Antioch, Admiral, 85: his bridge, 37
Gerba, 135
Germany: rulers of, see individual rulers; Sicilian diplomacy in, 83n
Ghent, 196
Giacomo Bonbello [G], 189, 200
Giacomo Manerio, podestà [G], 211
Gibelet, 53, 232, 236
Gionata Cavarunco [G], 184, 194
Gionata Ciriole [G], 106–7, 219
Gionata Crispino, G noble, 98, 224
Giordano de Molino [G], 102–3, 240, 243
Giordano Ricerio [G], 186, 197–8
Giovanni di Bonbello, G banker, 160, 200, 258–9, 274–5
Giovanni Busca [G], 269, 278
Giovanni Cristiani [G], 247–8
Giovanni di Donato, notary of S, 23
Giovanni Faber, 256, 259
Giovanni di Guiberto, notary of G, 19n
Giovanni Mazamorro [G], 179, 187
Giovanni Scriba, G notary: career of, 17–18, 97, 112; register of, 12–13, 16–18, 22, 155, 217, 224; techniques of, 12, 226
Giovanni Tarasco [G], 159, 162, 167
Girgenti, 38, 93–4, 126, 218: abp of, 83n
goats, 36, 37
gold: flow from Regno, 223, 225, 255, 267–73; Genoese holdings of, at Messina, 207; leaf, 46; oriental, 91; treasure of Sicilian kings, 126n, 128; see also paiole; tari

grain
of Apulia, 35
of Calabria, 71–2, 148
of Maremma, 72–3, 136n, 210
in Pisa, 51n, 152
in Provence, 71–2, 272n
of Sardinia, 71, 123
of Sicily: 36–7; in Genoa, 71, 91, 92, 123, 160, 224–5, 273–6; in Pisa, 51n; royal controls on, 40–1, 275–6; in Tunisia, 27, 40
see also barley; grana; wheat
grana, red dye, 200
Graziano Guaraco [G], 107, 228
Greece, 31, 84: Norman attacks on, 80–3, 138n, 163–5, 171; see also Almyra; Constantinople; Greeks
Greeks: as craftsmen in Sicily, 136; in Italy, 32; as merchants in Africa, 109; as monks in Italy, 36
Grillo, G family, 177, 178, 179, 241
Grimoald, Prince of Bari, 77
Gubbio, 133
Guercio, G family, 233
Guglielmo Burone the elder, G noble: investments of, 115; as politician, 130, 232
Guglielmo Burone the younger, G noble: investments of, 168; as politician, 169; wife of, 176
Guglielmo Cassinese, notary: and Lucca, 24; pupil Giovanni of, 19n; work of, 17, 18–19, 22, 183
Guglielmo or Guglielmoto Ciriole [G], 106, 134, 159, 228, 244–5
Guglielmo Filardo [G], 102n, 113, 228, 234
Guglielmo Fornario [G], 159, 185, 211
Guglielmo Malfigliastro, G businessman, 169, 176, 185, 186, 228, 236
Guglielmo Malocello [G], 115, 190
Guglielmo de Meleto, 184
Guglielmo Rataldo [G], 175, 200
Guglielmo Scarsaria [G], 218, 225, 230–1, 233–4, 235, 236, 282n
Guglielmo da Sori, notary, 11n, 19, 184–5, 212
Guglielmo Vento, G noble: as ambassador, 90, 122; as businessman, 102,

Index

Liège, *see* Jean de Liège
linen cloth, 218–19; *see also* flax; fustian
loca, shares in ships, 186, 190, 220
Lombardy: Frederick I and, 114, 124, 133, 137; Genoese trade in, 99, 121; peace of Venice and, 145-6; textiles in, 135, 218–19; Venice and, 133–4; *see also* Longobards
Longobards, of southern Italy, 32, 75, 134: in Constantinople, 134, 164, 203; 'Lombards' of Piazza, 278
Lothar, Emperor, 61, 114: in letter-book, 74
Lucania, *see* Basilicata
Lucca: cartularies of, 24; cloth of, 154, 201, 256-8, 260; expansion of, 260; Frederick I and, 132–3; Genoa and, *see* cloth of L., merchants of L.; Henry VI and, 260–1; merchants of, 19, 24, 154, 193, 200n, 201, 219, 227, 255–61; money of, 271; piracy against, 140; Pisa and, 51, 124, 140, 260–1; as textile centre, 258; *see also* Coenna; Paxio of L.
'Lupus, king of Spain', 108n, 115
Lyons, 201

Maastricht, 201
Maghrib, *see* Africa, Norman; Africa, North
al-Mahdiyyah: Genoese and Pisans at, 50, 52–3; Norman rule in, 86; Norman mint at, 109; Roger I and, 40; trade with Sicily, 40, 53, 86, 156
Maio of Bari: Hugo Falcandus and, 24n; king's minister, 85–91, 116–18, 122; his legate Elia, 98; 'Lombard' resistance, 278; murdered, 117
Majorca
  Genoese and planned invasion of, 129; Genoese trade with, 104, 105, 111, 157, 158, 161, 167, 174, 182, 228, 229, 243; Genoese treaties with, 157, 158, 174, 228; Pisans and, 157n; Sicilian invasion of, 156–7, 164
Malfigliastro, G family, 235-6, 237n, 239
Mallone, G family, 19, 183, 233, 234, 238, 252
Malocello, G family, 19

Malta: cotton of, 218; Genoese counts of, 103n, 207, 213; Pisan trade near, 163n; *see also* Margarito of Brindisi
Manduel, merchants of Marseilles, 23
Manegold of Brescia, *podestà* of Genoa, 181, 186
Mantua, 133
Manuel Komnenos, Greek emperor: and Genoa, 20, 89, 114, 115–16; and Peace of Venice, 145; and Pisa, 139; and Sicily, 80-2, 88, 133, 138n, 141-2, 145, 163; and Venice, 78, 80-2, 88, 133, 139, 141-2
Maragone, *see* Bernardo Maragone
Marchese Castagna [G], 242, 246, 252
Marchesio della Volta, G noble, 178, 201, 260n
Marchione della Volta, G noble, 122, 233n, 245: as merchant, 115, 233n, 245; as politician, 122, (murdered), 136
Maremma: Genoese trade in, 72–3, 99, 104, 105, 113, 154–5, 158, 161, 166, 174, 177, 182, 188, 260; grain of, 72–3, 136n; Pisan-imperial treaty (1162) and, 124; Provençaux and French in, 127
Margarito of Brindisi, Count of Malta, 191, 207, 213
de Mari, G family, 19
Marino di Marino [G], 212
Marino Sanudo, 88
Markward von Anweiler, 19, 206-8
Marsala, 108
Marseilles: Gaeta and, 186; Genoese, rivalry with, 95, (trade in) 174, 177; Pisan alliance, 95-6; notaries and charters of, 23, 238
Martinus, S notary, 23n, 265
Matteo di Marino [G], 212
Mazara, 43-4, 94, 100, 104, 127: in Pisan-imperial treaty, (1162) 124, 126, (1191) 180; cotton of, 218
Mazara, Val di, Sicily, 36, 281
meat, of Sicily and S. Italy, 22
medical goods, 221, 225: euphorbium, 220
Melgueil, money of, 243, 280
Merseburg, 84n

Index

Messina
  Calabria and, 72, 118
  city of: castle, 62, 208; church of St
    Peter in Canniccio, 280; monasteries,
    92n, (of Cistercians) 261, (of S.
    Maria Latina) 222, (of San Salva-
    tore) 77n; street of Florentines, 261;
    street called 'Magistra', 282
  cloth imports of, 219, 227, 263, 264
  cotton of, 218
  earthquake, 153n
  French and English kings in, 178n
  Genoese and: contracts for, 22, 106,
    110, 111, 118–21, 155, 195–7, 201,
    219; hospice and warehouse, 62-4,
    70, 92, 207, 279; scales in, 272;
    seized by Genoese, 206; struggle
    with Pisans, in (1129) 71, in (1194)
    207–8; treaty of 1156 and, 92–4;
    treaty of 1162 and, 132
  merchants of, 42, 134, 136
  Pisans and: colony of, 23, 205, 279–80;
    seized by Pisans, 206; struggle with
    Genoese, in (1129) 71, in (1194)
    207–8; trade in, 155; treaty of 1162
    and, 124, (1191 renewal) 180
  Robert Guiscard and, 40
  Roger I and, 52
  Savonese in, 65, 68
  tariffs, 92, 274
  trade routes, 53, 103, 230; in eleventh
    century, 44–5
  William I and, 41, 71, 116–19
Michele Simitecolo [V], 160–1, 203
Michiel, V family, 147: see also Domeni-
  co M.
Milan, 130n, 134, 219
Milazzo, 184
Molfetta, 150
da Molin, V family, 78, 79, 144, 149
Molise, 31: geography of, 35
Monaco, 71, 95, 127, 191n
Monreale, 30, 277–8, 280–1
Montpellier, 188, 233, 268, 280
Morocco, 115, 138n, 155-6, 249
myrrh, 110

Naples
  Amalfi and, 49, 184, 266; bankers of,

265–6; Calabrian grain and, 72;
  cloth imports of, 184, 264; commune of, 173, 266; Genoese contracts for, 154–5, 162, 165, 166, 168,
  174, 177, 179, 182–8, 269, 277;
  Genoese investment in, 19, 62, 168,
  183, 187; Genoese loss of interest in,
  202; geography of, 34; Henry VI
  attacks, 190, 191, 206; merchants
  of, 74, 96, 265–6; North French
  merchants in, 262; Pisa and, (in
  treaty of 1162) 124, (in treaty of
  1191) 180; Tancred and, 173; see
  also Campania, Capua
Naso, fief of, 206; see also Rubaldo de
  Platea Longa
Navarre, see Sancho
Negropont, 138n
Nice, 200, 263
Nicola Embriaco [G], 162, 166–7
Nicola Lecanoce (Leccanuptias) [G],
  194–7, 210–11
Nicola Mallone [G], 165, 210
Nicoloso Doria (De Oria) [G], 198
Noli, 170
Notaries, 9, 75: cartularies of, 11–13, 73;
  development of techniques, 226;
  Genoese, 8, 11, 16–24; Lucchese,
  24; Marseilles, 23; Neapolitan, 265;
  Pisan, 23–4, 51; Savonese, 22–3,
  265; Sienese, 24; manuals of, 11–12
Noto, 127
Noto, Val di, Sicily, 36, 130, 209; see
  also Simon, Ct of Syracuse

Obertino, son of Guglielmo de la
  Cazaira, of Verona, 75n, 144
Oberto Corso [G], 109, 260
Oberto de Olivano, podestà of G, 208
Oberto de Placentia, notary, 11n, 19n,
  183, 212, 261n
Oberto Scriba de Mercato, notary of G:
  career of, 11n, 18, 154, 183; invest-
  ments by, 167–8; and Lucca, 24;
  undated work by, 19n, 20
Oberto Spinola, G noble, 106, 115, 122,
  232
Odo de Melazo, 184, 189, 193n, 194,
  195, 277

Index

Ogerio (Ogerius Capra), G consul, 62–4, 67–8, 207
Ogerio Pallio or de Pallo, [G], 168, 175, 248
Ogerio Porco [G], 188, 194
Ogerio de Ripa, agent of Solomon of Salerno, 102–3, 240
Ogerio di San Lorenzo, G factor, 178, 200–1, 259
Ogerio Scoto [G], 185, 188
Ogerio Vento [G], 241; *see also* Oglerio V.
Oglerio Arloto [G], 160, 274–6
Oglerio Vento [G], 160, 176, 177, 274–5
oil: olive, 37; Pisan, 152; Spartan, 83
oil merchant, 85
olives, 35
Oliverio da Pavia, 229, 243
Olivier de Verdun, 227
Oran, 260n
Oto de Castello, *iudex*, 186; Oto *iudex*, 199, 248, 269
Oto *vicecomes* or Visconte [G], 268–9, 276
Otone Mallone [G], 168, 228
Ottobono Scriba, G notary, 12, 205, 206, 210
Ottone di Carreto, *podestà* of G, 208–9, 210–11
Otranto, 76–7, 82n
ovens, 129, 207

Paganus of Messina, 134, 136
paiole gold, 98, 225, 267, 271–2
Palermo
    archives of royal palace, 8, 28, 42
    city of: bridge of George of Antioch, 37; church of St James, 211; church of St Mark, 78, 79, 135, 143–4, 204, 231, 282; Khalsa quarter, 211; Seralkadi quarter, 79, 135; street of the Amalfitans, 49
    cotton of, 93, 218
    Genoese contracts for, 21, 107–8, 118–21, 189, 195–7, 228, 234, 236, 262, 268; Genoese estates near, 281; Genoese quarter, 211; Genoese stocks in, 221; treaty of 1156 and, 93–4

Henry VI seizes, 209
    Jews and, 44
    Muslims of, 42, 249
    Pisans: and attack of 1063 on, 52, 62; and, in treaty of 1162, 124; and, in treaty of 1191, 180
    Robert Guiscard and, 40, 125
    Solomon of Salerno, Eliadar and, 241
    trade routes and, 43, 52, 221
    Venetians and: Venetian quarter, 135, 150, *see also* Church of St Mark *supra*; treaty of 1175 and, 143
    William I and, 41, 118
    wool and fleeces of, 93, 218
paper, 11, 38
Papienses, coins of Pavia, 30n
papyrus, 38
parchment, from lambskins, 38, 93
Partinico, 281
passagium, 41
passports, 199n
Paterno, 39: Count Bartholomew de Lucy, 261; Count Henry, 39n; Count Simon, 39n
Pavia: coins of, 30n; Genoese visit (1162), 127; Germans at, 122, 211; merchants of, in Genoa, 227, 229, 235, 247
Paxio of Lucca, 201, 256, 259
pedagium, 41, 127
pedaticum, 127
pepper: as credit, 270; in Egypt, 240, 245; in Genoa: 176, 224, 242, (for export to Sicily) 236; in Pisa, 152
Perasco, 256–8, 268
Pescara, 10n, 75n, 144
Peschiera, 10n, 75n, 144
Philip II, King of France, 178n
Piacenza: Arnaldo Stricto of, 186; cloth of, 75, 219; and Frederick I, 130n, 133; merchants of, in Genoa, 227
Piazza Armerina, 278
Picardy, cloth of, 110, 219, 227
Pietro Ziani, V noble, 147–8
pigs, 36, 92
Pisa
    Alexandria, Pisan shipping at, 140, 141n
    Amalfi and, 59

Pisa *(cont.)*
 Annals of, 25; *see also* Bernardo
  Maragone
 Baptistery of, 90n
 Campania and, 60–2
 cathedral of, 278n
 church of San Sisto, 52
 colony of, in Messina, 23, 63, 205,
  279–80
 Constantinople: and ambitions in,
  139, 142; expulsion from of P, 1182,
  161, 164; P quarter in, 89, 116; and
  Siculo-Greek war (1185), 164
 crusade, Pisans and First, 53
 Egypt and, 54
 Gaeta and, 71
 Genoa and: co-operation with, 84,
  154, 155, 174; conflict with, 71,
  138–40, 207–8; trade with, 113, 174,
  182; *see also* Messina; Sardinia
 growth of, 49–54
 Henry VI and: 172, 178, 181, 205–10;
  embassy to (1193), 205; renews
  1162 treaty (1191), 180, 187; again
  (1193), 204
 Lucca and, 51, 124, 140, 260–1
 al-Mahdiyyah, Pisans in, 52
 Majorca and, 157n
 Malta and, 163n
 Marseilles and, 95–6
 notaries of, 23–4
 Palermo, Pisan raid, 52
 Roger II and, 61, 117n, 138
 Sardinia and, 114, 136, 154; trade, 23n
 Syracuse and, 208, 213
 Tancred and, 172, 202, 205–8
 trade of: in Sardinia, 23n, 154; in
  Sicily, 51
 treaty of 1162 and, 123–7, 129, 172
 Tunis and, 156
 Venice and: Pisans in V, 140; Vene-
  tians in P, 153n
 William I: and confiscation of goods,
  138; support of P for, 117n, 138n
 William II and, 139–40, 152
pitch, 41, 207
plateaticum, 41
Porcio de Catonibus, 212
portaticum, 41

Portovenere, 95, 123–5, 127
portulanus, 42
pottery, 45
profits of trade, 223–5, 228, 250
Provence: Genoese trade in, 71, 99, 105,
  108, 111, 113, 119, 154, 158, 166,
  177, 182, 188, 229, 244, 253; grain
  of, 272n; merchants of, 70, 95, 100,
  127, 239, 241; money of, 280;
  salt of, 72; Savonese trade in, 170n
Provesini, coins of Champagne, 30n,
  270–1
Provesini Senatus, coins of Rome, 270–1
purple, cloth of, 176

quittances, 10, 17

rabbits, 152–3, 221–2
Ragusa (Dubrovnik), and Sicily, 150–2,
  203: trade of, 49; treaties of, 29, 69,
  150–1; in Venetian treaties, 88, 143
Raimondo Unaldo [G], 195, 197–8
Rainald von Dassel, 132
Rainaldo Sardena [G], 67, 168, 171
Rainaldo de Tusa, Sicilian, 97
Rainulf, Count of Alife, 60
Rapallo, 72, 189
Ravenna, 133
Registro a catena, *see* Savona, Roger II
  and
Reggio Calabria, 36, 42, 84
regnicolo, native of Sicilian *Regno*, *see*
  Sicilians
Rialto (modern Venice), *see* Venice
Ribaldo de Sarafia, 101, 104, 225, 235–6,
  238, 253
Ricerio, G family, 198
Richard I, King of England, 178n
Richard, bishop of Syracuse, 97, 157
Robert, Prince of Capua, 60
Robert Guiscard, Duke of Apulia, 39,
  44, 150
Roberto di San Giovanni, 87
Roger I, the Great Count, 32: and
  Aleramici, 39, 65; and Pisa, 52; *see
  also* Aleramici
Roger II, K. of Sicily
 career of: minority, 64; Count of
  Sicily, 62; Duke of Apulia, 59–60,

Index

Index

Index

Walter de Moac, Sicilian admiral, 156–7
warehouses, Genoese, 129, 207
wax, 224, 252
weather, in Sicily, 37
weights and measures, 92: Genoese scales in Messina, 272
wheat
  of Sardinia, 175
  of Sicily and S. Italy, 22, 36, 41n, 148, 170, 281; Egyptian imports, 46; Genoese imports, 91–4, 137, 222, 274–5, 281, 283; North African imports, 77n, 222
  see also grain
William I, 'the Bad', K. of Sicily
  Frederick I and, 122–34, 136
  Genoa and, treaty of 1156, 28–9, 70, 86, 90–9, 101
  imprisonment of, 117
  Messina and, 41, 116–18
  Palermo and, 41, 118
  Pisa: contribution for Baptistery at, 90n; support of P in rebellion, 117n, 138n;
  Rubaldo Bisacia of G and, 115–16
  seizes Pisan property, 138
  Solomon of Salerno and, 239, 248, 251
  tari and, 30n
  Venice and, 78n, 83, 86–9, 133–4, 143
William II, 'the Good', K. of Sicily
  accession of, 137

achievements of, 171
Bubonoso his liegeman [G], 282
Constantinople, ambitions in, 94–5, 163–5
Dalmatian possessions of, 151, 171
Genoa and: embassy of 1168, 137; grant of 1174, 28–9, 137, 152
Manuel Komnenos and, 141–2
Monreale and, 278, 280–1
Nicola Embriaco and, 166–7
Pisa and: embassy of 1167, 139; embassy of 1169, 140
Sancho of Navarre and, 137
Venice and: grant of 1175, 28–9, 78–9, 88, 143, 147, 149, 152; Peace of Venice and, 145–6; relations with, 141–52
William III, K of Sicily, 207, 209
William, Duke of Apulia, 68, 77
wool, 93, 222
woollen cloth, 121; see also Flanders, cloth of

Xecha Bohahia, of Tripoli, 110, 131

Yemen, 45
Ypres, 196, 201, 262

Zara (Zadar), 150
Ziani, V family, 147